Salamanca 1812

Salamanca 1812

Wellington's Year of Victories

Peter Edwards

First published in Great Britain in 2013 by
The Praetorian Press
an imprint of
Pen & Sword Books Ltd
47 Church Street
Barnsley
South Yorkshire
S70 2AS

ISBN 978-1-78159-079-9

A CIP catalogue record for this book is
available from the British Library.

The publishers would like to thank Tim Saunders and Andrew Duff of BHTV
for providing the modern photographs in the plate section.

Typeset in 11/12.5 Ehrhardt by Concept, Huddersfield, West Yorkshire
Printed and bound in England by CPI Group (UK) Ltd, Croydon, CRO 4YY

Pen & Sword Books Ltd incorporates the Imprints of Pen & Sword Aviation,
Pen & Sword Family History, Pen & Sword Maritime, Pen & Sword Military,
Pen & Sword Discovery, Wharncliffe Local History, Wharncliffe True Crime,
Wharncliffe Transport, Pen & Sword Select, Pen & Sword Military Classics,
Leo Cooper, The Praetorian Press, Remember When, Seaforth Publishing and
Frontline Publishing.

For a complete list of Pen & Sword titles please contact
PEN & SWORD BOOKS LIMITED
47 Church Street, Barnsley, South Yorkshire, S70 2AS, England
E-mail: enquiries@pen-and-sword.co.uk
Website: www.pen-and-sword.co.uk

Contents

Maps

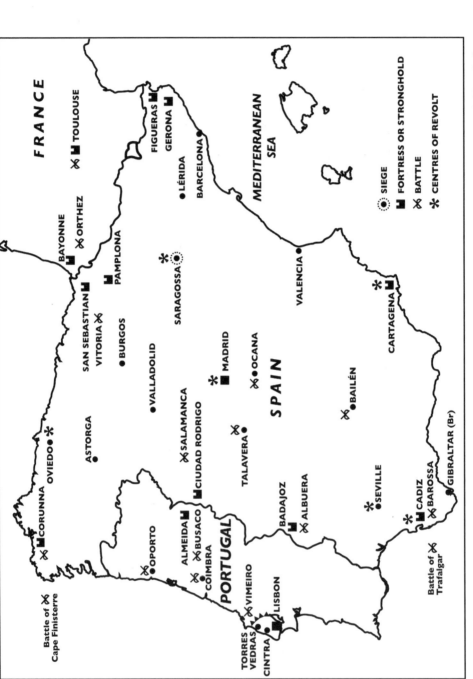

Map 1: The Peninsular War: Portugal, Spain and south-western France showing principal battles, sieges, fortresses or strongholds and places of revolt.

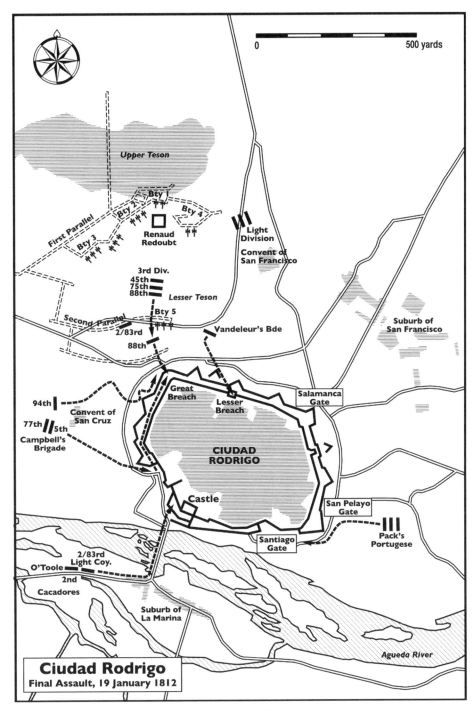

Map 2: *Ciudad Rodrigo: Final Assault, 19 January 1812.*

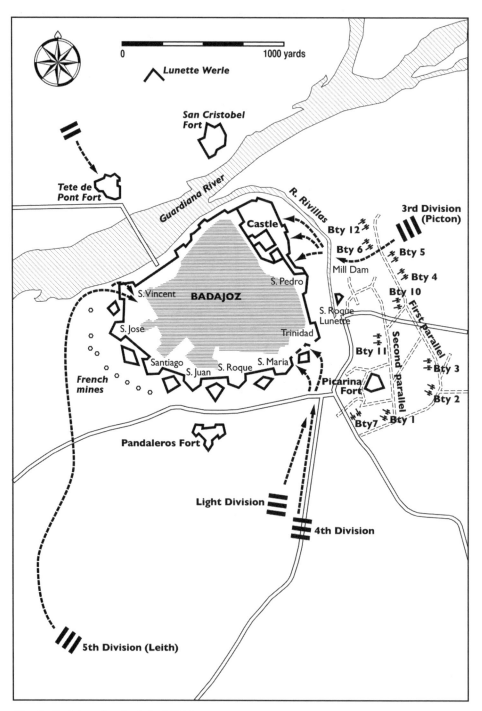

Map 3: Badajoz: Assault, 6 April 1812.

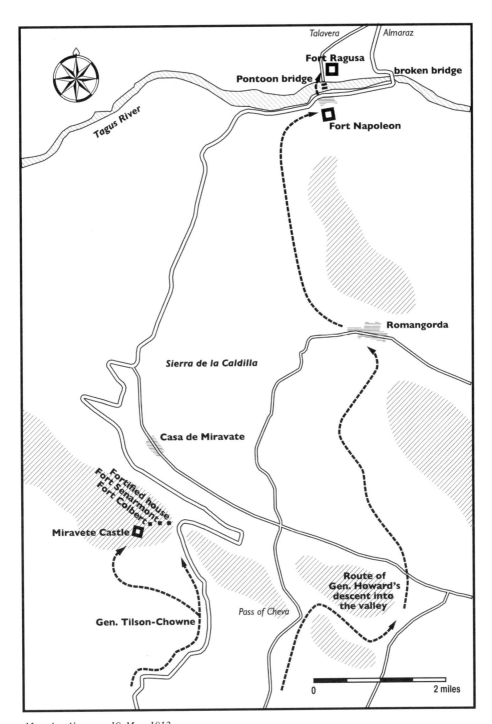

Map 4: Almaraz, 19 May 1812.

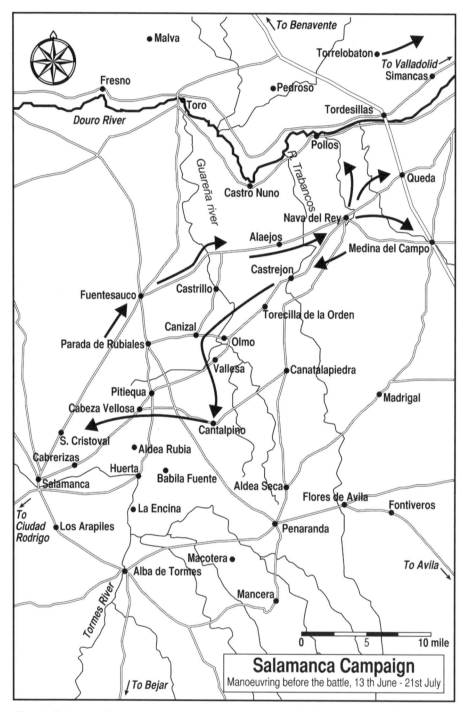

Map 5: Salamanca Campaign: Manoeuvring before the battle, 13 June to 21 July 1812.

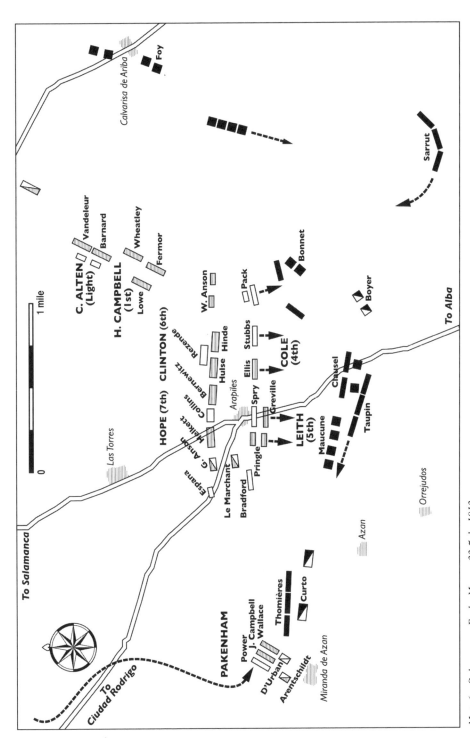

Map 6: *Salamanca: Early Moves, 22 July 1812.*

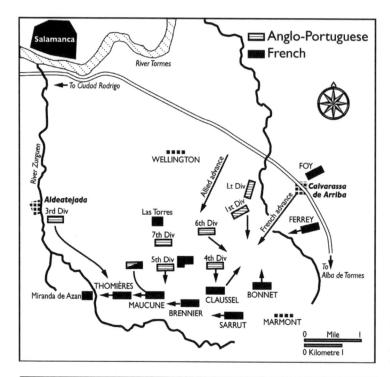

*Map 7:
Battle of
Salamanca,
22 July 1812.*

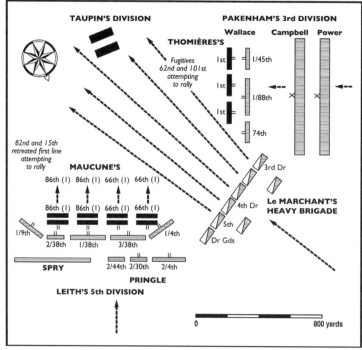

*Map 8:
Salamanca:
Le Marchant's
Charge.*

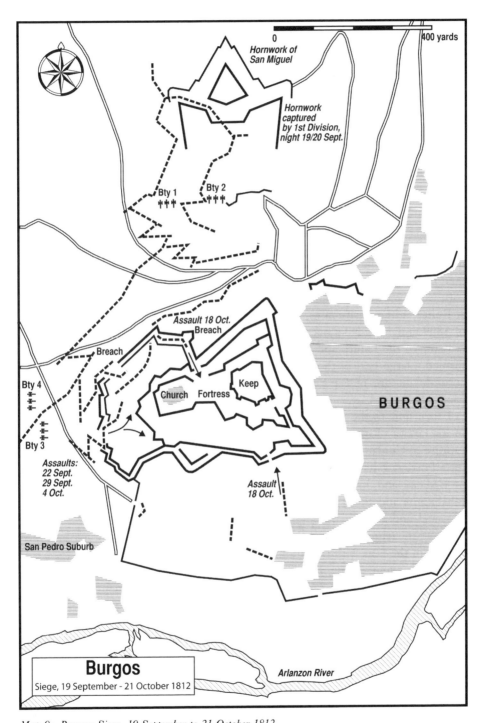

0   400 yards

Hornwork of
San Miguel

Hornwork
captured
by 1st Division,
night 19/20 Sept.

Bty 1   Bty 2

Assault 18 Oct.
Breach

Breach

Bty 4

Church   Fortress   Keep

BURGOS

Bty 3

Assaults:
22 Sept.
29 Sept.
4 Oct.

Assault
18 Oct.

San Pedro Suburb

Burgos
Siege, 19 September - 21 October 1812

Arlanzon River

Map 9: Burgos: Siege, 19 September to 21 October 1812.

Preface

*I look upon Salamanca, Vitoria and Waterloo as my three best battles –
those which had great and permanent consequences.*

My Regiment, the 48th (Northamptonshire), fought with Lord Wellington
throughout his Peninsular campaigns of 1808–14, notwithstanding in his
unfortunate absence from that fatal hill near Albuera in 1811, our 2nd Battalion
was well and truly knocked over, as were the Buffs, the Worcesters, the
Middlesex and the Berkshires. By 2pm that wet afternoon we were twenty-five
men lined up fit for duty, of 413 who had eaten breakfast. Over the years, the
48th were awarded thirteen Peninsular Battle Honours, absent from parade only
at Roliça, Vimeiro, Fuentes, and Ciudad Rodrigo. Our part in the campaigns
of 1809 and 1811 have been set out in my two earlier histories, wherein the
crossing of the Douro and the bloody battles of Talavera and Albuera rightly
formed a large part of those accounts; but I also endeavoured to give a fairly
accurate picture of the confrontations at Roliça, Vimeiro, Barrosa, Campo
Major, Sabugal, Los Santos, Fuentes, the 1811 Sieges of Badajoz and El Bodon.
  I turn now to the pivotal year of 1812, with Napoleon safely self-wrapped
in his faraway Russian adventure. And what a year it was to be: the surgical
capture of Ciudad Rodrigo, that northern key to the long road to the Pyrenees
(or a Portugese haven, if things went wrong); the shockingly unsurgical storm
of Badajoz and its subsequent sacking, entirely of the unpopular Spanish
inhabitants and their property; the near destruction of Marmont's Army of
Portugal and French fighting morale thereafter at Salamanca – oh! what a
victory!; the triumphant entry into Madrid; the step-too-far at Burgos; and the
closing of the year with that humiliating withdrawal which in various respects
echoed Corunna, Mons, Dunkirk and episodes in the Western Desert. That
the year ended on a sour note seems obvious, yet after Salamanca no French
general would now cheerfully tangle with our 'Atty. The strategic initiative
had already shifted to him the previous year, from the Lines onwards; now
his superb generalship around the Arapiles, and the staunch qualities of his
infantry and their mounted comrades, present for our admiration what must
surely be his finest victory. Yet while it was a testament to the previous four
years of learning, it was far more than a repetition of the defensive superiority
of the line versus column, of the proven sequence of volley–cheer–charge
emerging from a reverse slope, and of the formidable squares so adeptly formed

and which no French cavalry could breach. For at Salamanca we attacked with both foot and horse, and we smashed them, and so showed we were the complete, all-purpose fighting machine.

In the space of an hour at Salamanca, Lord Wellington demonstrated by his superb tip-toe balance his ready ability to fight a wide range of tactical scenarios. Having encouraged mystery in Marmont's mind, by moving overnight to place his mass just so, behind a ridge, at first light they were largely hidden. Thus Marmont was invited to guess their numbers, position and intentions. He held ground so lightly – one of the hardest things to do – that he effectively dared Marmont to attack. By 2pm, having stifled his frustration himself to attack, he was entirely ready to withdraw in the face of both turning and frontal movements, while so defensively placed by 2.30pm that the latter had no chance of success. The former – the puzzling march by Thomières – allowed that further versatility which would mark this day forever. At 2.45pm when his telescope whispered to him 'By God, that will do', he was able to transform his stance yet again into the stunning flank march by Pakenham and the stirring order to Le Marchant 'You must charge at all hazards' and which in Philip Guedalla's terse words was to launch 'twenty-eight battalions against seventy-eight and send them reeling eastwards into Castille ... the Army of Portugal hurried to shelter with a loss of 15,000 men and twenty guns.' One of the hurrying divisions was ably commanded by the thirty-seven-year-old General Foy, who six days later in his diary wrote handsomely of the conqueror of Salamanca:

> This battle is the most cleverly fought, the largest in scale, the most important in results, of any the English have won in recent times. It brings up Lord Wellington's reputation almost to that of Marlborough. Up to this day we knew his prudence, his eye for choosing good positions, and the skill with which he used them. But at Salamanca he has shown himself a great and able master of manoeuvring. He kept his dispositions hidden nearly all the day: he allowed us to develop our movement before he pronounced his own: he played a close game; he utilised the 'oblique order' in the style of Frederick the Great ... The catastrophe of the Spanish War has come – for six long months we ought to have seen that it was quite probable.

As a demonstration of off-the-cuff military virtuosity it is hard to think of a better. Waterloo was a mere slogging match. And as a precursor to the 1813 advance to Vitoria, Salamanca stood plain and upright, a promise of things to come. While the year 1812 began with Wellington's army concentrated for the siege of Ciudad Rodrigo licking its lips, it ended with a similar concentration under the same walls, this time licking its wounds. In between lay many months of efforts, of seizing opportunities, of evading an enemy four times his own strength and choosing so neatly where and when to strike. 'The beating of 40,000 men in 40 minutes' at Salamanca remains to this day a fine story, and I hope I do it justice. My effort so to do in large part is to acknowledge that my own Regiment lost half our twenty-two officers that day, and a fifth of our men. Since this was just twelve weeks after another 200 had been laid low in the bloody, desperate ditch at Badajoz, the campaign of 1812 remains understandably large in regimental folk memory, along with Talavera and Albuera.

It is that mention of Badajoz and the blood that was spilt on and under its walls which gives the year 1812 its shape, and its contrasts, for the modern reader to enjoy in the safety of his armchair. For if Rodrigo and Salamanca can both be viewed rightly with pride and no little amazement, Badajoz was the sombre filling in the sandwich. That, together with the concluding road back from Burgos, presents darker pictures. Darker because of the terrible casualties of the storm, and the subsequent shame of the sack. Yet, all in all, the year 1812 ended a good deal for the better. The two key frontier fortresses had been secured, the French effectively had been cleared out of southern Spain, and were leaching back to France as the Emperor sought to rebuild his forces after his gigantic losses in Russia – and 20,000 French prisoners had been taken. To quote Foy again, 'Lord Wellington has retired unconquered with the glory of the laurels of Arapiles, having restored to the Spaniards the country south of the Tagus, and made us destroy our magazines, our fortifications – in a word all that we have gained by our conquests.'

*   *   *

It will be seen that my narrative style leans heavily on eyewitness accounts, even (reluctantly) where these were written up long after the event, and in some cases where they may owe more than something to earlier narratives by Napier, Southey, Londonderry, John Jones etc., and which provided ready-made inspiration for veterans suffering temporary memory loss; although the more blatant copyings of course I spurn. For example, Sergeant Thomas Garretty, 43rd, published his *Memoirs* in 1835, devoting five pages to the attack on Ciudad Rodrigo, in which he was present on the Lesser Breach. One page (what a waste! one page!) described what he saw, the other four were precise regurgitations of Napier's very words, published eleven years earlier.

I am equally conscious of the danger of placing too great a reliance on any one account, if only because two accounts invariably prove *neither* participant could have been present at the same event, so differently do we all recall what we thought we saw. There is the related danger with multiple accounts that repetition can be boring or – when at odds one man with another – confusing; a good example are two of the accounts describing what happened at the right-hand top of Rodrigo's main breach. Each adamantly claims his Colonel, not the other's, was the first to cross the plank bridge – which is indeed confusing (if par for the course of regimental rivalry). One runs that risk, in seeking what journalists call verification: or, in this case, that there was indeed a plank bridge. One can but try.

It is also true that mid-Victorian writers are frequently over-florid, even sanctimonious, for our modern ears; at times much verbiage flows with little content. Today's reader should always feel free to skip our forebears' excesses, keeping alert for the historical nuggets. We just must put up with the boring bits.

Generally, eyewitnesses take the modern reader as close as he can get to a sense of 'being there', which presumably is what most of us seek. For example, read the description by Ensign William Grattan of his beloved Connaught Rangers watching in the gathering gloom before the assault on Rodrigo, as the 43rd passed them, going forward in the chill night air to the forming-up place. That may have been written in 1847, but what an immediate sense comes through of that moment, as the 43rd, shirt collars open, muskets slung, marched quietly into the bitter dusk to storm the Lesser Breach, their music fading to die away, for 'they had no drums'. Perhaps just six drummer boys piping on their fifes; but all old soldiers who have been so woken at reveille will feel the blood quicken at the thought. Grattan's memoirs, said Oman, 'are on the whole the most graphic and picturesque (of the many I have read) in giving the details of actual conflict ... his accounts above all of the storm and sack of Ciudad Rodrigo and Badajoz are admirable.' For his storytelling and his humour, Grattan appears often in this book.

On the subject of acknowledgements, I had hoped to illustrate this work by replicating the maps and plans of my good friend Ian Robertson, whose *Atlas of the Peninsular War* last year set such new standards via his brilliant cartographer Martin Brown. Unfortunately his publisher, Harvard University Press, have not felt able to match Ian's generosity of spirit. I can only urge readers to acquire Ian's *Atlas*.

I am also indebted to Nick Hallidie, late 19th (Green Howards) and Chairman of the Friends of the British Cemetery, Elvas, whose battlefield-tour knowledge gleaned from twenty-seven years of residence in Portugal, gave me most helpful guidance in my narrative of the two great sieges.

On a separate subject, I describe Lord Wellington's troops (as he did) as 'British', even though his officers in their memoirs invariably used 'English'; so too indeed his opponents to whom we also were always 'les Anglais'. The Norman French, like the Romans a thousand years earlier, never did make much progress in our wilder Scottish, Welsh and Irish peripheries, and so perhaps their descendants may be excused for apparently disregarding them in the Peninsula. However, a cursory glance at the surnames in the Parade States in the National Archives at Kew will confirm that, even in 'English' regiments such as my own, the Celtic (especially Irish) content was fortunately substantial, and thus truly British.

*   *   *

To readers of Spanish or Portugese blood, I apologise for writing in what fashionable English historians nowadays call an Anglo–centric manner, if thereby the reader feels diminished. Your forebears of course require no support from any Englishman, standing as they did so stoutly on their own feet at Busaco, Albuera, San Mascial, Alcaniz, Bailen, Tamares, or on the ramparts at Gerona and Zaragoza, or in the many extremely bloody partisan operations. It is condescending for we English to suggest otherwise. As it happens, the 1812 events I write about here somewhat preclude the multi-ethnic route now preferred by the politically correct. Napier, of course, is their big bogeyman and while they may well be right to criticise his powerful, sweeping *History* in its denigration of much that is Spanish, they are neither right nor patriotic to mock his admiration for Moore and Wellington, Soult and Napoleon, still less to blame him for inspiring the tone of all those many subsequent soldiers' memoirs which, they aver, copied his contemptuous descriptions of our Spanish allies. It is always possible, one supposes, such misguided opinions were sincerely held by our veterans before they ever came to read Napier in the 1830s.

A second area where I am vulnerable is my relaxed failure to quote chapter and verse for my eyewitness accounts. This will irritate scholars, who have never forgiven Sir Charles Oman for similar laxity (although unlike him, I do not re-write these accounts nor improve their grammar). My lazy excuse is a belief that proper Peninsula scholars are already familiar with the sources, while the rest of us aren't too interested in page numbers. Anyway, what follows is just a proud if limited tale of British effort to help free our allies from their French yoke – another populist battle-based account of a Wellington campaign if you will – and I leave to wider-ranging minds the writing of a better.

> *One more Charge, and then be Done.*
> *When the Forts of Folly fall,*
> *May the Victor, when He comes.*
> *Find my Body near the Wall.*

Introduction

We have certainly altered the nature of the war in Spain:
It has become, to a certain degree, an offensive on our part.

By the end of 1811 Napoleon had a quarter of a million soldiers sprawled across Spain in scattered concentrations, like ill-spread fertiliser on a pasture. The vast lands between lay fallow, never cooperative and grudgingly productive only when *force majeure* moved in, temporarily asserting rights of conquest. The arrogant imposition of Napoleon's Corsican brother Joseph as King of the proud Spanish people, the harsh requisitioning of his forage parties and the cruel treatment of the peasantry, guaranteed everywhere a sullen but passionate hostility. Bands of self-seeking guerrillas, partly armed and paid by the British, wrapped in patriotism and clothed in blooded blue French uniforms stripped from the ambushed and mutilated dead, roamed the hillside tracks seeking brutal revenge – and plunder. Always plunder or, more truthfully, second-hand loot. Unlike Napoleon's other European fiefdoms, the resulting need for strong garrisons, bridge guards, escort parties and reserves, reduced the man-power available to his generals to form the mobile armies necessary to eject Wellington. 1811 was not a good year for the Emperor and his marshals, who already sniffed at their inferior Spanish posting, sensing their master's grander ambitions to the East, pastures new, beckoning more urgently than their own rather boring Iberian difficulties, and with which they would be expected to cope and solve: a second eleven.

The Spanish ping-pong of 1811 had left Napoleon nonplussed, as he tried catastrophically to control affairs from Paris – with a reaction time stretching into so many weeks that credibility was removed from his eventual response.

The importance of the 1811 campaign lay in its pivotal role, its fulcrum position in the shifting British/French balance. Out of Wellington's strategic masterpiece of ultimate defence – the Lines of Torres Vedras – came the weakening through starvation of Massena's army, and his subsequent with-drawal, with huge losses, up to and beyond Sabugal. Soult had accordingly moved north to his aid (and in the process, amazingly, snatched Badajoz); to do this he had borrowed much of Victor's force from around Cadiz, which allowed Graham to earn his reputation at Barrosa – which in turn pulled the elastic on Soult, to drag him back. That in turn allowed Beresford the space for the first attempt at Badajoz, while his master dealt – just – with a resurgent Massena at

Fuentes d'Oñoro, that early close-run thing; and so up bounced Soult again, to try to save Badajoz, and to thwart him Beresford committed his command to the bloody confrontation at Albuera. Where my 2nd Battalion got knocked over in the rain, by the Lancers.

And yet patience is a French marshal's virtue. Should the Emperor's growing eastern ambitions reap a rich harvest, surely as in 1809 he would again turn his eyes, feet and resources to Spain? Now that was a thought worth hugging. Until then, his marshals must rub along as best they could, without getting into too many scrapes, particularly those self-inflicted by personal ambitions.

Apart from Suchet's 60,000 men in the Army of the Centre, now across in Valencia, and the royal stooge Joseph in Madrid (again hand-held by Jourdan) with some 10,000 effective marching troops, the thirty-eight-year-old Marmont held the pivotal ground with his 52,000 strong Army of Portugal, based on the Tagus with his headquarters in Talavera. Dorsenne's 48,000 strong Army of the North formed the French right, up beyond the Duoro, with Soult's 54,000 Army of the South correspondingly way down in Andalucia. Both Dorsenne and Soult had single divisions placed in advance, respectively at Salamanca and at Merida.

Thus given his strength and long sick list, any combination of two of the four French armies would of course present serious problems for Lord Wellington, as may be seen after the second attempt at Badajoz, when Marmont and Soult concentrated against him some 60,000 strong; and again in September when Marmont with help from the Army of the North re-provisioned Ciudad Rodrigo, defying his Lordship with some 58,000 men (and leading by chance to Picton's narrow squeak on the ridge at El Bodon). Hence as his army went into winter quarters, the Light Division adjacent to Rodrigo with the rest back around Guarda, consideration in the Peer's head would concentrate not so much on what his next step should be, but when it would be prudent to take it. That is, when the relative strengths would be favourable. He had had more than enough of rushed sieges, at a time when a quarter of his men were sick in hospital, especially those who had come out from recent service in Walcheren.

Encouragingly for Lord Wellington, as he pondered his options in the second half of October 1811, his headquarters at Frenada received two supportive pieces of gossip. The first came in the form of the captured governor – no less! – of Ciudad Rodrigo, scooped up by the guerrilla Don Julian Sanchez whilst riding foolishly outside his own walls. General Reynaud in his subsequent cups at Wellington's table – according to George Scovell, AQMG, and amongst other things the Peer's decypherer – made various derogatory comments on French morale and the distrust existing between commanders, and in particular that 'the different Armies in Spain are all independent and only acknowledge the Emperor's order'. And a week later, Scovell decoded a captured message from Marmont to General Foy (who had earlier incurred King Joseph's wrath for foraging too close to Madrid), saying, 'As a general principle you must not obey any order given to you in the name of the King, if it runs counter to my stated aims'. As Wellington commented, '[Marmont's letter] shows how these gentry are going on: in fact each Marshal is the natural enemy of the King and of his neighbouring Marshal.' These indications that all was not sweetness and light between the French leadership gave his Lordship a superior comfort. And they were promptly followed by proper intelligence of the first grade. For whether he believed it or not, in order to calm his commanders in Spain prior to milking them for his eastern ambitions, Napoleon insisted that the English had been so weakened by sickness that they 'are unable to undertake anything' (to Marmont in November); and 'the English will not undertake anything from now until the month of February, and there is reason to believe they will remain on the defensive' (to Joseph in mid-December).

On Christmas Eve 1811 came a reliable report that one of Marmont's southerly divisions (Brennier's) had quit its quarters in Plasencia three days earlier and was headed to Navalmoral, near the Tagus. Further astounding reports confirmed the cavalry of Dorsenne's Imperial Guard had returned to France, and that the infantry of the Guard had left Valladolid northwards towards France. Then on 29 December came news that Clausel's division near Salamanca had left Marmont for Avila, halfway to Madrid, replacing an unnamed division now moving ever further east.

So from this patchwork of intelligence it emerged that a general eastwards movement was underway, presumed by Lord Wellington firstly in part to be a search for fresh food supplies, partly to reinforce Suchet, and latterly en route to the snows of Russia. Deduction: Marmont was less and less able to concentrate his army fully or quickly and Ciudad Rodrigo was becoming exposed.

His moment had come. He wrote to his political boss Liverpool on New Year's day 1812, 'I propose therefore to make an attack upon Ciudad Rodrigo'; and to his brother on 3 January 'I propose to invest Rodrigo on the 6th and to break ground, if possible, on that night. The weather is however now very bad: the whole country now being covered in snow.'

CHAPTER 1

Part I – Ciudad Rodrigo
The Renaud Redoubt
8 January 1812

The attack on Rodrigo had been Wellington's settled strategy for months and like Torres Vedras was another major example of his far-sighted vision. Orders to the trusted gunner Captain Alexander Dickson were given verbally no less than six months earlier, in July 1811: 'His Lordship informed me that it was his intention to attempt the siege of Ciudad Rodrigo and he wished ... I should superintend the conveyance of the English battering train up the Douro to Lamego and thence by land ... to its ultimate destination.' The previous day Lord Wellington had written to the Earl of Liverpool setting out the strengths of the French relative to his own, and discussing briefly

> with this force whether any and what operation should be undertaken ... for with the prospect of the renewal of hostilities in the north of Europe, I am most anxious not to allow this moment of the enemy's comparative weakness to pass by without making an effort to improve the situation of the allies in the Peninsula.

Marmont's Army of Portugal at that stage was thought to comprise up to 40,000 bayonets and 6,000 sabres, the allies some 42,000 and 4,000 respectively. Thus, said his Lordship to Liverpool, 'you will observe that our numbers are but little superior; and that we are inferior in that principal arm in this open country, cavalry', and so any success might not be decisive, especially weighed against the inevitable losses due to the heat, the marches, and the lack of water inherent in manoeuvring Marmont to battle on the plains of Estremadura. Similarly, in the summer heat, a third attempt at Badajoz was unappealing, and 'Soult could without difficulty increase the army in Estremadura from 10,000 to 15,000 men and the enemy would again have the superiority of numbers in the field.'

Nor could he turn south against Soult directly, for any attempt to relieve Cadiz would see the Army of Portugal descend upon his rear and his communications: 'We should meet in Andalucia the whole force which lately obliged us to raise the siege of Badajoz, with the addition to it of the force which was left before Cadiz.'

Hence Rodrigo beckoned. Wellington's 1811 experiences before Badajoz ensured that this next siege should of course be conducted with proper artillery, and since it would take two months or so for the battering train to conclude its snail-pace journey, the summer's heat would by then be passing. Further, the Army of Portugal, 'which was destined to oppose us in whatever point we should direct our operations, was not likely to be so strongly supported in the north as in the south'. The train would then be safely and conveniently in a restored Almeida; the long umbilical cord of support to Lisbon could increasingly switch to Oporto, via a Douro to be made more navigable by Dickson's passage of the train; Rodrigo was but weakly garrisoned. Lastly Marmont might well be kept as ignorant of his Lordship's plans as his predecessor the previous year was ignorant of the Lines.

The British battering train was simply enormous when assembled on dry land: guns, howitzers, mortars, shot and shell, powder, carts, limbers, bullocks, mules and men. It had been sitting in the Navy's transports for the past two years, too big a task to get quickly to Badajoz for the first attempts, but clearly already in the Tagus at that time. (His Lordship had written to Admiral Berkeley on 20 March expressing his wish 'to disembark the ordnance store-ships (with the exception of the battering train) ... I am keeping the battering train on board because, whenever we may need it, it will be convenient to transport it part of the way by sea.') The Peer judged there was insufficient time to allow such a tardy convoy to be committed in 1811 to such a journey; nor had he then the confidence in Alexander Dickson he was later to enjoy. The train comprised thirty-four iron 24-pounders, four 18-pounders, eight 10-inch howitzers, two 8-inch howitzers, and twenty of the more conventional 5½-inch howitzers. The ammunition comprised 800 rounds per gun and 400 rounds per howitzer and mortar (including reserves), some 42,400 rounds in all, with 1,600 barrels of powder. The whole was transferred into 160 flat-bottomed boats at Oporto by two companies of English artillerymen and 300 Portuguese gunners, and reached Lamego fifty miles up the Douro where it was met by 1,000 carts and 8,000 bullocks, who then hauled the forty miles to Villa da Ponte, arriving by divisions during the first week of September. Captain Dickson faced and solved many difficulties during this period, such as the construction of 700 timber crates to take the shot and shell on the country carts; the replacement on eighty limbers of the horse shafts for bullock poles; the construction of sledges for the mortars; the making of 4,000 extra cartridges for the 24-pounders etc. etc., all at a time when he personally suffered recurring fevers and ill health generally. Much of his constant travelling was in a litter – a sort of large two-man sedan chair slung between two mules.

As the train began to arrive at Villa da Ponte, he wrote, 'About the middle of September I expect the first great convoy with all the heavy guns, will be at

Ciudad Rodrigo' and so too hoped his Lordship. But Dickson was wrong. He was to be stuck where he was until the middle of November, and it would be 1812 before the first 24-pounder ball crashed into the fortress of Rodrigo. As the engineer John Jones put it in his Journal, 'Just as the garrison of Rodrigo having become much distressed for supplies, and it was intended to try some immediate enterprise against it, the French made a great effort for its relief: on 28 September Marmont crossed the Agueda with an overpowering force.'

Wellington heard of Marmont's intentions to replenish Rodrigo on the last day of August but, with 14,000 sick, his 46,000 strength could not prevent the re-victualling – indeed, at El Bodon, it was all he could do to prevent Marmont's cavalry cutting up one of Picton's brigades. When the French eventually withdrew on 1 October, the deadlock on relative strengths continued, until ended by the need for dispersed winter quarters on both sides. Then the Emperor intervened in November with his orders to Marmont and to Joseph, to despatch troops to aid Suchet in Valencia and, a little later, the withdrawal of the unfortunate Guard regiments for Russia. There was now presented to his Lordship the opportunity for the attack on the fortress of Rodrigo that had long been in contemplation.

Ciudad Rodrigo's river Agueda was found by the Roman army to be easily fordable – except when the rains came down – and the adjacent slight hill, some 150 feet above the river level, neatly provided a defensible camp site. One guesses this was so in the time of Augustus, who turned the Mediterranean into a Roman lake. The Vandals, the Visigoths, the Arabs and the Crusaders were but a few of the many to have contributed to the construction and deconstruction of this town upon a hill. The true founding of the town came in the twelfth century, when it was repopulated by Ferdinand II, and the walls date from this period. The castle is thought to have been built by Henry II in 1372, and would therefore be medieval rather than Moorish. Yet the Moors mainly built castles with square towers, as at Rodrigo, whereas castles built by the Crusaders had round towers – so no-one can be too sure. The bridge is thought to have been constructed in the sixteenth century. The outer town wall was in a rough oval, some half mile by a quarter, of a plain perimeter construction, without bastions or angles, with a poor parapet. The masonry was now old, narrow and nowhere higher than thirty feet – all quite adequate for medieval defence but not against the subsequent invention of large calibre siege cannon. Thus there occurred the construction of a second, outer wall and the cutting of gun embrasures on the ramparts of the main wall. The outer was of faced packed earth, taken from without, thus creating a ditch-wall-ditch-wall sequence to test the attacker. The garrison's weakness, however, lay less than two football pitches to the north, a gentle ridge (the Lesser Teson) of stony soil which rose nearly to the height of the ramparts; and behind it by another 400 yards there was another slightly higher feature (the Upper Teson) which over-topped the ramparts by a significant thirteen feet or so. Hence the glacis and the first wall (which was set somewhat away from the main rampart wall) could not prevent aimed cannonfire being effective down onto the foot of the ramparts – the key 'open sesame' to any breaching operation.

The Tesons had two further attractions for the besiegers: they provided covered approaches via their dead ground; and the surfaces were diggable, unlike the western and eastern approaches which were not only open and rocky, but because of the slope of the land the guns would have to be much closer in to breach effectively. 'This would have been a tedious process,' Napier said, and any infantryman who has wielded a pick or, worse, a shovel on hard wintry ground will testify to that.

In 1810 Ney had made a lengthy and expensive meal of overcoming the Spanish garrison, and Lord Wellington knew he would be expected to choose the same route: for it was a proven key to the town and anyway re-opening old trenches and breaches is both hard to resist and quick to do. Accordingly the French had added fortified posts out beyond the town walls, to complicate and slow his efforts. These comprised the Renaud Redoubt (named after the recently captured Governor, but also known in some accounts as Fort Francisco) on the forward slope of the Upper Teson, and the Convents of Santa Clara, San Francisco, San Domingo and of the Trinity in the eastern suburbs, and finally that of Santa Cruz on the west. The Renaud Redoubt with its three guns, a dozen gunners and sixty bayonets, stood directly in the intended path, and was supported by another two guns and a howitzer on the flat roof of the Francisco convent just 400 yards away. The Redoubt had a palisaded ditch to the fore and plain palisades to the rear.

The town garrison comprised a battalion each of the 34th Léger and of the 113th Ligne, both from Thiebault's Division in Salamanca, together with two companies of artillery and some sappers – less than 2,000 all ranks – and was reluctantly commanded as a last-minute replacement by Brigadier General Barrié. Under his care he also had the battering train of Marmont's Army of Portugal, some 153 heavy guns complete with powder, shot and transport (but not the gunners). This was clearly a huge added bonus prize for the besiegers.

Lord Wellington's plan was to move up the undefended reverse slopes of the Upper Teson, taking the Redoubt at last light, sap forward to the Lesser and start constructing batteries on the forward slopes of both features. Those closest to the town would be a mere 200 yards from the walls. The Convents would also be dealt with. Unlike the previous year's abortive attempt at Badajoz, however, where once the breaches at Fort Christobal were considered (wrongly) to be practicable, and he had assaulted with just two grenadier companies, here for the Renaud Redoubt – like Christobal garrisoned by a weak company – he was to use eight British companies and two Portuguese.

The Light Division which had been blockading the town, moved to besiege it on 8 January, crossing the Agueda at a ford four miles above. Previous days had seen falls of sleet and snow, but this day was milder, albeit with ice on the river edges. The Division made a point of examining the entire perimeter during the afternoon, without overt or regular investment, and withdrew behind the Upper Teson. Johnny Kincaid, 95th:

> There was a smartish frost, with some snow on the ground and when we arrived opposite the Fortress, about midday, the garrison did not appear to think we were in earnest, for a number of their officers came out, under the shelter of a stone wall within half a musket-shot and amused themselves in saluting and bowing to us in ridicule ...
> We lay on our arms until dark.

A cold time it would have been in the wind, on open slopes, even wrapped in greatcoats.

The assault on the Renaud Redoubt was most unusual in Peninsular terms. Silent night attacks on entrenched positions necessarily dispense with preliminary artillery fire, in turn demanding for success a huge element both of surprise and of superiority of numbers, swiftly to overcome the natural advantages of the defender. There can be no room for doubt or hesitation, since control and changes of plan in darkness are at their most vulnerable to errors. The thirty-three-year-old Lieutenant Colonel John Colborne, 52nd, as commander of this venture therefore – and thankfully – issued orders that were simple, clear and to be carried out with compelling force.

The Redoubt's rear face was a plain low loop-holed wall without a ditch but with a gate set in it; the other faces comprised a wall with a ditch eight feet deep and about the same wide, with a timber palisade much the same height. In places this was quite close to the counter-scarp, or the near side of the ditch. A guardhouse was set in the rear. Four companies (two each from the 52nd and the 95th), around 300 men, half having Baker rifles, were to provide point-blank covering fire from the edge of the ditch against the one company's worth of French heads above the parapet; a further two companies (each from the 43rd and the 52nd) were to break in, while a further company was to circle the Redoubt to break in from the rear. The remaining three companies were in reserve – although some doubt still exists as to whether the two Portuguese companies were present in effective numbers. Additionally, a party of sappers under Captain Thomson RE were to carry the necessary scaling ladders and fascines. Awaiting success and standing by with picks and shovels was a 700-strong working party. They were immediately to commence digging trenches both in rear and forward of the Redoubt.

As the town clock struck 8pm half a mile away, the sound echoing up over the dark crest before them, John Colborne sat his horse at the front of the four fire support companies in the dead ground behind the Upper Teson. In the lead was No. 8 Company, 1st/95th, Captain Crampton's. The ladder parties came next, and then the assault or escalading companies.

Many years later Colborne described what happened:

> In this order we started and advanced, after a caution had been given
> by me in respect of silence, and each captain had been instructed
> precisely where he was to post his company and how he was to
> proceed on arriving near the redoubt. An officer of the 95th and two
> sergeants had been stationed before dark on the brow of the hill to
> mark the angle of the redoubt covering the steeple of the church in
> Ciudad Rodrigo. When we reached the point marked by the officer
> of the 95th, I dismounted and again called for the four captains of the
> advance guard and ordered the front company to occupy the front
> face and the 2nd the right, &c. Captain Mulcaster, of the Engineers,
> suggested that it would be better to wait for the light ladders which
> were coming up. I, however, thought that no time should be lost, and
> proceeded with the very heavy ladders which had been made during
> the day. When about fifty yards from the redoubt I gave the word
> 'double-quick'. This movement and the rattling of canteens alarmed
> the garrison; but the defenders had only time to fire one round
> from their guns before each company had taken its post on the crest
> of the glacis and opened fire. All this was effected without the least
> confusion, and not a man was seen in the redoubt after the fire was
> commenced. The party with the ladders soon arrived and placed
> them in the ditch against the palisades, so that they were ready when
> Captain Mein, of the 52nd, came up with the escalading companies.
> They got into the ditch by descending on the ladders and then
> placing them against the fraises. The only fire from which the
> assailants suffered was from shells and grenades thrown over from
> the rampart. During these proceedings Gurwood of the 52nd came
> from the gorge and mentioned that a company could get in by
> the gorge with ladders. I desired him to take any he could find.
> Thompson, of the Engineers, had no opportunity of being of use;
> the whole arrangements were executed by the exertions of captains
> of companies, and the order preserved by them. We entered the
> redoubt by the ladders safely; no resistance or opposition was made.
> The company at the gorge had tossed open the gate, or it had been
> opened by some of the defenders endeavouring to escape. Captain
> Mein, I believe, was wounded by a shot from one of our own com-
> panies as he was mounting on the rampart. Most of the defenders
> had fled to the guard-house Not one man was killed or wounded
> after we entered the redoubt ... Had the redoubt not been taken,
> five days would have been required to attack it regularly ... The
> Governor (of Rodrigo) had been in the redoubt half an hour before
> we attacked it.

Colborne suffered only six men killed and nineteen wounded, capturing some fifty all ranks (unwounded), (according to Captain John Ewart, 52nd, three officers and forty-seven men) with just a dozen Frenchmen wounded, three killed. That seventy-five per cent of the garrison suffered no ill would seem to indicate a remarkable lack of resolve on their part. Indeed, Colborne made comment later about the French taking refuge under the guns, with some muskets found to be piled, and not in the garrison's hands. Sergeant Garretty, 43rd, tells how 'when we entered the place I observed several packs of cards, with which the men had been amusing themselves.'

This stout little battalion-sized effort therefore achieved the surprise upon which it entirely depended, and the superiority of numbers brought to bear shows Lord Wellington had learnt lessons from the previous year at Badajoz. (It also shows he had overcome his Indian antipathy towards night operations.) It was a necessary but, nonetheless, neat coup-de-main, which saved much time overall. It showed how a concentrated close-range rifle fire will subdue rampart defenders, and thus give escaladers space to climb and swiftly conquer: a demonstration sadly not to be properly followed at Badajoz, with bloody results. And in passing, it is pleasing to speculate how John Colborne would have applauded another John in his regiment – Major John Howard – who 132 years later, in another silent night attack with two companies of the 52nd (now the 2nd Oxfordshire & Buckinghamshire Light Infantry), captured by glider-borne coup-de-main the two bridges at Ranville in Normandy, to secure the left flank of that great Invasion. The two Johns shared more than the cap badge.

CHAPTER 1

Part II – Ciudad Rodrigo
The Plan

Now that the siege proper could begin, just what was facing the British force on the other side of the Lesser Teson? The main town wall was about thirty feet high – nearly six men's height – and in places almost as wide, with a parapet rather too thick for defending with muskets, not easily able to command the ditch below, that is, with aimed fire, without leaning out to expose the body. The same problem attended the gun embrasures cut in the parapet, which were designed to cover the glacis and beyond, firing over the *fausse braie*, but not able to fire with depressed barrels into the ditch. This would not matter if the main wall had bastions or angles to afford ancillary flanking fire, but there were none, except at the point some 300 paces to the east of Lord Wellington's intended breaching site, in the form of a medieval tower.

The main wall ditch was some seven paces wide, up to the 'outside' wall, or *fausse braie*, which was twenty feet high, i.e. well below the main wall. The outer ditch below the *fausse braie* was another seven or eight paces wide, edged by the glacis but only to a height of some ten feet. So not only was the main wall's designed protector – the *fausse braie* – too short to prevent shot and shell striking the main wall, the *fausse braie*'s designed protector – the glacis – was too short in turn to protect it either.

Thus given the close 200 yards range of the Lesser Teson ridge and the superior height advantage (thirteen feet) provided by the Upper Teson ridge, once the Redoubt had been secured, the reduction of Rodrigo became a matter of establishing battering batteries forward on both ridges. A start was made within minutes of Colborne's coup-de-main: 'the force under my command was collected outside (having secured the Redoubt) and marched down to the rivulet at the bottom of the glacis of the place, and covered the working parties opening the first parallel, til moonlight.' As Rifleman Ned Costello, 95th, said:

> We expected to be marched back to our quarters at El Bodon, but instead were ordered to break ground, and we commenced the task of throwing up entrenchments in the face of the city. Being unsheltered from the enemy's shot, their grape and cannister occasionally played among us, so although the night was remarkably cold – it was freezing

at the time – we had no reason to complain of not having a good fire! Now was the time to cure a skulker, or teach a man to work for his life. There we were, in twos, each provided with a pick axe and shovel, digging with a vengeance into the frozen mould, and watching for the glances of the shot and shell. We stuck to our work like doubles, sometimes pitching ourselves to our bellies to avoid their being purged with grape or cannister.

A view echoed by John Cooke, 43rd:

A furious fire of shot and shell opened on us while digging a parallel close to the captured fort; the earth was thrown up on the town side. The land was arable and strewn with loose stones, which flew on all sides from the impulse given by the cannon balls and bursting shells. They exploded on every side, killing and maiming many soldiers.

But by first light on 9 January 150 yards of the old 1810 French parallel had been re-opened to a depth of three feet or so, adjacent to the Redoubt, continuing back over the crest onto the reverse slope, 'a trench sufficiently large to cover a Brigade' according to Lieutenant Madden, 43rd.

Costello reminds us of the conditions:

The following day (the 9th) we were relieved and marched back to our quarters, cold, hungry and fatigued. It was very annoying to have to cross the Agueda getting to the trenches and returning to them. Pieces of ice were constantly carried down this rapid stream, and they bruised our men so much that the cavalry were ordered to form four deep across the ford, under the lee of whom we crossed comparatively unharmed. Nevertheless, by the time we reached our quarters, our clothes were frozen and icy.

Lieutenant George Simmons, 95th, noted further how 'Our poor fellows had to cross the river nearly up to their shoulders, and remain in this wet state until they returned to their quarters.'

The garrison of course had the range to the digging work, and its fire concentrated on the battery sites and magazines, 'Their round shot causing many casualties' according to the engineer John Jones. Some thirty guns were positioned on the northern ramparts and 'The garrison adopted the expedient of firing shells filled with powder and having long fuses in salvos. Some of these falling together into the parapets, blew away in an instant the work of hours.'

On 11 January thirty-eight heavy guns from the battering train arrived, together with two days' expenditure of ammunition.

Next day the Light Division stood duty once more. In an effort to suppress the French fire, Simmons writes, 'Thirty riflemen were ordered to get as close as possible, dig holes sufficiently deep to cover themselves, and take deliberate aim at the enemy's embrasures which a good marksman could easily do by observing the flashes of their cannon, although it was dark.' That night, the cold was so intense, says Jones, that 'The same men were incapable of working the whole night through so that reliefs were regulated, a thousand men at dusk (soon after 5pm) and five hundred men at one a.m.'

On 13 January three of the four battery positions prepared in rear of the Redoubt on the Upper Teson received a total of twenty-seven guns. That night the garrison at the Convent of Santa Cruz situated just 200 yards from the intended line of the second parallel across the Lesser Teson, were ejected by 300 German troops from the 60th and the King's German Legion.

Next morning work on the second parallel commenced, prompting a sortie by 500 of the garrison, which recaptured Santa Cruz and destroyed much of the work on the new trenches. The garrison's Governor, General Barrié, had stationed an officer lookout on the steeple of the Cathedral, to observe and report the commencement of the relief by Wellington's duty division; a lazy drill had been fallen in to, which Jones describes as 'A bad custom ... The works were left unguarded for some time during each relief.' However, the incoming Division restored order and at 4.30pm fire commenced from the batteries on the Upper Teson. Two 18-pounders opened onto the walls of the Convent of San Francisco, and the other twenty-five pieces commenced battering the *fausse braie* and main wall at Lord Wellington's chosen breaching site – the same as Ney's in 1810 – the north-western corner of the town. Darkness fell soon afterwards, and the guns fell silent, but a start had been made and doubtless General Barrié went to bed with a good deal on his mind. It was not made any more tranquil a few hours later when news came that his small garrison in the Convent of San Francisco had been driven out, by three companies from the 40th – another silent night attack – leaving behind the guns which would have enfiladed the second parallel, and which had been making the diggers' lives uncomfortable in the first parallel. William Lawrence, 40th, was there:

> We were annoyed all the time by three guns which were situated on a fortified Convent a little distant from the town. As the Convent was near to where our Brigade's operations were in progress, our Colonel volunteered to storm it. The offer was accepted and several companies, my own included, advanced under cover of darkness. Unobserved by the enemy we took the Garrison by surprise and succeeded in effecting an entrance, but the Garrison managed to decamp. I and a few others volunteered to march up to the tower where the guns were situated. There were no French there, only three shattered cannon whose condition was hardly improved when we were ordered to throw them down. The only French left in the

Convent – or at least all I saw there – were two of their wounded.
However they were good enough to leave us a room full of cabbages,
which came in very handy indeed.

The removal of the threat from San Francisco, and the successful progress next
day battering the old breached site, decided Lord Wellington to locate a fourth
battery in the first parallel (just to one side of the Redoubt) with the role of
opening a second breach, at the medieval tower some 300 yards to the left (as he
saw it) of the main breach. It was his intention, however, to hold back the fire
onto this new breach, until the old one was imminently practicable. That day,
it was the turn of the 3rd Division. Private Donaldson, 94th, aged nineteen:

> The French kept up a very destructive fire on us during the whole
> of our operations, and while forming the second parallel they threw
> out some fire balls to enable them to see where we were working, that
> they might send their shot in that direction; one of them fell very
> near where a party was working, and by its light completely exposed
> them to the view of the enemy; a Sergeant belonging to our regiment,
> of the name of Fraser, seeing the danger to which they were exposed,
> seized a spade and, jumping out of the trench regardless of the
> enemy's fire, ran forward to where it was burning, and having dug a
> hole tumbled it in and covered it with a sod.

On 16 January a thick fog descended in the morning, enabling the embrasures
and gun platforms to be repaired as required, free from interference, by the
working party now numbering some 700 men. It was the Light Division's turn
once again and George Simmons, 95th, tells us:

> I had charge of a party to carry earth in gabions [wicker baskets] and
> plant them upon the advanced saps in places where the ground was
> an entire rock and could not be penetrated. The enemy fired grape
> and consequently numbers fell to rise no more from the effects of it.
> I ran the gauntlet here several times and brought gabions of earth,
> always leaving some of my poor fellows behind when I returned for
> more. Glad enough I was when the engineer said 'We have now
> sufficient'.

Once more riflemen that night sniped at the French gun teams from pits sunk
well forward. Next day (the 17th) the fog lifted around noon, and the battering
continued until darkness fell. A good part of both the main wall and the *fausse
braie* had been tumbled into the ditches, but the garrison's accurate fire, shot,
shell and grape, saw mounting casualties including amongst the riflemen in the
pits, and the working parties, and a 24-pounder which suffered a direct hit in
No. 2 Battery. That night the fourth battery on the first parallel was completed,

including its magazine, and seven 24-pounders with their ammunition were heaved into position. Their target was the second breach or tower, and was calculated at 550 yards range.

At daylight on 18 January fire commenced from thirty-two guns, and by evening the main breach was considered practicable. For this reason the tower was also engaged, and promptly came down 'like an avalanche'. By nightfall it was deemed prudent to play on the main breach throughout the dark hours, with three howitzers, 'to prevent the garrison from clearing the rubbish out of the ditch, as they had done on previous nights, and these did some execution, as the French said they had lost thirty men' (Captain John Ewart, 52nd, quoting a French journal later found in Rodrigo). The total expenditure of ammunition up to midday on 18 January was 5,544 rounds of 24-pounder and 490 rounds of 18-pounder, with a second 24-pounder out of action through a burst barrel.

By the afternoon of the 19th, the main breach was described as 'extremely good' and the tower breach 'nearly beaten down'. Lord Wellington decided to assault that very day, and sitting down under cover of the advanced trenches, wrote his orders. It was twelve days now since he had invested Rodrigo. His assessment of Marmont's eastwards movement, and his inability quickly to aid the fortress, had fully justified that decision. He had allowed himself the same twenty-four days to get the job done, as Ney had taken in 1810. Thus on the 19th he had every reason to be satisfied. That sentiment was doubtless the more satisfactory given his knowledge of 'the other side of the hill'. Four days earlier, writing to the Earl of Liverpool, he summarised Marmont's strength as being (apart from Thiebault at Salamanca) two divisions on the march from Toledo to Valladolid, one at Navamoral on the Tegus, forty miles west of Talavera, and one about Talavera itself. That is, all many marches distant. Marmont's headquarters was moving from Talavera also to Valladolid and 'I have reports that troops were to be collected at Salamanca . . . (but) it is not probable that a sufficient force can be collected to oblige us to raise the siege, at least for some days.'

For Marmont knew precious little. The Governor of Salamanca, General Thiebault, had been crying wolf too often to be believed, with his reports of the construction of fascines and gabions, the movement of the British battering train, and the possible construction of a bridge over the Agueda. Thiebault's own intelligence suffered particularly from the closing of the roads between Rodrigo and Salamanca by the guerrillas of Julian Sanchez. It was 13 January before Thiebault heard from General Barrié that the siege had begun six days previously. That very day Marmont at Valladolid (only a week's march away) was writing to Napoleon's chief of staff that he doubted Wellington would cross the Agueda! So when late the next day Thiebault's undeniable news arrived, telling him that Wellington with at least five divisions had been battering Rodrigo for nearly a week, it was most unwelcome news. Marmont knew who to blame, of course:

> The Emperor chose to cut down the number of his troops in Spain, and to order a grand movement which dislocated them for a time, precisely at the instant when he had increased the dispersion of the Army of Portugal, by sending a detachment of 12,000 men against Valencia. He was undoubtedly aware that the English Army was cantooned in a fairly concentrated position on the Agueda, the Coa, and the Mondego. But he had made up his mind – I cannot make out why – that the English were not in a condition to take the field: in every despatch he repeated this statement.

That Marmont shared that final sentiment is obvious, evidenced by his lack of reaction to the earlier reports from Thiebault and which he treated as 'Wild and whirling words'. But what to do? Working on the twenty-four day precedent set by Ney, he would need to confront Wellington by the end of January, and with good numbers if the British were fielding by then six or seven divisions. Once Rodrigo fell it would be too late, for his battering train was actually within the fortress. Marmont had but four divisions only loosely concentrating towards Salamanca, with others much farther afield. And if Wellington captured Rodrigo before he could relieve the place, would the English not then make for Badajoz, and would not that leave Marmont, if closing on Rodrigo, again in the wrong place?

We are fortunate that Wellington's detailed orders have survived, as hurriedly written that cold afternoon in the trenches before Rodrigo. Hurried because the day was wearing on, it would be dark soon after 5pm, and much of that which had to be done was best completed in daylight. The orders were in plain narrative style of who was to do what, where and when and with what, without a wasted word and not a single urgent sentiment nor supportive flattery. 'Once more unto the breach' was not the Peer's style. But they do present some insight into that calm and thoughtful intellect which penned them, racing across the page as time diminished, as shot and shell moaned overhead, and his staff stood waiting, hopping in the mud from foot to foot. The orders are attached at Appendix 1.

The plan, to be appreciated best, follows a brief description of the breached sites and the French defence. It is not known in what detail these measures were anticipated by the attackers, since none of them had ever been up a breach slope before; the two attempts against the walls of Badajoz the previous year had failed in the ditch, clutching ladders that were too short. Yet outside Fort San Cristoval they had certainly met canister and grape, hand grenades and rolling shells, the defenders each with maybe six or seven loaded muskets to hand, and, had they mounted the breach, there at the top would have been the upturned carts and chevaux-de-frise of blades set in massive timbers chained to the walls.

General Barrié had placed three infantry companies and a dozen gunners at the main breach, and a company of voltigeurs at the smaller. The latter was only ten paces wide at the bottom, and half that at the top, where it was all but closed by a 24-pounder cannon placed sideways across the gap in the town wall. There was space of a yard, however, between the muzzle and the wall. No retrenchments had been cut. The slope behind the breach down into the town, unlike the steep climb up to it, was quite gentle and the narrow alley beyond was blocked by only one up-turned cart. Bearing in mind the defenders had some two hours of darkness after the cannon-fire ceased, and before the assault, it was plain that no urgent effort had gone into the garrison's last minute defensive preparations.

The main breach was a much harder proposition. It was three times wider, if less steep, powerfully defended parapets above, including enfilading cannon, and flank entrenchments the details of which were unknown; those survivors of the assault still moving forward would plunge down sixteen vertical feet of the remaining town rampart, onto what Jones describes as 'A variety of impediments, such as iron crow's feet, iron chevaux-de-frise, iron spikes fixed vertically, and the whole being encircled with the means of maintaining a barrier of burning combustibles'. Finally, as Napier tells us, 'The houses behind (about twenty yards back) were all loop-holed and garnished with musketeers.'

Lord Wellington chose 7pm as assault hour partly to give the troops time to assemble their kit and move some way to their waiting areas in daylight, and latterly under cover; and partly to allow but a couple of hours of darkness for the garrison to clear rubble and effect repairs around the breaches (another lesson learned from the previous year at Badajoz).

Picton's 3rd Division was to take the main breach, Crauford's Light Division the lesser, with two diversionary attacks: Lieutenant Colonel O'Toole with one Portuguese battalion and Brigadier General Pack with two, to distract attention to the town walls furthest away. The two main divisional attacks were to go in after the diversions had stirred things up and, hopefully, diverted French reserves. The diversions were to kick off at 6.50pm, with O'Toole leading the 2nd Caçadores, strengthened by the Light Company 2nd/83rd, to rush across the unblocked Roman bridge to seize an outwork at the far end, beneath the Castle, and within which two guns were positioned to cover the gate to their right, where the ditch joined the main wall. Brigadier General Pack, with the 1st and 16th Line, was to attempt the outworks at the Santiago gate on the eastern walls. Both Pack and O'Toole were to take ladders in case their diversions met little opposition, and so might be developed into real escalades.

Now, there is little subtlety in taking a town: men have to climb defended breaches. In making two, and with two more threatened escalades, Wellington sought to disperse the defenders. He also sought to protect the flanks of his main attempt when it went in, by occupying the ditches on either side, by pre-positioned separate parties. These were to work their way along the ditches from right and left, sweeping out any of the garrison and any obstacles they discovered, and then forming a reserve force on arrival at the breach.

Campbell's brigade was given this task for the main breach, while Picton's other 3rd Division brigade (MacKinnon's) was to carry out the main assault. The 2nd/5th, under Major Ridge, was to leave the cover of the convent Santa Cruz, go east 400 paces to where the ditch and *fausse braie* abuts the town wall, cut down the gate (assuming O'Toole had silenced the covering guns) mount the *fausse braie*, and clear it for the quarter of a mile up to the breach. The 94th was to provide two columns of five companies each, each to leave Santa Cruz, for a similar but shorter role – get into the outer ditch, but rather closer to the breach, and again clear to it. Of Campbell's other two regiments, the 77th was to remain at the Convent as a reserve for the 5th, and the 2nd/83rd was to remain lining the second parallel, to provide fire support (and presumably to form a further reserve).

The 5th and the 94th were to leave the convent of Santa Cruz at 6.50pm, the same time as O'Toole's battalion. Similarly, three companies of the Light Division's 95th were to leave cover from the right side of the convent of San Francisco, get into the outer ditch half way between the two breaches, turn right and with axes clear the ditch of any obstructing palisades up to the main breach. Thus the two breaches would mutually support one another with the passage of reserves.

The assault on the main breach by MacKinnon's brigade was to be preceded not only by these ditch clearances, but immediately by a party of 180 unarmed sappers each carrying two hay bags to be tossed into the outer ditch at the breach, to break the ten-foot fall of the storming party. These sappers were to be immediately followed by the Forlorn Hope who, together with the main assault troops, were to have come forward into the trenches connecting the first and second parallels. The Hope was to be commanded by Lieutenant Mackie, 88th, and was limited to thirty volunteers from MacKinnon's assaulting battalions – 1st/45th, 75th and 1st/88th. The storming party comprised 500 volunteers to be led by Major Manners, 74th. The Divisional Reserve was to be Powers' Portuguese 9th and 21st Line, to be located in the second parallel.

The Lesser Breach on the left was again to be approached by the convent of San Francisco first by a hay sack party, from the 3rd Caçadores, then the Forlorn Hope of twenty-five volunteers from 1st/52nd under Lieutenant John Gurwood, with the main storming party of 300 volunteers led by Major George Napier, 52nd. These were all troops from Vandeleur's Brigade (1st/52nd, 2nd/52nd, four companies 1st/95th and 3rd Caçadores). Barnard's Brigade (1st/43rd, 1st/95th less four companies, 2nd/95th) were to be formed in reserve behind the convent.

Lord Wellington's orders specified that once up the first or *fausse braie* breached wall, Vandeleur was to detach five companies down the ditch to his right, to assist the 3rd Division; and once up the town wall, to turn right along the ramparts, again to link with the 3rd Division. A third task, once the two divisions had joined, was to open the Salamanca Gate, just 200 paces to the left of the Lesser Breach. And that was that. The orders are silent beyond the plan of attack on the walls. Nothing is said of subsequent operations within the town. We may therefore assume Wellington assumed the Garrison would yield. He had already formally summoned Governor Barrié to surrender three days earlier, on the foggy 16 January, after commencing the battering of the lesser breach; but to no avail. Poor Barrié, like all Napoleon's garrison commanders, was barred from adopting the old custom of surrendering after a practicable breach had been established by the enemy (a sensible custom that usually excused a garrison from slaughter). The Emperor had expressly forbidden surrender before the enemy should have made his first attempt, some say three attempts.

What actually happened is best told by those who were there, like Rifleman Edward Costello, 95th, who volunteered for the storming party:

> Volunteers were now required from the different regiments of our Division, and many of our men came forward with alacrity for this deadly service. With three others from my company I had, as I then considered, the good fortune to be chosen. This was a momentous occasion in the life of a soldier, and so we considered it.
>
> At the time, we were in the trenches in front of the city, from whence came a very smart fire of shot and shell, which gave us an idea of the warm reception we might expect on our visit that night. The entire company gathered round our little party, each pressing us to have a sup from his canteen. We shook hands with friendly sincerity, and speculated on whether we would outlive the assault. If truth must be told, we also speculated on the chances of plunder in the town. I gave my father's address to my comrade before starting, in case of accident.
>
> In our regiment, there were four or five volunteers from each company, and we were led by Captain Mitchell and Lieutenants Johnston and Kincaid. The storming division was commanded by Major George Napier of the 52nd Regiment.
>
> Darkness closed over the city, and our imaginations became awake to the horrors of the coming scene. The stormers – in all about 120 men – were ordered to 'fall in' and 'form', and we moved to a convent occupied by the 40th, the walls of which protected us from the enemy's shot.

The Light Divison with Lord Wellington present had moved under cover of the Convent of San Francisco and were drawn up as follows (Lieutenant Johnny Kincaid, 95th):

> First, four companies of our battalion, under Colonel Cameron, to line the crest of the glacis and fire upon the ramparts. Second, some companies of Portuguese carrying bags filled with hay and straw, for throwing into the ditch to facilitate the passage of the storming party. Third, the forlorn hope, consisting of an officer (Lt Gurwood of the 52nd) and 25 volunteers. Fourth, the storming party, consisting of three officers and 100 volunteers from each regiment; the officers from ours were Captain Mitchell, Mr Johnston and myself ... Fifth, the main body of the Division under General Craufurd, with one brigade, under Major General Vandeleur, and the other under Colonel Barnard.

Lieutenant John Cooke, 43rd, also went forward into the ringside seats:

> Soon after 3 o'clock we moved toward the ground occupied by the foot guards, who were halted one and a half miles from the suburbs of Ciudad Rodrigo. These troops came forward to wish us success, and our band struck up the 'Fall of Paris'. The 3rd Division occupied the trenches. The garrison must have observed the march of the Light Division from the ramparts. Extra troops! The governor should have pondered on it. He must have expected the assault for there were two breaches effected in the walls of this town.
>
> At 6.30, the Light Division formed behind the convent of San Francisco, near the suburb, almost exactly opposite to the small breach and about 400 yards from it. The 3rd Division, under General Sir Thomas Picton, was formed behind the ruins of Santa Cruz, and in the trenches opposite the large breach. The two divisions were to attack without knapsacks. All was silent, except for four or five shells thrown by the enemy into our left battery, which fell not a great distance from our column. If the governor thought that the assault was preparing, he ought not to have fired at all from the ramparts, as it prevented the approach of the troops from being discovered by the ear.

At some early point Wellington was there too, according to the anonymous source quoted by Napier:

> The Duke of Wellington, standing on the top of some ruins of the convent of Francisco, pointed out to Colonel Colborne and to Major Napier, commanding the storming part of the light division, the spot where the small breach was. Having done this, he said, 'Now do you

understand exactly the way you are to take so as to arrive at the breach without noise or confusion?' He was answered, 'Yes, perfectly.' Some one of the staff then said to major Napier, 'Why don't you load?' He answered, 'No, if we can't do the business without loading we shall not do it at all.' The duke of Wellington immediately said, 'Leave him alone.'

And the soon-to-die commander of the Light Division also had something to say to his men:

General Craufurd led us in person. While we stood formed under the wall, he addressed us upon the nature of the duty assigned us. On this memorable occasion his voice was more than ordinarily clear and distinct: 'Soldiers! The eyes of your country are upon you. Be steady, be cool, be firm in the assault. The town must be yours this night. Once masters of the wall, let your first duty be to clear the ramparts, and in doing this keep together.'

With hearts beating, we waited watchfully for the signal, with our Division formed immediately in our rear, ready to second the effort. We were on the brink of being dashed into eternity, and among the men there was a solemnity and silence deeper than I ever witnessed before.

The convent the division had formed behind was held by the 40th. There William Lawrence, spectator-safe, commented: 'The business those men were about to undertake was about the worst a soldier can undertake. For scarcely anything but death stares them in the face. They were silent, watching with intense anxiety for what, to many, would be the fatal signal.'

CHAPTER 1

Part III – Ciudad Rodrigo
The Attack
19 January 1812

Over on the right, the 5th, 77th and 94th were also on the move. An anonymous officer of the 77th wrote:

It was six o'clock – the firing on both sides had slackened, but not ceased – their instructions had been for some time in the possession of our chiefs, who were all bustle and mystery. Soon the 5th and 77th were ordered to fall in, and we proceeded some distance to the extreme right of the ground occupied by the division, where we halted; and whilst the men hammered at their flints, and made the customary preparations for business, the order was communicated to us. (Here follows part of Wellington's orders):

The 5th regiment will attack the entrance of the ditch at the junction of the counterscarp with the main wall of the place. Major Sturgeon will show them the point of attack. They must issue from the right of the convent of Santa Cruz. They must have twelve axes, in order to cut down the gate by which the ditch is entered at the junction of the counterscarp with the body of the place. The 5th regiment is likewise to have twelve scaling ladders, twenty-five feet long; and immediately on entering the ditch, are to scale the Fausse Braie, *in order to clear it of the enemy's parties, on their left, towards the principal breach. It will throw over any guns it may meet with, and will proceed along the* Fausse Braie *to the breach in the* Fausse Braie, *where it will wait until Major-General McKinnon's column has passed on the main attack, when it will follow in its rear. This regiment will make its attack at ten minutes before seven o'clock. The 77th regiment will be in reserve on the right of the convent of Santa Cruz.*

We of the 77th looked somewhat blank at the idea of remaining in reserve; and our colonel – a regular fire-eater – issued his directions with a grim countenance and a voice fierce from disappointment. Rest your souls in peace, brave Ridge and gallant Dunkin! O! though peace was little to your tastes in life. Finer fellows never cheered men to an assault; but Dunkin wanted that moderation and discretion which tempered Ridge's bravery. They alone ordered the colours to accompany their regiment – a rash act – considering that our united numbers little exceeded three hundred firelocks, and one that might have much embarrassed us in the work we had in hand: but it was Dunkin's fancy. Whilst waiting in the gloom, somewhat impatiently, for the return of the men sent for the ladders, and for Major Sturgeon's appearance, we mingled in groups of officers, conversing and laughing together with that callous thoughtlessness which distinguishes the old campaigner. I well remember how poor McDougall of the 5th, recently joined from the staff, was quizzed about his dandy moustaches. When next I saw him, in a few short hours, he was a lifeless and a naked corpse. Suddenly a horseman galloped heavily, but hastily towards us – it was Picton. He made a brief and inspiriting appeal to us: said he knew the 5th were men whom a severe fire would not daunt, and that he reposed equal confidence in the 77th. A few kind words to our Commander, and he bade us God speed – pounding the sides of his hog-maned cob as he trotted off in a different direction.

The 94th also moved up, as told by their anonymous officer:

From the engineer's stalls, there were given out to the 94th regiment a number of knotted ropes to assist in descending the ditch, and of felling-axes to remove and break down the impediments supposed to exist about the breach.

Lieutenant Colonel Campbell, having set his watch at the head-quarters of the Division, moved his regiment forward as soon as evening permitted, to the Convent of Santa Cruz, and to post under a loop-holed wall to the left of it, along which it had been intended to form a ditch which, however, was excavated to only the depth of a foot or two. This position was enfiladed by two light brass guns, mounted en-barbette on a projection of the *Fausse Braie*, but as the moon threw the shadow over the wall on this half-formed ditch, we were enabled to approach unobserved to within a hundred and twenty yards of the outer defences of the place. Here we waited until the moment arrived, at which as Colonel Campbell had been told, the storming party would leave the trenches; for although we had less ground to pass over to reach the breach than they, it was of import-ance that we should be there before them, in order to perform the duty of removing whatever might embarrass the attack.

And in the dead ground behind the Upper Teson, and destined to assault the main breach, the 88th (Connaughts) were waiting for news, as Ensign William Grattan tells us:

> It was now five o'clock in the afternoon, and darkness was approaching fast, yet no order had arrived intimating that we were to take a part in the contest about to be decided. We were in this state of suspense when our attention was attracted by the sound of music; we all stood up, and pressed forward to a ridge, a little in our front, and which separated us from the cause of our movement, but it would be impossible for me to convey an adequate idea of our feelings when we beheld the 43rd Regiment, preceded by their band, going to storm the left breach; they were in the highest spirits, but without the slightest appearance of levity in their demeanour – on the contrary, there was a cast of determined severity thrown over their countenances that expressed in legible characters that they knew the sort of service they were about to perform, and had made up their minds to the issue. They had no knapsacks – their firelocks were slung over their shoulders – their shirt-collars were open, and there was an indescribable something about them that at one and the same moment impressed the lookers-on with admiration and awe. In passing us, each officer and soldier stepped out of the ranks for an instant, as he recognised a friend, to press his hand – many for the last time; yet, notwithstanding this animating scene, there was no shouting or hazzaing, no boisterous bravadoing, no unbecoming language; in short, every one seemed to be impressed with the seriousness of the affair entrusted to his charge, and any interchange of words was to this effect: 'Well, lads, mind what you're about to-night'; or, 'We'll meet in the town by and by'; and other little familiar phrases, all expressive of confidence. The regiment at length passed us, and we stood gazing after it as long as the rear platoon continued in sight: the music grew fainter every moment, until at last it died away altogether; they had no drums, and there was a melting sweetness in the sounds that touched the heart.
>
> The first syllable uttered after this scene was, 'And are we to be left behind?' The interrogatory was scarcely put, when the word 'Stand to your arms!' answered it. The order was promptly obeyed, and a breathless silence prevailed when our commanding officer, in a few words, announced to us that Lord Wellington had directed our division to carry the grand breach. The solders listened to the communication with silent earnestness, and immediately began to disencumber themselves of their knapsacks, which were placed in order by companies and a guard set over them. Each man then began to

arrange himself for the combat in such manner as his fancy or the moment would admit of – some by lowering their cartridge-boxes, others by turning theirs to the front in order that they might the more conveniently make use of them; others unclasping their stocks or opening their shirt-collars, and others oiling their bayonets; and more taking leave of their wives and children. This last was an affecting sight, but not so much so as might be expected, because the women, from long habit, were accustomed to scenes of danger, and the order for their husbands to march against the enemy was in their eyes tantamount to a victory; and as the soldier seldom returned without plunder of some sort, the painful suspense which his absence caused was made up by the gaiety which his return was certain to be productive of; or if, unfortunately, he happened to fall, his place was sure to be supplied by some one of the company to which he belonged, so that the women of our army had little cause of alarm on this head. The worst that could happen to them was the chance of being in a state of widowhood for a week.

The 77th approached the Convent of Santa Cruz soon after 6.30.

The awful stillness of the hour was unbroken, save by the soft-measured tread of our little columns as we passed over the green turf, or by the occasional report of a cannon from the walls, and the rush and hiss of its bore as it flew past us, or striking short, bounded from the earth over our heads ... We had approached the Convent, and whilst passing under its walls, we found there the Light Company of the 94th awaiting the hour of 7, when they were to commence brisk fire against the ramparts from the glacis, to distract the attention of the enemy.

And there at the Convent the 77th were meant to halt. But instead they pushed on, 'right forwards to the walls, which now loomed high and near'. He commented that 'I imagine there must have been some new directions communicated by Sturgeon, who led us to our point of attack.' Although his earlier reference to Donkin being 'a regular fire-eater ... [who] lacked moderation and discretion' hinted at a Colonel bitterly disappointed with his Regiment's supporting role, and who was prepared to reject it.

Anyway, forward they marched:

We reached the low glacis, through which we discovered a pass into the ditch, somewhat resembling a wide embrasure, heavy palisadoed, with a gate in the centre ... Through the palisadoes were visible the dark and lofty old Moorish walls, while high over our heads was the great Keep or Citadel, a massive square tower which, as it was relieved against the sky, seemed like a giant frowning on the scene.

We still were undiscovered, though we could distinguish the arms of the men on the ramparts, as they were levelled and fired from the parapets, in idle bluster, the balls whistling over us. The men with hatchets began to cut a way through the palisadoes, but the sound of the blows would not, I think, have been heard by the enemy who were occupied by their own noises, had it not been for the enthusiasm so characteristic of his country, which induced a newly-joined ensign, fresh from the wilds of Kerry, to utter a tremendous war-whoop as he saw the first paling fall before our efforts. The cheer was immediately taken up by the men and we all rushed through the opening, the two regiments mingled together.

Sergeant John Jones, who was Orderly Sergeant to the 5th's Major Ridge (who of course had preceded the 77th forward), said:

> After the first or second blow of the axes, the French sentinel directly over our heads called out, 'Qui va la? Sacre bleu, Anglais' and fired his musket . . . Major Ridge now mounted one of the ladders and I closely followed him; at the same time he called out to Ensign Canch, who carried one of the Colours, to mount and show the men the way.

So the 77th had caught up the tail of the 5th, doubtless to Major Ridge's surprise, and thanks to Lord Wellington's prescience in sending O'Toole's Portuguese across the old Roman bridge to silence the cannon covering the ditch, the entry could have been worse:

> We were in the ditch heavily fired on from rampart and tower with musketry, but I do not recollect that they had any cannon bearing on us there; however, they tossed down lighted shells, and hand grenades innumerable, which spun about fizzing and hissing amongst our feet. Some smashed men's heads in their descent, while others exploding on the ground tossed unlucky wretches in the air. I have seldom passed three or four minutes less comfortably; I think that time was consumed in bringing in and fixing the ladders against a wall to our left about twenty-five foot high, which I understood to be the extremity of the *Fausse Braie*. We crowded towards the ladders. Amongst the first to mount was the gallant chieftain of the 5th, but so many of his soldiers followed on the same ladder that it broke in two, and they all fell, many being hurt by the bayonets of their comrades round the foot of the ladder. Ridge's ankle was sprained . . . On raising my head to the level of the top of the wall, I beheld some of our fellows demolishing a picket which had been stationed at that spot ... Our ascent of the ladders placed us in the *Fausse Braie* – a broad deep ditch – in which we were for the moment free from

danger. When about 150 men had mounted we moved forward at a rapid pace along the ditch, cowering in close to the wall, whilst over our heads we heard the shouts and cries of alarm and preparation. Our course was soon arrested by the massive fragments and crumbling ruins of the main breach, extending half across the ditch.

So they had done their job. The ditches and *fausse Braie* were clear and no threat would imperil the men of MacKinnon's brigade who, they supposed, would by now be clawing up the debris of the breach. They had been joined at the breach by the 94th under Campbell, on their shorter route, but where was MacKinnon? For, as the officer of the 77th wrote:

> The situation in which we now were placed was one of extreme danger and embarrassment. Instead of falling into the rear of a column supposed to have already carried the breach, we stood alone at its base, exposed to a tremendous fire of grape and musketry from its defences ... For a minute we seemed destined to be sacrificed to some mistake as to the hour of attack. On the appearance of the 94th, the fire of the garrison was redoubled – but after a moment's consultation between the seniors, it was decided to die like men on the breach than like dogs in the ditch, and instantly with a wild hoorah, all sprang upwards, absolutely eating fire.

Ridge's Orderly Sergeant, John Jones, adds that he called out, 'Up, my brave men! He and I ascending at the same time, and the mould being knee height and deep at each step.'

The 94th too saw the chance for glory: 'The breach was clear for attack ... and knowing that we would be immediately supported by the parties approaching the breaches [Colonel Campbell] gave the word to fix bayonets and mount ... And, not to lose a second of time.' The French drums were beating to arms.

MacKinnon's brigade should by now have moved forward for, as the sapper John Burgoyne tells us, 'The whole would be regulated by the attack of the 5th Regiment, ten minutes after which the rest would commence.' But earlier, when MacKinnon and Campbell's brigades were both still in their forming up places, 'General Crauford, being late, an order was sent to detain General MacKinnon ... [who] hesitated, in consequence of the foregoing order, and some time was lost.' When he did move, it was into the teeth of direct shot, shell and canister from the rampart embrasures and its forty-three guns and howitzers. The full moon had earlier been concealed by cloud, but now it thinned and cleared, and as Gratton with the 88th tells us, 'The enemy had a full view of all that was passing; their batteries, charged to the muzzle with case-shot, opened a murderous fire upon the columns as they advanced.' The 3rd Division lost heavily crossing the open ground to the glacis, 'Ravaged by a tempest of grape from the ramparts,' as Napier puts it, and some delay was further occasioned, right under the guns, whilst the hay-bag parties got forward to the outer ditch. Thus MacKinnon eventually arrived to find Campbell, Ridge and Donkin – his flank support – sweeping ahead onto the rough scree of the breach slope.

No-one of course knew what lay in wait at the top, since no close reconnaissance had been practicable. It was probably for the best not to know in advance. Gratton gives the soldiers' philosophy clearly enough:

> Men going to storm a breach generally make up their minds that there is no greater probability of their ever returning from it; and whether they die at the bottom or top of it, or at the muzzle, or upon the breach of a cannon, is to them pretty nearly the same.

What was known, however, to every man in the storming parties was that the garrison had had enough time to prepare their surprises. Of particular nastiness, the flat top of the rampart wall – the promenade, shall we say – had been trenched across either side of the breach with breastworks protecting those firing out over the trenches. Since the breach was situated on a near-right-angle turn in the town wall, fire from these breastworks above the trenches would not only fall onto their direct attackers but could also be directed onto the backs of those parties attempting their neighbour. The trenches were ten feet wide and ten feet deep, that on the French left being a double trench, that on their right possibly a single; but above each flanks' pits crouched a 24-pounder cannon triple-charged with canister. And that was not the end of the defensive arrangements, as we shall see. The 45th and the 88th were destined to take a closer look.

The 45th's History tells us:

> Whilst waiting for the hour fixed for the assault, an order arrived from Sir Thomas Picton to form a forlorn hope. The officers commanding companies were therefore called together and ordered to bring to the head of the column six men from each company for the purpose. They soon returned declaiming that every man present volunteered for the pre-eminence, and wished to know how they were to act, for the older soldiers claimed it as their right. The moment for the assault had arrived, and there was no time to be lost, so Captain Martin, commanding the Grenadier Company, put an end to all difficulties by requesting leave to lead as he stood with his company at the head of the regiment. This was very reluctantly acquiescenced in there being no time to make other arrangements.

The Division and Brigade commanders (Picton and McKinnon) rode up on the frosty grass, the former calling out, 'Rangers of Connaught! It is not my intention to expend any powder this evening. We'll do the business with the cauld iron.' Both generals having dismounted and placed themselves at the head of the 45th, the signal gun sent off Lieutenant William Mackie's twenty-strong forlorn hope from the Connaughts, the 180 hay-bag sappers and Major Manners' storming party of 300 volunteers drawn from the brigade as a whole.

To their left, the Light Division measured up to take the Lesser Breach. Three companies of the 95th had already got forward into the ditch half way between the two breaches, turning right to clear MacKinnon's left flank. The forlorn hope was twenty-five men under Lieutenant Gurwood of the 52nd, and Major George Napier of his regiment commanded the 300-strong storming party. At the very last minute, Lieutenant Theodore Elliot, who was present only as an off-duty engineer, was ordered to guide Napier to the breach (the officer named in Fletcher's orders had not turned up). 'At the Convent,' said Captain Ewart, 52nd,

> we found Lord Wellington, General Graham, with Marshal Beresford, and nearly all the general officers of the army. The 2nd Battalion 52nd were formed in column of three men in front (the 2nd Battalion close in rear of the 1st, both left in front) with the 43rd Regiment, formed in column of three in front, right in front, upon the right of them; so that the two regiments should enter the breach at the same time, preceded by the 300 men. The 95th Regiment and 3rd Caçadores were ordered to carry the ladders and bags filled with wool to enable the troops to get over the ditch easier. At a few minutes after 7p.m. the whole moved towards the breach.

Johnny Kincaid of the 95th said,

> As soon as we turned the corner of the convent wall the space between us and the breach became one blaze of light with their fire-balls, which, while they lighted us on to glory, lightened not a few of their lives and limbs; for the whole glacis was in consequence swept by a well-directed fire of grape and musketry ... The Portuguese sack-bearers mostly lay down behind their bags to await the result.
>
> The 300 yards of ground to the crest of the glacis was cleared at a run and the men jumped down the scarp, a depth of eleven feet, and rushed up the *Fausse Braie* under a smashing discharge of grape and musketry. The bottom of the ditch was dark and intricate, and the forlorn hope took too much to their left; but the storming party went straight to the breach. (Napier)

But Kincaid got lost:

> We had some difficulty at first in finding the breach, as we had entered the ditch opposite to a ravelin, which we mistook for a bastion. I tried first one side of it and then the other, and seeing one corner of it a

good deal battered, with a ladder placed against it, I concluded that it must be the breach and calling to the soldiers near me to follow, I mounted with the most ferocious intent, carrying a sword in one hand and a pistol in the other; but when I got up I found nobody to fight with except two of our own men, who were already laid dead across the top of the ladder. I saw in a moment that I had got into the wrong box and was about to descend again when I heard a shout from the opposite side that the breach was there; and, moving in that direction, I dropped myself from the ravelin and landed in the ditch opposite the foot of the breach, where I found the head of the storming party just beginning to fight their way into it.

As we have seen, the Light Division was running late, and Captain James Fergusson, who was commanding the 100 volunteers from the 43rd, heard the engineer officer (the stand-in Elliot) call out, 'You are wrong, this is the way to the breach.'

Lieutenant Cooke, 43rd: 'Although the enemy were firing rapidly from the top of the wall, the troops on first descending to the bottom of the ditch, were still in total darkness.'

Captain Fergusson, 43rd:

> Immediately calling the men to come on, we ascended the breach in the *Fausse Braie* and soon reached the breach in the body of the place without the use of ladders. We remained for a few moments on the breach, until we had collected about twenty or thirty officers and men.

Then, as more men arrived, as Captain John Dobbs of the 52nd said, they and the 43rd went up the breach 'In sections of threes, side by side,' that is, six men broad.

Over on the much-wider main breach, the 3rd Division's regiments – such a mixture of the 5th, 45th, 77th, 88th and 94th – were fighting as much for space to climb the shifting footholds as much as getting at the French, for as the 77th officer wrote, 'The ascent ... consisting as it did of a nearly-perpendicular mass of loose rubble, in which it was extremely difficult to obtain a footing.'

He described what happened when their front

> Reached the top of the rampart as one man ... Two guns pointed downwards from the flanks, and had time to fire several rounds of grape, working fearful destruction particularly on the 94th ... A strong train of gunpowder was fired from the enemy's left which, passing across the breach, kindled and exploded a great number of shells, by which many were killed and wounded, and all who had gained the top were thrown down and stunned.

And if that were not warm enough for an opening welcome, 'On the margin of the breach were ranged a quantity of shells, which were lighted and rolled down amongst us,' while for any who managed to show their face over the lip of the breach, 'A brisk fire was opened from a breastwork a little distant from the rear of the breach ... the space between this breastwork and the interior scarp of the wall, which was entire and sixteen foot high, was filled with carriages of different kinds, chevaux-de-frise etc.'

The 45th and 88th had joined this devilish cauldron, in time to be caught on the crest of the glacis and at the foot of the breach, by 'A heavy fire from a distant flanking demi-bastion,' which Sergeant Brazill of the 88th said was 'On our left'. Then, as they faced the rubble slope, showered by grenades and grape, eyewitness accounts as to the sequence of events then becomes doubtful. We can but describe them: the subjugation of the French defence of the two transverse trenches on the attackers' right; that of the trench on their left; the suppression of the musketry from the breastwork in rear of the breach and the explosion of a mine, which killed General McKinnon and many others. There is even doubt whether the explosion was a mine deliberately fired among the breach rubble or an ammunition reserve accidentally ignited on the rampart.

We are fortunate to have detailed accounts of the fighting at the main breach. Both Sergeant John Jones of the 5th and the anonymous officer of the 94th wrote to the *United Services Journal* in 1843, claiming their Commanding Officers were first up the right-hand side and over the twin trenches; there is another account by Sergeant Brazill of the 88th dealing with the left side, and one by William Grattan.

Here is the heroic single-combat crossing of the right hand trenches by Lieutenant Colonel James Campbell, leading the 94th:

> On this side the enemy had prepared a double retrenchment, con-
> sisting of two ditches (each ten feet deep, and the same in width) and
> two parapets formed across the rampart. It appeared that they had
> been communicating with the breach from this side at the moment
> we mounted, by means of two strong planks laid across the ditches
> on the inner edge of the rampart. In the confusion of the surprise,
> the plank traversing the ditch next to the breach was only drawn
> a little back, so that one end fell to the bottom of the ditch, while
> the other rested on the interior lip. In this position it furnished the
> assailants with the means of passing. This was eagerly seized, and,
> by mutual assistance, they rapidly cleared the first ditch. The plank
> laid over the second ditch having been left undisturbed, Colonel
> Campbell proceeded forthwith to take advantage of it. While he was
> on the plank, a French officer sprung forward, and, calling on his
> men to fire, made a lunge with his sword at the colonel; he parried the
> blow, and closed with the Frenchman, and both were instantaneously

borne within the second retrenchment by the ardour of our men who were pressing on. At this instant, the 5th regiment reached and mounted the breach with a vehement cheer. This corresponding in the rear most opportunely with the exertions of those in front, startled and appalled the French soldiers at the critical moment at which, by supporting their brave officer, who was forced to yield his sword, they might have successfully defended their post. The advantage thus lost their assailants were too energetic to permit them, whatever efforts were made, ever to regain; but springing one after the other within the retrenchment, each, as he came up, threw himself on the enemy, of whom the foremost soon lay lifeless on the terre-plein, and the rest, who were beyond the immediate reach of the bayonet, turned and fled in panic, without a thought but to save themselves.

Before we hear from another eyewitness, also part of this small group on the ramparts, we can usefully continue the 94th's version: 'Colonel Campbell stopped the pursuit at a place where a street coming from the centre of the town, nearly at right angles with the rampart, is terminated by the retaining wall, but ascends by a ramp on the left to the terre-plein.' There Campbell sensibly decided he had gone far enough.

Beyond this ramp, the houses encroach on the rampart, and narrow it at one point to a few paces, whence it slopes gently down as far as the Agueda gate. A post was thus formed, which those who had reached it could have defended against any number of the enemy, had they recovered themselves.

At this point the 94th's eyewitness was just congratulating Campbell on his success:

When the tread of a considerable body of the enemy descending the street gave warning of their approach. A sufficient number of our men having been posted to close the rampart where it was narrowest, the rest were moved down the ramp to receive the enemy on the bayonet, as they should turn at the foot of the street. They came down at a steady step until within twenty or thirty paces of us, but then, hearing a call given to those who were on their way from the breach to move on, they all at once halted, seemed to listen for a moment and then, throwing down their arms, fled with precipitation.

Our party was now joined successively by Captain C. Campbell, of the 94th, (brother of the Colonel); Captain Laing, 94th, wounded through the wrist; Major Ridge of the 5th, limping, having sprained his ankle; the Sergeant Major of this last regiment and several

men. Still in all it did not number above forty. Patrols were sent
out, who went to the old Moorish Castle, to the Agueda gate, which
was strongly barricaded with stones, to remove which would have
required the labour of many hours, and to the different streets and
lanes which touched the ramparts in this direction, and which were
found deserted and strewn with arms.

With so few men Campbell would not be keen to venture into the streets,
away from his blocking position on or above the ramp. Indeed, he sent officers
back to the breach, to bring more men across the trenches:

But they were unable to gain their attention, which was entirely
occupied by the fire kept up on them from the retrenchment on that
[left] flank, and from the breast work raised in rear of the rampart.
This fire had brightened up, and become very close, it having evidently
been reinforced at the same instant that the parties approaching us
had given way, and our troops were dropping fast, and had opened
their fire in return. As the dazzling light in front, and the smoke
which hung over the breach, through the ditch and flank by which
we had crossed into complete obscurity, no persuasion could prevail
on them to follow in that direction. The storming party, and the
other brigade of the 3rd Division, on arriving afterwards, were in like
manner attracted by the fire of the enemy, and without searching for
entrance but where that fire appeared, eagerly strove to bring their
own to bear on it.

A different version of the passage of the two trenches on the right of the
breach was given by ex-Sergeant John Jones of the 5th, writing thirty years
after the event but in direct response to the above account of the 94th's part,
which had been published in a letter to the *United Services Journal* of 1843.
Jones says:

I was Orderly Sergeant to Major Ridge ... [with him] I was now
moving from the breach to the right on the ramparts when by the
light of the guns and musketry, I saw a plank laid across a trench cut
in the ramparts and which the enemy had neglected to withdraw.
This I pointed out to the Major and assisted him over it; and I verily
believe we were the first of our army that gained the ramparts ... We
then pushed on the ramparts with more of our men who joined us,
to the distance I suppose of fifty yards. There appeared but few of
the enemy here, and they retreated before us; but an incessant and
destructive fire was still kept up from behind an entrenchment
opposite the breach. At the place about fifty yards to the right of
the breach, a wall or gable end of a house joined the ramparts. Here
we made a halt, with our backs to the said wall. A few more men now

joined us from the breach, and Colonel Campbell of the 94th amongst them. We were now about thirty men, the Colonel and Major Ridge being the only officers.

We now heard the awful explosion of the mine beneath the breach, by which General MacKinnon and a great number of men were killed. The firing at this point almost ceased for a moment or two, and Colonel Campbell said to Major Ridge 'I fear all is lost, and we are prisoners.' A minute afterwards we heard the attack commence at the lesser breach and the cheers of the Light Division. Colonel Campbell then proposed to Major Ridge that we should move on around the ramparts. To this the Major replied 'We had better keep our position, for if we move, we may fall on Colonel O'Toole's men – they were ordered to escalade about this part.' Our little party of the 5th, and about half a dozen of the 94th mixed, were placed two deep with our backs to the wall, and looking over the ramparts. By order of Major Ridge I told them off into two sub-divisions, with instructions to be ready to wheel up to the right or left, to fire a volley if directed, and wheel back again and reload, while the second sub-division should replace them. Shortly after this we heard foot-steps advancing; Colonel Campbell challenged and no answering being received, the men were wheeled up, fired and fell back again to their places. The fire was not returned.

Now, whether Campbell or Ridge were the first over the planks, (and we can even add a third claim: the 45th's History is adamant that it was 'the 45th, followed by their supporting regiments, (which) rapidly swarmed [over the planks]') there is agreement that their small joint party halted some way down the walk-way, and formed a static post; and that some time now passed, when neither the post was reinforced, nor the left trench of the breach was forced, because of what Jones called 'The incessant and destructive fire kept up from behind the entrenchment opposite the breach.' With this lull at the main breach, therefore, we can turn to examine events at the Lesser.

There, we left the Light Division, somewhat late, mounting it with the 43rd and 52nd side by side, joined by some of the 3rd/95th (who were meant to be providing fire support from the glacis). John Cooke of the 43rd:

> The French swore they should not enter, and fought most desperately on the crest of the breach, throwing down large stones and missiles, and keeping up a most deadly fire. Here many brave officers and soldiers fell. On the glacis, while cheering on the main body of the Division, General Craufurd received a mortal wound and Major General Vandeleur and Colonel Colborne were also wounded. How the troops contrived to force the breach I know not, but it was well done. It was exceedingly steep, being about five yards wide at the top,

with a cannon of heavy calibre placed sideways to block up the passage. However, there was a clear yard from the muzzle of the gun to the wall, sufficient space for one or two soldiers to enter at a time, besides those who would pass underneath the muzzle or over the wheels of the carriage.

James Fergusson also mentions the cannon:

A gun was stretched across the entrance, near which some of the enemy were bayoneted, and among the number some deserters from the Light Division, in arms defending it against their countrymen. A soldier of the name of Jonathon Wilde, 43rd, was the first man that mounted the breach in the faux brais, but no individual could claim being the first that entered the breach; it was a simultaneous rush of about twenty or thirty. The forlorn hope was thrown in some degree behind, being engaged in fixing ladders against the face of the work, which they mistook for the point of attack. Major Napier was wounded at the moment when the men were checked by the heavy fire and determined resistance of the enemy, about two thirds up to the ascent. It was then that the soldiers, forgetting they were not loaded, as the Major had not permitted them, snapped all their firelocks.

Lieutenant John Cooke, thought to be in Captain John Duffy's 9th Company, 43rd, the leading company in the Light Division, following the storming parties says:

On ascending the small breach directly after it was carried, I found myself with the crowd. Lieutenant Colonel McLeod, with the assistance of some other officers, managed to collect on the rampart about two hundred soldiers of our regiment, and was exalting them to keep together. At this time, with the exception of a few stray shots from the opposite buildings, there was no firing on us, but their sharp musketry still at the great breach.

And the commander of the 43rd's storming party, James Fergusson, says:

Upon carrying the breach, the parties moved as before directed by Major Napier; that is 52nd to the left, 43rd to the right. At this time the great breach had not been carried, and was powerfully defended by the enemy. The houses being on it were loop-holed and a deep trench lined with musketry bearing directly upon it; the flanks of the breach were cut off, and the descent into the town from the ramparts at the top of it appeared considerable.

Around this time, Fergusson was wounded in the body and was 'Carried back by one of the men a little way on the rampart, when an explosion took place.' Lieutenant Harry Smith, 95th, was also moving to clear the ramparts 'When the horrid explosion took place which killed General MacKinnon of the 3rd Division on the spot, and many soldiers, awfully scorching others . . . I shall never forget the concussion when it struck me, throwing me back many feet.'

Now the explosion which killed MacKinnon was one of three or four observed by General Harvey, watching the assault from the Tesons:

> I stood on rising ground and watched the progress of the attack. The great breach was attacked first. At the top of it the 3rd Division opened their fire heavily, and it was returned heavily, but there was a distressing pause. The small breach was carried first, and there was one considerable explosion and two or three smaller ones on the ramparts.

William Grattan of the 88th was present on the main breach when the explosion occurred: 'A frightful explosion near the gun to the left of the breach, which shook the bastion to its foundation and completed the disorder.' He goes on to say how that gun was dealt with:

> There was at this time but one officer alive upon the breach (Major Thomson, of the 74th, acting engineer): he called out to those next to him to seize the gun to the left, which had been so fatal to his companions – but this was a desperate service. The gun was completely cut off from the breach by a deep trench, and soldiers, encumbered with their firelocks, could not pass it in sufficient time to anticipate the next discharge – yet to deliberate was certain death. The French cannoniers, five in number, stood to, and served their gun with as much sang froid as if on a parade, and the light which their torches threw forth showed to our men the peril they would have to encounter if they dared to attack a gun so defended; but this was of no avail. Men going to storm a breach generally make up their minds that there is no great probability of their ever returning from it to tell their adventures to their friends; and whether they die at the bottom or top of it, or at the muzzle, or upon the breach of a cannon, is to them pretty nearly the same!
>
> The first who reached the top, after the last discharge, were three of the 88th. Sergeant Pat Brazill – the brave Brazill of the Grenadier Company, who saved his captain's life at Busaco – called out to his two companions, Swan and Kelly, to unscrew their bayonets and follow him; the three men passed the trench in a moment, and engaged the French cannoniers hand to hand; a terrific but short combat was the consequence. Swan was the first, and was met by the two gunners on the right of the gun, but, no way daunted, he engaged them, and plunged his bayonet into the breast of one; he was about to

repeat the blow upon the other, but before he could disentangle the weapon from his bleeding adversary, the second Frenchman closed upon him, and by a coup de sabre severed his left arm from his body a little above the elbow; he fell from the shock, and was on the eve of being massacred, when Kelly, after having scrambled under the gun, rushed onward to succour his comrade. He bayoneted two Frenchmen on the spot, and at this instant Brazill came up; three of the five gunners lay lifeless, while Swan, resting against an ammunition chest, was bleeding to death. It was now equal numbers, two against two, but Brazill in his over-anxiety to engage was near losing his life at the onset; in making a lunge at the man next to him, his foot slipped upon the bloody platform, and he fell forward against his antagonist, but as both rolled under the gun, Brazill felt the socket of his bayonet strike hard against the buttons of the Frenchman's coat. The remaining gunner, in attempting to escape under the carriage from Kelly, was killed by some soldiers of the 5th, who just now reached the top of the breach, and seeing the serious dispute at the gun, pressed forward to the assistance of the three men of the Connaught Rangers.

Sergeant Brazill's own account puts a different slant on the gun's location. Writing in a letter to the *United Services Journal* in 1843 he says 'There was a great panic following the explosion through fear of a second.' And he then

Distinctly heard a voice from the centre of the breach 'Are there any brave fellows who will come forward to push up the breach?' I am certain it was Captain Thompson, 74th regiment, who called from the breach into advance. I pushed forward with two of my own company, and immediately topped the breach by moving up by the left side, where there was a good passage about eighteen inches wide which reached to the top of the breach. That side of the breach was secured with gabions, well packed with clay, and covered the breach for their musketry, which they used in gallant style.

On reaching the top of the breach I pushed forward to the left, about forty yards, and attacked a large brass gun and took it, with the loss of one of my brave comrades, who fell while we were bayoneting the gunners that served the gun, which had done great damage, being only forty yards from the breach and pointed to rake the small passage left for us to gain either side of the breach. I then moved close to the parapet wall to see if I could obtain any assistance from the forlorn hope of the Light Division, when about a hundred yards from the taken gun I saw approach a man – immediately challenged him – the answer, an officer of the 52nd regiment. There was no individual with him, he was a brave soldier; I am sorry I did not know his name, as he raised my heart thinking I would be relieved from my perilous situation. Immediately I returned to the gun, and from the gun to the breach, where I found Lieutenant Mackie collecting as many as he could muster of all regiments of the 3rd Division.

Sergeant Brazill's estimate, that his cannon was as much as forty yards from the breach, seems curious: it certainly could not sweep the rubble slope beneath the breach, if so located. Others (in the 94th) used the description '[guns] pointing downwards from the flanks'.

Whether Picton's men eventually succeeded unaided by the Light, is arguable – and many of the Light Division did so argue, especially the 43rd. However, an officer of the 94th comes close to conceding it was a joint affair:

> Those officers and men of the 94th and 5th regiments who attacked the retrenchment on the left flank of the main breach, clung to it to the last, and suffered severely in their constant efforts to overcome the obstacles to their entrance; but it was an utter impossibility, so long as those behind stood firm. The instant however that they wavered, these brave men sprung over – and both they and the Light Division each thought themselves first into the town.

It is clear, and very understandably so, that the 3rd Division were sensitive to accusations of a slow assault and that their eventual success was due only to the appearance of the Light. So sensitive that there were counter-claims, that the Light, arriving later at their breach than the 3rd, owed their 'easy conquest' to the latter's prior efforts! A likely conjecture is that the French officer in charge of setting off the mine – one clearly and deliberately of mighty power – would have been watching the small party led by Campbell and Ridge successfully make it onto the walkway, with no quick reinforcements. He had in his hand the match to put to the powder trail; but as a last-ditch blow he would be loath to fire it, so long as he still had men at and behind the breach, putting up an effective defence. Then he would see the gun crew on his right bayoneted by the 88th, with an increase in the fire over the lip of the breach at the loop-holed defenders in rear; and as the final straw, he would see the men of the 43rd and the 95th running along the rampart from his right. As Cooke says 'The moment the magazine blew up, all the firing had nearly ceased, for the enemy had literally jumped over the right entrenchment to save themselves from the bayonets of the Light Division.' That is when he blew the mine, for all was then clearly lost. From this interpretation, if correct, we may say the 3rd Division had to all intents and purposes forced their breach, without help from the Light Division; but only just.

We next descend down into the town, inside the walls of Rodrigo, and consider the unappealing drunken aftermath. It is therefore appropriate here first to comment on this major assault, particularly since it was the Peer's third formal siege in the Peninsula, and preceding that at Badajoz, a far greater challenge to his engineers, gunners and, above all, to his dauntless infantry.

That lessons from the previous efforts against Badajoz had been learned is obvious: the greater application of manpower, employment of proper and ample artillery used at closer ranges, the element of surprise in overcoming the Renaud Redoubt rather than the well-signalled attempt at Fort San Cristobal, the application of close-range suppressive rifle fire to prevent rubbish clearance, the prior provision of adequate supplies of all kinds, the pre-training of infantry in sapper work. It is hard to fault this swift and vigorous siege, bar the unnecessarily long and exhausting marches required to get the Divisions from their different cantonments, six or eight miles distant from their work in the trenches. (Crossing the half-frozen Agueda river, as the 52nd's historian comments, made sure 'A pair of iced breeches were usually the accompaniments of each man, on twenty-four hours sharp duty.')

On the French side, Governor Barrié appears negligent in not adding trenches etc. to the Lesser Breach – it was high and narrow, and a little effort would have gone a long way. He had warning on the morning of the 19th, from deserters, that the Light Division had moved up out of turn for digging, so he should have known the assault was nigh; even that evening, as the 5th began to clear the ditches, and an officer was captured and taken to him, he was not believed to be involved in an attack. And there is a report that a demi-bastion with parapet, which flanked the Lesser Breach, was abandoned early on, even though damaged by the battering. As the 77th's officer noted, the French officers captured 'subsequently acknowledged that they never contemplated the assault being made that night'.

Marmont himself was at fault in garrisoning with only 1,700 or so men – in 1810 Massena was held for twenty-four days by Herrasti's 6,000. As Napier says 'When there are enough of men the engineers' art cannot be overcome by mere courage.'

The price of his Lordship's success in human terms has been set by Oman at nine officers killed and seventy wounded, and other ranks 186 and 846 respectively, with ten missing. That is, a total of 1,121 men. Of these, 562 or fifty-nine officers and 503 rank and file, fell in the actual storm. Unfortunately, the strengths of each battalion, before operations commenced, are not known, so percentage losses are not calculable. The figures, however, are in line with events: Ridge's 5th lost ninety-four all ranks killed or wounded (including nine officers): Campbell's 94th lost sixty-nine all ranks (eight officers); Donkin's 77th lost fifty all ranks (five officers) and the 45th lost forty-eight all ranks (seven officers). The Connaught Rangers got off fairly lightly with thirty-four all ranks (four officers).

At the Lesser Breach the Light Division lost altogether just 113 all ranks, over a third being from the 43rd of whom presumably many were struck down by the explosion; while the Portuguese troops had surprisingly high casualties totalling 114. It is a puzzle how that arose, unless they suffered particularly during the earlier siege operations. The Light Division's commander, General Craufurd, was mortally hit by a ball while on the glacis, shot through his arm and two ribs to shatter the spine; his second-in-command Vandeleur was simultaneously wounded, as was John Colborne at the head of the 52nd, and the commander of the stormers, Major George Napier. Perhaps modern eyes will question that officers of 'high rank and estimation' – even more so in Craufurd's case 'an ornament to his profession' – should be expected to place themselves at the head of their columns climbing a breach, given the statistical probability of being hit. The deaths of Craufurd and MacKinnon, and the serious wounding of Vandeleur and Colborne, were grave blows to Lord Wellington's command structure. At Badajoz, as we shall see, it was even worse: Generals Picton, Colville, Kempt, Walker and Bowes wounded; and at the Salamanca Forts the latter was killed. Officers of their value and skills – at brigade and higher levels, say – might with advantage be kept a little in rear, one would think: their personal reputations would scarcely suffer, if it had been the Peer's requirement?

CHAPTER 1

Part IV – Ciudad Rodrigo
Entry into the Town and Aftermath

Compared to the disgraceful events a few weeks later, inside the captured fortress of Badajoz, the next part of our story is tame. Still, a small taste of things to come. It is useful therefore to remind our modern minds of the practice prevailing two centuries ago, with respect to behaviour by victorious besieging troops towards their conquered enemy, and indeed the civil inhabitants, of a garrisoned town. That behaviour was condoned as part of the universal belief that a defender should surrender once his wall had been breached, and was open – 'practicable' – to a successful assault. Resisting rather than capitulating, from that point on, caused the attacker what he regarded as unnecessary further casualties; commanders knew that in the loose combat conditions of a siege, they had not that iron control of their men enjoyed in disciplined fire fights in the open. The condonement was simply an acknowledgement that, once inside disputed walls, any garrison was likely to be hunted down. And righteous retribution was a happy cover for both a thirst to be assuaged, and a knapsack to be filled with loot.

The men well knew they had licence to free-range once inside the walls, at least for some hours. There was a presumed connection between storm and sack, with many eyewitness accounts using phrases such as 'the immemorial privilege of tearing the town to pieces' or 'the men were permitted to enjoy themselves'. Indeed, officers largely recognised the impossibility of stemming alcohol-fuelled excesses, which (as Dobbs of the 52nd observed) it were best 'found necessary to let take its course'. Wellington would share this acquiescence at Badajoz, it would seem, when after a good eighteen hours of the town's possession he eventually issued the order 'it is *now* full time that the plunder of Badajoz should cease'.

Yet at Rodrigo the garrison were not in fact slaughtered – except as we shall see for some Italians – a surprising fact which presumably became rapidly known to the garrison down in Badajoz, and the more rapidly just because it was deemed surprising. The knowledge no doubt contributed to their sturdy defence, which was thus conducted without – they hoped – the traditional fear of retribution. In so doing they acted with a sense of a calculated risk, of course, but very likely also upon their reading of the British character, witnessed now during four years of campaigning, and with many expressions of mutual humanity. Lord Wellington himself in later years ruefully pondered that:

> I shall have thought of myself justified in putting the garrisons to the sword, and if I had done so at the first [Rodrigo] it is probable I should have saved five thousand men at the second [Badajoz]. I mention this to show you that the practice which refuses quarter to a garrison that stands an assault is not a *useless* effusion of blood.

Whether his soldiers would have agreed to obey such an order remains unknown, for on the night of 19 January 1812 no man knew what the next few hours would see. None present had previous experience in the business of successfully storming a proper European fortress. It was a novel operation for the Peninsular field army.

The only genuine report of part of the garrison being put to the sword – literally correct in that the 95th's Baker rifles were fitted with what they called swords, not bayonets – occurred to a party of Tuscan soldiers of the 113th Ligne. They had fired from a flanking ravelin onto the Light Division's breach and, the breach taken and their position untenable, they threw down their muskets and then cried out 'Poveros Italianos' to Kincaid's riflemen 'to excite our pity; but our men have somehow imbibed a horrible antipathy to Italians, and every appeal they made in that name was invariably answered with 'so you're not French but Italians, are you? Then, damn you, here's a shot for you', and the action instantly followed the word'. Yet at the time Kincaid's party were intent on moving rapidly around the ramparts, and his words tend to imply no more than that, as they hurried past, they fired down at the unarmed and cringing Italians whose cries, they would sense, were in the circumstances unduly cheeky. That is quite far from a massacre, and very much what one would expect: the custom, after all, if you wished to surrender yourself, was to discard your arms. Both sides generally honoured this mutually advantageous custom. Henry Ridge, writing a few days later, described 'throwing away their arms' as French soldiers' 'most effective means to obtain mercy', for even though they had not capitulated with two practicable breaches lying open, and therefore 'their lives became forfeit,' it was 'glorious to see Britons incapable of slaying *unarmed* men'.

Fresh from potting Italians, Kincaid's 95th Riflemen

> continued our course round the rampart until we met the head of the column which had gone by the right, and then descended into the town … Finding the current of soldiers setting towards the centre of the town, I followed the stream, which conducted me into the great square, on one side of which the late garrison were drawn up as

prisoners, and the rest of it was filled with British and Portuguese intermixed without any order or regularity. I had been there but a very short time when they all commenced firing without any ostensible cause; some fired in at the doors and windows, some at the roofs of houses and others at the clouds; and at last some heads began to be blown from the shoulders in the general hurricane, when the voice of Sir Thomas Picton, with the power of twenty trumpets, began to proclaim damnation to everybody, whilst Colonel Barnard, Colonel Cameron and other active officers were carrying it into effect with a strong hand; for, seizing the broken barrels of muskets which were lying about in great abundance, they belaboured every fellow most unmercifully about the head who attempted either to load or fire, and finally succeeded in reducing them to order. In the midst of the scuffle, however, three of the houses in the square were set on fire; and the confusion was such that nothing could be done to save them.

The 77th also progressed to the town square, from the main breach:

we dropped from the wall into the town. At first we were among ruins; but having extricated ourselves from them, we made our way into a large street leading nearly in a straight line from the principal breach to the plaza or square; up this street we fought our way, the enemy slowly retiring before us. At about half a length of the street was a large open space on our left hand, where was deposited an immense battering train of the Army of Portugal, and its material. Amongst this crowd of carriages, a number of men ensconced themselves, firing on us as we passed, and it required no small exertion on our part to dislodge them. Such of them as were caught suffered for their temerity. In the meantime, those of the enemy ahead of us were lost to sight, having entered the square; from which place we pushed on with as many men as we could lay hands, formed, without distinction of regiments, into two or three platoons; for the great proportion of those who had stayed with us had gradually sneaked off into the by-streets for the purpose of plundering, which business was already going on merrily. As we reached the head of the street (which entered the square at one angle), and wheeled to the left into the open space, we received a shattering volley from the enemy, which quickly spoiled our array. They were drawn up in force in the square, and under the colonnade of the cathedral, and we were for the moment checked by their fire, which we returned from the head of the street, waiting for a reinforcement. At length, when we were meditating a dash at the fellows, we heard a fire opened from another quarter, which seemed to strike them with a panic, for on our giving a cheer and moving forward, they to a man threw away their arms as if by word of command, and disappeared in the gloom like magic. It was the Light Division which entered the square by a street leading from the little breach, and their opportune arrival had frightened the game which we had brought to bay, leaving the pavement of the square covered with arms and accoutrements.

But it was at this point, when successful feelings were general and relief the greater, that the mind naturally turned to rewards in general and to alcohol in particular. Costello, with many others, had by now reached the town's square:

In a short time, a regiment of the 3rd Division entered the square and, commanded by their officer, something like order prevailed. When the British colours were planted in the centre, proclaiming the town to be taken, three cheers were given by the whole. When this was over, they commenced firing in the air, as well as at windows where any light appeared. Seeing the confusion, a number broke into squads, which went in different directions and entered different streets according to the fancy of their leaders. Myself and about a score of others took a large street to the right. The night was dark and as the city was not lit, we had to grope our way along. We had not gone far when we got mixed up with a quantity of French muskets, which had been thrown on the ground with their bayonets fixed. These pricked the legs of one or two of the men, who swore they had come to a chevaux-de-frise.

Groping about we came across a wounded French soldier, who told us in Spanish that we were close to the barracks. Knowing the French would not resign their liberty without a struggle, I expected a volley to be sent amongst us from the barracks, and began retracing my steps towards the square. However, I had only gone a short distance when I saw another party advancing towards me with a lighted candle. Hearing the noise of the first party in their front, they commenced firing as they advanced. Squeezing myself edgeways against a door, I awaited their arrival, then I begged them to desist from firing because there were some of their own men lower down. I then went with them and joined the first party.

The wounded French soldiers pointed to a large gateway, and told us it was the barracks. Having a light we entered, and mounted a large stone staircase. We found ourselves in a French hospital, full of sick and wounded. Those who were able to sit up in bed did so, supplicating mercy, but they had no occasion to do so for our fellows were kind to them, and wrapped the bedclothes round them. Shortly afterwards a third party came down. Seeing a light in our window they commenced firing. The poor fellow who held the candle was shot through the head, and one or two others were wounded. The rest lay down while the firing continued, but then one man, more daring than the rest, flew to the window and cried out that they were firing on their own men.

When this panic was over, I came downstairs, anxious to meet some of my own company to know how things were. I found a few outside, and we started in another direction, to a place with a large white house that had been used as a commissary's store by the French. Here a crowd had assembled to break it open. They were warned off by a sentinel, a German, who was posted to guard the premises. Not heeding his threat, the throng rushed at the door. The poor sentry, true to his trust, attempted to oppose their entrance, and was run through the body by a bayonet.

The house contained several puncheons of spirits, which the men present immediately tapped by striking in the heads. Some became madly drunk. Several wretches, who mounted the steps that had been placed against the butts to enable them to obtain the rum, fell into the liquor head first and, unnoticed by the crowd, perished. Several fights took place, and it was only the drunkenness of the parties which prevented mischief being done. To crown the whole, a light fell into one of the barrels of spirits and the place was set on fire. Many poor wretches, incapable of moving from the quantity of liquor they had swallowed, were consumed in the flames.

The 43rd also were sucked in to the general ill-discipline. John Cooke:

when the troops had sipped wine and the cognac brandy in the stalls, the extreme disorders commenced. To restore order was impossible; a whole division could not have done it. Three or four large houses were on fire, two of them in the market place, and the town was illuminated by the flames. The soldiers were drunk and many of them, for amusement, were firing from the windows into the street. At 1 a.m. I was in the square talking to the regimental barber, Private Evans, when a ball passed through his head. He fell at my feet dead, his brains lay on the pavement. I sought shelter.

I found Colonel McLeod with a few officers in a large house, where we remained until daylight. I did not enter any other house in Ciudad Rodrigo. If I had not seen it, I never could have supposed that British soldiers would become so wild and furious. It was quite alarming to meet groups of them in the streets, flushed as they were with drink and desperate in mischief.

And what of the 88th? Grattan tells us of one desperate single combat, and then turns to the growing disorder:

> Each affray in the streets was conducted in the best manner the moment would admit of, and decided more by personal valour than discipline, and in some instances officers as well as privates had to combat with the imperial troops. In one of these encounters Lieutenant George Faris, of the 88th, by an accident so likely to occur in an affair of this kind, separated a little too far from a dozen or so of his regiment, and found himself opposed to a French soldier who, apparently, was similarly placed. It was a curious coincidence, and it would seem as if each felt that he individually was the representative of the country to which he belonged: and had the fate of the two nations hung upon the issue of the combat I am about to describe, it could not have been more heroically contested. The Frenchman fired at and wounded Faris in the thigh, and made a desperate push with his bayonet at his body, but Faris parried the thrust, and the bayonet only lodged in his leg. He saw at a glance the peril of his situation, and that nothing short of a miracle could save him; the odds against him were too great, and if he continued a scientific fight he must inevitably be vanquished. He sprang forward, and, seizing hold of the Frenchman by the collar, a struggle of a most nervous kind took place: in their mutual efforts to gain an advantage they lost their caps, and as they were men of nearly equal strength, it was doubtful what the issue would be. They were so entangled with each other their weapons were of no avail, but Faris at length disengaged himself from the grasp which held him, and he was able to use his sabre; he pushed the Frenchman from him, and ere he could recover himself he laid his head open nearly to the chin. His sword-blade, a heavy, soft, ill-made Portuguese one, was doubled up with the force of the blow, and retained some pieces of the skull and clotted hair! At this moment I reached the spot with about twenty men, composed of different regiments, all being by this time mixed pell mell with each other. I ran up to Faris – he was nearly exhausted, but he was safe. The French grenadier lay upon the pavement, while Faris, though tottering from fatigue, held his sword firmly in his grasp, and it was crimson to the hilt. The appearance of the two combatants was frightful! – one lying dead on the ground, the other faint from agitation and loss of blood; but the soldiers loudly applauded him, and the feeling uppermost with them was, that our man had the best of it! It was a shocking sight, but it would be rather a hazardous experiment to begin moralising at such a moment and in such a place.

Those of the garrison who escaped death were made prisoners, and the necessary guards being placed, and everything secured, the troops not selected for duty commenced a very diligent search for those articles which they most fancied, and which they considered themselves entitled to by 'right of conquest'. I believe on a service such as the present, there is a sort of tacit acknowledgement of this 'right'; but be this as it may, a good deal of property most indubitably changed owners on the night of the 19th of January 1812. The conduct of the soldiers, too, within the last hour, had undergone a complete change; before, it was all order and regularity, now it was nothing but licentiousness and confusion – subordination was at an end; plunder and blood was the order of the day, and many an officer on this night was compelled to show that he carried a sabre.

The doors of the houses in a large Spanish town are remarkable for their strength, and resemble those of a prison more than anything else; their locks are of huge dimensions, and it is a most difficult task to force them. The mode, adopted by the men of my regiment (the 88th) in this dilemma was as effective as it was novel: the muzzles of a couple of muskets were applied to each side of the keyhole, while a third soldier, fulfilling the functions of an officer, deliberately gave the word, 'make ready' – 'present' – 'fire!' and in an instant the ponderous lock gave way before the combined operations of the three individuals, and doors that rarely opened to the knock of a stranger in Rodrigo, now flew off their hinges to receive the Rangers of Connaught.

The chapels and chandlers' houses were the first captured, in both of which was found a most essential ingredient in the shape of large wax candles; these the soldiers lighted, and commenced their perambulations in search of plunder, and the glare of light which they threw across the faces of the men, as they carried them through the streets, displayed their countenances, which were of that cast that might well terrify the unfortunate inhabitants. Many of the soldiers with their faces scorched by the explosion of the magazine at the grand breach; others with their lips blackened from biting off the ends of their cartridges, more covered with blood, and all looking ferocious, presented a combination sufficient to appal the stoutest heart.

Scenes of the greatest outrage now took place, and it was pitiable to see groups of the inhabitants half naked in the streets – the females clinging to the officers for protection – while their respective houses were undergoing the strictest scrutiny. Some of the soldiers turned to the wine and spirit houses, where, having drunk sufficiently, they again sailed out in quest of more plunder; others got so intoxicated that they lay in a helpless state in different parts of the town, and lost what they had previously gained, either by the hands of any passing Spaniard, who could venture unobserved to stoop down, or by those of their own companions, who in their wandering surveys happened to recognise a comrade lying with half a dozen silk gowns, or some such thing, wrapped about him. Others wished to attack the different stores, and as there is something marvellously attractive in the very name of a brandy one, it is not to be wondered at that many of our heroes turned not only their thoughts, but their steps also, in the direction in which these houses lay: and from the unsparing hand with which they supplied themselves, it might be imagined they intended to change their habits of life and turn spirit-vendors, and that too in the wholesale line!

By some mistake, a large spirit store situated in the Plaza Mayor took fire, and the flames spreading with incredible fury, despite of the exertions of the troops, the building was totally destroyed: but in this instance, like many others which we are obliged to struggle against through life, there was something that neutralised the disappointment which the loss of so much brandy occasioned the soldiers; the light which shone forth from the building was of material service to them, inasmuch as it tended to facilitate their movements in their excursions for plunder; the heat also was far from disagreeable, for the night was piercingly cold, yet, nevertheless, the soldiers exerted themselves to the utmost to put a stop to this calamity. General Picton was to be seen in the midst of them, encouraging them by his example and presence to make still greater efforts; but all would not do, and floor after floor fell in, until at last it was nothing but a burning heap of ruins.

Some houses were altogether saved from plunder by the interference of the officers, for in several instances the women ran out into the streets, and seizing hold of three or four of us, would force us away to their houses, and by this stroke of political hospitality saved their property. A good supper was then provided, and while all outside was noise and pillage, affairs within went on agreeably enough. These instances were, however, but few.

Oman estimated 7,000 troops were now inside the town, some five times the surrendered garrison, and in the narrow streets nowhere in bodies much above a dozen or so, few with officers, of whom even fewer were silly enough to attempt to impose control. Officers and drunken soldiers never mix well, for that deference from which flows a normal acquiescence to orders is invariably diluted by the alcohol; it is a short journey from minor verbal insubordination to minor physical aggression, and beyond, especially if the officer wears a different cap badge. Just as the Great Breach gave eventual access to the mixed bayonets of seven battalions, and the Lesser to those of another six, so the mixture continued into the town, there to meet the Caçadores of O'Toole's Portuguese via the Castle's sally port, and Pack's via the Santiago gate, all free of the discipline of the ranks and knowing your place, the first successful assault of a French garrison by the Peninsular field army. It was a heaven-sent opportunity for that tenth part of every regiment (described later by Sir John Colborne as 'in every regiment we must say there are from fifty to a hundred bad characters that neither punishment nor any kind of discipline can restrain.') The opportunity led first to the wine warehouses and then, for the majority, to the prospects of plunder.

Colonel MacLeod's 43rd at least tried: 'he immediately detached officers with guards to take possession of all the stores they could find, and to preserve order. These parties ultimately dissolved themselves. If they had not done so, they would have been engaged in the streets with our own troops.' Yet the disorder was mild by later sieges, accordingly to Jonathan Leach:

> No town taken by assault suffered less than Rodrigo. It is true that soldiers from all regiments got drunk, pillaged, and made great noise and confusion in the streets and houses. But bad and revolting as such scenes are, I never heard that either the French garrison after its surrender, or the inhabitants, suffered personal indignities or cruelty from the troops.

Sometime after midnight some order was returning: 'We succeeded in getting a great portion of our battalion together by 1 o'clock in the morning and withdrew with them to the ramparts, where we lay by our arms until daylight.' (Kincaid). George Simmons too passed the night on the ramparts, but in much more comfort:

> My battalion formed up upon the ramparts and made fires, as the night was a clear and frosty one. Some men brought me wine, ham, and eggs. I soon made a hearty meal, and washed it down with some good French burgundy, put my feet to the fire, and enjoyed as calm a sleep as I ever did in my life before, for three or four hours.

It was McLeod who also tried to restrict the taking away of plunder. According to John Cooke, he:

> Ordered Lieutenant Wyndham Madden of the 43rd to descend the small breach with twenty-five men and continue at the foot of it during the night to prevent soldiers leaving the town with plunder. At eleven o'clock that night I went to see him. He had no sinecure and had very judiciously made a large fire which showed to perfection the delinquents attempting to quit the town with plunder, in the garb of friars, nuns or enveloped in silk counterpanes; or who were laded

with silver forks, spoons, and church plate. All of this was taken from them and piled up to hand over to the proper authorities on the following day. He told me that no masquerade in point of costume, or of grotesque figure, could rival the characters he stripped that night. The fire was large, and surrounded by the dead bodies of those who fell on the first onset at the foot of the breach.

Madden was on guard until late the next day. Typically not averse to the general benefits of captured French possessions, he later noted that 'many of our officers have got horses and mules. William [his brother in the 52nd] has got two beautiful animals, and he has promised to give me one of them.' We must hope they enjoyed their new rides: ten weeks later William was dead, and Wyndham severely wounded, both at Badajoz.

Next morning, at eleven o'clock on 20 January, as the fires were finally brought under control, Cooke again made his way through the corpses on the streets, this time to see the scene at the main breach.

The ascent was not as steep as the small one, but there was a traverse thrown up at each side of it on the rampart; hence there was no way into the town, as the wall was quite perpendicular behind the breach. When the 3rd Division had gained the top of the rampart, they were enclosed and hemmed in. They had nowhere to go and the enemy continued to fire upon them from some old ruined houses 20 yards distant. I counted more than 63 soldiers of the 3rd Division dead on the terre-plein of the rampart between the traverses. I did not see one dead soldier of that Division on the French side of those traverses, but I saw some of the Light Division.

I saw General MacKinnon lying dead on his back, just under the rampart on the inside, i.e. the town side. He was a tall, thin man, and was stripped of everything except his shirt and blue pantaloons; even his boots were taken off. There were no other dead near him, and he was not on the French side of the traverse either. There was no possibility of getting at the general without a ladder, or without traversing a considerable distance along the ramparts to descend into the town, passing through several narrow lanes, ruined houses, and over broken stone walls. The distance was at least a quarter of a mile. No human being could have accomplished it during the night.

It is said that he was blown up, but there was no indication that such had been his fate. Neither the state of his skin, nor the posture in which he was lying led me to think it. I should think that when a man is blown up, his hands and face could not escape. I never saw any whose face was not scorched, but MacKinnon's was pale, and free from the marks of fire. How strange that, with the exception of the General, I did not see a soldier of the 3rd Division who had been stripped. Neither was there any officer among the dead, or else they had been carried away. I wonder if the General had been killed with all the others between the traverses, and some tender-hearted followers of the army, having taken his clothes off, had just given him a hand over the wall to place him in the position described?

The greater portion of the Light Division lay in the ditch at the foot of the small breach. They fought on the slope, and rolled down in succession as they were killed. On gaining the ramparts – there being no interior defences – they followed the right and left as the French retreated panic-struck into the interior of the city, keeping up a running fire from the different streets, or from the massive stone buildings.

The 3rd Division, at the first onset, had been fired on from the parapets of the ramparts, and assailed by summit of the wall. The enemy did not stand on the crest of the great breach to oppose their ascent. If they had, it would have been impossible to escape behind their traverses. They had left a space on the left of the right traverse for one man to pass at a time, but expecting the attack, they had previously blocked it up with barrels filled with earth, having placed others behind to stand on for the purpose of firing over them. Before the morning, all these barrels, except one, were thrown down the scarped wall.

The 3rd Division had mounted to the terre-plein with facility, but when on the rampart, they were fired on in front and both flanks as described. In this small space they suffered a tremendous loss of nearly 500 heroic officers and soldiers. During the fighting, their dead and wounded were piled one on top of the other. The wounded cried out in agony as they were trampled upon, or they impeded the progress of others exerting themselves in vain amongst such havoc to carry the traverses. The moment the wooden magazine blew up, all firing had nearly ceased, for the enemy had literally jumped over the right entrenchment onto the terre-plein of the breach to save themselves from the bayonets of the Light Division.

About the same time that morning-after, as Cooke stood contemplating the scene at the main breach,

a great explosion took place a few yards to the right of the small breach, blowing up the terre-plein of the rampart, four yards in breadth and ten in length. The fatal explosion was accidental: some sparks of fire ignited barrels of gunpowder in a casement. It happened while the French garrison were marching out of the city by the small breach. This had become so hard owing to the numbers of soldiers walking up and down it, that ascent was nearly impracticable. The

French, as well as the British soldiers, were carried up into the air, or were jammed sticking out of the earth. I saw one of the unfortunate soldiers in a blanket with his face, head, and body as black as a coal; he was cased in a black substance like a shell, his features no longer distinguishable, and all the hair singed from off his head. The unfortunate man was still alive. How long he lived in this horrible situation I cannot say.

A tall athletic soldier of the 52nd lay on his back amongst the dead at the foot of the breach, his arms and legs at their full extent. The top of his head, from the forehead to the back part of his skull, was split in twain, and the cavity entirely emptied of the brains. It was as if a hand grenade had exploded within, expanding the skull and forcing it into a separation. The parts were ragged like a saw with a gaping aperture nine inches in length, and four in breadth. For a considerable time I looked on this horrible fracture, to define by what missile or instrument so wonderful a wound could have been inflicted, but without being able to come to any conclusion.

Cooke moved on to see a wounded friend, said to be at the San Francisco convent:

The interior was crowded with wounded soldiers lying on the hard pavement. A soldier of the 3rd Division was sitting against a pillar, his head bent forward, his chin resting on his breast, his eyes open and an agreeable smile on his face. I stopped with surprise to observe him sitting in so contended a posture, surrounded by the groans on his companions. At length I addressed him. No answer being returned I called a doctor, under the impression that the man was delirious – on the contrary, we found he was quite dead.

Towards noon, when the evacuation of the town by the assault divisions was completed, Grattan of the 88th also went sightseeing:

The breaches presented a horrid spectacle. The one forced by the Light Division was narrower than the other, and the dead, lying in a smaller compass, looked more numerous than they really were. I walked along the ramparts towards the grand breach, and was examining the effects our fire had produced on the different defences and the buildings in their immediate vicinity, but I had not proceeded far when I was shocked at beholding about a hundred and thirty or forty wounded Frenchmen, lying under one of the bastions and some short distance up a narrow street adjoining it. I descended, and learned that these men had been performing some particular duty in the magazine which blew up and killed General Mackinnon and so many of the 3rd Division. These miserable beings were so burnt that

I fear, notwithstanding the considerate attention which was paid to them by our medical officers, none of their lives were preserved. Their uniforms were barely distinguishable, and their swollen heads and limbs gave them a gigantic appearance that was truly terrific; added to this, the gunpowder had so blackened their faces that they looked more like a number of huge negroes than soldiers of a European army. Many of our men hastened to the spot, and with that compassion which truly brave men always feel, rendered them every assistance in their power; some were carried on doors, others in blankets, to the hospitals, and these poor creatures showed by their gestures, for they could not articulate, how truly they appreciated our tender care of them.

I next turned to the captured gun, so chivalrously taken by the three men of the 88th. The five canonniers lying across the carriage, or between the spokes of the wheels, showed how bravely they had defended it; yet they lay like men whose death had not been caused by violence; they were naked and bloodless, and the puncture of the bayonet left so small a mark over their hearts, it was discernible only to those who examined the bodies closely.

I turned away from the breach, and scrambled over its rugged face, and the dead which covered it. On reaching the bivouac we had occupied the preceding evening, I learned, with surprise, that our women had been engaged in a contest, if not as dangerous as ours, at least one of no trivial sort. The men left as a guard over the baggage, on hearing the first shot at the trenches, could not withstand the inclination they felt to join their companions; and although this act was creditable to the bravery of the individuals that composed the baggage-guard, it was nigh being fatal to those who survived, or, at least, to such as had anything to lose except their lives, for the wretches that infested our camp attempted to plunder it of all that it possessed, but the women, with a bravery that would not have disgraced those of ancient Rome, defended the post with such valour that those miscreants were obliged to desist, and our baggage was saved in consequence.

We were about to resume our arms when General Picton approached us. Some of the soldiers, who were more than usually elevated in spirits, on his passing them, called out, 'Well, General, we gave you a cheer last night; it's your turn now!' The General, smiling, took off his hat, and said, 'Here, then, you drunken set of brave rascals, hurrah! We'll soon be at Badajoz!' A shout of confidence followed; we slung our firelocks, the bands played, and we commenced our march for the village of Atalaya in the highest spirits, and in a short time lost sight of a place the capture of which appeared to us like a dream.

Kincaid says that when the 95th marched out 'most of their swords were fixed on the rifles and stuck full of hams, tongues, and loaves of bread, and not a few were carrying birdcages.'

One of his riflemen, Costello, also noted how they left the town:

> As we marched over the bridge dressed in all varieties imaginable, some with jack boots on, others with white French trousers, others in frock coats with epaulettes, some even with monkeys on their shoulders, we met the 5th Division on their way to repair the breaches. They immediately formed upon the left of the road, presented arms, and cheered us. I was afterwards told that Lord Wellington, who saw us pass, inquired of his staff 'Who the devil are those fellows?'

The 5th and the Light were again to pass one another a few days later, when Lord Wellington buried Robert Crauford at the foot of the Lesser Breach, near the spot where he fell. He was borne by six sergeant majors, with six dismounted field officers as pall-bearers, 'in a plain coffin with a sheet over it' (Captain John Ewart, 52nd), preceded by bands playing mournful music and, immediately, by a chaplain; followed by Wellington, Castanos, Beresford, Stewart and all the staff and general officers, and the regiments of the division with arms reversed. They passed through a double rank of the 5th Division's men, also with reversed arms. It was said that the clergyman's voice – the only sound to be heard – faltered over the words 'I am the Resurrection and the Life'.

A far different planting six feet under is told by Harry Smith of the Rifles, touching on the botched execution of the Light Division's deserters:

> After the siege we had a few weeks holiday, with the exception of shooting some rascals who had deserted to the enemy. Eleven knelt on one grave at Ituero. It was an awful ceremony, a military execution. I was Major of Brigade of the day. The Provo-Marshall had not told the firing off, so that a certain number of men should shoot one culprit, and so on, but at his signal the whole party fired a volley. Some prisoners were fortunate enough to be killed, others were only wounded, some untouched. I galloped up. An unfortunate Rifleman called to me by name – he was awfully wounded – 'Oh Mr Smith put me out of my misery,' and I literally ordered the firing party, when reloaded, to run up and shoot the poor wretches. It was an awful scene.

On the same subject, Grattan tells us that earlier 'Lord Wellington had extended mercy to everyone who could procure anything like a good character from his officers.'

We will close this chapter on a more cheerful note, with Grattan's picture of the 88th's auction of their loot, quite plainly an authorised activity, and which rather therefore questions the value of Wyndham Madden's search party at the main breach.

> The soldiers busied themselves in arranging their different articles of plunder; many of them clad in the robes of some priest, while others wore gowns of the most costly silk velvet; others, again, nearly naked; some without pantaloons, having been plundered while drunk, of so essential a part of their dress; but all, or almost all, were occupied in laying out for sale their different articles of plunder, in that order which was essential to their being disposed of to the crowds of Spaniards who had already assembled to be the purchasers; and if one could judge by their look, they most unquestionably committed a breach in their creed by 'coveting their neighbour's good'. And had the scene which now presented itself to our sight been one caused by an event the most joyous, much less by the calamity that had befallen the unfortunate inhabitants of Rodrigo, to say nothing of the human blood that had been spilt ere that even had taken place, the scene could not have been more gay. Brawny-shouldered Castilians carrying pig-skins of wine on their backs, which they sold to our soldiers for a trifling sum; Bolero-dancers, rattling their castanets like the clappers of so many mills; our fellows drinking like fishes, while their less fortunate companions at Rodrigo – either hastily flung into an ill-formed grave, writhing under the knife of the surgeon, or in the agonies of death – were unthought of, or unfelt for. Sick transit Gloria Monday! The soldiers were allowed three days congé for the disposal of their booty; but long before the time had expired, they had scarcely a rag to dispose of, or a real of the produce in their pockets.

For modern minds, the auction seems like a drunken car boot sale set to music, all goods being offered for sale without legal title by the vendors, and doubtless in some cases, actually sold back to those from whom they had been forcibly acquired.

That day of the 88th's auction, news reached Marmont of Rodrigo's capture – a mere week after he had first heard of its encirclement. During that week he had sought as best he could to concentrate his reduced Army of Portugal on Salamanca (four days' march from Rodrigo). But his divisions were still widely dispersed. He – and Napoleon – had been caught out by supposing the British sick list would hobble Wellington; that the time of year was inappropriate for active operations; and – a failing common enough among military men – disregarding fresh intelligence that did not fit his interpretation of a situation for which he had already deployed. He lost thereby the essential base for possible future operations by the Emperor into Portugal, a base moreover that would now function in reverse for his enemy; and ironically he had lost within it the very item necessary to its re-capture – his siege train.

The day after he heard Rodrigo was lost, Marmont wrote to Berthier, 'On the 16th the English batteries opened their fire at a great distance. On the 19th the place was taken by storm and fell into the power of the enemy. There is something so incomprehensible in this event that I allow myself no observation.' He was indeed speechless. But not so the Peer's employers: he received a Spanish dukedom from the grateful Cortes, a marquisate from Portugal, an earldom from the Prince Regent, and an annuity of £2,000 from Parliament.

For at quite the wrong time of year, on rocky ground and in incessant rains, with ill-trained amateur sappers, with forethought, secret planning and speedy execution, while no-one was looking he leapt on this great frontier fortress with its vast magazines of warlike stores, gateway to the future; and he seized it in eleven days flat, start to finish. It had been a brilliant operation, soundly conceived and timed and swiftly executed.

CHAPTER 2

Part I – Badajoz
Setting the Scene

Within three or four days of the fall of Rodrigo, the new Earl of Wellington and Ducque de Ciudad Rodrigo had turned actively to his next task. Having arranged for the breaches to be cleared, the trenches filled, two new redoubts to be traced out on the Tesons, and for a Spanish garrison of 3,000 men, on 25 January 1812 (the same day Craufurd was buried at the foot of the Lesser Breach) he instructed Captain Dickson to commence the move of powder, shot and stores back the way they had so laboriously come, by road, river and sea via Oporto to Setubal, below Lisbon, and thence by road to Elvas, convenient for Badajoz. Sixteen heavy 24-pounder howitzers would travel overland. By 8 March a battering train of fifty-two pieces (including twenty additional Russian 18-pounders cheatingly provided by the Navy) and sixteen 24-pounders in transports in the Tagus, had come together at Elvas. His seven infantry divisions gradually slipped south from behind the Agueda and the Coa, except for the 5th and the KGL Hussars who, together with his Lordship, his Lordship's pack of hounds and his Headquarters, remained ostentatiously in the shop window. The 5th left on 9 March, and Headquarters three days earlier. By the second week of March some 60,000 men had been concentrated west of Elvas, the garrison of which had long been employed making gabions and fascines for the coming siege.

Wellington's two reliable lieutenants, Hill and Graham, were detached north-east to Merida and south to Llerena, with 14,000 and 19,000 men respectively, to hold Marmont and Soult should either approach individually or seek to combine. Beresford was given the 3rd, 4th and Light Divisions (some 11,000 men) to invest Badajoz, an operation which now commenced on 16 March.

As for the French, all was muddle and counter-order. Whereas in January Marmont had been scrambling to concentrate on Salamanca, in February he was scrambling to shift south, getting three divisions on the Tagus, from which an attempt to relieve Badajoz (a siege he now saw coming), could be launched; but in the middle of that month Napoleon intervened from 700 miles distance, to insist upon the concentration around Salamanca, from whence Marmont was improbably to threaten Portugal, the Douro, Almeida and the Asturias and thus force Wellington to leave Badajoz, to protect his bases.

> I suppose you consider the English mad, for you believe them capable of marching against Badajoz when you are at Salamanca, i.e. of allowing you to march to Lisbon before they can get back. They will only go southward if you, by your ill-designed schemes, keep two or three divisions detached from the Tagus: that reassures them, and tells them that you have no offensive projects against them.

Marshal Marmont, Duke of Ragusa, and understandably irate, now fired off to Paris a series of letters protesting at the detailed (and largely irrelevant) instructions being received, and which he knew were not only strategically wrong but administratively impractical, due if only to his desperate lack of supplies. Finally, in a reply from Napoleon's Chief of Staff, Berthier, which arrived with Marmont eleven days *after* Badajoz was invested, he was given a conditional freedom to aid Badajoz, but far too late. So the French were running to catch up, and not very successfully. In brief, Lord Wellington had space to tackle Badajoz, not entirely at his leisure but with a fair window of opportunity.

The fortress shared common features with Rodrigo. Both were sited on slight hills adjacent to substantial bridges over major rivers; and both contained castles, of sorts. The scale of Badajoz however dwarfed Rodrigo by the order of two or three: 5,000 yards of ramparts not two; three times the acreage; the river twice as wide; four outworks to one; walls to forty-six feet not thirty feet; 140 guns on the ramparts to 109; nine huge bastions to none; seven garrison battalions (two being German) to two, and so on, to say nothing of the relative resource and energy of the respective Governors.

So the 3rd and Light Divisions, with their experiences at Rodrigo, and now the main part of the force earmarked to take Badajoz, on 16 March looked at their new objective through narrowed eyes. They too could multiply the Rodrigo figure. They were right to go quiet, since the relative human costs were indeed to be in the same order as the physical: the capture of Rodrigo saw 1,100 killed and wounded, Badajoz would see 4,700. In both cases, about a fifth of those knocked over were never to rise again, the same proportion as at the bloodbath of Albuera. And there the officers killed were some four per cent of the British dead; at Badajoz it would be eight per cent.

And those who had been present in 1811 at the first and second sieges would now see that the fortress had in their absence been further strengthened. For in addition to the nine massive four-sided bastions (see map and photographs) stretching from the Guadiana river in the west, round beneath the southern walls to the Castle in the north, six triangular ravelins lay out front of the old town curtain walls, between the bastions, which themselves were over a hundred paces across. Three of these ravelins were much improved, and in front of that between the Trinidad and Santa Maria bastions a small but deep ditch had been dug and flooded, in the ditch itself. The water came from a huge inundation, up to 200 wide and 1,000 yards long, created along the east front of the town, by damming the bridge in the rear of the San Roque Lunette. Fort San Cristobal on the northern heights beyond the Guadiana, and which in 1811 formed Wellington's preferred route, had had the ditches deepened, the glacis raised and the rear secured; 200 to 300 yards away up the slope, where the 1811 breaching batteries stood, there was now a formidable redoubt with ditches blasted into the rock three-men deep – the Verlé Lunette.

To the south, the Pardaleras fort had been properly closed off, with a loop-holed wall, the ditches deepened and joined to the garrison, with powerful covering batteries. In front of the two western ravelins the approaches were prepared for mines, although fortunately a French sergeant major of sappers had deserted with a map. The explosives had not yet been put in place. The shafts had indeed been sunk and the galleries formed, so mines could be put under any breaching batteries approaching the glacis, all 'in case of necessity'. But Colonel Lamare, as the garrison's commanding engineer, tells us 'This resolution was not persevered in, on account of the absolute want of powder towards the end of the siege.'

Oman gives the garrison's infantry strength as 3,861, but up to 300 men were sick in the hospital and Lamare with hindsight said 'The garrison was not strong enough' and should have been around 7,000. But at least Governor Philippon had engineers – 260 all ranks. The British had half that (twenty-three engineer officers and 150 sappers), a remarkable improvement on the pathetic first outing at Badajoz the previous year (forty-seven all ranks), but of course a pitiful specialist strength with which to set about a modern European fortress. It was one that Lord Wellington was to lobby hard if belatedly to change. His efforts to urge Horse Guards to create a trained pool of sappers and miners were to bear fruit eventually (in time for San Sebastian), but for now his ad-hoc solution – as at Rodrigo – was fairly limited: to train half a battalion's worth of infantry in the practices of sapping and lend them, together with any soldiers with carpentry etc. skills, to Colonel Fletcher. However, because of the casualties suffered at Rodrigo, the half-battalion was down now to 120 men, and the carpenters to eighty.

The garrison had provisions for forty days, which was adequate in one sense: their estimate was that the walls and powder could not hold beyond twenty or twenty-five days of open trenches. The poor 4,000 or so civilian inhabitants – a quarter of the usual population – who had not fled the scene, were worse supplied.

The Governor of the garrison was Armand Philippon, thirty-four years a soldier and now a baron and an energetic major general. He and his staff, including the gunner and engineer commanders, had been in the town for just over a year, and therefore knew it well. The defence of Bastions 1 (San Vincent) and 2 (San José) next to the town's river frontage, on the north-west, were allocated to the 3rd/9th Léger; Bastions 3 (Santiago) and 4 (San Juan) to the similarly-sized 1st/28th Léger; No. 5 (San Roque) Bastion alone to the 1st/58th Ligne; Bastion 6 and 7 (Santa Maria and Trinidad) the 3rd/103rd Ligne and Bastions 8 (San Pedro) and 9 (San Antonio) and the Castle to the two battalions of the Hesse-Darmstadt Regiment.

It is futile to attempt to tell how these individual battalions would have set about deploying on their respective bastions, since that would wait until the breaches were advanced enough to require it. But the simplest sums quickly confirm Lamarc's view that the garrison was far from excessive. Taking the bastions that will most interest us, 6 and 7 (Santa Maria and Trinidad), and their connecting town wall together with a fair extension either side of it, some 700 or 800 yards of rampart were the responsibility of the 3rd/103rd, at that time with a strength of about 540 men in six companies. Allow one company as reserve at each bastion, and allow ninety men for each of the other four companies, and those 360 men on 800 yards of ramparts would only be a meaningful defence against an escalade or a breach when concentrated. If there were to be two or three simultaneous attempted break-ins, Governor Philippon would need to shuffle his pack of cards with some urgency. And it must be noted that the strength figure for the 3rd/103rd was according to the parade state of 15 March, and so before the losses incurred in the Sortie and the capture of Fort Picurina (see below), as well as the many sick in the hospital.

The 3rd/88th Ligne were designated the reserve, together with the forty-two cavalrymen; the last sub-units of infantry, two companies of the 64th Ligne, who had entered the town as convoy escort shortly before the envelopment snapped shut, were doled out to the gunners, so too fifty surplus sappers. For Colonel Picoteu, commander of the artillery, had only his 260 men for 140 rampart guns, and more hands were needed.

Another early decision by Philippon was to form a company of what today we would call snipers – if such a description can be applied to muskets – by taking the best marksmen from the seven battalions, to harass the British once the trenchwork approached close enough to the walls.

On 16 March, as the 3rd, 4th and Light Divisions under Beresford invested the town, the Chief Engineer, Colonel Fletcher, sent out ostentatious reconnaissance parties to view the south and north fronts, while he concentrated on viewing the eastern Bastions (6, 7 and 8) and Fort Picurina, from a vedette on the Sierra de San Michael, some 600 yards east of the latter. It had already been settled that previous endeavours against Fort San Cristobal and the Castle were no longer practicable, due as much to the additional works by Philippon as to the experience of the previous year's failures. Bastions 8 and 9 would be under the guns of the Castle and Fort San Cristobal, and would need the prior capture of the Lunette San Roque, and *that* would need the prior capture of Fort Picurina. At the other end of the defences, the western abutments onto the Guadiana at Bastions 1–4 were held to be equally unattractive, partly because of the defensive mining, which Fletcher's stretched manpower could not contend with, partly because four breaches might be required, beyond the scope of the battering train in the time available.

There was a stretch of the wall's defences which met the prime rule of all battering: place your early shots onto the base of the wall, not higher up. Hit high and you aid the defender, for the loosened debris will fall down to deepen and shelter the front of the wall, before it has received any damage, and the resultant breach slope will be steep and to a height. To hit low at any distance, however, requires the gunner to have a sight line, and it is to conceal the line that garrisons construct high glacis or *fausse braies*, or counterguards. Now the counterguard in front of the right face of the Trinidad Bastion was, unaccountably, unfinished. Consequently a gun on the heights of San Miguel, the slight hill occupied by Fort Picurina, could hit low down on the base of the bastion's walls. Ironically, the garrison itself regarded one of their weak points to be 500 yards farther north, the town wall between Bastions 8 (San Pedro) and 9 (San Antonio). According to Lamare, the foot of the wall could be seen 'From the country at a distance of eight hundred yards, and having but a simple curtain, without a parapet, ditch or counter scarp, behind which it was impossible to construct an entrenchment ... [hence] we constructed in front of this weak curtain a small retrenchment' on some piles of earth which the Spaniards had formerly dumped to turn into a ravelin. If Fletcher had spotted this possibility, it was not mentioned as one of the 'courses open' by John Jones, presumably because it was immediately overlooked by the Castle complex.

Thus guns there must be on San Michael, but first the Fort must be captured. This prerequisite formed the starting point for his Lordship's planning, notwithstanding that the capture would add to the length of the business. At least the similar early capture of the Renaud Redoubt at Rodrigo was an encouraging precedent.

The plan therefore envisaged the excavation of a zig-zagging approach trench, from the engineer park nearly a mile from Fort Picurina and which, some 300 yards short of the Fort would branch right and left (north and south) to curve around the Fort, on the right straightening to end nearly opposite the Castle, on the left running down to the Rivillas stream – over two miles of digging. Batteries adjacent to this First Parallel would then put fire onto and into the Fort, as well as keeping down the interference from the town itself, until the Fort might be assaulted. New batteries would then be added in a Second Parallel, and seek to breach both the right face of the Trinidad Bastion and the opposite or left flanking face of the Santa Maria Bastion. Since the garrison would almost certainly react by retrenching behind the two breaches as they developed, a third breach in the old connecting town walls – and which it was hoped might be knocked down within the last day's firing – would allow the assault troops to turn such inner defences. So they would use two breaches, with a third last-minute addition if it turned out to be required.

CHAPTER 2

Part II – Badajoz
The Trenches and Fort Picurina
16 March–5 April

Following in the mud of the investing troops, on 16 March, were the first convoys of engineer stores – six score bullock carts – and 1,000 Portuguese militiamen from Elvas, with 500 gabions. The dumps were commenced a mile from the town walls, hidden behind the heights of San Michael. Over coming days there were built up 1,200 gabions, 700 fascines, and the same number of tracing fascines (all such labour!), 3,000 picks and shovels, 80,000 sandbags and the large quantities of timber required for gun platforms, magazines and bunkers. The first gun convoy set out from Elvas, consisting of eight 24-pounders, eight 24-pounder howitzers and ten 18-pounders. Shot for these old Russian 18-pounders was of such random circumferences, that it was necessary to divide them into three sizes, and paint them, each cannon allocated a particular colour.

During 17 March, some seven battalions (the whole 3rd Division) were warned for duty for that night, as the working (digging) party of 1,800 men and their covering (protection) party of 2,000 men. Colonel Fletcher with a thirty-man guard at last light walked forward to the top of the San Michael feature, and staked his line of curving trench, to be dug around Fort Picurina. The trench lay in places only 160 yards from the Fort's covered way and it was thus fortunate that the heavy rain and wind helped conceal the noise of the subsequent digging. Harder work of course for the diggers, and just plain miserable for the covering party, lying huddled in their hundreds, cold and soaked, in position just behind the line of the workmen – to be in front would have put them almost in the French lap. Not many would have trusted their powder to be dry, nor for many days thereafter. As Kincaid wrote, 'We had scarcely taken up our ground when heavy rain commenced, and continued without intermission, for about a fortnight (or so it seemed).'

By dawn the four zig-zag approaches were 1,400 yards long and the parallel some three feet deep and much the same wide; work continued with fresh troops the next day, harassed by frequent heavy showers of both rain and musketry from the Fort, together with occasional howitzer and cannon fire, from the town. 'In working,' wrote Major Charles Cocks, 16th Light Dragoons,

> it is usual to allow at night one man to each four feet and to calculate that in twelve hours they will have got themselves under cover, that in twenty-four hours there will be cover for infantry and in forty-eight the trenches will be completed to the breadth of nine feet and depth of three. Parallels require another day as they must be twelve or fourteen feet wide, provided with a better parapet and should have two banquettes. Batteries may be finished in forty-eight hours ready for the guns and the guns may be got in in a night. Our zigzags are to be ten feet by three and our parallels twelve by three.

The excavated spoil of course allowed a parapet giving an effective depth of at least six feet.

That night, 18/19 March, the parallel was further extended, and two battery positions traced out: No. 1 for three of the 18-pounders and three 5½-inch howitzers; and No. 2 for four 24-pounders, all for use against the Fort and its approaches, from a range of about 250 yards. It would be four days before the guns could move in, but they and their ammunition were this day drawn up in readiness to the engineer park.

Also in the park, shortly after 1pm, to the clear horror of the many unarmed men going about their lawful businesses, suddenly there erupted the rare and dreaded sound of cantering cavalry, forty blue-clad sabre-wielding French hussars splashing through the mud, most unwelcome guests, arriving unbidden from the back of the covering heights.

For 'in a dense vapour, issuing from the Guadiana and Rivillas, caused by the heavy rain' Philippon had sent out a sortie, to raid and disrupt the trench work – three battalions of infantry, who had lined up unobserved along the trench connecting the Fort with the San Roque Lunette. Actually, Ensign William Grattan of the 88th did observe:

> Having a little more experience than the officer who commanded the party, I observed with distrust the bustle which was apparent, not only in the Fort of Picurina, but also along the ramparts of the town. Without waiting the formality of telling the commanding officer what I thought, I on the instant ordered the men to throw by their spades and shovels, put on their appointments, and load their firelocks. This did not occupy more than three minutes, and in a few seconds afterwards the entire trenches to our right were filled with Frenchmen, the workmen massacred, and the works materially damaged; while at the same moment several hundred men attempted to throw themselves into the Battery we occupied.

They were into the parallel before the workmen could reach their arms or the covering party form up in good order. Sergeant William Lawrence, 40th, wrote,

> I myself killed a French Sergeant. I was in the trenches and he came on the top. Like me, he had exhausted his fire, and so made a thrust at me with his bayonet. He overbalanced and fell, and I pinioned him to the ground with mine. The poor fellow expired. I was sorry afterwards and wished I had tried to take him prisoner, but with the fighting going on all around, there had been no time to think, and he had been a powerful looking man, tall and stout, with a moustache and beard which almost covered his face, he had been as fine a soldier as I have ever seen in the French army. If I had allowed him to gain his feet I might have suffered for it, so perhaps what I did was for the best? At such times it is a matter of kill or be killed.

Both the working and covering parties were forced out of the works, but were quickly rallied some fifty yards in rear, then turning to eject the French, including the small party of sappers brought out to fill in the digging. Lieutenant John Cooke, 43rd, wrote:

> Two or three French dragoons having approached within a few yards without being perceived, fired their pistols into the trenches. We had just entered the mouth of the first parallel and all joined in a simultaneous attack on the enemy's Infantry, without regard to trenches or anything else. The French were beaten out of the advanced lines and retired. They formed a line under the Castle, having two field pieces on their left flank. I cannot say how they entered the town because there was so much smoke near the walls. General Philippon knew his business well. The day was fine, and the time well-selected. The sortie took place while we were filing into the trenches. He concluded that the front parallel would be vacant while the relief were coming in, but there was an order against that.

It is thought the sortie was to cover the hussars' reconnaissance into the dead ground of the engineer park. Cocks says 'they took some officers but could not get them off; I do not think they learnt much. Our guns were parked in a hollow and I do not believe they saw them . . . they nearly took General Picton.' Apart from that near-coup, little else was achieved with respect to filling in the trenches, but 200 picks and shovels were taken, a demeaning little loss. Philippon had offered a reward of a dollar per tool. The French lost thirty men killed and 287 wounded, quite a high price – some eight per cent of the garrison's infantry. The besiegers suffered 150 men killed and wounded, including Lieutenant Colonel Fletcher, hit in the groin by a ball which drove a silver dollar piece to a depth of an inch, and which would see this important man spend the rest of his siege on a litter. Wellington visited to consult him each morning at 8am.

Wellington – we hate to imagine his irritation – immediately placed a signal post on the far hillside, from which observation would in future be kept on the reverse of the Fort, and a dragoon squadron was ordered to take position behind the San Michael heights.

And then, at 3pm, 'A heavy and uninterrupted rain began to pour down' and continued through the night of 19/20 March. John Jones notes that 'there was little fire kept up on either side', but the parallel was somehow extended another 600 yards, stopping just 300 yards up the slope adjacent to the narrow ending of the Inundation on the Rivillas. Little further progress could be made, the trenches being now full of water, dug soil changing to sliding mud; but over the dark hours of 20/21 March three more battery positions were commenced: No. 4 for six 24-pounders and a 5½-inch howitzer, No. 5 for five 18-pounders and No. 6 for three 24-pounder howitzers, for enfilading fire respectively against the right face of the Trinidad and San Pedro bastions and the same for the San Roque Lunette. Some concern was felt for the security of these new works, which were but 300 yards from the Lunette, and this entire parallel now a mile in length: so No. 4 and No. 5 Batteries were sited actually a little in rear of the parallel itself.

The rains continued during 21 March, and that night a further battery position, No. 3, was marked out for four of the 18-pounders, to add to the fire onto the Lunette. Once more, however, continuing heavy rains washed out any prospects and next morning the lower trenches were so full that bailing-out parties were at work; fascines were placed to stand on. Then, at four o'clock, occurred what Jones describes as 'One of the heaviest showers imaginable, which again filled the trenches', carrying away the pontoon bridge over the Guadiana, with eleven other pontoons sunk at their anchors, and leaving the flying bridge working, with difficulty, in the rapid currents.

Perhaps encouraged by the sight of his drowned opponents floundering in the mud, General Philippon added to the pressures. A further but smaller sortie had been made on the night of the 20th/21st, and attempts to establish a two-gun position on the San Cristoval feature, and adjacent to Fort Pardaleras, had to be seen off by rifle picquets. On the night of the 21st/22nd three field guns were deployed on the far bank of the river and these, throughout the 22nd, put a destructive long-range fire into the Parallel, such that Wellington was forced to order General Leith's 5th Division to march in from Campo Major, and cover that side. Philippon also commenced a communication trench from the Trinidad gate to the back of the Lunette San Roque. At 300 yards range this strongpoint could put fire into the flanks and rear of the attack anticipated on what they saw as the weak point, between the San Pedro and San Antonio Bastions. In a labour-saving plan to be copied in other trenches a century later, theirs was lined above ground with a canvas curtain, frustrating the British riflemen. On 22 March further strengthening work was continued on the dam behind San Roque to secure the Inundation; and additional 24-pounder platforms and embrasures were readied on the Castle, to bring added fire to bear on the batteries of the parallel opposite. Altogether some 800 men of the garrison were employed in the above works.

That night, with the men sinking knee-deep into the mud in places, the ten pieces earmarked for Batteries No. 1 and No. 2 were put in place, the platforms being laid with much difficulty; next day (23 March) the rain holding off until 3pm and the ground improving, the other battery platforms were also laid. Lord Wellington was cheered to be brought a letter, from Philippon to Soult, no less, by a Spaniard paid 512 dollars by the former, saying 'Within these few days the English works have assumed a formidable appearance; that he will do his best to prevent being taken by a coup vivre, but if not relieved must alternatively surrender.'

The afternoon rain continued through to the morning of 24 March, and was accompanied by a much heavier fire by the garrison onto the trenches. The fire being mainly cannon not howitzer, the parapets kept the men reasonably well covered. Captain John Dobbs, 52nd, was an expert witness:

> The enemy's shells at Rodrigo were more destructive than at Badajoz, the surface being hard the shells did not sink into the ground, consequently fell in all directions, while at Badajoz they sank into the clay, and you could lie quite close to them without danger, the splinters flying upwards. To persons who had not read on the subject it may be well to state that, in every Battery there is a person on the lookout who crawls out at every discharge from the enemy, ball or shell as it may be; when the former each person covers himself behind the parapet, if the latter it was watched as it took its course through the air 'til it fell; if close, you fell flat on the ground, 'til it exploded; if at a distance you had to take your chance.

Much the same scene was noted by Captain James MacCarthy, 50th:

> I sat down with two men of the Corps of Artificers watching the fall of numerous shells thrown at the work, when one of the men said 'A shell is coming here, Sir'. I looked up and beheld it approaching me like a cricket ball to be caught; it travelled so rapidly that we only had time to run a few paces and crouch, when it entered the spot on which I had been sitting and, exploding, destroyed all our night's work.

That day, 24 March, by 3pm, Leith's 5th Division completed the invest-ment of Fort San Cristobal and the French field pieces were withdrawn. By now it is no surprise to read these damp and resigned sentences by the engineer John Jones:

> The rain which fell had so saturated the ground, that the water stood everywhere in pools; the earth lost its consistency and would not retain any form, but fell into the ditch as fast as thrown out; the revetments of the Batteries also fell, and no solid foundation could be obtained upon which to lay the remaining platforms. [In any case] the guns could not travel along the parallel or across the fields into the Batteries, and no progress was made with the attack.

The deluge had lasted four days and nights, and perhaps the equivalent of just one day's work had proved possible. All were excessively tired, cold and soaked, and this was the seemingly endless period when a good many of the mud-coated infantry had private thoughts, and short words, regarding the inside of Badajoz. For it is to be recalled that many old soldiers knew the inside rather well, and not a few of the women and wine bars – they had been there in 1809, after Talavera. Their treatment by the Spanish inhabitants, many felt, deserved retaliation.

While the rains prevented digging, the men were employed completing the batteries, draining the trenches and carrying shot to the batteries. A hundred shot per piece was the complement.

But the rains stopped again in the middle of the 24th, and during the later dark hours, with great exertions, which thankfully were spared undue interference by the garrison, fourteen guns and four howitzers with ammunition were got into Batteries 3 to 6. At eleven next morning a brisk fire was opened generally by a total of twenty-one guns and seven howitzers. Batteries 1 and 2 quickly succeeded in silencing the French artillery in Fort Picurina but, according to Cocks,

> they did not produce all the effect that was expected, the ditch at Picurina is very deep and the scarp mostly cut out of solid rock; it is likewise so well covered by its glacis that it cannot be seen. The parapet is of earth, well rammed to a stiff, adhesive nature and left at the natural slope. The only injury the fort suffered was in the embrasures and a few palisades near the salient angle.

Lord Wellington promptly decided to attack that night, being very much in touch with progress as a frequent visitor in the forward positions. Captain James MacCarthy, 50th but for now a volunteer engineer, had been in a trench when his Lordship appeared with others:

> Gently walking in the trench, where shot and shell were flying, as tranquilly as if strolling on his own lawn in England, and on approaching the medical officers, they made their obeisance and offered their

glasses, one of which his Lordship politely received, and also placed in the same scallop: at that instant the besieged (perhaps seeing cocked hats) fired the gun, the shot hummed as it passed over Lord Wellington's head, he smiled, but made his inspection and returned the glass.

Rifleman Ned Costello, 95th, also had an encounter:

Occasionally, Lord Wellington would pay us a visit during the work, to make observations and examine the trenches. One day when Crawley and myself were working near each other, a shell fell inconveniently close to us. Tom was instantly half buried in mud awaiting the explosion. The shell had sunk itself deep into the earth because the fuse was too long, so I decided to play a trick upon Crawley – when the shell exploded I was going to throw a large lump of clay on his head, to make him believe himself wounded. To obtain the clod I sprang at the other side of the trench, and in doing so exposed myself to a grape shot. It splashed me from head to foot with mud, and I had to throw myself back into the trench upon Crawley who, believing that a shell had fixed itself upon his rear, roared like a bull. In an instant however the sunken missile burst, and when the smoke dispersed I beheld the Duke, crouched down, his head half averted, drily smiling at us.

General Philippon's guns answered the British cannonade, the engagement on both sides only ceasing at dusk. Efforts were then made to repair the parapets at Fort Picurina using woolpacks and fascines, the parapets only twelve feet wide at the front angle and now much damaged. The garrison of 200 men could not venture into the open until darkness, such was the marksmanship of the men in the batteries 150 yards away. At the salient or front angle, four small galleries had been cut facing backwards into the ditch, to give a reverse or flanking fire. The top of the ramparts stood thirty feet above the bottom of the ditch, the front edge of which was about nine feet beneath the glacis, but only the first fourteen or sixteen feet of the wall was perpendicular. A continuous row of fraises or sharpened stakes, was driven into the wall at that level leaning outwards, and the upper half of the wall then sloped back, being therefore then climbable. At intervals, suspended from the fraises, were 'Very large earthen vessels – oil jars – filled with combustibles, and furnished above them with bundles of hemp, pitch etc. . . . to give light when ignited, and to drip fire into those pots below and cause explosions' (Captain James MacCarthy, 50th).

The rows of palisades at the rear had a large gate set in them and a bridge of planks connecting over the Inundation to the town. Around the ramparts grenades, powder barrels and loaded shells were stock-piled, to be hurled down at the attackers. Each defender had extra muskets ready loaded. Most of the twin rows of palisades, three rows at the rear, still stood in spite of the battering, the two main walls some seventy paces long, twenty at the sides, all these preparations had been reported to Wellington by a Spanish deserter. With seven guns and a colonel in command, it was altogether a formidable position.

So, taken all in all, the Fort was rather more than a minor impediment and the busy French commanding engineer regretted in hindsight only that 'Two hours more would have put this work in a sufficient state of defence', with the troops fully deployed; and a second regret that the 200-strong composite garrison was drawn from across the various battalions in the town, rather than from two or three regular companies under their own officers. Otherwise, it was as strong an outwork as Philippon and Lamare, experienced and energetic as they were, could devise.

Major General Sir James Kempt, commanding No. 1 Brigade in the 3rd Division, since MacKinnon's death at Rodrigo, and the day's duty commander in the trenches, formed three attack columns: 200 men of the 74th under Major Shaw; 200 of the 77th under Major Rudd; and 100, mostly from the 2nd/83rd under Captain Powis. Each column would be preceded by the engineer officers Lieutenant Gipps, Stanway and Captain Holloway respectively, who each were to take twelve sappers carrying ladders and axes, six miners with crowbars, and six carpenters with saws. Both Rudd and Shaw's columns were to move out from the parallel on the same signal from No. 4 Battery, Rudd skirting the right flank of the Fort to come at its rear, and Shaw by the left flank, to drop off half his force as a block between the force and the San Roque Lunette, the other half joining Rudd in the rear; and Powis to remain formed in No. 2 Battery but ready to climb the damaged salient angle of the walls should Rudd and Shaw fail to break in from the rear. Three additional battalions stood ready in the trenches to come forward on success, to guard against a counter-attack. The attack was timed for 9pm, but Jones tells us it was another hour before all the preparations were completed, no doubt to the Peer's irritation: the extra hour of dark gave the French more scope to clear the rubbish, and jam woolpacks and fascines into the damaged structure.

Ensign William Grattan did not take part himself (he was deputed to command a party of thirty-two sappers, tasked to dismantle the Fort after its capture) but fellow 88th officers were part of the assault, and he would have heard the story from their lips:

> At about three o'clock in the afternoon of the 25th March, almost all the batteries on the front of La Picurina were disorganised, its palisades beaten down, and the fort itself, having more semblance of a wreck than a fortification of any pretensions, presented to the eye nothing but a heap of ruins. But never was there a more fallacious appearance: the work, although dismantled of its cannon, its parapets

crumbling to pieces at each successive discharge from our guns, and its garrison diminished, without a chance of being succoured, was still much more formidable than appeared to the eye of a superficial observer. It had yet many means of resistance at its disposal. The gorge, protected by three rows of palisades, was still unhurt; and although several feet of the scarp had been thrown down by the fire from our battering, it was, notwithstanding, of a height sufficient to inspire its garrison with a well-grounded confidence as to the result of any effort of ours against it; it was defended by three hundred of the elite of Philippon's force, under the command of a colonel of Soult's staff, named Gaspard Thiery, who volunteered his services on the occasion. On this day a deserter came over to us from the fort, and gave an exact account of how it was circumstanced. Colonel Fletcher, the chief engineer, having carefully examined the damage created by our fire, disregarding the perfect state of many of the defences, and being well aware that expedition was of paramount import to our final success, advised that the fort should be attacked after nightfall.

At half-past seven o'clock the storming party, consisting of fifteen officers and five hundred privates, stood to their arms. General Kempt, who commanded in the trenches, explained to them the duty they had to perform; he did so in his usual clear manner, and everyone knew the part he was to fulfil. All now waited with anxiety for the expected signal, which was to be the fire of one gun from No. 4 Battery. The evening was settled and calm; no rain had fallen since the 23rd; the rustling of a leaf might be heard; and the silence of the moment was uninterrupted, except by the French sentinels, as they challenged while pacing the battlements of the outwork; the answers of their comrades, although in a lower tone of voice, were distinguishable – 'Tout va bien dans le fort de la Picurina' was heard by the very men who only awaited the signal from a gun to prove that the response, although true to the letter, might soon be falsified.

The great Cathedral bell of the city at length tolled the hour of eight, and its last sounds had scarcely died away when the signal from the battery summoned the men to their perilous task; the three detachments sprang out of the works at the same moment, and ran forwards to the glacis, but the great noise which the evolution unavoidably created gave warning to the enemy, already on the alert, and a violent fire of musketry opened upon the assailing columns. One hundred men fell before they reached the outwork; but the rest, undismayed by the loss, and unshaken in their purpose, threw themselves into the ditch, or against the palisades at the gorge. The sappers, armed with axes and crowbars, attempted to cut away or force down the defence; but the palisades were of such thickness, and so firmly placed in the ground, that before any impression could be made against even the front row, nearly all the men who had crowded to this point were struck dead. Meanwhile, those in charge of the ladders flung them into the ditch, and those below soon placed them upright against the wall; but in some instances they were not of a sufficient length to reach the top of the parapet. The time was passing rapidly, and had been awfully occupied by the enemy; while as yet our troops had not made any progress that could warrant a hope of success. More than two-thirds of the officers and privates were killed or wounded; two out of the three that commanded detachments had fallen; and Major Shawe, of the 74th, was the only one unhurt. All his ladders were too short; his men, either in the ditch or on the glacis, unable to advance, unwilling to retire, and not knowing what to do, became bewildered. The French cheered vehemently, and each discharge swept away many officers and privates.

Shawe's situation, which had always been one of peril, now became desperate; he called out to his next senior officer (Captain Oates of the 88th) and said, 'Oates, what are we to do?' but at that instant he was struck in the neck by a bullet and fell bathed in blood. It immediately occurred to Oates, who now took the command, that, although the ladders were too short to mount the wall, they were long enough to go across the ditch! He at once formed the desperate resolution of throwing three of them over the fosse, by which a sort of bridge was constructed; he led the way, followed by the few of his brave soldiers who were unhurt, and forcing their passage through an embrasure that had been but bolstered up in the hurry of the moment, carried – after a brief, desperate, but decisive conflict – the point allotted to him. Sixty grenadiers of the Italian guard were the first encountered by Oates and his party; they supplicated for mercy, but, either by accident or design, one of them discharged his firelock, and the ball struck Oates in the thigh; he fell, and his men, who had before been greatly excited, now became furious when they beheld their commanding officer weltering in his blood. Every man of the Italian guard was put to death on the spot.

Meanwhile Captain Powis's detachment had made great progress, and finally entered the fort by the salient angle. It has been said, and, for aught I know to the contrary, with truth, that it was the first which established itself in the outwork; but this is of little import in the detail, or to the reader. All the troops engaged acted with the same spirit and devotion, and each vied with his comrade to keep up the character of the 'fighting division'. Almost the entire of the privates and non-commissioned officers were killed or wounded; and of fifteen officers, which constituted the number of those engaged, not one escaped unhurt! Of the garrison, but few escaped; the Commandant, and about eighty, were made prisoners; the rest, in endeavouring to escape under the guns of the fortress, or to shelter themselves in San Roque, were either bayoneted or drowned in the Rivillas; but this was not owing to any mismanagement on the part of Count Philippon. He, with that thorough knowledge of his duty which marked his conduct throughout the siege, had early in the business ordered a body of chosen troops to débouche from San Roque, and to hold themselves in readiness to sustain the fort; but the movement was foreseen. A strong column, which had been placed in reserve, under the command of Captain Lindsey of the 88th, met this reinforcement at the moment they were about to sustain their defeated companions at La Picurina. Not expecting to be thus attacked, these troops became panic-struck, soon fled in disorder, and, running without heed in every direction, choked up the only passage of escape that was open for the fugitives from the outwork, and, by a well-meant but ill-executed evolution, did more harm than good.

Grattan's timings seem adrift, and his reference to 'the Italian guard' is a puzzle, but otherwise it all rings true. Napier, writing thirteen years earlier, noted that 'Powis, Holloway, Gipps and Oates of the 88th, fell wounded on or beyond the rampart; Nixon of the 52nd was shot two yards within the gate; Shaw, Rudd and nearly all the other officers had fallen outside.' Oman reckons Wellington lost twenty officers and 300 men, killed or wounded, of the 500-strong force; while on the French side the Fort commander, Colonel Gaspard Thierry and 145 men were taken, eighty killed and wounded, and just one officer and forty men of the Hessian regiment escaped into the town. By any standard, the British loss, of two-thirds, was very severe and so no wonder the Governor loudly signified displeasure at the weak resistance of this work. For with only the equivalent of two full British companies left on their feet, and with very few officers, the outcome was quite finely balanced. Philippon blamed the under-usage of the grenades,

> loaded shells and combustibles lying ready on the parapets and on the glacis, of which the effect had been so fortunate at the two assaults of the breach of San Cristoval in 1811, thanks to the wounding of the commanding gunner, Captain Mareillac, and his replacement by an unnamed captain who did not show the same courage (Lamare).

The attack had lasted just under the hour. The horizontal fraises high on the ramparts had proved a blessing, lodging points for the ladders, but also allowing the stormers to gather thereon before making the final climb, up the sixteen feet of the massive sloping earth parapet, untouchable by the defending bayonets until the last. The ferocity of that final close struggle was shown afterwards, by the discovery of 'Several officers and many men, shot dead or severely wounded, found lying on the fraises ... The defenders certainly disputed the parapet.' (Jones)

Just as at the two breaches at Rodrigo, the Light and 3rd Divisions again exercised their inter-tribal vanities. A hundred men from the former, under Lieutenant James Stokes, 95th, had been required by General Kempt to collect and carry the ladders for use by the 3rd Division stormers. Harry Smith tells us:

> The working party were sent to the engineer park for the ladders. When they arrived [at the Fort], General Kempt ordered them to be planted ... The boys of the 3rd Division said to our fellows, 'Come, stand out of the way', to which our fellows replied, 'Damn your eyes, do you think we Light Division fetch ladders for such chaps as you to climb up? Follow us'. And springing on the ladders, many of them were knocked over.

It was said (probably by a Rifleman) that Stokes (who was to die twelve days later) was the first man into the Fort. So the Rifles here showed again that they saw no reason to limit themselves to their orders – whether merely to clear the ditch at Rodrigo, or merely to carry a ladder at Picurina, they pop up early at the very sharp end, on the walls, desperate for glory.

Grattan's reference to the failed French counter-attack reflects well on Kempt's decision to post, as a block, a strong company from Shaw's column, precisely to counter such a threat. The flight of the French force, the 3rd/103rd after the loss of only seventy men (according to Lamare), implies a great disaster, and it was unfortunate that the 520 or so remainder sought the same escape route over the Inundation (a partly destroyed plank bridge) as the fleeing remnants from the Fort. In the dark confusion, weighed down by boots and equipment, many would drown.

By this stage, around 11pm, the Garrison were unsure whether a further attempt on the main walls was imminent. The move forward of the three reserve battalions may have been misinterpreted. For an hour or so alarms continued to be heard within the walls, and intermittent if random fire from both cannon and muskets took some time to die down. By morning the sappers had smoothed a ramp on the breach, up the front or salient angle of the Fort, and this was connected by trench back to the First Parallel. A start was made on the Second Parallel, running left-handed down to the Inundation, but throughout 26 March the garrison's cannon and howitzers put heavy fire over and through the rear palisades, making the inside of the Fort thoroughly unhealthy.

Yet even so, the Fort's capture marked an important step forward in Lord Wellington's plans. After eight days of open trenches he was now between 350 and 500 yards from the Trinidad and Maria bastions (albeit across 100 yards of water), and he had now to construct the necessary batteries. These were to be in the Fort's gorge, a very hot place to be. We have Lamare to thank for the description of those who would make it so: 'more than eighty pieces of cannon against that point [the Fort] from the guns of bastions Nos 5, 6, 7, 8 and 9, from the Castle, from the Lunette San Roque, and Fort Pardaleras.' And that fire, in their view, would have made the British fail in their attack on the Maria and Trinidad bastions given only that 'we had a sufficient quantity of ammunition'. But they didn't. They thought Wellington was making a mistake, to choose the strongest bastions, subsequent to the capture of Picurina across the way, rather than what they believed to be the weakest link in their defensive chain – Bastions 8 and 9, and which they thought had been his Lordship's original plan. That was never the case, of course, 6 and 7 always having been the intention.

The daylight hours after the Fort's capture – like the previous dark hours – were notable for the ferocity and volume of the French fire at and around the Fort, even at an oblique angle from the Castle, and from Fort San Cristobal a mile away. But when Colonel Picoteau, Philippon's artillery commander, was given the figures for the day's ammunition expenditure, they made unhappy reading. Another 12,000lbs of powder had been fired off, making 82,000lbs used since the siege began. This was half their total stock. It was reluctantly decided that fire rates must be reined back.

The British batteries Nos 1, 3, 4, 5 and 6 replied vigorously. A feature of the British shooting was for Nos 4 and 5 Batteries to fire on reduced charges against the enfiladed gun line on the Trinidad and San Pedro right-flank walls. This ricochet technique of lobbing a shot just over the parapet from the side, to roll along a line of guns, could be very rewarding, given a slice of luck. (The French had used the same reduced charge idea at Talavera, to roll shot through the British battalions lying down behind the Medellin.)

That night, 26/27 March, one of the new battery positions (No. 9) was started in the Fort's gorge, for eight 18-pounders, to fire on the breach site on the left flank of Santa Maria; also No. 7 Battery was started down next to the Inundation, for twelve 24-pounders, to breach the right face of Trinidad; and No. 10 up on the First Parallel, next to No. 4, for three 24-pounder howitzers, to enfilade any workmen in the ditch before the principal breach at Trinidad. Nos 1 and 2 Batteries, used against Picurina, were dismantled.

Over the next three days the Second Parallel was with difficulty extended above the San Roque Lunette, eventually closing to forty paces. Casualties were heavy. The aim of this extension was to take possession and then unblock the Inundation at the dam in rear. To this end Wellington ordered up another six guns from Elvas, to form a further battery, No. 11, just 200 yards from the Lunette, in the Second Parallel. In addition, the platforms were laid for No. 9 Battery in the gorge, and No. 8 was commenced next door for another of the six 18-pounders, also to fire on the left flank of Maria. In front of both batteries a trench was dug for riflemen to provide covering fire. Captain John Dobbs, 52nd, tells us:

> I happened to be in the covering party, and occupied a trench in its front, running parallel to the battery; the enemy opened a tremendous fire upon it, and in a short time dismounted several guns and disabled others. On this a message came to us requesting that we would endeavour to stop the enemy's fire. Accordingly we opened fire on their embrasures, and the effect of the fire was such that in about twenty minutes they had to stop them with gabions. Some of the shots struck the sides and glanced right and left – others went right through the centre, so that the gunners could not stand to their guns. I do not remember our distance from the walls, but the trench ran along the front of the batteries, about fifty yards nearer to the walls.

This was the sap the marking out of which caused a brave French sapper, Corporal Stoll, to creep out, re-aligning the tapes to the guns on the Castle, so that the trench so dug would lay exposed. Fortunately a sapper officer, Captain Ellicombe, spotted and corrected what was initially thought to be a mischance, not a deliberate act. We get a flavour of the dangers when working in close sapping from Ensign Grattan:

> We were frequently obliged to run the flying-sap so close to the battlements of the town that the noise of the pick-axes was heard on the ramparts, and, upon such occasions, the party was invariably cut off to a man … When a fire so destructive as to sweep away all our gabions took place, men would run forward with a fresh supply, and under a fire in which it was almost impossible to live, place them in order for the rest of the party to shelter themselves, while they threw up a sufficiency of earth to render them proof against musketry.

On the other side of the Inundation, the French continued to raise the counterguard in front of Trinidad, since by now they were in no doubt of the besiegers' intentions. That evening Philippon ordered a sortie by 400 men of the 3rd/9th Léger, to destroy the line of trenchwork in hand by the 5th Division, some 600 yards beyond the Tête de Pont and San Cristobal and linking with a new small square fort (Lunette Werle) on the Knoll of Atalaya. But according to Colonel Lamare 'the enemy brought up the whole force which he had on that bank, and obliged them (the sortie) to return without having achieved any object.' Strangely, no mention of this sortie on the 29th is made in any British account.

On the night of 29/30 March, eight 18-pounders were got into Battery No. 9, and three 24-pounder howitzers into No. 10, the former opening fire on the left-flank wall of Santa Maria next morning. Time began to press. News came of Soult's marches, and in consequence the 5th Division left Badajoz for the south.

Philippon and Lamare now began constructing retrenchments behind and between Santa Maria and Trinidad, as was anticipated. In addition and independent of the retrenchments 'we caused a second enclosure to be formed in rear, by making use of the garden walls and houses adjacent, and loopholed them in such a way as to compel the enemy to repeat his assaults. The streets we cut across with ditches and traverses.'

By the end of April Fool's Day, three days hard pounding at the bastions was just beginning to bear fruit, there now being twelve 24-pounders operating against Trinidad, eleven 18-pounders and three 24-pounders against Maria, and enfilading fire from Batteries 3, 5 and 10. The French meanwhile added another four feet in height to the counterguard in front of the Trinidad breach. The bottom third of the wall was now obscured from the breaching gunners, who were understandably not best pleased with their enfilading brethren, who had not been sufficiently active during the night. The commanding officer (Picton) 'Is determined to report every officer to Lord Wellington who shall neglect this duty.' The next night the enfilading batteries fired continuously.

The garrison also worked hard at night in clearing the rubbish now beginning to form at the breaches, so as to aggravate the climb, the men being 'exposed for four or five hours to grape shot and the projectiles of every description.' Cocks says the French working party was 200 strong, and a deserter reported forty killed and wounded. Lamare quotes overall casualties to this point from 16 March at some 700. And British losses were also mounting up, with the French firing some 5,000 cannon balls on 31 March alone.

But the walls still stood at Trinidad and Maria. The facing stones had come away but the solid clay interior remained, jammed obstinately tight between the buttresses inside the structure. Not so the parapets now shattered alongside the supporting revetments. The garrison endeavoured to replicate new parapets at the breach sites, a little in rear, using sandbags and wool and cotton bales; but these proved short-lived. Case shot and shell were running low and – more importantly – powder began to fail. This was accordingly rationed to 6,500 pounds a day and on that basis was due to be expended on or by 9 April. Presumably this calculation became general knowledge amongst Philippon's men – certainly it is implied in Lamare's account. While he lavished praise on the troops for their 'noble devotion ... zeal and ardour' etc. in the declining circumstances, and how indignant the lowest soldier would be 'had anyone uttered a thought of capitulating', he did interestingly add 'Before they had repulsed several assaults'. Implicit therein lies the expectation of eventual failure.

On the night of 2 April, because progress sapping up to the Lunette was too slow, Wellington put in hand an alternative attempt to drain the Inundation – and thus open up his possible routes for the assault – by blowing down the masonry dam and sluice across the Rivillas to its rear. For the Inundation was a serious hindrance, made worse by the endless rains of 20–22 March. It allowed but a narrow approach across the Valverde road from the south, not from the trenches to the east as would be wished, and where last preparations could safely be made under cover, and, possibly, without detection. Lieutenants Stanway and Barney – the former had guided Major Rudd's 77th's stormers at Fort Picurina – took twenty sappers and a covering party of thirty men forward to the Lunette as soon as it was dark. They dropped down into the bed of the Rivillas, turned left, and quietly approached the dam. Sentries on the bridge twice challenged and once fired upon the men carrying the two heavy cases of powder. It would seem the darkness had by then fully fallen and, the sentries not investigating further, the powder cases containing a massive 450lbs of explosive were placed, by touch, against the dam wall (but not quite against it, for a clay buttress had been built against the wall, and water was pouring over it). Stanway had also brought sandbags, to be jammed over the cases to direct the force of the blast inwards; however, he judged a further carrying party would be discovered. A train was laid, the match lit, Stanway withdrew – and the match failed. The Lunette guard discovered the party in the ditch, and opened fire. Stanway returned under fire to relight the match, but the resultant explosion unfortunately failed to disturb the dam. Moorsom, in his excellent *Historical Record* of the 52nd, maintains that an hour later Lieutenant Robert Blackwood and three sappers were ordered to make another (equally unsuccessful) attempt on the dam.

Attempts to sap to the dam continued next day but were finally abandoned due to the very high casualties involved. His Lordship now reluctantly accepted the limitations imposed by Philippon's Inundation, which the Peer doubtless described, no pun intended, as a damned inconvenience.

On 3 April No. 11 Battery, having been armed during the night with six 18-pounders, opened initially (and possibly as a feint), since no breach had been considered there, on the curtain wall between Trinidad and San Pedro. Jones tells us that this soon switched to the Lunette, 'the wall proving very hard'. Lamare, however, says this new battery fired ricochets at the workmen on Trinidad. In either event, such was their shortage of ammunition, the French batteries 'could reply only feebly' to the British artillery this day, consisting of 'forty pieces of cannon, eighteen or twenty-four pounders, which fired incessantly'. By evening both the breaches were very promising and, there now being no parapet from the main Trinidad breach, the terre-plein behind was quite open to view. As at Rodrigo, on either side of the breach lay a ditch and parapet, across the breadth of the terre-plein, and the retaining wall behind the rampart was fourteen feet deep. The French themselves considered the breaches were becoming practicable and the efforts of the workmen clearing rubbish at night to be proving inadequate. After dark the breaches had each been test-climbed by French NCOs in full kit, and thus proved; and earlier a convoy of wagons loaded with scaling ladders had been spotted moving forward. So General Philippon assembled his Counsel of Defence to issue his final orders. Colonel Lurat and his 3rd/103rd Ligne was to hold the retrenchments behind Trinidad; Colonels Barbot and Maistre of the 3rd/88th and the Hessian Regiment were to hold the breaches with some 350 men each, coming from the grenadier and light companies in the garrison, together with gunners and sappers. Another 1,000 men, changing in shifts, worked on the retrenchments clearing rubbish, destroying the ramps, and working in the Castle both as a last safe haven and also to create another large battery, to overlook the approaches to the Trinidad breach. The threat from this latter battery next day caused Lord Wellington to order a counter-battery of fourteen iron howitzers to fire shrapnel, but only in the assault, to be positioned right at the end of the Second Parallel in enfilade as No. 12 Battery.

In the trenches, destruction continued in both directions. Lieutenant George Simmons, 95th, tells us:

> I was with a party of men behind the advanced sap, and had an opportunity of doing some mischief. Three or four heavy cannon that the enemy were working were doing frightful execution amongst our artillery men in their advance Batteries. So I selected several good shots and fired into the embrasures. In half an hour I found the guns did not go off so frequently ... and soon after gabions were stuffed into each embrasure to prevent our rifleballs from entering. They withdrew them to fire, which was my signal for firing steadily at the embrasures. The gabions were replaced without firing a shot. I was so delighted with the good practice I was making against Johnny, that I kept it up from daylight until dark, with forty as fine fellows as ever pulled trigger. These guns were literally silenced.

Also on 4 April came news that Marshal Soult and 24,000 men, having joined with Drouet, and Dericau, was now at Llerena seventy miles or four or five marches away. His progress from Seville had been delayed by concerns of the Spanish threat from the Ronda hills; but he was also convinced Philippon, on the previous year's outcomes, was in no immediate danger. Sensing that Marmont wanted no part in a joint force, Soult's modest strength was thus a sufficient cause of tardiness. He wrote a week later:

> The best accounts give Wellington 30,000 men, and some make him as high as 40,000; ... If the Army of Portugal had joined me with 25,000 men Badajoz would have been saved or retaken; and a great victory would throw the English back into their lines ... (but) I was not strong enough alone.

Graham fell back towards the old battlefield at Albuera, one day's march south of Badajoz, and Hill, having destroyed the two centre arches of the bridge at Merida, to Talavera Real, one march east. Fortunately, in compliance with his Emperor's orders, Marshal Marmont was away in the other direction; yet time now again became a pressing factor, perhaps with a second battle of Albuera looming for the covering forces.

With this in mind, and after another day's busy breaching, at noon on 5 April Wellington himself went forward to the farthest sap, to make his personal reconnaissance. He returned to give a warning order for the assault that evening, but subject to further reconnaissance by Colonel Fletcher, now fortunately again on his feet. The Chief Engineer took particular trouble to make what he could of the defensive works behind the breaches and, as a result, formed the view that the principal breach would form 'an obstinate and protracted resistance'; that is, the breach itself and what lay behind it in the form of a second line. On hearing this at 4pm, Lord Wellington cancelled his warning order, and directed that, next morning, fire be opened on the curtain wall between the bastions, and grape during the night to interrupt the garrison's working parties.

When 6 April dawned, fourteen 24-pounder howitzers had been put into No. 12 Battery during the night, ready to fire upon the new battery on the Castle, overlooking Trinidad. Another fourteen guns in the breaching batteries opened on the old curtain wall, the base of which was visible to them, and by 4pm proved easily effective against the poor masonry. Lord Wellington went forward to satisfy himself on the state of all three breaches and returned to confirm the assault for 7.30pm that evening. His orders having been written up the previous day, before the attack on the curtain wall was settled, a separate order was sent to the 4th Division for that purpose; and similarly for the 5th, to attempt to climb the San Vincent bastion. Lord Wellington's orders are attached at Appendix 2.

For the garrison had run out of time. They had done all they could. The three breach sites had replacement parapets of fascines, woolpacks and sandbags, with shells, barrels of combustibles, casks filled with tar and straw, powder and loaded grenades, and multiple muskets for each man with cannon double-charged with canister, all lay ready. There was even a large boat anchored in the flooded ditch in front of Trinidad, full of soldiers to enfilade the breach with musketry. General Philippon issued his orders which Lamare paraphrased as 'to prolong the defence by every obstacle which courage and art could oppose: everywhere to make the most determined resistance and to make the enemy pay with the blood of his best soldiers'.

He also made one small but ultimately fatal re-allocation of troops to tasks: to hold the new third breach he took a grenadier company of Hessians away from the Castle. All in all, however, General Philippon had created a robust, ingenious defence, and had fought the progress of the British tooth and nail. Yet he had only three days' powder and Soult lay more marches than that away, and with a battle to fight en route. The garrison appeared lost, unless a successful repulse of the British, imposing heavy casualties, could gain a day or even two while Soult's approach itself put increasing pressure on the besieging divisions. And the British acknowledged their position, in preparing to attack breaches without first blowing the counter-scarps into the ditch, thus easing the descent into the ditch; the failure to do so gave the garrison added scope for deepening the drop and laying explosive trains. The drop from the counter-scarp was now up to eighteen feet, partly flooded, and anyway blind to the approaching attackers, who would naturally seek to form up there. What a place for sixty 14-inch shells, four paces apart, and barrels of powder connected by covered train to the ramparts! What a place for rope entanglements, old carts, fascines, broken boats, deep holes: all in advance of the breaches, covered in crowsfeet, beams studded with nails, doors with long spikes, and at the summit of each breach chevaux de frises formed by Spanish sabres stuck in foot-square timbers and chained down. And behind all that, a second line of trenches, loop-holed houses with cannon with canister and massed men with multiple muskets at each stage. As Lamare wrote of their endeavours 'Heroic resolution! And such as merited better success!'

CHAPTER 2

Part III – Badajoz
Wellington's Plan of Attack

We will preface his Lordship's plans by reminding ourselves of the mood that night of his men. Charles Oman's Introduction in 1902 to Ensign Grattan's *Adventures* praises his treatment of the 'psychology of the stormers at Badajoz', saying that nowhere else has he seen it described so convincingly:

> There was a certain something in their bearing that told plainly that they had suffered fatigues, which they did not complain of, and had seen their comrades and officers slain while fighting beside them without repining, but that they smarted under the one, and felt acutely for the other; they smothered both, so long as their minds and bodies were employed; now, however, that they had a momentary licence to think, every fine feeling vanished, and plunder and revenge took place. Their labours, up to this period, although unremitting, had carried on with a cheerfulness that was astonishing, hardly promised the success which they looked for; and the change which the last twenty-four hours had brought in their favour, caused a material alteration in their demeanour; they held the present prospect as the mariner does the disappearance of a heavy cloud after a storm, which discovers to his view the clear horizon. In a word, the capture of Badajoz had long been their idol. Many causes led to this wish on their part; the two previous unsuccessful sieges, and the failure of the attack against St Cristobel in the latter; but above all the well known hostility of its inhabitants to the British army, and perhaps might be added a desire for plunder, which the sacking of Rodrigo had given them a taste for. Badajoz was, therefore, denounced as a place to be made an example of; and most unquestionably no city, Jerusalem excepted, was ever more strictly visited to the letter than was this ill fated.

These considerations were not, of course, limited to Grattan's 88th Connaughts; as a further example, hear Sergeant William Lawrence, 40th, who with two friends volunteered for their Forlorn Hope:

All three of us had been quartered at Badajoz after the battle of Talavera so we knew where the shops were located. Having heard a report that, if we succeeded in taking the place, three hours plunder would be allowed, we arranged to meet at a silversmith's shop ... [later] I saw some of our men launch a naked priest into the street and flog him down it – they had a grudge against him for the way they had been treated at a convent, when they were in the town previously.

In the orders setting out his plans, Wellington's final paragraph urges his commanders 'to impress upon their men the necessity of their keeping together and formed as a military body after the storm, and during the night' ostensibly to repel counterattacks, but also with a passing reference to 'the honour of the Army'. There is no doubt – especially after Rodrigo – that every one of his officers knew their collective honour was all set to be tarnished.

The Earl's plan to capture the town was in two parts. One was obvious to all, having been on the menu for the French to read for some days; the other was a matter of pot-luck surprise, designed to cause Philippon to redeploy his companies in the bastions, and disperse or commit his reserve, thus lightening the resistance to the three main attempts. These were, of course, the left and right flanks respectively of the Maria and Trinidad bastions, together with the linking curtain wall. All three rubble slopes were in an area perhaps some 200 yards wide by 100 yards deep (see Napier's sketch). Perhaps not much more than a football pitch, and into which some 6,500 men were to be decanted in the coming darkness. Clearly the centre breach would not be easy, protected as it was by flanking fire from the others, and set behind a deeper killing zone. It and the two bastion breaches were to be defended by the ten grenadier and light companies from the garrison's five battalions, with four fusilier companies from the 3rd/103rd Ligne as an immediate reserve, manning the entrenchments in rear. Oman estimates the flank companies totalled some 700 men, the fusiliers another 400 or 500. We do not know if he meant this to be just the number of bayonets, or whether he also included associated gun teams and sapper parties. If the former, it puts an impossibly high average manning figure on the infantry, bearing in mind earlier losses. These (some 600) probably had reduced the companies to around fifty men. A small confirmation is Lamare's comment that four companies of the 88th Ligne 'amounted to about two hundred men'.

These fourteen companies were under the command of Colonel Barbot, whose own 3rd/88th Ligne formed Philippon's reserve back in the Cathedral Square; the two Hessian battalions under Colonel Maistre held the Castle, the San Roque Lunette, the San Pedro and San Antonio bastions. The 3rd/9th Léger, the 3rd/28th Léger and the 1st/58th Ligne, less their flank companies, manned the other bastions. Allowing fifty bayonets per company, this meant the 9th Léger would be defending San Vincente and San Jose bastions with fewer than 200 men on each – bearing in mind they also had the long run of the connecting curtain wall. Lamare subsequently indicated that San Vincente was allocated just two and a half companies. The 28th Léger would be even more thinly spread, with not only the San Jago and No. 4 Bastions but also two lengths of curtain; and the 58th Ligne would also have its hands full with No. 5 Bastion, two lengths of wall, and the communications out to Fort Pardaleras. Altogether the French bayonet strength was quite inadequate, and the greater the demands upon it, the weaker would be the response. This consideration would especially apply where defences were less pre-arranged than they were at the breaches. Surprise was all, and Lord Wellington fully intended to stretch his enemy. General Philippon, aware of that, 'frequently reconnoitred our works ... from the tower of the Cathedral, (it) being very high'.

But at Trinidad and Maria, there could be no surprise. Only weight of numbers could steamroller a passage, the overwhelming surge of two whole divisions flooding across the glacis, jumping down into the very deep ditch, climbing over and through the obstacles and forcing the breach. Nor could they even reach the glacis with much chance of surprise, since Philippon's Inundation channelled any approach from the south across the Calamon stream which paralleled the Valverde road, passing the Stone Quarries on the left, with the head of the waters on the right, just hundreds of yards down the slopes from Fort Pandeleras. The approach therefore ended with a right-angle left turn to face up to the glacis. The turn would be made under the garrison's guns, and to maintain control in the dark Wellington's plan required the two divisions – Light on the left and the 4th on the right – to move either side of the convenient axis of the Calamon stream. The line of Quarries running parallel to the Valverde road had its northern end perhaps 170 yards from the Maria covered way, and the Light Division was to throw forward a hundred men in advance, to close up on the covered way, in readiness to engage the French on the bastion and the covered way once the main storming parties were discovered, coming from their right. Separate firing and storming parties, to a strength of 500 men for each division (300 stormers, 200 firers), were to form the two advance guards each equipped with a dozen ladders, twelve carpenters with axes, a gunner party of an officer and twenty artillery men, and the Forlorn Hopes to carry hay sacks to drop into the deep ditch (the counterscarp not having been touched). The Light Division's advanced guard would precede the 4th's, and all formed bodies in their approach march were to keep as close to the Inundation as they could, i.e. away from the Valverde road. The firing parties on arrival at the glacis would take up firing positions, the hay sacks would be jettisoned to the left and right of the unfinished ravelin for each division, and the Forlorn Hopes and the stormers would descend, the 4th making for Trinidad and the Light turning left for Santa Maria. The firing parties, curiously, were 'to follow immediately in the rear of their respective storming parties'. Curious since the stormers would then have no overhead suppressive fire onto the breaches and the neighbouring gun embrasures. In this context, Kincaid had an interesting idea, after it was all over:

> The defences on the tops of the breaches ought to have been cleared away by our batteries before the assault commenced. But failing that, I cannot see why a couple of six-pounders (or half a dozen) might not have been run up along with the storming party, to the crest of the glacis. Our battalion took post there, and lay about ten minutes unknown to the enemy, and had a few guns been sent along with us, I am confident that we could have taken them up with equal silence.

Both Divisions' main bodies would follow in column of brigades, two British brigades sandwiching the Portuguese, and were initially ordered to concentrate and remain in the Quarries until the breaches had been ascended. Each was to leave 1,000 men behind as reserves. (Lord Wellington on second thoughts allowed that 'the heads of the columns should be brought as near as they can without being exposed to fire,' fearing that the Quarries might not be close enough for the main bodies quickly to join the fray.) On achieving the ramparts, both divisions were to send parties outwards, to link up with others and open up the various town gates. Fire support from the fourteen heavy howitzers in No. 12 Battery was to be put onto the enfilading cannon located on the Castle and the San Antonio demi-bastion.

As to the third breach, in the town wall, Wellington wrote a separate memorandum the next day (6 April) to enlarge on the bald note to his orders of the 5th 'That General Colville will observe that a part of the advance of the 4th Division must be allotted to storm the new breach in the curtain.'

That then is the outline for the assault on the San Maria and La Trinidad bastions. Neither division was at full strength: the 4th was that night providing the trench guard, and some of the Light's riflemen were detached, giving strengths respectively of 3,500 and 3,000 men, or thereabouts.

Half a mile east of Trinidad, beyond the San Pedro bastion and the San Antonio demi-bastion, the Castle sat hunched above the Rivillas, where it joins the Guadiana river. Its walls varied from eighteen to twenty-four feet in height, but the ditch had been deepened along the rocky foot of the walls, which raised their effective height very considerably. In places the parapets were narrow and defenders could with ease reach out, to ward off ladders. The walls were to be climbed by Picton's 3rd Division, setting out from the First Parallel near No. 6 Battery, and crossing the Rivillas stream below the broken bridge, taking long ladders, slightly right of the San Antonio demi-bastion. His orders quite specifically directed his escalade to that part of the Castle 'in rear of the great battery constructed by the enemy to fire on the bastion of La Trinidad ... The attack should be kept clear of the bastion of San Antonio'; that is, the battery being constructed upon San Antonio, the division should keep to its right, as seen from the trenches.

Picton's British brigades (commanded by Kempt and Campbell), together with Champalimaud's Portuguese brigade, were to move off before 10pm, but not to attack before that time, since Lord Wellington wished all his attacks to be simultaneous. The exception to this was the proviso that if the engagement of the 3rd Division by the French was earlier, that was to be the signal for the fourth attack, upon the Lunette San Roque. This outwork would threaten the flanks and rear of Picton's approach. Four hundred men of the 4th's covering party under Major James Wilson, 48th, who was commanding in the trenches that night, were to capture the Lunette and blow in the dam in rear which was containing the Inundation. Half his force was to leave the Second Parallel and make for the rear of the Lunette; half from the sap head then to cover the short distance to the covered way's salient angle, to put musket fire onto the defenders, keeping them occupied and undecided as to where exactly they should concentrate.

Four further attacks were added to this complex plan: false escalades by Power's Portuguese brigade on the Tête de Pont and on Fort San Cristobal, across the Guadiana; another false demonstration by the 5th Division's Portuguese against Fort Pardeleras; and a real escalade by one of Leith's British brigades of the 5th Division, against the riverside San Vincente bastion or, if easier, the curtain wall round the corner towards the bridge. This was the bastion which was held by just two and a half companies of the 3rd/9th Léger.

We have now explained Lord Wellington's plans and, this not being the place to comment upon them, we will press on to the narration of their execution.

CHAPTER 2

Part IV – Badajoz
The Attack
10pm to Midnight, 6 April 1812

A Lt-Colonel or cold meat in a few hours.

At half past seven o'clock, the light now failing, the British guns ceased their fire. Philippon's working parties rushed out again at each breach, to make good the debris and re-arrange the obstacles. By 8pm the attacking regiments had assembled, piled arms and sunk again to rest, preparatory to the various fatigue parties setting off (if not having done so earlier) for the engineer park, to collect ladders, hay sacks, axes etc. It was also the time for confirmatory orders by the divisional generals to their brigade and battalion commanders, and the synchronisation of watches.

The men, having been earlier disappointed by the previous day's postponement of the attack, and with the sodden hardships of long days digging mud whilst randomly having their heads blown off, were spoiling for a fight. The prospects of plunder and revenge even fuelled the competition to join the Hopes. Bugler William Green, 95th:

> Our Bugle Major made us cast lots which two of us should go on this momentous errand; the lot fell on me and another lad. One of our buglers who had been on the Forlorn Hope at Ciudad Rodrigo offered the Bugle Major two dollars to let him go in my stead. On my being apprised of it, he came to me, and said 'West will go on the Forlorn Hope instead of you'. I said 'I shall go where my duty calls me.' He threatened to confine me to the guard tent. I went to the adjutant and reported him; the adjutant sent for him, and said 'So you are in the habit of taking bribes;' and told him he would take the stripes off his arm if he did the like again! He then asked me if I wished to go? I said 'Yes, sir.' He said 'Very good,' and dismissed me. Those who composed this Forlorn Hope were free from duty that day, so I went to the river, and had a good bathe; I thought I would have a clean skin whether killed or wounded, for all who go on

this errand expect one or the other … At nine o'clock at night, we were paraded – it was then dark – and half a pound of bread and a gill [a quarter pint] of rum was served out to each man on parade.'

The Light Division's Forlorn Hope was composed of 350 men from the 43rd, 52nd and 95th Rifles, all volunteers and two buglers from each regiment. Even the officers' servants insisted on their place in the ranks, such that 'I was obliged to leave my baggage in charge of a man who had been wounded some days before' (Kincaid, 95th); and the forty-one-year-old Lieutenant MacCarthy, 50th, on duty as an assistant engineer attached to Picton's 3rd Division, even used the word 'hilarity' to describe how the men packed their knapsacks and fixed their best flints 'All forming in column with the utmost alacrity, to march to the assault'.

And march they did. The 3rd Division assembled three miles distant, according to MacCarthy, who had volunteered for the unenviable task of guiding the irascible Picton forward. Upon reaching the west-east road to Talavera, the general dismounted to lead on foot, beside MacCarthy. Before reaching the First Parallel, however, musketry broke out up ahead which 'becoming brisk, increased the general's anxiety … lest any occurrence should retard the operation of his Division'. That is, get him into the Peer's bad books for lateness. For all attacks were meant to be simultaneous at 10pm, and brisk musketry, occurring while he was not yet even in the First Parallel, either meant something unplanned, or he was very late indeed. His pocket-watch no doubt reassured him, that it was about 9.30pm, for having then progressed up to the end of the Parallel, he was met by 'The enemy's volcanic fire [which] burst forth in every direction long and far over the Division, and in every kind of combustible' such that it seemed 'all the stars, planets and meteors and firmament, within numerable moons emitting smaller ones in their course [were] descending upon the heads of the besiegers' (MacCarthy). General Picton whereupon exclaimed 'Some of them are too soon; what o'clock is it?' and comparing his watch with others, saw 'The time was a quarter before 10 o'clock'.

So he at least had approached nicely before time, and was according to plan, ready to go; but Major James Wilson it was who had jumped the gun, for some reason having disregarded his Lordship's injunction to attack the Lunette 'as soon as' i.e. not before, the 3rd Division was spotted. For the firing can only have been Wilson's, and Lamare confirms this 'At 9.30 at night a numerous Artillery were throwing a shower of projectiles in every direction. About the same time a brisk fire of musketry began at the Lunette San Roque: the besiegers attacked it.'

Wilson carried out Wellington's plan to the letter. He took 200 men round the right rear ready to escalade the barrier and gate leading to the bridge, whereupon his other 200 men crossed the few yards from the saphead to the salient angle, and opened their fire. Lieutenant Robert Knowles, 7th, was with Wilson's party:

> When the 3rd Division advanced to commence their attack upon the castle, we advanced to the ravelin, and after considerable difficulty succeeded in placing one ladder against the wall, about twenty-four feet high. A corporal of mine was the first to mount it, and he was killed at the top. I was the third or fourth, and when in the act of leaping off the wall into the fort I was knocked down by a discharge from the enemy, the handle of my sabre broke into a hundred pieces, my hand disabled, and at the same time I received a very severe bruise on my side, and a slight wound, a piece of lead (having penetrated through my haversack which was nearly filled with bread, meat and a small stone brandy bottle for use in the trenches during the night) lodged upon one side of my ribs, but without doing any serious injuries. I recovered myself as soon as possible, and by the time seven or eight of my brave fellows had got into the fort, I charged along the ramparts, killing or destroying all who opposed us. I armed myself with the first Frenchman's firelock I met with, and carried it as well as I was able under my arm. The greater part of my party having joined me, we charged into the Fort, where they all cried out 'Prisoners'.

It would seem that the fire in front kept the defenders so busy that Wilson was able to get round behind and climb the walls almost without opposition. For this action, a fortnight later Major Wilson was to receive brevet promotion to lieutenant colonel. His part in the plan had achieved the prime object: it removed the possibility of flanking fire to the left of the 3rd Division battalions as they crossed the Rivillas; and it allowed work to commence on unblocking the dam that restrained the water itself. Lieutenant Wright RE on Brigade Major Jones' orders was 'immediately on carrying the Lunette' to fix three cases containing (possibly) 670lbs of powder against the dam – an enormous charge – more firmly than on the earlier two attempts by Stanway and Blackwood, 52nd, four nights previously. The new attempt must have failed, however, since Ensign Grattan tells us he, with Major Thomson, acting engineer, and a small party of sappers, was still placing casks of powder under the dam 'in front of San Roque . . . long after the Castle had been carried'. We must assume Grattan was fourth time lucky?

James MacCarthy's *Recollections of the Storming* are interesting if somewhat confusing, written twenty-four years later, for he it was who guided Picton personally to the First Parallel. There, with much relief, he was able to hand the old fire-eater over to the engineer Major Burgoyne. (Picton at one stage, near the Talavera road, as the brisk musketry served to excite his anxieties as to whether his guide was lost 'Said that I was blind and going wrong and, drawing his sword, swore he would cut me down.')

And since MacCarthy had the further job of assisting the placing of the ladders, and the control of the men queuing to climb, his narrative is most helpful, up to the point when he is wounded (a compound fracture of the thigh). He confirms the statement by Sergeant Joe Donaldson, 94th, that the passage across the Rivillas was very constricted: 'We reached a sort of moat about fifty yards wide, formed by the inundation of the river; here we had to pass rank entire, the passage being only capable of admitting one at a time ... when we reached the other side we formed again.'

MacCarthy's own description of the final approach was:

> I was walking between General Picton and General Kempt, when General Picton stumbled and dropped, wounded in the foot. He was instantly assisted to the left of the column, and the command devolving on General Kempt, he continued to lead it with the greatest of gallantry. On arrival at the mill–dam (extremely narrow), over which the troops were to pass, streams of fire blazed on the division: the party with ladders, axes etc. which had preceded, were overwhelmed, mingled in a dense crowd, and stopped the way ... rushing through the crowd (numbers were sliding into the water and drowning), I found the ladders left on the palisades in the fosse, and this barrier unbroken; in the exigence, I cried out 'Down with the paling!' and aided by the officers and men in rocking the fence, made the opening at which the Division entered; and which being opposite the before-mentioned mound, then, 'Up with the ladders!' – 'What! Up here?' said a brave officer of the 45th. 'Yes!' was the reply – and all seizing the ladders, pushed and pulled each other with them up the acclivity of the mound, as the shortest way to the summit.'

Another account of the 3rd Division's rush to get to grips with the Castle is that of Volunteer George Hennell, 94th, published in London later in the year. His account is unusually detailed as to measurements which, since it was written within weeks, we may hope can be trusted:

> On the fireballs striking near us, we moved out of the road to the green sward, but the cannonballs hissed by us along the grass, and the musket balls flew like hale above our heads; we immediately began therefore to run forward, til we were within about a hundred yards of the bridge across the ditch, and then the balls came on so thick, that as near as I can judge, twenty must have passed in the space of a minute, within a yard of my head.
> While we were running on the grass, one or two men dropped every minute and were left behind; but now they fell faster; when we

came to the bridge, which was about two yards wide and twelve yards long, the balls came so thick that I had no expectation of getting across alive. We then began to ascend the hill and were as crowded as people in a fair. We had to creep upon our hands and knees, the ascent being so steep and rocky and, while creeping, my brother officer received a ball in the brain and fell dead.

Having got up this rock, we came to some palisades within about twenty yards of the wall; these we broke down: but behind them was a ditch three feet deep, and just behind that a flat space about six yards broad and then a hill thrown up, eight foot high. These all passed, we approached a second ditch, and then the wall itself which was twenty-six foot high, against which we planted six or seven ladders.

The hill is much like that of Greenwich; about as steep and as high. Just as I passed the palisaded ditch, there came a discharge of grapeshot from a twenty-four pounder directly into that flat space, and about twelve fine fellows sunk upon the ground, uttering groans that shook the oldest soldier to the soul. Ten of them never rose again and the nearest of them was within a foot of me, the furthest not four yards distant. It swept away all within its range. The next three or four steps I took was upon this heap of dead! You read of the horrors of war, yet little understand what they mean. When I got over this hill or escarpment into the ditch, under the wall, the dead and wounded lay so thick, that I was continuing treading upon them. A momentary pause took place about the time we reached the ladders, occasioned I apprehend by the grapeshot, and by the numbers killed from off the ladders.

For the question put to MacCarthy of 'What, up *here?*' had been a very good one. His opening of the palisade fencing beyond the mill-dam led directly to the curtain wall between the San Pedro and San Antonio bastions, precisely where Lord Wellington had expressly warned Picton not to go. The attack was rather to be upon 'That part of the castle which is on the right, looking from the trenches, and in the rear of the great battery constructed by the enemy to fire on the bastion of La Trinidad.' MacCarthy had put the 3rd Division directly under that great battery, and was in fact attacking the curtain wall, not the Castle. It makes one wonder what Major Burgoyne was doing, to allow it: he was the senior, professional engineer whose amateur assistant MacCarthy was, and who was with MacCarthy at the time:

I was visited by General Kempt and Major Burgoyne, although this place and the whole of the wall, being opposed by the guns of the citadel, was so swept by their discharges of round shot, broken shells, bundles of cartridges and other missiles, and also from the top of the wall, ignited shells etc., that it was almost impossible to twinkle the eye on any man before he was knocked down.

As Lamare commented, this being the wall they regarded as their weakest link: 'Three hundred Hessians and the gunners on the rampart vigorously resisted this attack.'

Donaldson of the 94th said:

When we reach the other side (of 'a sort of moat fifty feet wide') we formed again (from single files) and advanced up the glacis, forcing our way through the palisades, and got down into the ditch. The ladders by which we had to escalade the castle were not yet brought up, and the men were huddled on one another in such a manner we could not move; we were now ordered to fix bayonets. When we first entered the trench, we considered ourselves comparatively safe, thinking we were out of range of their shot, but we were soon convinced of our mistake, for they opened several guns from angles which commanded the trench, and poured in grapeshot upon us from each side, every shot of which took effect, and every volley of which was succeeded by the dying groans of those who fell. Our situation at this time was truly appalling.

The 88th also found there was little safety in getting under the walls, as Lieutenant Parr Kingsmill tells:

By quickening our pace we succeeded in getting so close under the wall that the guns could not bear upon us; but the brilliant fireballs, which mocked all our efforts to extinguish them, burned so vividly as not only to enable them to direct their musketry, but also to hurl with fatal precision every kind of missile upon us.

Similarly the 45th (William Brown):

The point at which we descended into the ditch was between two bastions, from both of which we experienced a dreadful fire of musketry, while from the body of the wall the enemy continued to pour, by means of boards placed on the parapet, whole showers of grenades, which they had arranged in rows and, being alighted with a match, the whole was upset, exploding amongst us in the ditch with horrid destruction. Coils of rope, in a friable state, strongly impregnated with tar, pitch and oil, were likewise employed by the enemy as a means of annoyance, which completely answered the purpose intended by scorching and scalding numbers in a dreadful manner.

One of Brown's officers, and an unnamed Brigade Major, got five ladders up.

> Four of my ladders with troops on them and an officer on the top of
> each were broken successively, near the upper ends, and slid into the
> angle of the abutment – dreadful their fall ... On the remaining
> ladder was no officer, but a private soldier at the top, in attempting
> to go over the wall, was shot in the head as he appeared above the
> parapet, and tumbled backwards to the ground. (MacCarthy)

Donaldson:

> When the ladders were placed, each eager to mount, crowded them
> in such a way that many of them broke, and the poor fellows who
> had nearly reached the top were precipitated thirty or forty feet,
> and impaled on the bayonets of their comrades below; other ladders
> were pushed aside by the enemy on the walls, and fell with a crash on
> those in the ditch; while more who got to the top without accident
> were shot on reaching the parapet, and tumbling headlong, brought
> down those beneath them.

And no wonder Picton's lead brigade (Kempt's) of the 45th, 88th and 74th
were stuck. As William Grattan, 88th, tells us:

> A host of veterans crowned the wall, all armed in a manner as imposing
> as novel; each man had beside him eight loaded firelocks; while at
> intervals, and proportionably distributed, were pikes of an enormous
> length, with crooks attached to them, for the purpose of grappling
> with the ladders. The top of the wall was covered with rocks of
> ponderous size, only requiring a slight push to hurl them above the
> heads of our soldiers, and there was a sufficiency of hand grenades
> and small shells at the disposal of the men that defended this point, to
> have destroyed the entire of the besieging army; while on the flanks
> of each curtain, batteries were charged to the muzzle with grape and
> case shot, and either swept away entire sections or disorganised the
> ladders as they were about to be placed; and an incessant storm of
> musketry, at the distance of fifteen yards, completed the resources
> the enemy brought into play.

Lamare has told us that Grattan's 'host of veterans' was the 300 Hessians
and gunners under Colonel Webber; but of course immediately to their left
were the Castle's garrison of 'at least eighty (Hessians) as well as twenty five
Frenchmen, and a small detachment of artillery', all under Colonel Knoller.
Picton's seven battalions therefore were being held by the equivalent of a small
battalion, that is, odds in his favour of say seven to one. But the French and
Germans were more than holding their own. An hour had passed, without
success. Kempt was carried off wounded, the 88th was down to half strength

and the other battalions little better, as Grattan summarised with succinct understatement 'Picton became uneasy.' He had after all earlier told his commanders 'Some persons are of the opinion that the attack on the Castle would not succeed, but I will forfeit my life if it does not!' And perhaps come eleven o'clock the boast was returning uncomfortably to his mind. For he must have known he had thrown his division (or somehow allowed it to throw itself) absolutely where – for all obvious reasons – his commander had so wisely banned. While Picton was himself not present, being wounded, it remains a puzzle that Kempt and Major Burgoyne did not immediately take robust action to correct MacCarthy's direction of the ladder parties, there being by all accounts no shortage of illumination. Colonel Lamare's comment was simply 'The enemy ... crossed the Rivillas and in vain attempted to escalade the front (marked 8 and 9)'– on his map the San Pedro and San Antonio bastions. Talk about walking into a three-sided cauldron of fire. Picton's Division this night suffered over 500 casualties, including fifty-three officers, the great majority of whom were knocked over in this first hour, in this haphazard misdirection.

A possible cause for Picton's navigational difficulties may lie in a letter written by General Kempt in 1833 and quoted by Napier. Kempt's brigade was always meant to escalade the Castle but, in Wellington's first arrangement, Picton's two other brigades 'were to have attacked the bastion adjoining the Castle' i.e. San Antonio. However:

> On the day before the assault took place, this arrangement was changed by lord Wellington, a French deserter from the Castle (a sergeant of sappers) gave information that no communication could be established between the castle and the adjoining bastion, there being (he said) only one communication between the castle and the town, and upon learning this, the whole of the 3rd Division were ordered by lord Wellington to attack the castle.

Might it be this change of plan was not fully passed down?

The same hour had also passed for Lieutenant General Sir James Leith's 5th Division, tasked to get into the San Vincente bastion, next to the Guardiana, whilst also making a false attack on Fort Pardaleras. The latter was energetically enacted by one of his Portuguese battalions, but the bastion itself remained safe and sound, quite unmolested. For his ladder parties had got lost, coming back from the engineer park. The two British brigades, perhaps near 3,000 men, sat and shivered; they were faced by less than 200 Frenchmen in three weak companies of the 9th Léger, plus gunners, who presumably were also shivering, depending on how long the respective brandy and rum issues had lasted.

By eleven o'clock, therefore, it may be said that while Major Wilson had successfully stolen the Lunette, neither Picton on the right nor Leith on the left were at all happy men. As the clock ticked, both felt a growing frustration with their own situations, magnified by the never-ending sounds of mayhem and stubborn resistance coming from the breaches. Guilt, too, that neither was helping the main effort.

So let us now cross the Calamon over the small stone bridge, or the temporary one next to it of wood, go up the side of the Inundation, pass the Quarries on the left, and join the Light and 4th Divisions, 3,000 and 3,500 men strong; of whom it is feared every fourth man was about to be hit by something: cannon ball or canister or grape, musket ball or improvised shot, blown up or burned by shell, powder kegs, tar barrels or grenades, struck down by rocks, cartwheels or timbers, impaled on sword, pike or bayonet blades, or drowned, or smothered under bodies. Or various combinations, for every fourth soldier.

All was quiet near the Quarries. The night was dark and damp, with a cold vapour hanging in the air about the town, the remains it was said of the dense smoke of the day's firing. The Light Division's column was headed by four Rifle companies commanded by Colonel Campbell, and with Johnny Kincaid as his temporary adjutant. They were to line the glacis and fire over the heads of the stormers, at the defenders on the ramparts and on Santa Maria:

> The enemy seemed aware of our intentions. The fire of artillery and musketry, which for three weeks before had been incessant, both from the town and trenches, had now entirely ceased as if by mutual consent, and a death-like silence of nearly an hour preceded the awful scene of carnage.
>
> The signal to advance was made about nine o'clock and our four companies led the way. Colonel Cameron and myself had recon-noitred the ground so accurately by daylight that we succeeded in bringing the head of our column to the very spot agreed on, as opposite to the left breach, and then formed line to the left without a word being spoken, each man lying down as he got into line, with the muzzle on his rifle over the edge of the ditch between the palisades, already to open. It was tolerably clear above, and we distinctly saw their heads lining the ramparts; but there was a sort of haze on the ground which, with the colour of our dress, prevented them from seeing us, although only a few yards asunder. One of their sentries, however, challenged us twice, 'Qui Vive' and receiving no reply he fired off his musket, which was followed by the drums beating to arms; but we still remained perfectly quiet, and all was silent again for the space of five or ten minutes, when the head of the Forlorn Hope at length came up.

Preceding the Forlorn Hope were six volunteers of the 95th led by Lieutenant William Johnston 'Carrying ropes prepared with nooses, to throw over the sword blades (of the chevaux de frise) as the most likely method of displacing them and dragged them down the breach'.

The Light Division's Hope was led by Lieutenant Horatio Harvest, the 43rd's senior subaltern and who had already been promised his company. He had nevertheless volunteered, because in the Light Division it was the custom for the senior subaltern to insist on the right to lead such endeavours, and not to do so, as Surtees put it 'Might be construed to the detriment of his honour'. Harvest seemed to know he was to die, for he had said that afternoon to his brother officer John Cooke, 'My mind is made up, I am sure to be killed.' Behind Harvest and his men were 300 volunteer stormers led by Major O'Hare, 95th, being each 100 men from the Rifles under Captain Crampton, 100 from the 43rd again (as at Rodrigo) led by Captain James Fergusson, and 100 from the 52nd under Captain Jones. Behind the stormers came the Division's main party, in column of sections.

The sentry's solitary musket shot was also heard by Lieutenant John Cooke, in the 43rd's column:

> The Division drew up in the most profound silence behind the large quarry, three hundred yards from the three breaches made in the bastions of La Trinidad and Santa Maria. A small stream separated us from the 4th Division. Suddenly, a voice from that direction giving orders about ladders broke the stillness of the moment. It was so loud that it might be heard by the enemy on the rampart. Everyone was indignant. Colonel Macleod sent an officer to say that he would report the circumstance to the General-in-Chief. I looked up the side of the quarry fully expecting to see the enemy come forth and derange the plan of attack. It was nine thirty this happened. The ill-timed noise ceased and nothing could be heard by the loud croaking of the frogs.
>
> At 10pm a carcass was thrown from the town. This was a most beautiful firework which illuminated the ground for a hundred yards. Two or three fireballs followed and fell in different directions. Showing a bright light they remained burning. The stillness that followed was a prelude to one of the strangest scenes that the imagination of man can conceive.
>
> Soon after 10pm, a little whispering announced that the Forlorn Hope were stealing forward, followed by the storming parties. In two minutes the division followed, with the exception of the two regiments of Portuguese, who were left in reserve in the quarries, many of whom afterwards came forward to the breaches. One musket shot, no more, was fired near the breaches, who was on the look out.
>
> We gained ground leisurely, but silently. There were no obstacles. The 52nd, 43rd and part of the Rifles closed gradually up to column

at quarter distance. Left in front. All was hush. The town lay buried in gloom. The ladders were placed on the edge of the ditch.

The French were standing-to, but without light had nothing to aim at, and mere suspicion of British presence did not justify using up further precious fireballs – but not for long. The town clock told the hour of ten, and the sentries along the walls successively gave their usual cries of 'Sentinelle, guard a vous' translated by the besieging infantrymen as 'All is well in Badahoo'. Lamare wrote:

> The very dark night, only feebly lit by a quarter moon, favoured their approach ... The columns of attack arrived on the glacis without being seen; the heads of these columns instantly leapt into the ditches and arrived at the foot of the ruins. The clinking of arms was heard; a sudden cry was raised: 'There they are! There they are!'

Captain Harry Smith, 95th: 'The breach and the works were full of the enemy, looking quietly at us, but not fifty yards off and most prepared, although not firing a shot.' The 52nd's ladder party, led by Ensign George Gawler, let down six ladders against the counterscarp. He and 'about 12 or 15 men descended into the ditch when, with a blinding blaze of light and a regular chorus of explosions of all kinds, the enemy's fire opened.' (Leeke's Regimental History)

Bugler William Green, 95th: 'As the hay bags were thrown and the men descended, the enemy threw up blue lights,' because they needed now to see – and wait for – the attackers to congregate in numbers in the ditch. As John Cooper, 7th, wrote 'As our men kept going down the ladders, the whole ditch was soon filled with a dense mass.'

That is what French Lieutenant Maillet of the Miners was waiting for. He was charged with blowing them up.

> We had arranged at the foot of the counter scarp immediately in front of the breaches sixty fourteen inch shells ... This officer seized the proper opportunity ... powder hoses (were) set fire to as the assailants were crossing the ditch to reach the breaches. The explosion took place with a most tremendous noise; the fire which darted from the shells and barrels, with a noise like that of thunder, illuminated the horizon and presented the most awful spectacle. (and) Six hundred or seven hundred of our men, each furnished with three muskets, fired at the English at their very muzzles ... The dead and the wounded were heaped in the ditches and on the glacis. (Lamare)

'The whole rampart was in a blaze; mortars, cannons and muskets roared and rattled incessantly.' (John Cooper, 7th)

'The earth seemed to rock under us.' (John Cooke, 43rd)

And who can resist quoting Napier here?

> The Forlorn Hopes and storming parties of the Light Division, about
> five hundred in all, had descended into the ditch without opposition
> when a bright flame shooting upwards displayed all the terrors of the
> scene. The ramparts crowded with dark figures and the glittering of
> arms, were seen on the one side, and on the other the red columns
> of the British, deep and broad, were coming on like streams of burn-
> ing lava; it was the touch of a magician's wand, for a crash of thunder
> followed, and with incredible violence the storming parties were
> dashed to pieces by the explosion of hundreds of shells and powder
> barrels.

Ned Costello, 95th, was a ladder man in the Light Division's Forlorn Hope.
It took six of them to carry it, encumbered as they were also with a hay bag, and
a rifle, (but only two hands) per man. Just before the glacis his party bumped
into the stormers from the 4th Division, closing in on their right. As they
reached the glacis three of his party were shot dead, while the 'remainder of
the stormers rushed up … many were shot and fell upon me, so that I was
drenched in blood.'

The ditch, some said, was twenty-four foot deep with two unfinished
ravelins. Napier's sketch shows these with the Inundation artificially extended
by cunettes – ditches dug within the main ditch. The cunette before the
Maria breach was seven feet deep. John Dobbs was in one of the 52nd's rear
companies:

> The ladder I descended was at the edge of the Inundation, and I got
> into about a foot of water to begin at first. I turned to my right, and
> finding the water got deeper, I retraced my steps and came to the
> unfinished ravelin (which I fancied to be one of the breaches).

Dobbs was not the only man to turn right. John Cooper, 7th, noted that
some of his fellow fusiliers, and some of the 23rd and 48th 'Went further to the
right and jumped into that part of the ditch that was filled with water, and were
drowned.'

Costello, having extracted himself from the bodies, descended a ladder and
'Rushed forward to the right, but to my surprise found myself immersed to my
neck in water … Diving through the water – I was a good swimmer – I gained
the other side but in doing so I lost my sword.'

Bugler Green:

> Our men were in the ditch, while the enemy had shells loaded on the
> top of the wall about two yards apart. As they were fired they rolled
> into the ditch, and when they burst, ten or twelve men were blown
> up in every direction. Some of them arrived at the breach, but a great

many, both killed and wounded, lay around me. The balls came very thick about us and we were not able to move. At length the whole of the Light Division came past me ... and made for the breach.

George Simmons:

Our storming party was soon hotly engaged. Our columns moved on under a most dreadful fire of grape that mowed down our men like grass. We tore down the palisading and got upon the glacis. The havoc now became dreadful. My Captain (Gray) was shot in the mouth. Eight or ten officers and men innumerable fell to rise no more. Ladders were resting against the counterscarp from within the ditch. Down these we hurried, and as fast as we got down, rushed forward to the breaches, where a most frightful scene of carnage was going on.

The Inundation being deeper to the right, in front of Trinidad, the 4th Division naturally sought to pass it to the left, thus mingling with the Light – but also taking them towards the unfinished ravelin. So with all the engineer guides having been hit, this wide ravelin misled many into thinking they had reached the main breach. Men of both divisions put up ladders and climbed the broken slope, to take what they thought at the top of the mound must be the prize; only to emerge into the massed musketry of the defenders 'Every man mounting being swept down, and the whole ditch crowded with men, dead and alive'. The men of the 52nd, having pushed up the unfinished ravelin,

In the hope of tracing a practicable passage to the central breach [found] the summit, in the very focus of fire, rendered still more untraversable by a field piece in the flank of Santa Maria, which powered incessant charges of grape across the ravelin, and onto the covered way to the Trinidad, on which now appeared the head of the 4th Division endeavouring to plant its ladders.

The assault now having reached a frustrating mixture of lack of leadership, disorientation and regiments no longer acting as formed bodies, the kiss of death began to confront Lord Wellington's endeavours. The confused scene is well described in Moorson's History of the 52nd:

The two massive (divisional) columns were first checked almost hopelessly on the crest of the glacis, under the fire within sixty yards of the veteran soldiers well covered, with several firelocks each, adding to their bullets wooden cylinders set with slugs, then officers and men, British, German, Portuguese of various regiments, became practically undisciplined mobs at the foot of the ladder. There were desperate rushes, in which the confused mass divided into three parties, according to each man's fancy for a particular breach. Then came the lighted fireballs and tar barrels, the explosion of heavy shells, powder barrels and fougasses, and the crashes of logs of wood rolled incessantly from above. Then, halfway up the breach, were barrows turned the wrong side upwards and planks studded with pointed nails ... Chevaux etc. . . . and from these projected the muzzles of muskets of grenadiers, with their recollections fresh of two previous defences.

Only two of the Light Division's officers in the storming party were still on their feet. All their men were brightly illuminated, silhouetted against the carts, gabions and boats etc. placed as obstacles in the ditch, all ablaze from the explosion of the mines; and the men tended to drift towards the Trinidad breach, rather than the Light Division's real objective to the left; and no-one of the 4th made straight ahead to the curtain – at least, few corpses were there next morning.

There was no shortage of efforts to mount the Trinidad breach, nonetheless: 'The whole of the Division made for the breach. A tremendous fire was going on. I heard the Bugle Major sound the advance and double quick . . . I rolled on my back (he was wounded on the glacis) and repeated the sound.' (Bugler Green)

Ned Costello (having swum the flooded ditch):

> I now attempted to get to the breach, which the blaze of musketry from the walls clearly showed me. Without rifle, sword or any other weapon, I succeeded in clambering up a part of the breach where there was a Chevaux de Frise, consisting of a piece of heavy timber studded with sword blades, turning on an axis. Just before I reached it, I received a stroke on the breast. Whether it was from a grenade, or a stone, or the butt end of a musket, I cannot say, but down I rolled senseless, drenched with water and human gore.

Harry Smith:

> We flew down the ladders and rushed at the breach, but we were broken and carried no weight with us, although every soldier was a hero. The breach was covered by a breast work from behind and ably defended on the top by Chevaux de Frise of sword blades, sharp as razors, chained to the ground; while the ascent to the top of the breach was covered with planks with sharp nails in them. However, devil or one did I feel at this moment. One of the officers of the Forlorn Hope, Lieutenant Taggard, of the 43rd, was hanging on my arm – a mode we adopted to help each other up; for the ascent was most difficult and steep. A rifleman stood among the sword blades at the top of one of the Chevaux de Frise. We made a glorious rush to

follow, but, alas! in vain. He was knocked over ... I had been some seconds at the revetment of the bastion near the breach, and my red coat pockets were literally filled with chips of stones splintered by musket balls. Those knocked down were driven back by this hale of mortality, to the ladders.

Costello – and who can blame him – by this time had wisely decided that discretion was appropriate:

I could not have laid long in this plight, and when my senses started to return, I saw our gallant fellows still rushing forward, each seeming to meet a fate more deadly than my own. The fire continued in one horrible and incessant peel, as if the mouth of the infernal regions had opened to vomit forth destruction upon all around us. Even more appalling were the fearful shouts of the combatants, and cries of the wounded that mingled in the uproar ... Strange to say, I now began to feel my arms and legs were entire. At such moments a man is not always aware of his wounds. I had lost all the frenzy of courage that had first possessed me, and felt weak, my spirit prostrate. Among the dead and wounded bodies around me, I endeavoured to screen myself from the enemy's shot. While I lay in this position the fire continued to blaze over me in all its horrors, accompanied by screams, groans, and shouts, the crashing of stones and the falling of timbers. For the first time for many years, I uttered something like a prayer.

John Cooke:

Death and the most dreadful sounds encompassed us. It was a volcano! Up we went; some killed and some impaled on the bayonets of their own comrades, or hurled headlong among the outrageous crowd. These Chevaux de Frise looked like innumerable bayonets. When within a yard of the top my sensations were extraordinary; I felt half strangled, and fell from a blow that deprived me of sensation. I only recollect feeling a soldier pulling me out of the water, where so many men were drowned. I lost my cap, but still held my sword; on recovering, I looked towards the breach. It was shining and empty! Fireballs were in plenty, and the French troops standing upon the walls, taunting and inviting our men to come up and try it again. What a crisis! What a military misery! Some of the finest troops in the world prostrate – humbled to the dust.

These descriptions of the scene should leave most modern readers feeling bludgeoned. At the risk, therefore, of extending the shellshock, we really cannot move on without Major William Napier, 43rd. He missed these joys at Badajoz, being back in England still with a ball in his back (perhaps just as well for all those memoir-writers later inspired by his great History):

> Now a multitude bounded up the great breach as if driven by a whirlwind, but across the top glittered a range of sword blades, sharp pointed, keen edged on both sides, and firmly fixed in ponderous beams, which were chained together and set deep in the ruins; and for ten feet in front, the ascent was covered with loose planks studded with sharp iron points, on which the feet of the foremost being set the planks moved, and the unhappy soldiers falling forward on the spikes, rolled down upon the ranks behind. Then the Frenchmen, shouting at the success of their stratagem, and leaping forward, plied their shot with terrible rapidity, for every man had several muskets ... Again the assailants rushed up the breaches, and again the sword blades, immovable and impassable, stopped their charge; and the hissing shells and thundering powder barrels exploded unceasingly. Hundreds of men had fallen, and hundreds more were dropping, but still the heroic officers called aloud for new trials, and sometimes followed by many, sometimes by a few, ascending the ruins; and so furious were the men themselves, that in one of these charges, the rear strove to push the foremost onto the sword blades, willing even to make a bridge of their writhing bodies; but the others frustrated the attempt by dropping down; and men fell so fast from the shot, that it was hard to know who went down voluntarily, who was stricken, and many stooped unhurt that would never rise again. Vain also would it have been to break through the sword blades, for the trench and parapet behind the breach were finished, and the assailants, crowded into even a narrower space than the ditch was, would still have been separated from their enemies, and the slaughter would have continued.

Lord Wellington's plan for the three adjacent breaches to be assaulted together never happened. Almost the entire effort was attracted to Trinidad, like iron filings to a magnet. The curtain wall was farther into the crossfire and protected by obstacles; yet the freshest breach, made that very morning, had nothing like the sophisticated defences Philippon and Lamare had concocted for the others. Napier quotes an anonymous officer:

> I consider that the centre breach at Badajoz was never seriously attacked. I was not at the centre breach on the night of the assault, therefore I cannot positively assert what took place there. But there were not bodies of dead and wounded at the centre or curtain breach in the morning to indicate such an attack having been made upon

it, and being in the curtain it was far retired from the troops, and the approach to it was made extremely difficult by deep cuts, and I think it passed unobserved except for a straggling few. I consider that Chevaux de Frise were placed upon the summit of the centre breach during the assault. I was there at daybreak. The approach to it was extremely difficult, both from the difficulty of finding it, and from the deep holes that were before it, which to my recollection resembled the holes you see in a clay field, where they make bricks. Another great obstruction was the fire from the faces and flanks of the two bastions, which crossed before the curtain.

As to the Santa Maria breach, there is little reference to it in the memoirs, bar the story that Lieutenant James Shaw, 43rd, saw the last engineer officer on his feet, Captain William Nicholas, trying unsuccessfully to mount the breach. Shaw collected some fifty men of various regiments in the ditch near him, to support the effort, but it petered out in the face of a concentrated fire of musketry and grape, two thirds of the way up the ascent. Nicholas' wounds (from which he died eight days later) were described as 'one through the lungs, and two ribs broke, left arm broke below the elbow, left knee touched on the cap, left calf and right thigh grazed with musket balls.'

Captain James Currie, 52nd, according to their *History*, in desperation examined the counterscarp to the left, beyond the Maria breach, and found a narrow ramp which the garrison had not fully destroyed. Mounting it, he ran the short distance to Wellington's tactical headquarters, on a hillock near the Quarries. 'Can they not get in?' was the Earl's anxious and emphatic question. On Currie's reply, 'That those in confusion in the ditch could not, but that a fresh battalion might succeed by the descent he had discovered,' a reserve battalion was ordered to follow Currie; 'These men as they got in [the ditch] became mixed up with the confused parties rushing at or retiring from the breaches, and this last hope vanished.' For it was now plain that the French defence was simply too strong. Innumerable attempts had piled up further layers of bodies, not all of whom, it must be said, would be corpses or be badly wounded – but some who judged the job was just not practicable. Men who felt the same but who would not sink to feign death were more numerous: 'I had seen some fighting, but nothing like this. We remained passively here to be slaughtered, as we could do the besieged little injury from the ditch.' (George Simmons). For despair was in the air. Read again Costello: 'I had lost all the frenzy of courage ... and felt weak, my spirit prostrate ... I endeavoured to screen myself from the enemy's shot ... For the first time for many years I uttered something like a prayer.'

There is even reference, we must hope mistaken, to a retrograde movement. Harry Smith who had just helped the mortally wounded Colonel Macleod of the 43rd to get away up a ladder, and onto the glacis, in search of a doctor:

I did so, and came back [down the ladder] again. Little Freer and I said 'Let us throw down the ladders; the fellows shan't go out.' Some soldiers behind said 'Damn your eyes, if you do we will bayonet you.' And we were literally forced up [the ladder] by the crowd. So soon as we got on the glacis, up came the fresh brigade of Portuguese of the 4th Division – I never saw any soldiers behave with more pluck. Down into the ditch we went again, but the more we tried to get up [the breach], the more we were destroyed.

There was said afterwards to be rumour in the ditch that the garrison was making a sally from the two flanks, hence the retrograde panic, if that is the right word; also that Harry Smith had not heard the order to retire. Who can tell?

Lord Wellington, with the Prince of Orange and Lord March alongside, was joined by Surgeon James McGrigor, who later wrote:

Soon after our arrival, an officer came up with an unfavourable report of the assault, announcing that Colonel Macleod and several officers were killed, with heaps of men, who choked the approach to the breach. At the place where we stood, we were within hearing of the voices of the assailants and of the assailed; and it was now painful to notice that the voices of our countrymen had become fainter, while the French cry of 'Avancez, etrillons çes Anglais' became stronger. Another officer came up with a still more unfavourable report, that no progress was being made; for almost all the officers were killed and no more left to lead on the men, a great number had fallen. At this moment I cast my eyes on the countenance of Lord Wellington, lit up by the glare of the torch held by Lord March; I shall never forget it til the last moment of my existence, and I could even now sketch it. The jaw had fallen, and the face was of unusual length, while the torchlight gave his countenance a lurid aspect; but still the expression of the face was firm.

Two hours had now passed and it was nearing midnight. Wellington knew only that he had suffered most severely, without success and with no such prospects on current reports, neither in front, nor out left with the 5th, or on the right with the 3rd. The losses were truly dreadful. Of 3,000 men present with the Light Division, 915 officers and men had been killed or wounded – nearly one in every three; of the 4th Division's 3,500 men, 925 men out of it – one in every four. The Portuguese lost another 400, so a total of 2,244 all ranks had fallen in the storm. The glacis, the wide ditch and the breach slopes were covered with bodies. And all for nothing?

The buglers of the reserve were then sent to the crest of the glacis to sound the retreat; the troops in the ditch, grown desperate, at first would not believe it genuine, and struck the buglers in the ditch who attempted the sound; but at length sullenly re-ascended the counter-scarp as they could ... As the last stragglers crossed the glacis the town clock was heard again, heavily tolling twelve. (52nd's *History*)

CHAPTER 2

Part V – Badajoz
The Attack
Midnight to Dawn

Whilst the Light and 4th Divisions had been dying on Trinidad, the 3rd Division, likewise with great losses, had failed to get Kempt's Brigade up the ladders, unfortunately placed under the San Antonio demi-bastion. The 1st/45th, 74th and Connaughts were down 300 men. Champlemond's Portuguese brigade had followed them into the ditch and also had got nowhere. The defensive artillery crossfire was just too strong. Kempt was wounded and nearly a third of his officers were dead or wounded; baffled, a hotchpotch of five battalions huddled for shelter in the ditch and under the rocky slopes. Picton, now partly recovered and having spent twenty minutes on the glacis, got forward his last hope, Campbell's brigade of the 2nd/5th, 77th, 2nd/83rd and the 94th, and directed that the ladders should be tried farther to the right. So there were now nine battalions crammed under the walls – say nearly 4,000 men – along a very narrow strip little more than 300 paces long, and lightly opposed by three companies (two of which were Hessian) and the French gun teams, not more than 300 men and probably rather less. That gave Picton a substantial thirteen to one advantage. In addition, and crucially, his final attempt to escalade being made a bit farther round the Castle's corner to the north, it was therefore partly masked from the guns on San Pedro and the muskets on San Antonio.

Grattan tells us two ladders were laid by the 5th's commander, Henry Ridge, and by Lieutenant Canch, his Grenadier officer, while Lieutenant William MacKie, 88th, laid a third, and each officer led the way upwards followed by their carrying parties. By choice ladders went adjacent to gun embrasures, because of their lower entrance level, and not all of the embrasures contained cannon. Ridge and Canch fought their way in, and held the parapet whilst more men joined; another 88th officer, Lieutenant Parr Kingsmill, chose an embrasure where the French did have a gun team. Unfortunately his ladder was too short, and an interesting tableau is described:

> I found that no exertion I could make would enable me to gain the
> embrasure or to descend. In this unhappy state, expecting immediate

death from the hands of the ferocious-looking Frenchmen in the embrasure, I heard a voice above call out, 'Mr —, is that you?' I answered 'Yes'. And the same voice cried out, 'Oh, murther! murther! what will we do to get you up at all, at all, with that scrawdeen of a ladtherr? But here goes! Hold my leg, Bill'; and throwing himself flat on his face in the embrasure, he extended his brawny arm down the wall, and seizing me by the collar, with Herculean force, landed me, as he said himself, 'clever and clane', on the ramparts.

I found myself standing amongst several French soldiers, who crowded round the gun in the embrasure. One of them still held the match lighted in his hand, the blue flame of which gave the bronzed and sullen countenances of these warriors an expression not easily forgotten. A grenadier of the 103rd leaned on the gun, and bled profusely from the head; another, who had fallen on his knees when wounded, remained fixed in astonishment and terror. Others, whose muskets lay scattered on the ground, folded their arms in deep despair; and the appearance of the whole group, with their huge bushy mustaches, and mouths blackened with biting the cartridges, presented to the eye of a young soldier at least an appearance sufficiently formidable.

'Don't mind them fellows, Sir,' said Tully O'Malley; 'they were all settled jist afore you came up; and, by my soul, good boys they war for a start, and fought like raal devils, so they did, till Mr S and the grenadiers came powdering down on them with the war-whoop. Och, my darlint, they were made smiddreens of in a crack, barring that great big fellow you see there, with the great black whiskers, bleeding in the side, and resting his head on the gun-carriage. He was the bouldest of them all, and made bloody battle with Jim Reilly: but 'tis short he stud afore Jim. He gave him a raal Waterford puck that tumbled him like a nine-pin in a minute; and, by my own sowl, a puck of the butt-end of Jim's piece is no joke, I tell you, for he tried it on more heads nor one on the hill of Busaco.'

Another whose ladder was too short by some three feet, was Lieutenant James Macpherson, 45th. Appointed to command his battalion's best shots – 100 sharpshooters – he had reported a spot to Picton where the Castle was least well defended; shouting to his men below to push the ladder nearer the wall, hence raising the top to which he clung, he was shot at point-blank range by a defender on the rampart. The ball struck a Spanish silver waistcoat button, ricocheting off but breaking two ribs. Unable to climb further, Macpherson descended somehow down the rear of the ladder, to collapse unconscious in the ditch. More and more men from various regiments reached the ramparts, and Henry Ridge took them in hand with the cry 'Come on my lads, let's be the first to seize the Governor'. The French had largely withdrawn to the open space by the main gate into the town, quickly sensing their numbers were inadequate. They had not, however, run: the British progress, made somewhat prudently through the darkened ways, egged on by Ridge's 'Why do you hesitate? Forward!' was met by a volley and which did for Ridge, shot in the chest. The French were forced out through the gates, closing both inner and outer as they went, but leaving a small wicket gate open in the latter. 'A heavy fire was kept up on those who attempted to pass it.' (According to an anonymous officer of the 5th) Lieutenant Colonel James Campbell, 94th, commanding the British 3 Brigade and (Kempt being wounded and Picton unable to ascend the ladders) temporarily in command of the division, ordered the regiments as they came together to form in column facing the gates. Presumably the intention was to march upon the breaches. However, all the gates being found bricked up or securely barred, the columns stayed put.

A Spanish lieutenant colonel in the French service had earlier rushed in a panic to Governor Philippon with the false news that the San Maria bastion had been entered. Correctly disbelieving this, and checking it out by a quick dash to the bastion, Philippon subsequently also disbelieved a second report, brought by dragoon Lieutenant Lavigne, that the British were escalading the walls of the Castle. Time passed – precious time – before the Governor on second thoughts sent forward his reserve of four companies of the 88th, even though the Hessian colonel commanding the Castle had sent no report. 'But fortune had abandoned us,' wrote Colonel Lamare 'The enemy, already master of the Castle, had shut the gate on the side next to demi-bastion number nine (San Antonio) ... These companies arrived too late: they were received by a heavy fire of musketry ... And the soldiers were disbursed after having made a vain attempt to retake the Castle.' Two companies of the 9th Léger had also been called up, from the San Vincente bastion, but got sucked into the battle raging at the breaches. The failure of these two counter attacks – with no other reserves now left – markedly hit French moral. The Castle had been their last redoubt, and contained their reserves of food and ammunition, which now all being lost 'Shook the courage of some of the officers, and disorder began'.

The 3rd Division continued up the ladders, James Macpherson among them now conscious again and mobile, despite his broken ribs; his determined search for individual fame called for no less than the capturing of the French Colour, up on the flagstaff at the top of the Castle's tower.

> I at length found my way to the tower where I perceived the sentry still at his post. With my sword drawn I seized him, and desired him in French to show me the way to the colours. He replied 'Je ne sais pas'. I, upon this, gave him a slight cut across the face, saying at the same time 'Vous avez prison,' at which he dashed his arms to the ground and, striking his breast, said as he raised his head and pointed

to his heart, 'Frappez, je suis Français!' His manner at the same time indicating that the colour was there, I could not wait to provide for the safety of this brave fellow; so I called out loudly for a non-commissioned officer to take charge of him so that he should not be hurt. One stepped forward, when, giving him instructions to protect the gallant soldier, I ascended the tower; but my precaution was vain, for I afterwards discovered that this noble fellow was amongst the dead.

Macpherson struck the colour and hoisted his own red coat as a British substitute. (The colour was subsequently presented to Lord Wellington, on Picton's instruction. Sadly for Macpherson's ambitions, however, it was another three years before he achieved his captaincy, and that in a garrison battalion.) He would, however, be gratified, 200 years later, to know that, on 6 April each year, a red coat is hoisted up the flagpole on Nottingham Castle.

Back at the breaches, the Light and 4th Divisions had withdrawn some 300 yards from the ditch, down towards the Quarries. One can only imagine the coming together of the survivors, as each company fell in (literally in many cases) on their right markers. The calling of the rolls, the first aid for those fit enough to be patched up, the muddle of instant promotions of the second and third elevens, where available, the passing of water bottles (and stronger – Oh for a drink!) the attempts in the dark to replace flints, and then the sinking to the earth in a stupor.

Now at this stage in the proceedings, it is not known where his lordship – in his own mind – thought they stood. Why should we know, his mind always kept closed to others? The indications are that first light would see a separate, new plan, for the 3rd Division seemed to need time and tools (not readily to hand) to force open the iron-bound gates blocking egress from the Castle to the ramparts and the breaches. Though why exits could not be instantly blown with – presumably – the readily available French powder barrels, is not clear. Lack of engineers? Anyway, whether Picton's ADC knew of this problem and its implications, and reported them when he got to his Lordship, we know not.

It was of course academic, since the key to the Badajoz lock was even now being turned by Lieutenant Colonel Brooke, commanding the 4th (King's Own) nearly a mile away around the ramparts, at the San Vincente bastion. He had approached along the banks of the river, closing on the garrison's guard-house on the waterside track, the noise of the flowing Guadiana smothering all. Behind him crept the light companies of Walker's 4th, 30th, 38th and 44th Regiments, supported by his own battalion companies – say 700 men, with the 30th and 44th back in reserve under Walker. The 5th's divisional general, Leith, had already sent in a Portuguese battalion to create a major disturbance at the outwork Pardaleras, and a noisy mock attack across the river at the bridge-head.

Brooke's light companies quietly spread out on the glacis. Captain Edward Hopkins, 4th, tells what next happened:

> The column halted a few yards from a breast-work surmounted with a stockade and a 'chevaux de frise' concealing a guard-house on the covered way, and at this moment a most awful explosion took place, followed by the most tremendous peals of musketry. 'That is at the breaches,' was the whisper amongst our soldiers, and their anxiety to be led forward was intense, but their firmness and obedience were equally conspicuous. The moon now appeared. We could hear the French soldiers talking in the guard-house, and their officers were visiting the sentries. The engineer officer who preceded the column, said, 'now is the time'; the column instantly moved to the face of the gateway. It was only at this moment that the sentry observed us, and fired his alarm-shot, which was followed by musketry. The two companies of Portuguese carrying the scaling-ladders threw them down, and deaf to the voices of their officers, made off. This occurrence did not in the least shake the zeal and steadiness of our men, who occupied immediately the space left, and shouldering the ladders moved on. We could not force the gate open, but the breast-work was instantly crowded, and the impediments cut away sufficiently to allow of two men entering abreast ... The engineer officer was by this time killed. We had no other assistance from that corps, and the loss was most severely felt at this early period of the attack.
>
> The troops were now fast filling the ditch; they had several ladders, and I shall never forget the momentary disappointment amongst the men when they found that the ladders were too short ... The enemy took advantage of this to annoy us in every way, rolling down beams of wood, fireballs, &c. together with an enfilading fire.
>
> We observed near us an embrasure unfurnished of artillery, its place being occupied by a gabion filled with earth. A ladder was instantly placed under its mouth, and also one at each side. This allowed three persons to ascend at once, but only one at a time could enter in at the embrasure. The first several attempts were met with instant death. The ladders were even now too short, and it was necessary for one person to assist the other by hoisting him up on the embrasure.

The walls were after all twenty feet high, with a twelve-foot slope above that; a great many men were swept off the ladders, and a cunette in the ditch six feet deep by the same wide had compressed the light company men prior to the mine's detonation. Colonel Brooke found a spot further to their left, eventually, where the ladders were just long enough for a practicable escalade.

We must remember that Philippon had about this time withdrawn two companies of the 9th Léger to reinforce the Castle, leaving San Vincente with a

single company plus gunners – well under 100 men. So Walker had an overwhelming advantage, even greater than Picton about this time enjoyed at the
Castle – thirty companies against the one? It was therefore indeed a feat of arms
for this skeleton defence to wreak such losses on Walker. By the end of the
night's work he had lost over 500 men, although of course many of these would
have been laid low subsequently on the ramparts or in the town.

So the Vincente ramparts were necessarily thinly manned, and the light
companies pushed on along them, progressing into and through the first three
bastions. The fourth, San Julian, opposite Pardeleras, was, however, a bastion
too far, and General Walker near here being wounded, and a perceived bright
flash exciting a cry of 'Mines!', the panicking invaders reversed their progress. They were helped by a counter attack of 400 men of the 28th Léger
under Brigadier Veiland, Philippon's second in command. Fortunately, Walker
had placed Colonel Nugent with the understrength 38th as a reserve on San
Vincente, and upon whom Brooke now reformed, and the 38th's solid volley
reversed the situation. Colonel Lamare's account implies Veiland should not
have had to intervene with this counter attack: for the 28th Léger themselves
on bastions three and four had 'Made no [early] movement to succour bastion
number one'.

Brooke's 4th, under Major John Piper, got down into the town's streets
with a view to reaching the breaches on the far side. With him went Captain
Hopkins:

> Some shots were fired from a building in the town, and Colonel Piper
> was sent with a party to dislodge the enemy, while General Walker,
> at the head of his brigade, attempted to clear the rampart to the right.
> The enemy retired from the building on our approach, and Colonel
> Piper did not return to the ramparts but moved into the body of
> the town. Could we have divested our minds of the real situation
> of the town it might have been imagined that the inhabitants were
> preparing for some grand fete, as all the houses in the streets and
> squares were brilliantly illuminated, from the top to the first floor,
> with numerous lamps. This illumination scene was truly remarkable,
> not a living creature to be seen, but a continual low buzz and whisper
> about us, and we now and then perceived a small lattice gently open
> and re-shut, as if more closely to observe a singular scene of a small
> English party perambulating the town in good order, the bugleman
> at the head blowing his instrument. Some of our men and officers
> now fell wounded; at first we did not know where the shots came
> from, but soon observed they were from the sills of the doors.

The 4th progressed to the main square – the Place de St John – which had
been Philippon's tactical headquarters. Hopkins again:

We soon arrived at a large church facing some grand houses, in a sort of square. The party here drew up, and it was at first proposed to take possession of this church, but that idea was abandoned. We made several prisoners leading some mules ladened with loose ball cartridges in large wicker baskets, which they stated they were conveying from the magazines to the breaches. After securing the prisoners, ammunition etc., we moved from the square with the intention of forcing our way upon the ramparts. We went up a small street towards them, but met with such opposition as obliged us to retire with loss. We again found ourselves in the square.

The Governor now made a last desperate charge with forty or so dragoons against more of the 5th Division in the Place de las Palmas near St Vincente, but failed with heavy losses. Finding himself and General Veiland and about four dozen men cut off from the breaches, he crossed the nearby bridge to the Tête de Pont and Fort San Cristobal. It was one o'clock in the morning. He had sent Captain De Grasse to bring back the troops from the breaches, but the streets were blocked by the incoming British tide. It was the end. Lamare:

> The Governor could no longer communicate with his troops. Doubt and dismay took possession of their minds; they fled about the streets and fired in disorder. Cries of Victory! and frightful groans were heard; confusion was at its height ... The brave men who defended the breaches, receiving no orders, ceased to make further resistance, broke their arms and surrendered.

Hearing of the 5th's success, Lord Wellington now sent the Light and 4th Divisions forward once more into the breaches. George Simmons:

> I was lying upon the grass, having the most gloomy thoughts of the termination of this sad affair, when a staff officer rode up and said 'Lord Wellington orders the Light Division to return immediately and attack the breaches.' We move back to this bloody work as if nothing had happened. Never were braver men congregated together for such a purpose. We entered the ditches, and past over the bodies of our brave fellows who had fallen, and dashed forward to the breaches. Only a few random shots were fired, and we entered without opposition. Firing was now going on in several parts of the town and we were not long in chiming in with the rest of them.

Ned Costello (hardly conscious, in the ditch):

> I heard a cheering ... I now attempted to rise but, from a wound which I had received, but at what time I know not, found myself unable to stand. A musket ball had passed through the lower part of my right leg – two others had perforated my cap. At the moment this

discovery I saw two or three men moving towards me, who I was glad
to find belonged to the Rifles. One of them, named O'Brien, of the
same company as myself, immediately exclaimed 'What! Is that you,
Ned? – We thought all you ladder men were done for.' He then
assisted me to rise.

Kincaid:

> The enemy were abandoning the breaches, and we were immediately
> all ordered forward to take possession of them. On our arrival we
> found them entirely evacuated, and had not occasion to fire another
> shot, but we found the utmost difficulty and even danger, in getting
> in in the dark, even without opposition. As soon as we succeeded in
> establishing our battalion inside, we sent pickets into the different
> streets and lanes leading from the breach and kept the remainder in
> hand until day should throw some light on our situation.

Which gives a cosy view, with no hint that plunder, rioting and worse were
breaking out elsewhere, as Rifleman Costello, now inside the town with a rifle
as a crutch, indicates more robustly:

> We now looked round for a house where we could obtain refresh-
> ment, and if truth must be told, a little money, for wounded though
> I was, I had made up my mind to gain by our victory. At the first
> house we knocked at, no notice was taken of the summons, so we
> fired a rifle ball at the keyhole, our usual method of forcing locks. It
> sent the door flying open. As soon as we entered the house, we found
> a young Spanish woman crying bitterly and praying for mercy. She
> said she was the wife of a French officer. When O'Brien demanded
> refreshment, she said there was nothing in the house but her poor
> self. However, she produced some spirits and chocolate, and being
> very hungry and faint I partook of them with much relish. But the
> house looked poor, so we soon quitted it in quest of a better and went
> in to the direction of the market place, O'Brien and the Frenchman
> supporting me.
>
> It was a dark night, and confusion and uproar prevailed in the
> town. The shouts and oaths of drunken soldiers in quest of liquor,
> reports of firearms, the crashing in of doors, and the appalling shrieks
> of hapless women, made you think you were in the regions of the
> damned.

Robert Blakeney, 28th, also remembered the noise:

> the howling of the dogs, the crowing of cocks, the penetrating cackle
> of geese, the mournful bleating of sheep, the furious bellowing of
> wounded oxen maddened by being continuously goaded and shot

at and ferociously charging through the streets, were mixed with accompaniments loudly trumpeted forth by donkeys and mules, and always by the deep and hollow baying of the large Spanish half-wolves, half-bloodhounds which guarded the whole. Add to this the shrill screaming of affrighted children, the piercing shrieks of frantic women, the groans of the wounded, the savage and discordant yells of drunkards firing at anything and in all directions, and the continuous roll of musketry kept up in error on the shattered gateway; and you may imagine an uproar such as one would think could issue only from the regions of Pluto; and this din was maintained throughout the night.

For the town had at last been captured, and would now pay the price for earlier perceived unfriendliness, and the rain and mud, shot, shell, ball and fire, mines, Inundation, too-short ladders, broken ladders, chevaux de frises and all similar torments; all of which were clearly the fault of those inside the walls, whether in uniform or not. A general opinion was that an implicit licence had been granted; one indeed applicable to all, including camp followers:

A couple of hundred women (wives) from the camp poured into the place, when it was barely taken, to have their share of the plunder. They were, if possible, worse than the men. Gracious God! Such tigresses in the shape of women! I sickened when I saw them coolly step over the dying, indifferent to their cries for water, and deliberately search the pockets of the dead for money, or even divest them of their bloody coats. (Lieutenant von Hodenberg, KGL).

CHAPTER 2

Part VI – Badajoz
The Sacking, 7–9 April

Now commenced that Wild and Desperate Wickedness,
Which tarnished the Lustre of the Soldier's Heroism.

It was the drink they wanted, all 10,000 men. Many had arranged to meet up at wine shops they knew from earlier days – or at silversmiths, the early birds catching the worms. The men knew they would be allowed their heads – the 45th were specifically given two hours leave to go 'wherever we pleased', the 40th 'three hours' plunder would be allowed'. They knew also that the narrow medieval alleyways would be no place for formed companies, moved in ranks, officers and sergeants in their due places; so the customary hierarchies and aids to discipline were to be absent and, once the alcohol got to work, heaven help those who would seek to re-impose them.

Contrary to this generality, however, were some who were kept to their duties, at least initially and despite their human inclinations. Johnny Kincaid's battalion, the 1st/95th Rifles, having returned to the breach after the midnight pause:

> Once established within the walls we felt satisfied that the town was ours. Profiting by his experience at Ciudad, our commandant (Colonel Cameron) took the necessary measure to keep his battalion together so long as the safety of the place could in any way be compromised. Knowing the barbarous licence which soldiers employed in that desperate service claim, and which they will not be denied, he addressed them, and promised that they should have the same indulgence as others, and that he should not insist upon keeping them together longer than was absolutely necessary; but he assured them that if any man quitted the ranks until he gave permission, he would cause him to be put to death on the spot. That had the desired effect until between 9 and 10 o'clock in the morning, when, seeing that the whole of the late garrison had been secured and marched off to Elvas, he again addressed the battalion . . . 'Now my men, you may fall out and enjoy yourselves for the remainder of the day, but I shall expect to see you all in camp at the usual roll-call in the evening.'

Colonel Cameron was to be disappointed at roll-call, but he had demonstrated a remarkable grip on his battalion.

Inside, Grattan's Irishmen would not be so patient:

> In the first burst, all the wine and spirit stores were ransacked from top to bottom: and it required just a short time for the men to get into that fearful state that was alike dangerous to all officers and soldiers, or the inhabitants of the city. Casks of the choicest wines and brandy were dragged into the streets, and when the men had drunk as much as they fancied, the heads of the vessels were stove in, or the casks otherwise so broken that the liquor ran about in streams.

Sergeant Joe Donaldson agreed the wine and spirit stores were top priority:

> The greatest number first sought the spirit stores, where having drunk an inordinate quantity, they were prepared for every sort of mischief. At one large vault in the centre of town, to which a flight of steps led, they had staved in the head of the casks and were running with their hat-caps full of it, and so much was spilt here, that some, it was said, were actually drowned in it.

The drownings did indeed take place, in the vault of the Cathedral, as told by the anonymous senior officer quoted in Maxwell's *Sketches*:

> On entering the cathedral, I saw three British soldiers literally drowned in brandy. A spacious vault had been converted into a spirit depot for the use of the garrison. The casks had been pierced with musket-balls, and their contents escaping, had formed a pool of some depth. These men becoming intoxicated had fallen head foremost into the liquor, the position in which I found them, and were suffocated.

According to *A Short History of Badajoz* published the following year, 'One of the chapels (of the Cathedral) was filled up to the roof with biscuit, and a vault contained so great a quantity of brandy, in casks, which were staved in, that three or four of our soldiers were actually drowned in spirit.' The corpses were observed three days after the assault, 9 April, and are thus a reminder that widespread inebriation much delayed collection of bodies generally, and the succour of the wounded in particular. William Surtees, 3rd/95th, came upon his friend Lieutenant Arthur Cary, apparently dead in the ditch:

> He was shot through the head, and I doubt not received his death-wound on the ladder, from which in all probability he fell. He was stripped completely naked, save a flannel waistcoat which he wore next to his skin. I had him taken up and placed upon a shutter (he still breathed a little, though quite insensible) and carried him to the camp. A sergeant and some men, whom we had pressed to carry him,

were so drunk that they let him fall from off their shoulders, and his
body fell with great force to the ground. I shuddered, but poor Cary,
I believe, was past all feeling, or the fall would have greatly injured
him. We laid him in his tent, but it was not long ere my kind,
esteemed, and lamented friend breathed his last.

The overwhelming volume of casualties combined with the drunken man-
power available, created an immense medical problem, inevitably slow to resolve.
Lieutenant MacCarthy, 50th, shot before midnight on the 6th, was still in the
ditch late on the 8th when

> I prevailed on an officer to allow his men to convey me to my tent;
> but they were unwilling, and though obliged to carry me, jostled
> and nearly rolled me out of the bier [blanket] in going over the mill-
> dam; they however laid me down on my left side at the end of the
> Second Parallel, leaving the bier under me, and joined the sports in
> the Town.

It is not as if MacCarthy was in some quiet spot, hidden away for those two
long days, for 'the dead and wounded were as close as a regiment laying down
in repose'.

Some early efforts were, of course, made to get the wounded out, and
William Surtees tells us how he and Captain William Percival did their best:

> and now he and I, hearing the heart-piercing and affecting groans
> which arose from the numbers of wounded still lying in the ditch,
> set to work to get as many of these poor fellows removed as was in
> our power. This we found a most arduous and difficult undertaking,
> as we could not do it without the aid of a considerable number of
> men; and it was a work of danger to attempt to force the now lawless
> soldiers to obey, and stop with us till this work of necessity and
> humanity was accomplished.
>
> All thought of what they owed their wounded comrades, and of
> the probability that ere long a similar fate might be their own, was
> swallowed up in their abominable rage for drink and plunder; however,
> by perseverance, and occasionally using his stick, my commandant at
> length compelled a few fellows to lend their assistance in removing
> what we could into the town. But this was a most heart-rending duty,
> for, from the innumerable cries of – 'Oh! for God's sake, come and
> remove me!' it was difficult to select the most proper objects for
> such care. Those who appeared likely to die, of course, it would have
> been but cruelty to put them to the pain of a removal and many who,
> from the nature of their wounds, required great care and attention
> in carrying them, the half-drunken brutes whom we were forced to

employ exceedingly tortured and injured; nay, in carrying one man out of the ditch they very frequently kicked or trod upon several others, whom to touch was like death to them, and which produced the most agonising cries imaginable.

But the task was too enormous, as Surgeon Walter Henry describes:

There lay a frightful heap of fourteen or fifteen hundred British soldiers, many dead but still warm, mixed with the desperately wounded, to whom no assistance could be given. There lay the burned and blackened corpses of those that had perished by the explosions, mixed with those that were torn to pieces by round shot or grape, and killed by musketry, stiffening in their gore, body piled upon body, involved and intermixed into one hideous and enormous mass of carnage; whilst the morning sunbeams, falling on this awful pile, seemed to my imagination pale and lugubrious as during an eclipse. At the foot of the castle wall, where the 3rd Division had escaladed, the dead lay thick, and a great number were to be seen about the San Vincente bastion at the opposite side of the works. A number had been drowned in the cunette of the ditch, near the Trinidad bastion, but the chief slaughter had taken place at the great breach. There stood still the terrific beam across the top, armed with its sharp and bristling sword blades, which no human dexterity or strength could pass without impalement. The smell of burned flesh was yet shockingly strong and disgusting.

If drink was the prime reason for the poor casualty evacuation, a choice between plunder and rape vied for second. Actually, rape was a term rarely used by our Victorian memorialists: vaguer references to 'violation by men mad with passion' and 'deeply injured females' being deemed preferable, and quite right too. Few Spanish ladies led a charmed life on the night of 6 April 1812, and the days and nights that followed. There were enough coded references: Costello's 'Appalling shrieks of hapless women', Blakeney's similar 'Piercing shrieks of frantic women', McGrigor's 'The shrieks of women', Cooke's 'The poor nuns in deshabille', Costello's 'Two daughters ... the mother too ... dragged from their hiding place ... without dwelling on the frightful scene that followed ...', Grattan's 'Perhaps not one female in this vast town escaped injury', and McGrigor's 'Very few ladies, old or young, escaped violation by our brutal soldiery, mad with brandy and passion.'

Surgeon McGrigor also related the story of Philippon's two daughters, and what happened to them – or didn't – by the 88th (Connaughts):

In one street, I met General Phillipon, the governor, with his two daughters, holding each by the hand; all three with their hair dishevelled, and with them were two British officers, each holding one of the ladies by the arm, and with their drawn swords making thrusts occasionally at soldiers who attempted to drag the ladies away. I am glad to say that these two British officers succeeded in conveying the governor and his two daughters safely through the breach, to the camp. At any other time, the rank and age of General Phillipon, bare-headed with his grey whiskers streaming in the wind, would have protected him from any soldiers. When I saw them pulling at these two ladies, and endeavouring to drag them away from their father, and two young officers who so gallantly defended them at the peril of their lives, I could not forbear going up, and endeavouring with threat to bring to the recollection of two soldiers of my old regiment, the 88th, how much they tarnished the glory which the Connaught Rangers had ever earned in the field, by such cowardly conduct.

Philippon was of course a special case, and his daughters ditto; but protection of the fair sex was not entirely absent. The nineteen-year old Joe Donaldson, 94th, tells us 'Many risked their lives in defending helpless females and although it was rather a dangerous place for an officer to appear, I saw many of them running as much risk to prevent inhumanity, as they did the preceding night in storming the town.' And then there is the romantic case of Captain Harry Smith, 95th, and the fourteen-year-old Juana Maria De Los Delores De Leon. Kincaid:

Was sitting at his tent flap outside the town when two young ladies approached. The elder, whose husband was a Spanish officer, begged protection and food. They had been assaulted – blood dripped where ear-rings had been torn out – and their fine house wrecked ... she stood by the side of an angel – A being more transcendently lovely I have never before seen – and one more amiable, I have never yet known! Fourteen summers had not yet passed over her youthful countenance, which was of a delicate freshness – more English than Spanish; her face, though not perhaps rigidly beautiful, was nevertheless so remarkably handsome, and so irresistibly attractive, surmounting a figure cast in nature's fairest mould, that to look at her was to love her; and I did love her; but I never told my love, and in the meantime another and more impudent fellow stepped in and won her! But yet I was happy, for in him she found such a one as her loveliness and her misfortune claimed – a man of honour, and a husband in every way worthy of her!

The impudent fellow was Harry Smith. Three days later they were married, Lord Wellington himself giving away the bride, the start of a long marriage and service in India and South Africa. Nearly thirty years after her death in 1872, her name was on every Victorian's lips as the scene of another famous siege – Lady Smith.

If alcohol was the first self-awarded indulgence for the stormers, and sex for some, coinage must always be high on the list of needs, preferably silver or the great dream – gold. The search for portable, concealable wealth drove much of the wrecking of house interiors and the deliberate violence towards the inhabitants, to discover where caches lay buried. For every Spanish resident, during the siege, would have thought long and hard as to the best hiding places for his wealth, bank deposits being unknown. The men from their Rodrigo experiences knew that in the next few hours they might just transform their personal finances. It was all a question of getting there first, into the finer properties.

Ned Costello, feeling faint from his wounds, entered a house off the market place:

> I sat at the fire, which was blazing up the chimney, fed by mahogany chairs broken up for the purpose. Then I heard screams for mercy from an adjoining room. I hobbled in and found an old man, the proprietor of the house, on his knees, imploring mercy of a soldier who had levelled his musket at him. With difficulty, I prevented him from being shot. The soldier complained that the Spaniard would not give up his money, so I immediately informed the wretched landlord in Spanish, as well as I was able, that he could only save his life by surrendering his cash. Upon hearing this, and with trembling hands, he brought out from under the mattress of the bed, a large bag of dollars enveloped in a night-cap. The treasure must have amounted to 100–150 dollars. By common consent, it was divided among us. The dollars were piled on the table in small heaps according to the number of men present, and called out the same as messes in a barrack-room. I confess that I participated in the plunder, receiving about 26 dollars for my own share.

Poor pickings for Costello. At Vitoria some fourteen months later he 'came by' over £1,000 pounds in gold and silver doubloons and dollars. Such were the dreams of many.

And when the alcohol produced its inevitable change to men's nature – an increased aggression – with perhaps for some the frustrations of unsatisfactory sex or not finding treasure, there also came a mindless urge to destroy. As John Cooke puts it 'The place was completely sacked by our troops. Every atom of furniture was broken and mattresses ripped open in search of treasure. One street was strewn with articles knee deep. A convent was in flames . . . the town was alive, with every house filled with mad soldiers, from the cellar to the once solitary garret.' Or Grattan: 'If they entered a house that had not been emptied of all its furniture or wine, they proceeded to destroy it.' Or William Brown with final succinctness: 'What could not be carried away they, in near wantonness, destroyed.'

And much was indeed carried away, to the various regimental camps, where an air of drunken freedom prevailed: 'Some of them had dressed themselves in priests or friars garments – some appeared in female dresses, as nuns etc.; and, in short, all the whimsical and fantastical figures imaginable almost were to be seen coming reeling out of the town, for by this time they were nearly all drunk.' (William Surtees). And in the 94th's camp 'The camp during the day, and for some days after, was like a masquerade, the men going about intoxicated, dressed in the various dresses they had found in the town: French and Spanish officers, priests, friars and nuns, were promiscuously mixed, cutting as many antics as a mountebank.' (Joe Donaldson).

Later that first afternoon, 7 April, with no sign of the indiscipline abating, the order was issued that 'It is now full time that the plunder of Badajoz should cease, and the Commander of the Forces requests that one officer and six steady NCOs of each regiment be sent into the town at 5am next morning to bring away any stragglers.' No notice being taken, however, by troops no longer in hand, next day a brigade of Portuguese entered the town – only to melt away to join the looters. Wellington saw and heard for himself the embarrassing drunkenness which prevailed: 'There he comes with his long nose, let's give him a salute.' And half a dozen musket-balls whistled over his head, and his staff's; a feu-de-joie too far, or too close, their disappearing cry of 'There goes the ol' chap who can leather the French' was too much. A further order was issued on 8 April at 11pm:

> The Commander of the Forces is sorry to learn that the Brigade in Badajoz instead of being a protection to the people, plunder them more than those who stormed the town. The Commander of the forces calls upon the staff officers of the army, and other officers of regiments to assist him in putting an end to the disgraceful scenes of drunkenness and plunder which are still going on in Badajoz.'

A triple gallows was put up in the main square next morning (9 April).

If it is true that the threat alone sufficed, Rifleman Castles for one came too close: 'I observed a sort of gallows erected,' said Rifleman Costello

> with three nooses hanging from them, ready for service. Johnny Castles, a man of our company, and as quiet and as inoffensive a little fellow as could be, but rather fond of a drop, but not that distilled by Jack Ketch and Co, had a near escape. He was actually brought under the gallows in a cart and the rope placed round his neck, but his life was spared. Whether this was done to frighten him or not I

cannot say; but the circumstances had such an effect on him that he took ill and was a little deranged for some time after.

Who wouldn't be?

Gradually, gradually, order was restored. Exhausted by the exertions of the storm and the poisonous alcohol of the sack, we can readily support Napier's view that 'The tumult rather subsided than was quelled.'

While many officers sensibly made themselves scarce during all this mayhem, some chose to walk back to the walls when daylight came, especially to the breaches which in darkness had proved so impossible; now a curiosity as to their nature was only natural. A further common reason to view old ground was to find the fate of friends, not seen thereafter.

George Simmons:

> I saw my poor friend Major O'Hare lying dead upon the breach. Two or three musket balls had passed through his breast. A gallant fellow, Sergeant Flemming, was also dead by his side, a man who had always been with him. I called to remembrance poor O'Hare's last words before he marched off to lead the advance. He shook me by the hand saying, 'A Lieutenant Colonel or cold meat in a few hours.' I was now gazing upon his body lying stretched and naked amongst thousands more.

John Cooke:

> One man only was at the top of the left breach (the heaps of dead had, as a matter of course, rolled to the bottom) and that was one of the 95th Rifles, who had succeeded in getting his head under the chevaux-de-frise, which was battered to pieces, and his arms and shoulders torn asunder with bayonet wounds ... Poor McLeod, in his 27th year, was buried half-a-mile from the town, on the south side, opposite our camp, on the slope of a hill. We did not like to take him to the miserable breach, where, from the warmth of the weather, the dead soldiers had begun to turn, and their blackened bodies had swollen enormously; we therefore laid him amongst some young springing corn, and, with sorrowful hearts, six of us (all that remained of the officers able to stand) saw him covered in the earth. His cap, all muddy, was handed to me, being without one, with merely a handkerchief round my bruised head, one eye closed, and also a slight wound in my head.
>
> The country was open. The dead, the dying, and the wounded, were scattered abroad: some in tents, others exposed to the sun by day, and the heavy dew by night. At length, with considerable difficulty, I found my friend Madden, lying in a tent, with his trousers on and his shift off, covered with blood, and bandaged across the body to

support his broken shoulder, laid on his back, and unable to move. He asked for his brother – 'Why does he not come to see me?' I turned my head away; for his gallant young brother [a captain of the 52nd] was amongst the slain.

Joe Donaldson:

Here all was comparatively silent, unless here and there a groan from the poor fellows who lay wounded, and who were unable to move. As I looked round, several voices assailed my ear begging for a drink of water; I went, and having filled a large pitcher which I found, relieved their wants as far as I could.

When I observed the defences that had been made here, I could not wonder at our troops not succeeding in the assault. The ascent of the breach near the top was covered with planks of wood firmly connected together, staked down, and stuck full of sword and bayonet blades, which were firmly fastened into the wood with the points up; round the breach a deep trench was cut in the ramparts, which was planted full of muskets with the bayonets fixed in the earth up to the locks. Exclusive of this they had shell and hand grenades ready loaded, piled on the ramparts, which they lighted and threw down amongst the assailants. Round this place death appeared in every form, the whole ascent was completely covered with the killed, and for many yards around the approach to the walls, with every variety of expression in their countenance, from calm placidity to the greatest agony. Anxious to see the place where we had so severe a struggle the preceding night, I bent my steps to the ditch where we had placed the ladders to escalade the castle. The sight here was enough to harrow up the soul, and of which no description of mine could convey an idea. Beneath one of the ladders, amongst others, lay a corporal of the 45th Regiment, who, when wounded, had fallen forward on his knees and hands, and the foot of the ladder had been, in the confusion, placed on his back. Whether the wound would have been mortal, I do not know, but the weight of the men ascending the ladder had facilitated his death, for the blood was forced out of his ears, mouth, and nose.

Robert Blakeney:

When I arrived at the great breach, the inundation presented an awful contrast to the silvery Guadiana; it was fairly stained with gore, which through the vivid reflection of the brilliant sun, whose glowing heat already drew the watery vapours from its surface, gave it the appearance of a fiery lake of smoking blood, in which were seen the bodies of many a gallant British soldier. The ditches were strewn with killed and wounded; but the approach to the bottom of the main breach was fairly choked with dead. A row of chevaux-de-frise, armed with sword blades, barred the entrance at the top of the breach and so firmly fixed that, when the 4th and Light Divisions marched through, the greatest exertion was required to make a sufficient opening for their admittance. Boards fastened with ropes to plugs driven into the ground within the ramparts were let down, and covered nearly the whole surface of the breach; these boards were so thickly studded with sharp pointed spikes that one could not introduce a hand between them; they did not stick out at right angles to the board, but were all slanting upwards. In rear of the chevaux-de-frise the ramparts had deep cuts in all directions, like a tanyard, so that it required light to enable one to move safely through them, even were there no opposing enemy. From the number of muskets found close behind the breach, all the men who could possibly be brought together in so small a place must have had at least twenty firelocks each, no doubt kept continually loaded by persons in the rear. Two British soldiers only entered the main breach during the assault; I saw both their bodies. If any others entered they must have been thrown back over the walls, for it is certain that at dawn of 7 April no more than two British bodies were within the walls near the main breach. In the Santa Maria breach not one had entered. At the foot of this breach the same sickening sight appeared as at that of Trinidad: numberless dead were strewn around the place. On looking down these breaches, I recognised many old friends, whose society I had enjoyed a few hours before, now lying stiff in death.

A final very sad and scarcely believable piece by Johnny Kincaid, showing how three days after the storm limbless men still awaited succour:

and, in passing the verge of the camp of the 5th Division, we saw two soldiers standing at the door of a small shed, or outhouse, shouting, waving their caps, and making signs that they wanted to speak to us. We rode up to see what they wanted, and found that the poor fellows had each lost a leg. They told us that a surgeon had dressed their wounds on the night of the assault, but that they had ever since been without food or assistance of any kind, although they, each day, had opportunities of soliciting the aid of many of their comrades, from whom they could obtain nothing but promises. In short, surrounded by thousands of their countrymen within calls, and not more than 300 yards from their own regiment, they were unable to interest any one on their behalf, and were literally starving. It is unnecessary to say that we instantly galloped back to the camp and had them removed to the hospital.

If both these men happened to be the most unpopular soldiers in the entire Army, they could not, it would seem, have been worse served by their comrades. Yet we know the aftermaths of all Peninsular battles are full of stories of the injured lying out quite unattended the following day, even without the competing immediate attractions of a rich town to plunder; it is all of a piece with equally consistent records of bodies being stripped, whilst warm; indeed whilst still living, if the stripper considered the wounds mortal – and the boots (or whatever) were the right size.

*   *   *

So it was all over. Governor Philippon before first light on 7 April sent out dragoons from Fort San Cristobal, through the Portuguese pickets, to carry his grim news to Soult (two marches away down near Villafranca). With 25,000 men to Wellington's 55,000, of whom Graham and Hill with 31,000 were standing in his way at Albuera, Soult sensibly about-turned to Andalucia. Philippon surrendered at seven o'clock under a white handkerchief on a bayonet, together with his staff and some 100 men, having been refused a discussion of terms by Lord Wellington's ADC, Fitzroy Somerset, and Beresford's, William Warre (the latter later claimed to be the senior officer present, but stopped short of claiming the surrender). The Fort captured, Lamare said it contained 'Scarcely thirty rounds of ammunition for cannon, and not a single ration of provisions.' The town itself had neither shells or grenades but 'Twelve thousand pounds of powder, one hundred and forty pieces of cannon and a pontoon train'.

Philippon's fight had been magnificent, a lesson in seeking initiatives, in eking out inadequate supplies of powder and making do with inadequate troop numbers; the latter so effectively that in conjunction with many imaginative field defences, they had imposed horrendous losses. Lamare puts their own at some 1,500, with the major part of the garrison, 3,500, marching out as prisoners. Need one add that a certain General Baron Armand Philippon quickly escaped from his prison in England, crossed the Channel, rejoined the colours, and fought again for his Emperor in Russia and Germany?

Wellington's losses were huge. Six generals wounded – Bowes, Colville, Hervey, Kempt, Picton and Walker; ten lieutenant colonels and nineteen majors killed or wounded, including the commanding officers of the 5th, 7th, 43rd, 44th, 48th, 52nd, 60th, 74th, 77th, 1st/95th and the 3rd Caçadores, and no less than the equivalent of seven battalions now lacking all their company commanders. Think of these figures – that's twelve battalions leaderless, and sixty-seven captains killed or wounded. What promotion for the lieutenants, however temporarily! A lieutenant colonel or dead meat indeed; but a captain by midnight was more likely. All told in round figures the Light and 4th Divisions were each down 1,000, the 3rd and 5th each 500, the Portuguese another 700;

and these casualties were suffered in the storm on 6/7 April; add another 1,000 for the previous siege operations and Oman calculates Wellington's losses total at 4,670 all ranks. Two thousand casualties alone at the breaches – effectively, that is at Trinidad – while several sources imply French losses there were less than three figures, with Lamare giving twenty dead: so a terrible price for a terrible British failure, with future echoes and for much the same reason: firepower and obstacles. A century later chevaux de frise would be replaced by wire, multiple muskets by machine guns, yet still the same old courage in fruitless efforts to dominate. The paucity of French casualties flowed from the obstacle courses Philippon designed to stand in front of his men. Thus it follows that when Lord Wellington chose to hit head on, his injuries were many times those suffered where his escalades more randomly met less prepared walls. The exception was the poor 4th Foot in Walker's brigade, who were hardest hit of all – a casualty rate of some forty-four per cent – presumably thanks to the counter-attack by the 28th Léger, which pushed them back along the ramparts, and also their subsequent fighting probe into the main square. Their 230 casualties were a higher casualty rate than the 341 and 320 of the Light Division's much larger 43rd and 52nd, but these figure are only marginally ahead of the 95th's and of the battalions of the 4th Division. Taking my own regiment, the 48th, in Bowes' Fusilier Brigade, we had nineteen officers and 154 other ranks knocked over or drowned in front of Trinidad. Among the former, Major William Brooke was severely wounded while serving as AQMG, his elder son William was killed, and his youngest son John was also severely wounded: a bad night indeed for the Brookes and I know of no other father-and-two-son casualty combinations.

*   *   *

William Napier concludes his fourth volume with typical passion. His hero Lord Wellington, who can do no wrong, at Badajoz was yet again faced by circumstances not covered by his engineers' pamphlets. Napier examines the various pressures and options open, concluding that, although the breaches in the event proved impregnable, Wellington had 'To strike without regard to rule, trusting in the courage of his men and to fortune to bear him through the trial triumphant,' and that 'the probable loss of a few thousand men, more or less' – if he succeeded – would lead to a 'Horizon ... bright with the comin glory of England.' By that he implied Salamanca, the stilling of domestic clamour from defeatist generals, and by politicians on the costs of the war, and the reviving hopes of the continental powers as they watched Napoleon, at the head of 400,000 men, stride across Russia.

Well, yes: but it is that unfortunate phrase 'a few thousand men' that cannot be passed by. Had the town fallen via Trinidad or Maria it would have been a different story but, like the Somme or Gallipoli or Arnhem, it dishonours the dead not to seek answers to such a catastrophically costly failure. One need not seek far, of course, nor we imagine did his Lordship when, next morning on the breach, Picton found him in tears. 'Good God, what's the matter?' he asked, to which years later Wellington commented, 'I bit my lips and did everything I could to stop myself, for I was ashamed he should see it, but I could not.' This near-unique show of weakness acknowledged a degree of personal culpability: for he knew he had asked too much of his men. Much lies in two of the Peer's letters. The first, quoted by Oman, went to Lord Liverpool and contains, of course, Wellington's strictures on his engineering resources but also for our purposes stressing that 'I have never seen breaches more practicable in themselves than the three walls of Badajoz, and the fortress must have surrendered with these breaches open, *if I had been able to "approach the place"*'. He was more specific to his old QMG George Murray:

> We could do no more, and it was necessary to storm or raise the siege ... I trust however that future armies will be equipped for sieges with the people necessary to carry them on ... and that our engineers will learn how to put their batteries on the crest of the glacis and *to blow in the counterscarp*, instead of placing them wherever the wall can be seen, leaving it to the poor officers and troops to get into and across the ditch as best they can.

Not dealing with the counterscarp not only broke up any cohesion among the stormers (who must then reform in the dark, once beneath it) it also allowed the garrison to mine, wire, inundate and generally turn the ditch into a lethal obstacle course and certainly not a place to reform troops under fire. Lamare mentions in a puzzled way the neglect to destroy the counterscarp, supposing that this lucky gift was 'From inexperience, or from other causes'. We saw how, on 29 March, sapping close to the Lunette had to be abandoned, due to the heavy casualties; sapping right up to the counterscarp to blow it in, with the lack of trained sappers, and with time and Soult pressing, was just not an option. Yet had not Rodrigo's breaches been won, with modest casualties, over intact counterscarps?

So to sum up Wellington's dilemma, while it could not be helped, it might be done, for it had already been done once.

The next consideration ought therefore to be whether the breaches, if breaches there must be, were the right breaches. But that 'if' needs examining briefly, since the French themselves held the view that rather than create laborious breaches 'If Lord Wellington had attempted an attack by sudden assault i.e. by escalade, when the place was first invested, he might have hoped for the same result as he obtained twenty one days later'. That is, due both to the then unprepared defences, and to the stunning surprise such action would achieve. Unfortunately, of course, his Lordship was not privy to his enemy's retrospective views, and it is impossible to imagine him ordering such a gigantic coup-de-main but for one recent thing: the Renaud Redoubt operation at Rodrigo. One does have to wonder if the memory of that silent and successful night attack, delivered within hours of the town being enveloped, crossed Wellington's mind at all? If so, it was a temptation put to one side, probably quite quickly, by a man who had once, in India, bitterly written 'I have come to a determination, when in my power, never to suffer an attack to be made by night upon an enemy who is . . . strongly posted, and whose posts have not been reconnoitred by daylight.' So, ten companies in the dark against the Renaud might fail and no great harm ensue; four divisions at Badajoz needed rather more caution.

We should not forget also that the British were entirely familiar with Badajoz town, headquarters being located there for several months in 1809. The outline plan of attack was thus settled well before Fletcher sent out his ostentatious reconnaissance parties. We know nothing about what discussion, if any, took place between the Peer and his engineer concerning sites other than Trinidad and Santa Maria; the French themselves were more sensitive towards next-door Pedro, and the demi-bastion Antonio up against the Castle. Lamare says:

> This is one of the weakest points, having but a scarp of masonry, the foot of which may be seen from the country at a distance of eight hundred yards, and having but a simple curtain, without a parapet, ditch or counterscarp behind which it was impossible to form a retrenchment.

When, on 21 March, they woke to find three new British batteries on the extreme right of the First Parallel, opposite the place of concern, this 'Occasioned us much uneasiness'; which, however, promptly dissipated when fire was opened instead on the right faces of Trinidad, Pedro and the Lunette.

The French concern was understood by Major John Burgoyne who, with MacCarthy, helped lead Picton forward and who had earlier advocated the town wall to be breached at this point. Whether he had any plan to get the assaulting divisions across the Inundation, other than the one-man-wide bridge necessarily used by Picton's men, we do not know.

That local difficulty did not apply way to the west, where the 5th Division escaladed. The problems there were the French defensive mines, tunnelled from the counterscarp under the glacis, the mines to be used should saps and batteries get close enough. For unlike the rest of the town's defences, which had the added covering strength of the outworks San Roque, Picurina and Pardaleras, nothing stood in front of the three western bastions. The mines were in this sense partly a substitution. We know the mines were known to Fletcher via the desertion of the French sergeant major of sappers clutching his map; we know from Lamare no explosives had yet been laid; we don't, however, know if that was also known. But in any event, Fletcher had already ruled out the southern fronts, much though Lord Wellington wished otherwise, according to John Jones. Fletcher found:

> It would require at least thirty pieces of ordnance, including mortars, beyond the number that could be made available for the operation, five or six times the number of gabions, and twenty times the quantity of timber and other materials, for which carriage was likely to be procured; and further, an additional number of well-instructed miners as well as sappers.

So however much his Lordship was desirous, it just could not be done, and instead one suspects that the final approval for attacks upon Trinidad and Santa Maria came from Fletcher's confirmatory reconnaissance from the vedette on the heights of San Michael, 600 yards from Fort Picurina, on 16 March. This showed that the right face of Trinidad with the still incomplete counterguard in front, could be hit low down by artillery from the Picurina hill. The attack plan flowed from that.

After the action, Fletcher's Brigade Major, John Jones (and therefore writing his Journal as a semi-official engineer spokesman?), stoutly maintained that the breaches were not only practicable but should have been taken. He believed it was the failure of the infantry to assault up them 'Properly in strong columns, closely formed up' that was the problem; indeed, he says it was more a case of 'Scarcely at any one time did more than fifty men ascend either breach in a compact body'. Jones belittled the existence of the chevaux-de-frise, saying that on Santa Maria 'Though excellent to resist individuals, [it] was incapable from its lightness and small base, to withstand the efforts of a body' while on Trinidad the chevaux 'Had been placed along its summit' as if (without chains, which are not mentioned) it could be as readily unplaced. This was just impossible: the timber was fixed beyond any instant moving, for according to John Patterson, 50th, who visited the breach whilst 'bodies of the slain (still) lay heaped about the ditch ... the chevaux de frise being a stout cylindrical block of timber, bristled with sharp pointed sword blades, its *extremities were mortised into the stonework* of the parapet, by thick iron staples'.

An infuriated Napier responded to Jones on behalf of all infantrymen everywhere that 'Engineers intent upon their own art sometimes calculate on men as they do on blocks of stone or timber, nevertheless where the bullet strikes the man will fall'. As he says, the rows of French muskets up front and the inability of British muskets behind (down) the breach slope to suppress the defensive fire across the heavy beams 'Rendered a simultaneous exertion impossible', i.e. their removal. The breaches to modern eyes as to Napier's were surely quite impregnable.

Picton's 3rd Division did indeed save the Army's honour and that of its leader, but no more than did Leith's 5th. Getting inside first, the former's success initiated the rumours that spread through the streets to the men loading muskets at the breaches, that caused reserves to mobilise and troops to be thinned out from in front of Leith. But it was the latter – and we really mean Walker's brigade of the 1st/4th, 2nd/30th and 2nd/44th, together with the 38th (who held off the counterattack) – who actively captured the town. Indeed, some say it was curious that Picton's division, perhaps because he himself was prevented by injury from climbing the ladders into the Castle, was surprisingly apathetic once inside the citadel. Gates leading to the breaches and their frustrated 4th and Light Division comrades might, one imagines, have been made to yield quite promptly with a few captured powder barrels. We shall never know. Anyway, the division being in the Castle soon after 11.30pm, a successful exploitation to the Trinidad breach – all of 500 paces away – would surely have saved many hundreds of lives in the final and despairing series of ad-hoc attempts by the 4th and the Light.

Equally, of course, had Leith's ladder men not lost their way, the same applies, although the two companies of the 9th Léger would not by then have been withdrawn and Walker would have had a much tougher fight. Had that proved impossible to win, however, the town would still have fallen, thanks to Picton – but not until first light, when presumably his Lordship would have co-ordinated a combined effort by the 3rd Division, the 4th and the Light. It would then have answered, one way or the other, those who, like the great Vauban, sometimes favoured daylight attacks over night. 'You wish,' he told Louis XIV at the siege of Valenciennes

> To spare the blood of the soldiers. You will spare it much better when they fight by daylight, without confusion and without tumult. We want to surprise the enemy. They always expect to be attacked by night. We shall surprise them much more effectively when, exhausted with the fatigues of their night watch, they will be under the necessity of encountering our troops refresh ... Night favours the coward, and is attended with the danger of one part of our troops firing upon the other; which indeed happens but too frequently.

And Louis concurred, and the garrison of 4,000 in Valenciennes was taken by storm, in daylight, at a cost of forty men.

Alternative hindsight also suggests capitalising on the French certainty that Trinidad and Maria were to be the main entrances, by launching only feint attacks upon them. By the time Philippon dare re-deploy his defence, Picton and Leith would have been up and over, and 2,000 casualties spared the 4th and Light. But when commentaries reach this 'what if' stage it is sensible to cease, and time to move on. The view from the armchair is always clearer and more farsighted.

We should also move on from Badajoz. The scale of both the casualties and the sack having been here perhaps too much dwelt upon, like the troops them-selves we can feel some relief in quitting the mud for a more open road. Part of that relief was to distance the soldiers' honour from their drunken excesses, and part, no doubt for a great many, was amazement at their personal survival. For just as modern men wonder at the disciplined lines going forward on the Somme, so do we wonder at their great-grandfathers' climbing of the ladders and of Trinidad's horrid slippery slope. Repeatedly, immense fortitude and resolution was shown, of a quite different nature to that required (say) on the Albuera slopes. Perhaps a superior courage? For to go forward to certain death as an individual, one of the few on a narrow front, each finding his own route in the dark, seems to call for more strength than passively waiting for death's random visit, when in line beside your comrades. To do so over a carpet of bodies, signalling earlier failure after earlier failure, is to reach the heights of human determination and valour. When all is said and done, the storm of Badajoz must be reckoned one of the most magnificent deeds in the history of the British Army. In an age when deference to class and position was assumed, it required officers to go up the ladders first, and their men to follow, and that they did; and they did so in the teeth of their traditional foe, their most gallant foe, who made up for an inadequate strength by an excess of energy and resolution. They held the breaches, but were too few to hold the walls. What would Philippon have done with another three or four of Marmont's battalions?

*   *   *

CHAPTER 3

The Affair at Villagarcia
11 April 1812

Having given up hopes of a quick move south to catch Soult, who had
withdrawn too far for that purpose, and with Marmont now running a little
too freely around and to the south of Ciudad Rodrigo (which was provisioned
only for another two weeks), four days after Badajoz fell Lord Wellington
necessarily turned north – possibly a temporary measure at this stage – to deal
with Marmont's Army of Portugal. The French had reached Rodrigo, to the
garrison's horror, by 30 March, but without a siege train, of course; Marmont
sent Clausel west to see if Almeida could be snatched and, that proving too
big a task, south to Castelo Branco (halfway to Badajoz), which he reached by
12 April. Marmont himself raided across to Guarda. Hearing on 15 April of the
fall of Badajoz, and especially the crossing the next day of the Tagus at Villa
Velha by Lord Wellington's advance guard, the entire French force concentrated back to Sabugal. Marmont was unaware, however, that Wellington's far
superior force was en route, and the latter took pains not to over-frighten his
enemy, at whose back ran the swollen Agueda. He remained for one week, until
22 April, when, his rationing having become quite desperate, he withdrew in
the nick of time. He did so without fully appreciating how his four divisions of
20,000 had had 40,000 men closing fast upon their backs.

Meanwhile, Hill with some 14,000 men of the 2nd Division, and Hamilton's
two Portuguese brigades, together with his cavalry, was left as an anti-Soult
blocking and observing force three marches south-east of Badajoz, around
Almendralejo and Villafranca.

Wellington's movement from Badajoz on 11 April had been led by the 11th
Light Dragoons. That same day fellow dragoons in the 12th, 14th and 16th Light
Dragoons, together with their heavier brethren in the 5th Dragoon Guards,
and with the 3rd and 4th Dragoons not far behind, all took part, sixty miles
away, in as neat a cavalry action as could be wished.

So after our previous muddy and bloody pages in the confines of Badajoz,
it will do the reader good to mount up and leap a few walls and ditches, wind
in his hair, and chase the French over a nearly five mile point. And we shall
be in the company of Major General John Le Marchant, who will feature so

stunningly three months later at Salamanca. It is no bad thing to get an early flavour of the important role to be played there by Wellington's British and Portuguese cavalry, particularly as the arm was so much stronger, with the reinforcements sent out to the Peninsula the previous summer and autumn – his Lordship now had fifteen regiments compared to seven in 1811.

Wellington was by background and necessity an infantry general, with the low opinion of the mounted arm which can only come from a superb horseman. Peninsular experience to date of disorderly conduct at Vimiero and Talavera (where he was present) outweighed stories of glory at Benavente, Sahagun and Usagre (where he was not), together with the misreported Campo Major, and formed a conviction that they were

> So inferior to the French from want of order, that although I considered one of our squadrons a match for two French, yet I did not care to see four British opposed to four French, and still more so as the numbers increased, and order of course became more necessary. They could gallop, but could not preserve their order. (Letter to Sir John Russell, 31 July 1826.)

It is true that at Vimiero the 20th Light Dragoons' Colonel Taylor 'Rode that day a horse which was so hot that not all his exertions would suffice to control it, and he was carried head long upon the bayonets of the French'. (Sergeant Landsheit.) It was true also that his two squadrons hilariously then jumped into an enclosure which 'Was fenced round to a great height, and had but a single aperture which ... the enemy immediately closed' and were saved from complete annihilation only by the coincidental advance of the 50th. And at Talavera, as any foxhunting man knows when suddenly confronted by a hidden ditch, order does loosen somewhat; yet it is also true that not everyone of sound mind would then continue, first failing in a charge against the 27th Ligne in four-deep square, then thrusting on with two squadrons – 160 men? – to charge the 10th Chasseurs, the 26th Chasseurs, the Polish Vistula Lancers and the Westphalian Light Horse – a mere 1,200 horsemen. Since just seven (not surprisingly) of the 23rd Light Dragoons survived to make it back up that Balaclava-like valley, watched no doubt by Sir Arthur from the Medellin, he of course had his prejudice strengthened.

And Campo Major? 'Mischiefs ... disorder ... undisciplined ardour ... rabble ... If the 13th Dragoons are again guilty of this conduct, I shall take their horses from them, and send the officers and men to do duty in Lisbon' (to Beresford, 30 March 1811, who was of course himself to blame for throwing away, by over-cautious inaction, the just desserts of a splendid charge and pursuit). Sir John Fortescue said the truth of it all: 'I know of nothing finer in the history of the British cavalry ... If he [Colonel Head, 13th Light Dragoons] had been supported and his trophies been secured, the action would no doubt have become a classic in the annals of cavalry.' Wellington's severe and public –

in a General Order – censure was partly mitigated later when given a fairer version of events by the field officers of the 13th, but he would not retract his reprimand. The 13th's consolation, as Napier wrote, was 'The unsparing admiration of the whole army'. For hundreds upon hundreds of infantry officers, mounted on their unfit narrow old screws, and boringly shackled to the three miles per hour of their marching companies, could well fantasise a rapid seven mile pursuit to the gates of Badajoz. What fun! Let's transfer to the 13th!

Charles Oman, of course, was pretty priggish about all this, unlike Fortescue, and his grudging account of Campo Major makes depressing reading; unfortunately, his views on the natural exuberance of British cavalry have coloured many subsequent accounts, so at least we must be grateful that of Villagarcia he managed to say 'The affair was very creditable to all concerned'. Wellington himself was typically not bowled over by Villagarcia – in forwarding to Lord Liverpool Sir Stapleton Cotton's report 'I have only,' he said, 'to add my commendation of the conduct of Lt–General Sir Stapleton Cotton, Major-General Marchant and the officers and troops under their command' which surely qualifies as coldly damning with the faintest of praise. Of course he was quite right to lack enthusiasm; his implied suspicion that Villagarcia was an exception that proved the rule was to be justified only weeks later at a place called Maguilla. For if Villagarcia stands high in the annals of horsed encounters, Maguilla – as we shall see – took the all-time biscuit for incompetence. And that lack of consistency much irritated the Peer and for good reason: it showed he could not rely on his cavalry not to get into scrapes. He did like best those he could rely upon.

Now, as to the events on 11 April, we really need the previous day to have been helped by a Lieutenant Penrice and two of his dragoons to climb the church steeple in Bienvenida, a modest town fifteen miles from Llerena. This observation post in late afternoon allowed the telescopes of Lieutenant General Cotton and his AAG Lieutenant Colonel John Elley to spot French cavalry ten miles away around a wood, in front of the village of Villagarcia. The newly-promoted Sir Stapleton Cotton had nine regiments in his 1st Cavalry Division, currently behind him by up to twenty miles in the triangle Los Santos–Villafranca–Ribera. Major General John Le Marchant had a Heavy Brigade comprising the 3rd and 4th Dragoons, and the 5th Dragoon Guards; Major General Sir John (Mad Jack) Slade's Heavy Brigade comprised the 1st (Royal) Dragoons, and the 3rd and 4th Dragoon Guards; and Lieutenant Colonel the Hon Frederick Ponsonby (vice Anson, who was at home on leave) the 12th, 14th and 16th Light Dragoons.

What the telescopes showed was a gap of several miles between the enemy cavalry and its supporting infantry and artillery, back around Llerena; the flat rolling terrain was inter-cut by some hill lines and would be quite familiar to Cotton and Elley. They saw the possibility of a surprise attack, in keeping with Wellington's supposed further move southwards. In particular a ridge of broken ground ran between the Villagarcia–Llerena and the Bienvenida–Llerena roads i.e. to the south of Villagarcia, and Cotton's developing plan was to send Le Marchant on a wide right hook to get behind the French cavalry, cutting them off from Llerena, whilst holding their attention in front with his light regiments. That idea was now forming in his mind.

The French cavalry were Marshal Soult's eyes, operated by Drouet D'Erlon, acting much the same role as Hill with two infantry divisions and Pierre Soult's division of dragoons around Llerena, of which a strong brigade under Lallemand and Peyremmont were four miles in advance at Villagarcia, comprising the 2nd Hussars, the 17th and 27th Dragoons. Drouet's orders were to fall back towards Seville should the British press hard, but preferably to remain, so as to keep up communications via Medellin, Truxillo and the Tagus with the Army of Portugal. Hill and Cotton, in furtherance of the Peer's wish to give the impression he was looking south to invade Andalucia, and not moving north on Marmont, were to push forward.

Thus Ponsonby, with the 12th and 14th, was ordered up to Usagre 'And to occupy it this evening, if the enemy does not occupy it . . . Should he, you will bivouac in view of the town, and advance at daylight the following morning'. The two heavy brigades were ordered to Bienvenida, and the 16th (who had not completed rationing) were to join Cotton at the latter place. Modern readers who are themselves horsemen may at this point be reminded of – and admire – Cotton's physical diligence in making these simple arrangements: he and Elley had already ridden twenty miles forward to the steeple; now twelve miles back to Zafra, there to tumble Le Marchant out of bed and give him his marching orders; fifteen miles to Villafranca and ditto Ponsonby, and finally twenty-two miles back to the steeple: a round trip of nearly seventy miles, of which the final fifty were in darkness! Quite a hack! There is little doubt such an energetic outing was evidence of a man eager for glory. It is said that Cotton had been present a month earlier at the dinner given by Lord Wellington at which Generals Graham and Hill were both presented with the insignia of the Bath. Cotton still smarted at his exclusion.

On the approach march, however, came news to Cotton that the French cavalry were no longer about Villagarcia. He accordingly sent a note to Ponsonby by hand of Lieutenant Wheeler, 16th Light Dragoons, 'I wish we had been allowed to follow them this day. I fear it is too late. The enemy have left Villagarcia. Push Cocks on in the morning to Villagarcia, and let him send on patrols to feel the enemy, whose rear I think he will find in Berlanga.' (Ten miles east of Llerena, on the Cordova road.) Now Frederick Ponsonby would interpret this quite plainly: his commander regretted earlier delays and wanted Cocks to locate the French even if this required a patrol of fourteen or fifteen miles to Berlanga, i.e. a potentially thirty-mile round trip to bring back information – certainly another three-hour delay. So, Ponsonby, you had better act now. Off went Major Charles Cocks, 16th Light Dragoons, with a squadron each from the 12th and 14th, and at first light he found and drove in the French vedettes from the hill above Villagarcia.

Meanwhile a second message to Ponsonby, carried by Captain Luard, 4th Dragoons, was on its way from Cotton. This was to delay entering Villagarcia, second thoughts suggesting the French (if they were still nearby) might thereby be forced prematurely back before the right hook from Le Marchant could come in behind them, and cut the road to Llerena. But, too late, for Ponsonby's two squadrons under Cocks clattered through the village at dawn and, progressing out the other side, ran into the main French force. In his despatch, Cotton says, 'I desired Colonel Ponsonby would show only three squadrons and endeavour to amuse the enemy in front'; by which we may assume Charles Cocks' two squadrons out front by themselves was a mistake, confronted now by the 17th and 27th Dragoons under Lallemand, with the 2nd Hussars under General Peyremmont coming up from support. That is 200 sabres being pushed by 2,000. Thus, far from amusing the French, Ponsonby hastened to save Cocks by joining him with the other four squadrons of the 12th and 14th, making six light squadrons against – we don't know for sure – between twelve and eighteen heavy squadrons. Enough anyway for General Peyremmont to be quite confident in pushing Lallemand forward.

Cotton himself with the 16th Light Dragoons was coming up between Ponsonby and Le Marchant anxious to join the former, who was now in trouble. Behind Ponsonby, in a defile, were several enclosures with stone walls which would limit movement. Le Marchant watched from the right on the edge of the olive groves as the six light squadrons faced the much more numerous French heavies, 400 yards apart. The 5th Dragoon Guards had just made a forced night march of over twenty miles, after more than the same again the previous day 'And the last four miles at a brisk pace through a country abounding with obstructions' says their Records. Le Marchant had taken them through a defile over the hills bordering the east of the plain, stumbling in single file up tortuous gullies strewn with boulders. Guided by Colonel Elley he had found his way down to the south-west of Villagarcia, and was hidden in rough terrain behind the ridge overlooking the plain, across which ran the road from Villagarcia south-east to Llerena. Only the 5th were with him, the 3rd and 4th Dragoons being not immediately available.

There is a nice reference in Le Marchant's *Memoirs* of 1841, written up by his second son Dennis, of some of the red-coated 5th Dragoons being spotted by General Lallemand emerging

> From an olive grove in his rear, and pushed boldly towards him across the plain. They were evidently no more than three hundred or four hundred men, and he could not see any troops near to support them. For a moment he supposed them to be a detachment who had mistaken their orders or lost their way; but on closer observation,

their compactness and precision with which they moved, aroused in his mind suspicions which he deemed prudent to communicate to General Peyremmont ... A few minutes elapsed before Lallemand could find Peyremmont; and when he did his suggestions were ill-received. Peyremmont insisted that the officer commanding the British detachment must be a blockhead, and was throwing himself upon certain destruction.

Lallemand apparently muttered something about if the British Commander was not a blockhead, he must be no ordinary soldier, to which remark Peyremmont smiled contemptuously and turned dismissively away – briefly – for then the redcoats surged forward, Le Marchant in advance of the centre squadron, each squadron in echelon, forming line as they went. Peyremmont checked his further movement towards Ponsonby's light troopers, prior to changing his position; some confusion reigned, and at this point the separate British regiments combined with unusual skill. Behind and to Ponsonby's right over a low hill appeared the 16th Light Dragoons. A wall lay between them and the plain. 'The French paid little attention to this reinforcement,' wrote Cotton's biographer in 1866, 'For between them and the enemy ran at the bottom of the hill a low stone wall, which appeared to render a direct advance of the 16th impossible.' The twenty-year-old Captain William Tomkinson rode that day with the 16th:

> When we came on the top of the hill, there were the 12th and 14th on our left, close in front of Villa Garcia. The enemy formed a quarter of a mile from them, and a small stone wall betwixt the 16th (our regiment) and the French. We came down the hill in a trot, took the wall in line, and were in the act of charging when the 5th Dragoon Guards came down on our right, charged, and completely upset the left flank of the enemy, and the 12th, 14th and 16th advancing at the same moment, the success was complete. The view of the enemy from the top of the hill, the quickness of the advance on the enemy, with the spirit of the men in leaping the wall, and the charge immediately afterwards, was one of the finest things I ever saw.

There was little the French commanders could do – Generals Lallemand and Peyremmont had walked into a trap which now closed as the three Light Regiments turned about and surged forward. Le Marchant, the designer of the light cavalry's sabre (1796 pattern) in use that day was to see its effectiveness (Tomkinson tells us of a 'French Dragoon ... his head nearer cut off than I ever saw before; it was by a sabre cut at the back of the neck').

It is not clear if either side had a formal second line in support. While Peyremmont's 2nd Hussars was probably up in his three regiment line, Le Marchant's 3rd and 4th Dragoons are only referred to as being 'In support' rather loosely, i.e. at a distance, to conform to his Lordship's best practice. 'The 4th Dragoons returned one man as wounded, detached with the skirmishers', as explained by Le Marchant, but otherwise were not present. Slade certainly was absent – unsurprisingly a late starter again.

The moral advantage lay with the British. For every Frenchman felt the wretched foolishness, and anger, that always follows being caught out and while their right arms were adrenalin-strong for a while, the inclination grew to turn and run, towards their infantry and guns some five miles back around Llerena. Thus there developed a splendid and no doubt exhilarating pursuit across the plain, halted temporarily when the French made use of a ditch, around the halfway mark, daring Cotton to charge over the obstacle. There was a hesitation at this point amongst the pursuers' leaders, as we shall comment upon later, but the immediate cause of delay was that Cotton was brought down, in a heavy fall, when his horse (which had covered such distances that day) fell at the ditch, dislocating a shoulder and having to be shot. Cotton suffered severe contusions, according to his biography. However, all that overcome, he first sent two squadrons of the 16th down the Llerena road around the French left, whilst charging with three squadrons of the 12th, and the French again turned and ran, until safely back inside their lines the other side of Llerena. Tomkinson again:

> We drove them quite close to Llerena, and Cookson, of Captain Cocks' troop, was killed in the town. To check us, the enemy fired (from the ground they held with 10,000 infantry close to the left of Llerena) a few cannon shots over our heads, not daring to hit us, being so intermixed with their own people. The Heavies [cavalry] supported us, and, on the cannon opening, we were ordered to withdraw on Villa Garcia.

So Cotton turned back with his prisoners (no fewer than four officers and 132 troopers) and the five-mile return hack would pass over the French dead and wounded, strewn where they lay. The total British loss was put variously at between fifty-one and fifty-eight all ranks, of whom the great majority (forty to forty-five) were dragoon guards. It is hard therefore not to suppose their cumbersome swords proved less handy in defence than the light dragoons' curved sabres, and which did such work: 'The prisoners are dreadfully cut, and some will not recover,' wrote Tomkinson. The French casualty figures were 'more than 100' according to Captain Thomas Fenton, 4th Dragoons, which with prisoners made an overall loss to Drouet D'Erlon of well over 200, four times the British loss. A more jaundiced view was that of William Bragge, 3rd Dragoons:

> The Big Wigs choose to consider this Affair a great Feather in Sir Stapleton's Cap but when the superiority in Numbers and Horses is

so much in our Favour together with the Ground, we ought not to think much in taking 4 officers, 140 Men and 114 of the worst Horses you ever beheld. The Loss of the 5th Dragoon Guards was 12 killed, 2 missing, 1 Officer and 35 Men wounded, and 24 Horses missing. It is worthy of remark that scarcely one Frenchman died of his wounds, although dreadfully chopped, whereas 12 English Dragoons were killed on the Spot and others dangerously wounded by thrusts. If our men had used their Swords so, three Times the number of French would have been killed.

There is one curiosity in the story. Some held that Cotton and Le Marchant, at that halfway ditch, meant to go no farther, doubtless recalling Campo Major and the Peer's subsequent strictures: it would be most unlikely that alarm bells did not ring. One clue is the exchange between Tomkinson and Le Marchant, when the latter turned to order the recall. Tomkinson was urging his men on whereas Le Marchant said ' "Halt and form your men". I said "The enemy are in greater confusion." "You must halt." "Must I call out 'Halt' "? I asked. Seeing the General hesitate (he would not give the order), I called to the men to come on, and we drove the enemy a mile, in the greatest confusion into Llerena.'

Now, it is to be wondered at, that the major general allowed the captain so flagrantly to disobey, unless he felt in his heart the latter was justified: for there was no sign of any French reserve.

Another clue is to recall that Colonel Ponsonby, commanding the three light dragoon regiments, had three years before (at Talavera with the 23rd Light Dragoons) experienced the disorder a ditch can create in formed ranks. That memory, too, would have rung bells and caused hesitation. So, too, – a third clue – the memory in the head of Lieutenant Colonel John Elley, Le Marchant's guide for the 5th's approach march: like Ponsonby he had been with the 23rd at Talavera. Indeed, as their guide that day, he it was who, out front, had jumped that ditch first, reining in and turning unsuccessfully to hold back the squadrons behind.

So several of the leading British officers probably hesitated at that halfway gulley, held back by past ghosts.

Overall, we should not view this very pleasing action at Villagarcia as a work of military genius, the whole trap meticulously planned, executed with perfect timing etc. 'To march divided, to fight together' is a military dictum rarely achieved – most especially in darkness – without a huge slice of luck. Here were four considerable but detached groups of British horse: Charles Cocks' two squadrons of the 12th and 14th out on the plain; Ponsonby arriving from behind with the other four squadrons; Cotton arriving separately with the 16th and Le Marchant clambering furiously up onto the ridge, his brigade trailing way behind. There is no suggestion of course that Cocks was sent forward deliberately under-strength, to entice the French dragoons into an ambush ready laid: he was simply back-pedalling because he had gone too far, too soon. That he did so was correctly in pursuit of Cotton's earlier encouragement to Ponsonby; so the former's subsequent criticism of the latter was, therefore, most unfair. He would have done better to have reserved his ire for Slade, whose presence on the field would have seen a French casualty rate much higher than the twenty per cent we can vaguely calculate. Even more does that apply to Le Marchant's two lagging regiments, and one can but suppose his final approach was necessarily in single file. Nose to tail, a regiment's 400 horses would stretch back nearly a mile. Had Le Marchant had the time to assemble the 3rd and 4th Dragoons – half an hour more would nearly have done it – Lallemand surely would have been encircled and captured entire. Le Marchant's plan was for the 3rd and 5th to be in the first line, and the 4th in the second as a reserve (he wrote to R. B. Long on 7 May), and 'Lord Edward Somerset and Major Clowes were mortified at not being able to share in the action, but the impediments of ground rendered it quite impracticable'.

The odd thing is, on Le Marchant's sketch accompanying his letter to Long, he marks four squadrons for each of his three regiments (should there not be three only?) climbing the defile, the 5th leading, the 3rd and 4th left and right behind – really quite closely behind. It is as if he then hurried the 5th forward, opening a gap. Or perhaps the sketch is merely as indicative as it is legible?!

Apart from the obvious mortification of the French, Le Marchant had through this affair 'Of no great consequence, brought myself and my brigade acquainted on essential points, and I have reason to believe that we are mutually well pleased with each other.' Salamanca was to show that to be correct.

It is said that, during their retreat, Lallemand took some small comfort from the sight of his superior Peyremmont, hatless and dusty, no longer quite so contemptuous of the British blockheads, 'Soiled and disordered ... Urging his steed along the slippery slopes of a hill which afforded but an insecure footing, some English Dragoons following at a distance, with a certainty of capturing him if the animal should fall ... None stopped to help him.'

Their leader's now deflated certainty stood token for the general effects of this British action at Villagarcia: the further proof that French cavalry were beatable, that British cavalry commanders could cobble together a halfway decent tactical manoeuvre, and that the strength of British right arms was more than adequate. Of Le Marchant's brigade of heavy horse, which is to star at Salamanca, we shall note the presence there, on the left of the first line, of the 5th Dragoon Guards, who had charged at Villagarcia; and on their right we shall note the presence of the 4th Dragoons, who had charged so effectively eleven months earlier at Usagre. The destruction of eight French battalions at Salamanca, and the general devastation of their centre, may largely be predicted by these earlier endeavours by two such fine regiments – and of their brigade commander. For Le Marchant set about three regiments with one of his own, not really knowing if the Light Dragoons to his left would – could – turn and join in, a triumph then ensuing as they did so: as he put it in his letter to Long, it was his charge with the 5th that broke the enemy 'And the Light Cavalry then joined in the pursuit'. And that pursuit, contrary to Wellington's and Oman's jaundiced expectations, was conducted without great loss of control – perhaps just a little, but nothing serious. It was indeed a neat enough day for British cavalry, and an embarrassment for the French.

* * *

CHAPTER 4

Hill's Raid on the Almaraz Bridge
19 May 1812

A major consideration in Lord Wellington's strategic thinking, in late 1811, part and parcel with plans to possess the twin fortress gateways to Spain, and the options of a left or right turn – Marmont or Soult – thereafter, was the broad and deep barrier to troop movement provided by the east-west run of the Tagus. While he now commanded the largest European troop numbers of his career and need not fear any one French army, Marmont and Soult together, with or without attachments from elsewhere, would give pause for thought. The Tagus barrier was not impervious. One of the joys of being in Badajoz again would be the change to British ownership of Soult's pontoon train. Without the means, therefore, to construct either a bridge of boats or flying ferries, French troop movement and communication between their armies must be across the sole bridge in French hands, that at Almaraz, seventy miles south of Salamanca. Along the rest of the Tagus, from Toledo way over to the east, forty miles beneath Madrid, and west right to the Portuguese border near Alcantara – 170 miles or more? – the French could not cross. It is true there were bridges at both Talavera and Arzobispo but the approach roads were inadequate for the heavy wheeled vehicles and guns of a marching army. Thus the Almaraz bridge was of prime importance to whichever marshal his Lordship chose to attack, for without it succour could come only through a massive 400 mile detour into New Castile.

Wellington had warned his reliable deputy, the newly-promoted Lieutenant General Sir Rowland ('Daddy' or 'Farmer') Hill of a possible operation to destroy the Almaraz bridge as early as January, and confirmed this with prescience both on 24 and 30 April, a few days before a captured despatch from Marmont to Jourdan came to headquarters, explicitly confirming the bridge's importance to Marmont, and with the pleasing information that Foy's Division, of 5,000 men at Talavera, was the only force within two days' march of Almaraz. A coup-de-main by Hill on the bridge and the defending forts was therefore very much on the cards, given due secrecy. Success would be a devastating blow to French movement.

The final decision to advance towards Salamanca and on Marmont, rather than a raid into Andalusia and on Soult, appears still not to have emerged a month after Badajoz. But continuing – and unresolved – problems with the mutinous Spanish garrison in Ciudad Rodrigo, so recently set a-trembling by Marmont's raid, presented Wellington with a vulnerable flank, should he (Wellington) move south of the Tagus, since not only would the garrison in his rear prove unreliable if attacked but the repair work still continued to be neglected. Marmont had the larger effective force, and was more easily mobile compared to Soult's, and Marmont himself had always shown a readiness to assist others, unlike Soult. Mobility, however, assumes provisions and Marmont had none – hence his present wide dispersion. Wellington, on the other hand, was well provided; the harvest north of the Tagus being later than in Andalucia, his northern enemy would therefore have a longer period of famine-induced immobility than his southern and thus be more vulnerable. He wrote on 13 May that 'they cannot undertake any operation till the harvest shall be ripe,' and the previous day (also to Liverpool) the deduction that 'the eventual success of the campaign depends upon my being able to move forward into Spain before the harvest'. The spin of the coin was turning towards Marmont: drive back his Army of Portugal, and Soult too must retire or be in danger of isolation.

Still, while his Lordship pondered these options, the destruction of the Almaraz boat bridge would clearly support either endeavour. Hill was given the go-ahead on 7 May. He collected his force at Merida on the 12th, the three brigades of the 2nd Division comprising the 13th Light Dragoons, Major General Kenneth Howard's 1 Brigade – 50th (West Kents), 71st (Glasgow Highlanders) and 92nd (Gordon Highlanders), plus a company of the 60th; Colonel Wilson's 2 Brigade – 28th (Gloucestershire) and 34th (Cumberland) plus another 60th company; and Colonel Charles Ashworth's Portuguese Brigade – 6th and 18th Line and 6th Caçadores. Engineers with explosives and a pontoon train, and two artillery companies, also joined, the latter commanded by Wellington's trusted Alexander Dickson. Hill left 11,000 men under Sir William Erskine to continue the watch on Drouet D'Erlon, taking some 7,000 men on his raid.

The boat bridge at Almaraz lay a good hundred miles from Merida, where Hill crossed the Tagus on the newly-repaired bridge. Three forced marches saw the column reach Truxillo on 15 May, where all baggage was dropped, save one camp kettle mule per company (the men to carry three days' bread, and bullocks for four days). The Almaraz road then crossed five tributaries running north-west to the Tagus, with mountain ranges between making the going strenuous; Jaraicejo was another twenty-mile march commenced at 2am taking the column discreetly to the foot of the Sierra de Miravete, just a night march short of the Pass of Miravete, itself within a four-mile striking distance of Almaraz. The Pass was well defended.

Hill's initial plan, made without close reconnaissance, was to form three attack columns, approach by night march, and attack at dawn on the 17th. As can be seen from the map, the road snakes through the Pass 150 feet below Miravete Castle, which lay some 700 yards to the west, with two small forts and a fortified house linking the Castle to the road. The Castle complex contained 300 men of the 39th Ligne, and eight guns, and consisted of an old Moorish tower to which the French had added a wall and twelve-foot rampart.

The idea was for Colonel Wilson's brigade and the 6th Caçadores, under Lieutenant General Tilson-Chowne (the Tilson who commanded a brigade on Talavera's Medellin) to escalade the Castle after an encircling movement to the west, whilst Ashworth and the artillery under Major General Long made a false attack from the road; and Hill with Howard's brigade would go for the boat bridge and its defending forts, via a bridle path through the mountains to the east.

The centre column of Portuguese and guns reached the pass beneath the Castle in good time before dawn; the left also reached the Castle from the west – or at least the 34th did. Ensign George Bell was their orderly officer this day and commanded the ladder parties:

> We crawled up this steep ascent with great caution and silence; but just as we approached the tower, a solitary shot was fired at the foot of the hill [presumably a negligent discharge], and the next moment the Castle was in a blaze. Luckily for us it was not yet daylight, and that a cloud of mist hung over the Castle top. We could not be seen ... too late to surprise our friends ... we retired a little way down ... there we lay all day waiting for fresh orders.

John Jones confirms General Chowne's column 'advanced close to the Castle' whereupon deciding – once he could see to judge – the nut was too hard to crack without siege cannon.

It was Howard's column, with Hill, that could not reach its target by dawn, and which caused the cancellation of his plan – not, as Oman and Fortescue have it, that 'by dawn neither (Chowne or Howard) had got anywhere near its destination' (Oman) or that by 'the coming of day all three columns were still far from their striking points' (Fortescue).

Surprise was therefore lost, and doubtless a horseman was already away carrying the news to Almaraz and on to Foy at Talavera. Hill now wisely spent time with his telescope. As he said in his Despatch, once he had lost the element of surprise he must defer an attack 'until we should be better acquainted with the nature and position of the works'. Better late than never! He rapidly saw that the Castle complex on its steep approaches, would not easily fall, while the road beneath it – the only approach to Almaraz that allowed wheeled access – was thereby blocked. Throughout 17 and 18 May strenuous efforts were made to find a way of getting guns forward to the Almaraz valley, but to no avail. A lesser man than Hill might now have abandoned the whole enterprise, especially since he had not yet even reconnoitred his target. Time, however, was on his side, and so too men, and he had ladders; and had not those elements twice proved successful at Badajoz? He also had local guides he trusted and, although the five-mile track beyond La Cueva via the hamlet of Romangorda was more suitable for goats, he resolved to press ahead.

His new plan was for Chowne to demonstrate noisily against the Castle at Miravete, with 2 Brigade under Wilson, whilst he led a strengthened 1 Brigade under Howard over the hills and down to the Tagus, to assault at dawn.

His target, the boat bridge, was anchored a mile downstream from the old broken stone bridge, with forts on the slopes above guarding each end. Fort Napoleon was 100 yards back from the river on the south side, connected to a stone tête de pont at the near pontoons. The fort had a central tower, loop-holed and twenty-five-feet high, and approached across a drawbridge. The ditch was palisaded but the scarp was formed curiously in two parts, with a berm or semi-platform, nearly flat and in places two-feet wide, running round halfway up. Fort Napoleon was manned by two companies of the 6th Léger and a company of the 39th Ligne, plus nine guns and twenty-five gunners and sappers – some 325 all ranks under a Major Aubert; the tête de pont held 250 men from the 6th and also the 4th Étranger. Fort Ragusa on the north bank comprised a tower twenty-five-feet high with two rows of loop-holes, surrounded by a five-sided ditch, with a frontage of about fifty yards; an angled fleche on the riverbank served as a basic tête de pont, since Ragusa sat a good quarter mile from the river, on the hilltop, and the fleche filled the gap. The fleche held fifty men of the 6th Léger and the Fort some 230 men of the 4th Étranger, with twenty engineers. There were twelve guns. Be it noted (not that Hill would know) the 4th Étranger were mostly Prussian prisoner turn-coats, and hence not utterly reliable.

So Hill's main task was to overcome 300 bayonets inside Napoleon, followed by a similar number in the tête de pont – say a batalion's worth of fire-power. He transferred the 6th Portuguese Line from Ashworth to Howard's brigade, making him up to four battalions, and an extra company of riflemen from the 60th, and the twenty-strong gunner detachment from General Chowne's, together with their lintstocks, spikes, prickers etc. and 100lbs of powder, in a good example of forward thinking. For if his own guns must stay behind, perhaps his gunners could find and use some French ones? Similarly practical was the decision to cut in half the thirty-two-feet-long scaling ladders, to make them more easily carried around the tight corners of the twisting path.

The column set off at 9pm. The march was 'Conducted by experienced guides in the mazy sheep-walks in the brushwood, which were considered impassable,' says Captain James MacCarthy, 50th. A soldier (anonymous) of the 71st wrote six or seven years later:

> A scaling ladder was given to each section of a company of the left wing, with the exception of two companies. We moved down the hill

in a dismal manner; it was so dark we could not see three yards before us. The hill was very steep and we were forced to wade through whins and scramble down rocks, still carrying the ladders. When daylight on the morning of the 19th at length showed us to each other, we were scattered all over the foot of the hill like stray sheep, not more in one place than were held together by a ladder. We halted, formed, and collected the ladders, then moved on.

The lead company of the 50th halted before first light (which fell at 5.05am) at the hamlet of Romangorda, two miles from the bridge. There had been a helpful three-quarter moon but this had set at 1.44am, and that's when the real delays commenced. The column became much elongated in the darkness, as always happens on poor going, and only the 50th and the 71st's left wing was immediately available, some 900 men. Sergeant Robertson of the 92nd was in charge of a ladder, using two shifts of eight men, and declared the path the roughest he had ever trod. When a ladder man lost his footing, down would go the whole party. But they made it, a descent (with ups and downs) of 1,200 feet to the Tagus from the Cueda Pass.

The 50th moved forward again, to a crest just 300 yards from Fort Napoleon. MacCarthy: 'By 6 o'clock when the sun was shining so resplendent, as each individual emerged from the labyrinth he was distinguishable, and thus obliged to lay down (in ambush) to avoid discovery from the battlements.'

Major Aubert, commanding in Fort Napoleon, knew the English were now a present threat, but the wooded terrain and the ridges had prevented early observation. He had failed, it seems, to put out standing patrols. He would now be one of the observers noted on the tower, watching puffs of smoke erupt around the castle, as Tilson-Chowne, as arranged, began his false attack with his howitzers. He was also sending skirmishers forward up the slopes towards the castle's sugar-loaf eminence. This, therefore, was Hill's time to assault Fort Napoleon, and although he had only one and a half of his four battalions ready to go, he was not inclined to delay – in any event, discovery would quickly follow if Aubert thought to send out a dawn patrol. Acquiescing therefore in the plea made by 50th's commanding officer, Lieutenant Colonel Stewart, three columns each of a five company wing were readied. Stewart led one, Major Harrison his other, and Major Cother that of the 71st. Hill left orders for the right wing of the 71st, and the 92nd, now beginning to arrive in numbers, to attack the tête de pont from the west.

Preceded by the ladder parties, the assault ran forward over the concealing crest into view of the French, and down towards separate parts of the ditch. They were at once met by a storm of fire, both the tearing hell of musket balls and grapeshot, and the thunder of round shot from the cannon. Once in the ditch, as so often before, it became apparent the ladders were too short. Some were lashed together there in the ditch, back to the original thirty-two feet length; some were used to gain precarious access to the intermediate berm on the face of the rampart, before being pulled up to the ledge to try the last leg. The 71st's chronicler:

> Their entrenchment proved deeper than we expected, which caused us to splice our ladders under the wall; during which time they annoyed us much by throwing grenades, stones and logs over it; but not a Frenchman dares to be seen on the top; for we stood with our pieces cocked and presented. As soon as the ladders were spliced, we forced them from the works.

Others spurned the ladders, seeing handholds in the scarp. John Patterson, 50th, wrote

> the French grenadiers whose great bearskin caps and whiskered faces ornamented the breastwork overhead, hurled down on us with ruthless vengeance an infinite variety of missiles ... fragments of rock, stones of huge dimensions, round shot, glass bottles and many other articles.

'Our soldiers were impatient,' said MacCarthy, 'And climbing dilapidated parts, pulled up their comrades, laid in the inner ditch until all were gathered, and then dashed forward – Colonel Stewart himself gallantly leading.' Captain Robert Candler was said to be first onto the rampart, first up his ladder but sadly to be blown to atoms, 'his shattered remains lying extended on the slope of the rampart'. But his No. 4 Company followed, the top was gained at several places and that was enough for the garrison. The Grenadier Company of the 39th Ligne was said to have led the way. Instead of making for the tower, the inner work that should have been their rallying point, those of the French 6th and 39th who did not immediately throw down their muskets made for the rear gate. Major Aubert, according to MacCarthy, with his back to the round tower

> Became frantic, refusing to surrender his sword and flourishing it in defiance, attempted to strike an officer of the 50, who was remonstrating with him, which a Sgt [Sergeant Checher] in the warmth of the moment, unfortunately wounded him with his pike, which was deplored as unnecessary (for) ... his (Aubert's) excitement must soon have subsided.

In another instance of the soldier's respect for honourable and courageous behaviour, the Frenchman was later 'buried at Merida with military honours, his remains being attended by the whole garrison, and the officers in command there'. (Patterson)

The 100-yard rush to the tête de pont was a mixture of five regiments, pursuers intermingled with the pursued. Neither the muskets of the Prussian garrison in the bridgehead nor their cannon could fire without striking down their own. In despair the garrison also now joined the fleeing crowd. The fifth regiment was the 92nd, who by then had formed and moved forward with the missing half of the 71st. The scene on the bridge of boats could therefore be readily imagined. The bridge was said to be 200 yards long, with some twenty pontoons. The weight in the centre, however, was taken up by a river boat, lighter and therefore able to be easily removed at night, or whenever security was in doubt. There had been some 575 blue coats on the south side of the river, and surely not more than a tenth now lay dead or wounded in Fort Napoleon, or along the 100-yard dash? So some 500 crowded onto the shaking bridge – which then broke, the two centre pontoons sinking beneath the crowd. Some say the bridge was deliberately cut by those fleeing, but too early; some say Aubert had the centre river boat removed at the outset, as a sensible (and temporary) precaution. But if so then neither of the two garrisons on the south bank could have escaped, bar by swimming – in full kit and boots? So if the bridge had been broken deliberately beforehand, Hill's report of taking 279 prisoners must surely have been nearer 500?

There then occurred an almighty slice of luck for General Hill. For, with the bridge broken, the Tagus could not be crossed nor the bridge repaired, under the guns of Fort Ragusa. Hill's designs would appear frustrated. But when the artillery detachment under Lieutenant Love turned the French cannon in Napoleon upon Fort Ragusa, and fired a few rounds, the Prussians promptly fled their responsibilities, accompanied by the half company of the 6th Léger in the fleche. This astonishingly rapid application of the old phrase 'Self preservation is nature's law' was later to result in the death penalty for Ragusa's commandant, who was shot in Talavera. The immediate result was that four grenadiers of the 92nd swam unmolested over to the far bank, returning with several boats. So Hill now had complete ownership, and began to burn, blow up, and generally destroy all he had won: the bridge of twenty large pontoons and its ancillary store of ropes, timbers, carriages, anchors and the associated workshops; round shot and shells were chucked into the river; the stores of food, clothing and musket cartridges were burnt; and with powder abundantly available the Fort towers were levelled, a process completed next morning. His soldiers, fed for three days on double beef but no bread or biscuit, were delighted with the captured French rations including the choicest wines: the soldier of the 71st showed a simple grasp of the basics when he wrote 'We ... found plenty of provisions ... filled our haversacks, and burned the town.' Captain Patterson of the 50th put it more poetically, describing what they found as 'Provisions to gratify the pallet of the most fastidious gourmand', describing the scene:

> Collected together in knots and parties, with the green sward for
> our tablecloth, forgetful of the past, and careless about the future, we

feasted most sumptuously, drinking to our foes in their own generous wine and wishing that, in future campaigns, our adventures might be terminated in an equally agreeable and fortunate manner.

His regiment's price for their 'adventures' was, however, not cheap. Of Hill's overall loss of 189 all ranks killed and wounded, the 50th comprised sixty-seven per cent: a total of 127 casualties of whom eight were among the officers. The left wing of the 71st suffered fifty-seven, the 92nd just two, with a further two outside the castle. On the French side, of course, the 4th Étranger was effectively destroyed: Oman quotes 'A parade state reduction between 15 May and 1 July as from 366 to 88, and puts the French total loss at around 400.' These included the mortally-piked Major Aubert, and the 39th's commanding officer Lieutenant Colonel Teppe, a prisoner; the trophies included a flag colour of the 4th Étranger taken by the 71st, eighteen guns, the huge powder stores and, of course, the pontoons – the second such train to have been captured or destroyed inside a few weeks.

There now remained for Hill the isolated French garrison in the Castle complex up at Miravete, and the destruction of that place. However, before he could set about the matter he received a letter from a panicking Sir William Erskine, back at Almendralego with the rest of the division, with respect to the (false) approach of Soult; consequently Hill returned to Truxillo on 21 May. In the end, the bridge never was rebuilt, events in coming months overtaking its importance – the French abandoned it on 11 July. Whether Hill could have taken the castle, perched as it is on a precipitous sugar-loaf hill, having only howitzers, is open to doubt. What is not, is that as Wellington put it in his covering letter to Hill's Despatch:

> The communications from the bridges of Arzobisbo and Talavera to the Guadiana are very difficult, and cannot be deemed military communications for a large army. The result then of Lieutenant General Sir R. Hill's expedition has been to cut off the shortest and best communication between the armies of the south and of Portugal which, under existing circumstances, it will be difficult if not impossible to re-establish.

As Jac Weller points out 'Even squadrons of cavalry used to convey messages safely through the hostile Spanish countryside (now) took five days longer each way ... For all practical purposes Marmont's army was cut off from Soult's.'

Following immediately upon Hill's Raid, Lord Wellington put into effect another bridge operation which had been in his strategic contemplation for some months. The old Roman bridge at Alcantara had been out of use since Mayne blew down an arch three years before. It lay across the Tagus on the direct route between Badajoz and Rodrigo. Now that both of these places were in his hands, the more westerly crossing at Villa Velha would become less well-favoured, since via Alcantara there would be a saving of 100 miles, or six marches. At the end of May the broken arch was accordingly replaced by an ingenious rope and cable suspension, and this repair, together with the results of Hill's operation at Almaraz, gave Wellington a time advantage over the French (in moving troops from north to south or vice versa) of some ten or twelve marches. It is hard to see what more he need now do, prior to advancing into Spain, bar the throwing of smoke and sand into the eyes of his opponents.

CHAPTER 5

Maguilla, San Cristoval and the Salamanca Forts June 1812

Napoleon having extracted for Russia 27,000 men of his Guard and Polish regiments, the French had some 230,000 effectives in Spain with many more thousands in hospital, so that Wellington's 65,000 were outnumbered four to one (in that general but not very relevant sense). His narrower interest lay for now in Marmont's Army of Portugal, which was around 52,000 but much dispersed: Hill also being detached, his own strength would be some 47,000. So it would never do for Marmont to get too much larger. His Lordship accordingly endeavoured to arrange various entertainments, mostly to be staged by his Spanish allies, to engage the attentions of the nearest French armies, of Caffarelli (48,000) and Soult (54,000) (the Armies of the North and South respectively) and also of Suchet (60,000) away on the east coast.

Hill's 18,000, of course, already stood between Soult's Drouet D'Erlon and Marmont, and to encourage Soult himself to stay in his Seville fiefdom the Spanish General Ballesteros was activated, to great effect. Outnumbering Conroux two to one, he nearly won a famous victory on 1 June at Bornos, between Seville and Gibraltar. As a result, Soult sent south two brigades as reinforcements, whereupon a week later Hill moved threateningly forward to Zafra, then Llerena, achieving what Oman nicely calls 'The see-saw of alternative distraction', and which was his Lordship's precise Machiavellian purpose. For Soult now sent north a full infantry division and one of cavalry, still being convinced that Wellington, like the bogeyman, was coming to get him.

Before listing the other diversions contrived by Lord Wellington, it is proper to note a cavalry clash on 11 June following Hill's latest rattling of D'Erlon's bars. The affair near Maguilla was a curious and embarrassing episode. It involved two regiments of horse on either side (by far the best descriptive analysis is in Ian Fletcher's *Galloping at Everything*). A bare outline follows here, enough to allow some thoughts on the leadership involved.

Major General Sir John Slade's Heavy Brigade, which missed the action at Villagarcia, charged Lallemand's 17th Dragoons with his 1st (Royal) Dragoons, the 3rd Dragoon Guards initially being in second line. Outnumbered two to one, and after Villagarcia duly suspicious and therefore cautious, Lallemand and the 17th back-pedalled eight miles under pressure to the broken ground around Maguilla, where his second line regiment, the 27th Dragoons, stood waiting. Both Slade's regiments were now – after such a long pursuit – intermingled and, of course, blown, with only one squadron kept back as a support. Predictably, Lallemand's fresh reserve charged, the 17th's survivors turning to join the 27th, and, amazingly, Slade's troopers showed their backs to the French. That is, they legged it all the way for another eight miles. In this nightmare, Slade lost forty-eight killed and wounded, a shaming 118 being taken together with 127 horses – he lost half a regiment's worth. Lallemand's loss was just fifty-one (100 of the 17th Dragoons taken prisoner in the first lap, being released during the second).

The question is not why was Slade stupid enough to allow both regiments to charge, thus having no support to fall back upon when needed – Slade just was stupid – but rather why 700 stalwart British troopers turned their backs on 600 Frenchmen, an unheard of and incomprehensible act. It is possible that his Lordship missed the point in his subsequent volcanic letter of condemnation to Hill, to address merely the out-of-control charge and the lack of support:

> I have never been more annoyed than by General Slade's affair, and I entirely concur with you in the necessity of enquiring into it. It is occasioned entirely by the trick our officers of cavalry have acquired of galloping at everything, and their galloping back as fast as they gallop on the enemy. They never consider their situation, never think of manoeuvring before the enemy; so little that one would think they cannot manoeuvre, except on Wimbledon Common; and when they use their arm as it ought to be used, viz, offensively, they never keep nor provide for a reserve.
>
> All cavalry should charge in two lines, of which one should be in reserve; if obliged to charge in one line, part of the line, at least one third, should be ordered beforehand to pull up, and form in the second line, as soon as the charge should be given, and the enemy has been broken and has retired. The Royals and the 3rd Dragoon Guards were the best regiments in the cavalry in the country, and it annoys me particularly that the misfortune has happened to them. I do not wonder at the French boasting of it; it is the greatest blow they have struck.

Of course, he wrote on the eve of his long-planned offensive – the first since Talavera – and one going into good cavalry country. His righteous anger, therefore, erupted out of concern at such a time for the self-esteem or general morale of his mounted arm. But he writes as if no problem lay within the regiments concerned, only that of the tactics used in taking them forward. This does not address the question of why the 'best regiments in the cavalry in the country' turned their backs and ran from inferior numbers.

The Royals' historian, C. T. Atkinson, expressed a strong belief – understandably biased – that their morale at this time had been weakened by the misfortune of being under the command of Slade and Erskine. In particular Atkinson implies the growth of a form of nervousness, a sort of panic-struck reaction to the French:

> By fidgeting and worrying the men, and by disturbing and depressing them with false claims and unnecessary retreats, they [Slade and Erskine] had robbed them of their confidence and of their sense of superiority over their enemies ... Slade's responsibility lies less in his tactical errors on June 11th than on his undermining of the regiment's morale before the action, for which Erskine must share the blame.

Atkinson implies this was certainly the common view of the Royals' officers, as expressed in entries made in the regimental Journal:

> Nervous, excitable and irresolute, Erskine was in constant alarm of an attack on his cavalry screen. He 'would order picquets in every direction but that from which danger was to be expected', and then abuse Brigadiers, Staff officers and Colonels for not carrying out his express orders. The merest rumour of a French advance would make him decamp without waiting for it to be confirmed. Slade was equally liable to sudden alarms. 'No sooner was it announced that the French were in motion, no matter where or at what distance, than an order was given to turn out, Jack (Slade) running about crying out, 'Bridle up, bridle up. The first dozen men for God's sake. God damn you, trumpeters: blow, damn you. Haste, haste. Gallop. God damn you. Corporal, tell those fellows to turn out and never mind telling off. Turn out, turn out: the baggage to Azinshal.' The consequence was that all was confusion: curbs were lost, surcingles were forgot, some of the men threw away their corn, others in the act of cooking threw aside their tins and meat and camp-kettles, while the batmen with the baggage half-tied on, by dint of beating, urged stubborn brutes into a jog.

So at the end of an eight mile point 'at a time' admitted Slade in his report 'when we were in confusion', the cry of 'Look to the right! Look to the right!' spreading through the mingled, panting groups might well fall on overly sensitive ears. 'All was now confused. Every man turned and made to the rear, and for a few seconds the extraordinary sight was to be seen of two forces running away from each other' (Atkinson). But only briefly, for the pursued 17th quickly grasped that the flank appearance of their brethren in the 27th Dragoons had stopped the pursuit in its tracks, and they could contemplate revenge, which they cheerily did for the next eight miles.

All in all Maguilla was not only a bad day for the immediate reputation of the two regiments involved but, sadly thanks to his Lordship's slightly misdirected anger, it tarnished the reputation of British cavalry generally. The astonishing thing is that Wellington allowed Slade to continue in command of his brigade for a further year. No-one – certainly not this author – has ever been able to understand why he was so tolerant in this case, when frankly so intolerant in others.

That aside, returning to Wellington's distraction measures, he next arranged through a co-operative Castanos for General Abadia's 16,000 effectives in the Army of Galicia to march upon the isolated garrison in Astorga and into the plains of northern Leon. This would not only invite Marmont to send help but would also threaten Bonnet's division in the Asturias, and his com-munications with Marmont. And if Astorga could be said to cover Marmont's rear, Zamora seventy miles to the south covered his right flank: thither four Portuguese militia regiments under General Silveira were directed to cross the border and blockade its garrison. D'Urban was detached from Beresford's staff with a small cavalry brigade, to nanny the somewhat over-enterprising Silveira.

Next, a series of measures were put in hand aimed at Caffarelli's Army of the North, adjacent to Marmont and sitting on his communications back to France. The Spanish General Mendizabal was loosely in command of two irregular bands, each several thousands strong, under Porlier and Longa, together with smaller guerrilla groups under Marino, Salizar, Saornil and others, all operating either side of the Cantabrian Mountains; Mendizabal was to cause trouble generally for Caffarelli, and this he willingly did – including several daring raids down into Old Castille, one of which caused consternation to the Burgos garrison. Mainly, however, the contribution of the Spanish irregulars in the north was to be in conjunction with a British sea-based force of two marine battalions and a naval squadron under Admiral Sir Home Popham. The plan was for Mandizabal's local troops to descend from the hills to blockade each port garrison from the land side, while the Royal Navy battered it from the sea. The first such action, Gijon, was made on 17 June, precisely when Marmont's plea for reinforcements would be reaching the Army of the North. As we shall see, an alarmed Caffarelli sent nothing. He was too busy marching up and down the coast at 3 mph while Popham went with the winds.

We can finally touch on another arrangement: the landing of an expeditionary force from Sicily, under Sir William Bentinck, upon the coast of Valencia or Catalonia. As Sir William put it some months earlier to London, 'The occasional disembarkation at different points of a large regular force must considerably annoy the enemy, and create an important diversion for other Spanish opera-tions.' Wellington quickly seized upon the general concept, and turned the proposed destination from Corsica or Elba to Barcelona or Taragona; in May plans looked good for an allied force 17,000 strong complete with siege train to descend on Taragona on 3 June. In the event, unhappily for reasons that need not detain us here, only 7,000 landed, and then only at the very end of July. But, nevertheless, the rumours of a large force readying itself in Sicily and Majorca came to Suchet's ears in early June, and of the undoubted movement of the transports, succeeded in worrying him, and his concern – like Caffarelli's – was such that he sent no troops either to Soult or to Joseph in Madrid.

Equally unhappily, two more of Wellington's distraction plans were to go off at half-cock: Silveira's militias were slow to mobilise and the Galician army delayed its advance, having chosen a bad moment to change commanders. It would be early July before Astorga and Zamora felt the heat. But the overall success of Wellington's various arrangements was writ large in a letter sent to Marmont from Jourdan in Madrid, the day after he set his army in motion:

> Your letter of June 6th says that Wellington will soon fall upon you. But we have similar letters from Soult, declaring that the blow is to be delivered against him: he encloses two notes of June 2nd and 5th from General Daricau in Estremadura, declaring that 60,000 of the allies are just about to begin an invasion of Andalucia. We are too far off from the scene of operations to determine whether it is you or the Duke of Dalmatia who is deceived. We can only tell you, meanwhile, not to be misled by demonstrations.

Do not be misled indeed – but too late! For Wellington was closing on Salamanca, the outskirts of which he reached without incident after four easy marches, on 19 June. There he learnt that the city had already been evacuated by the two divisions located there, bar a garrison of 800 men in its three forts. For Marmont, his divisions dispersed seeking provisions, was furiously concentrating twenty miles the other side, on the Toro road. News of Wellington's advance had reached him on 14 June, and by the 19th five of his infantry divisions and two cavalry were all in hand, with Foy and Thomiere nearly there as well, with Bonnet still closing from the Asturias. He had 38,000 bayonets, 2,800 sabres and eighty guns, less Bonnet (who would add a further 6,500). He also had good reason to expect help from the Army of the North. In reply to letters in late May and early June querying the availability of reinforcements (before Marmont heard of Wellington's advance), Caffarelli gave him to understand he could free 7,000 bayonets, 1,000 sabres and twenty-two guns. This encouragement was received on 19 June, the day Marmont concentrated his Army.

Wellington thus seemed for the moment to have the edge with his 43,000 bayonets, especially his 3,500 cavalry, but one must make two caveats: the British and KGL contingent numbered only 28,000 or two-thirds of the whole, his 15,000 Portuguese being the other third. The behaviour of some Portuguese at Badajoz had been worrying. Further, two of his three most senior officers were about to leave. Picton, Graham and Beresford had commanded his three columns in the approach to Salamanca, but the former's unhealed wound from Badajoz turned to a debilitating fever and his 3rd Division had to be taken over on 28 June by Wellington's brother-in-law, Edward Pakenham; and Graham's eyesight deteriorated to the point where he was to be sent home for treatment. That raised the question of who would be second to Wellington's command? The question, no doubt, was of lively concern for his divisional commanders, still more for the staff at Headquarters, but seemed to concern his Lordship not one jot. He was certainly against an officer being sent out immediately and especially for such a potential role. His reference in a letter to Bathurst in London of 9 July 'Sir William Beresford is here (i.e. knew the form) and would naturally have a considerable influence in the conduct of the operations', constitutes a clear guide to the short-term succession. This remains a surprise for many of us, post Campo Major and Albuera.

The news of the departures of Picton and Graham came within a few weeks of the capture of Wellington's best intelligence officer, Colquhoun Grant, and within days of news that the earlier departure of his Chief of Staff, Major General Murray, was to be permanent. His Lordship was rarely daunted by events over which he had no control, but the loss of these four individuals was most unfortunate.

Marmont's determination to fight is indicated by the recall of Bonnet from the Asturias – not something he would rush to tell Napoleon – together with the swift orders to concentrate generally. It would, of course, have to be at a time and place of his choosing, for the relative strengths were not pleasing – especially in cavalry. His views were shared by his opposite number, even though at that stage Wellington had neither an expectation that Marmont would flout his Emperor with respect to Bonnet's 6,500, nor that Thomières would march in from Zamora and Astorga. Thus even without reinforcements being sent by Caffarelli or Joseph in Madrid, the numbers would be tight. As he wrote, 'Marmont will not risk an action unless he should have an advantage; and I shall certainly not risk one unless I should have an advantage; and matters therefore do not appear likely to be brought to that criterion very soon.'

The entry into Salamanca on 17 June was a scene of genuine rejoicing by the city's people. It was well recorded by Captain Andrew Leith Hay, 29th:

> Lord Wellington entered Salamanca about ten o'clock in the forenoon: the avenues to it were filled with people clamorous in their expressions of joy; nothing could be more animating than the scene. The day was brilliant, presenting all the glowing luxuriance of a southern climate. Upwards of fifty staff officers accompanied the British General; they were immediately followed by the 14th Dragoons and a brigade of artillery; the streets were crowded to excess; signals of enthusiasm and friendship waved from the balconies; the entrance to the plaza

was similar to a triumph; every window and balcony was filled with persons welcoming the distinguished officer to whom they looked for liberation and permanent relief ... At the same time, the 6th Division of British infantry entered the southwest angle of the square. It is impossible to describe the electric effect produced under these circumstances by the music; as the bands of the regiments burst in full tones on the ear of the people, a shout of enthusiastic feeling escaped from the crowd, all ranks seeming perfectly inebriated with exultation.

However, the entry was not via the old bridge across the Tormes, for three convents had been converted into forts, and garrisoned, and the two guns of one of these commanded the bridge. The cheers of the crowds

> Annoyed the French men a good deal, and they revenged themselves by firing at everyone they saw in the cross streets leading to their works ... [but] nobody seems to trouble their heads about them, and walk about the streets, men, women and children, in perfect safety and with the greatest unconcern. (William Warre).

An operation to capture the three forts was of course put in hand immediately, but strangely by two brigades of the 6th Division, which, apart from the 1st and 7th, was Wellington's only division not to have experience in the popular art of besieging. Since it was not to succeed for a long week, and during that time four miles away a major battle with the Army of Portugal only narrowly failed to ignite, we shall park the story of the forts for now, and return to them in due course.

For Wellington sent his army straight to a ridge beyond San Cristoval, out on the Torro road. When he found time to reconnoitre the ground is not known, but that part of Spain is not short of defensible ridges. It is clear from his deployment that he hoped Marmont would attack, as yet under-strength but anxious no doubt not to have to report to the Emperor the loss of a third major town and river crossing – to say nothing of the immense stores of provisions so recently abandoned. The 800-strong garrison of the three forts has been likened to bait, which might lure a rescue attempt forward into an ambush, concealed behind a reverse slope across his path. The British position was four miles long, running between San Cristoval and Cabrerizos on the Tormes. The ground was held from the right in the order of the 7th Division, then the 1st, 4th, the Light, the 3rd and on the left the two Portuguese brigades of Pack and Bradford. In reserve lay the 5th Division plus Hulse's brigade from the 6th, and Espana's 3,000 Spaniards. Alten and Ponsonby's light cavalry brigades covered the right and left flanks, with Le Marchant and Bocks' heavy brigades in reserve in the centre. The ground was open for miles, a treeless, shrubless, waterless plain stretching across to the next tributary of the

Tormes, and onto the next ridge beyond that. Wheat grew everywhere and was nearly ripe. Wheeler of the 51st noted how 'It is beautiful to look down on the enemy at night, the whole plain is covered with fires. The position we occupy is of vast importance, the enemy cannot see a single man of our army, except those who go up to the brow out of curiosity.' For this was a classic Wellington battle scene with battalions hidden on the reverse slopes, reminiscent in various ways of parts of Talavera and Busaco – not impregnable having open flanks, but a nicely obscured invitation to the blue columns.

And on 20 June, three blue columns were indeed reported advancing from Fuente Sauco, sixteen miles away. They came up in fine style during the afternoon, deploying to within a half cannon shot at the foot of the heights. 'Their light infantry pushed close to the position, and had an affair with ours from the 7th Division. There was considerable fire on both sides ... The cannonade both sides was sharp, but holding the commanding ground they suffered much more than we did' (Tomkinson). The village of Castalliano was taken, in front of the centre of the heights, and then at dusk an attempt was made on another village half a mile towards the river, called Morisco. Wellington had however posted the 7th's 51st (West Riding) and 68th (Durhams) there, who repulsed three attacks before being withdrawn during the night.

There is a nice picture drawn by Tomkinson of his assembled divisional commanders grouped around his Lordship on the crest above Castalliano, as darkness fell:

> Whilst standing receiving the orders, several round shot came amongst them, and one close to Lord Wellington, he having a map in his hand. Very little confusion was occasioned – his Lordship moved a few paces, and continued his directions. I was with Sir Stapleton, and close to Lord Wellington at the time.

But a much more interesting observation is contained in the Journal of Captain James Stanhope, 1st Guards, one of Graham's ADCs, who relates that while watching the assembled blue lines, several times Wellington was heard to say 'Damned tempting! I have a great mind to attack 'em.' Whether his temptation became a rumour amongst the ranks is not known, but Tomkinson attests he and his fellow officers felt 'The opportunity for an attack was so favourable, we all agreed Lord Wellington had some unknown reason for not availing himself of their situation.'

That he did not choose to attack Marmont was much regretted, it has been suggested, by most of his senior officers including Graham, Picton, Leith, Cotton and Pakenham, whilst the latter, in a letter to Sir George Murray on 24 August, blames Beresford's caution for contaminating the Peer:

> Marmont you know advanced a day or two after, and committed his people disparity by running slap up against our position which covered

the town and fort and where he remained for two days playing the bully. Had it not been for a certain Marshal (whose nerves latterly have been worse than ever) Marmont would have been lost the first night of his approach, but I believe everything has ended for the best.

Pakenham's low opinion of Beresford's post-Albuera caution was shared by one of Wellington's ADCs, Major Ulysses Burgh, who meeting the Marshal soon after Wellington decided to attack at Salamanca, tellingly said, 'Well, we are going to attack at last, and *you can't prevent it*'.

So why didn't Wellington attack? Well, while Marmont had only five divisions present that afternoon, which Oman credits with a strength of 18,000 bayonets and less than 2,000 cavalry, two more divisions were closing fast with another 10,000 men. Wellington's advantage would then be slim at about three to two with his 40,000 bayonets (British, Portuguese and Spanish) and 3,500 horse. Two unstated reasons for caution were, firstly, the political scenario in England, and the effect there of a defeat in Spain; and secondly the possible impetuosity of his troops in attack (Talavera and so many cavalry actions) which could again be their undoing. Set these against the near-certainty on that day, the 20th, that Marmont meant to attack him next morning, and the attractions therefore of a successful defensive battle would appear overwhelming. He wrote to Liverpool on 25 June):

> Between the 20th and 22nd, I had a favourable opportunity of attack-ing the enemy, of which, however, I did not think it proper to avail myself for the following reasons. First; it was probable he had advanced with an intention to attack us, and in the position which we occupied, I considered it advantageous to be attacked; and that the action would be attended by less loss on our side. Secondly; the operations against the forts of Salamanca took up the attention of some of our troops; and although I believe the superiority of numbers in the field was on our side, the superiority was not so great as to render an action decisive of the result of the campaign, in which we should sustain great loss. Thirdly; in case of failure, the passage of the Tormes would have been difficult, the enemy continuing in the possession of the forts, and commanding the bridge of Salamanca.

That his Lordship seemed certain Marmont would attack, is indicated by an observation made by Lieutenant John Cooke, 43rd:

> The Duke of Wellington was stationary from morning til night, watching the enemy, generally alone and on foot, at the crest of the hill, and in the centre of the position. His Staff approached him one at a time to receive orders. At night the Duke slept on the ground, wrapped in his cloak.

It would not surprise us if Cooke had added, say, 'throughout this time he lay with his ear pressed to the ground', so clearly can we picture a general eager to have his prayers answered.

But Marmont did not attack. Foy, Thomières and a dragoon brigade were not yet up – they were expected during the 21st – and Marmont would need every man and gun he had. That evening he called his divisional generals (including Foy and Thomières, who were now present) to a Council of War, that time-honoured refuge for commanders in a dilemma. We are fortunate to have Foy's Diary:

> At dusk on the 21st there was a grand discussion, on the problem as to whether we should or should not give battle to the English. The Marshal seemed to have a desire to do so, but a feeble and hesitating desire. Remembering Vimeiro, Corunna, and Bussaco, I thought that it would be difficult to beat the English, our superiors in number, on such a compact position as that which they were occupying. I had not the first word: I allowed Maucune, Ferey, and La Martinière to express their views, before I let them see what I thought. Then Clausel having protested strongly against fighting, I supported his opinion. Just because we had left a small garrison in the Salamanca forts, we were not bound to lose 6,000 killed and wounded, and risk the honour of the army, in order to deliver them. The troops were in good spirits, and that is excellent for the first assault: but here we should have a long tough struggle: I doubted whether we had breath enough to keep it up to the end. In short, I saw more chances of defeat than victory. I urged that we ought to keep close to the English, 'contain' them, and wait for our reinforcements; this could be done by manoeuvring along the left bank of the Tormes above and below Salamanca. Clausel and I set forth this policy from every aspect. The Marshal was displeased: he fancied that his generals were plotting to wreck his plan: he wanted to redeem the blunder which he saw that he had made in leaving a garrison in Salamanca: he dreads the Emperor and the public opinion of the army. He would have liked a battle, but he had not determination enough to persist in forcing it on.

So even with a bare majority for attack, Marmont's own inclination was not strongly enough held, and he very wisely held off. For who can doubt the outcome, had he pressed forward? The nature of the ground behind him and Wellington's eleven cavalry regiments must surely have seen a complete rout develop.

On the morning of the 22nd, Marmont spent some time on his left flank, reconnoitring the high ground beyond Aldea Rubia, to which he was thinking of withdrawing. He also moved close enough to the picquets for a brief but unsuccessful attempt at capture, by two squadrons. Wellington then sought to provoke him, once first light had passed without the anticipated action. He moved six howitzers (brought up from the town siege) and the 7th Division farther to the right, two KGL battalions pushing away the French picquets, and the 51st and 68th taking a feature 200 yards in front of Morisco village. Wheeler was with the 51st:

> As we advanced the shot whistled brisker, Sir Thomas was in front, he wheeled round his horse, and ordered us to deploy on the 1st Division. Sir Thomas sat with his back to the enemy shading his eyes with his cocked hat, watching the companies deploy. He expressed his satisfaction at the manner we had performed the move-ment. As our line passed him he said 'my lads you shall give them a taste of your steel directly.' We was soon within point blank distance of their line. Sir Thomas then gave the word double quick, in a moment thirty buglars was sounding the charge and off we dashed in double quick time with three cheers, and away went the enemy to the right about. We had now gained the ridge without discharging a single musket, our bugles sounded the 'halt' and 'fire'. Two of our guns, on our right, opened on them, at the same time about a dozen of our Cavalry shewed themselves. The sight of the Cavalry induced the enemy to form square, what a glorious opportunity this gave us to pepper them. There they were about 150 yards from us in a cluster like bees descending the hill. What between our fire and the fire of our guns they were knocked about like nine pins. Having now gained our object Sir Thomas ordered us to fall back a few paces and lay down to cover ourselves from a battery of 14 guns they had opened on us. We were now comparatively safe. The square behaved very well under so sharp a fire, although their punishment was great they retired in good order.

In this and the earlier confrontation, the 51st and 68th lost thirty-two men, and the KGL twenty-three. The 1st and Light Divisions were readied to act in support should Marmont take the bait, which he didn't, and nor did he counter-attack, being content to await what he presumably expected would be Wellington's own general attack. No doubt the preparatory movements of the 1st and Light supported this opinion.

And that was that. Next morning the French were gone, the wheat slopes denied a bloody fertiliser. The bait of rescuing the forts' garrisons had proved marginally inadequate, thanks to Foy and Clausel, and who no doubt were much relieved. The Peer on the other hand was much disappointed, and thus correspondingly impatient to finish with the forts. That night the 6th Division was ordered to assault them. And – probably – also that night the Duke of Ragusa was mulling over the Englishman's caution. Was it not encouraging that his opposite number – winner of so many set-piece defensive battles with his predecessors – that day had not risked an attacking battle? What was wrong with the man? Some say Marmont did not himself realise just how vulnerable he had been, for those hours under the San Cristoval ridge. If that were so, allied to his coming success in out-manoeuvring this hesitant Wellington up on the Duoro, there may be an over-confident foot hovering over a banana skin.

* * *

The episode of the three forts inside Salamanca city was frustratingly painful, in time and casualties. Both would have benefited had adequate artillery been available – it goes without saying adequate sappers and miners would never have been available, whatever the fore-knowledge. It is odd that his Lordship 'was mistaken in my estimate of the extent of the means which would be necessary to subdue these forts', for two reasons: firstly, according to Jones, the enemy 'had been employed for nearly three years in constructing these works, but with increased activity for the last eight or nine months'; and secondly that in this period Father Patrick Curtis, surely his most diligent spymaster, had been sending his intelligence gatherings from the Irish College not 500 steps from the three Catholic convents concerned, all the buildings around which having been demolished, to provide proper fields of fire, and the builders with ready-shaped masonry. Something like twenty acres had been flattened – it was said to be a quarter of the city. Yet Jones tells that prior to the first reconnaissance, the information regarding them had been limited 'to the extent that some convents had been fortified (together with) a confused sketch of the buildings by a Spaniard, not a military man.' There is reference in a letter from Edward Pakenham (26 June) to 'the under-estimating of the works by those who made the secret report, which was some months since.' The picture, there-fore, in Wellington's mind no doubt was of shaky medieval structures, possibly with walls having windows stopped up, some loop-holed, with embrasures knocked into the upper storeys etc. – but not overall presenting much of a defensive obstacle. Perhaps Curtis could not see the import of what lay under his nose.

Instead, using stone blocks and timbers readily available, walls had been doubled in thickness, protected by proper perpendicular masonry scarps, casemated counterscarps, deep ditches, palisades, bomb-proofs, bastions, and covered ways. The largest fort, San Vincente, abutted a steep cliff above the Tormes and stood on dominating ground. The two smaller, San Cayetano and La Merced, also on elevated ground, were separated by 250 yards of open ground and a deep ravine, the fire of each helping to protect the other. The smaller forts mounted six guns, two in La Merced which commanded the Roman bridge into the city, and thirty more guns with the better part of a company of artillery, in San Vincente. The three garrisons totalled some 800 men in six companies. These were not mere converted convents. An unidentified officer of I Troop, Royal Horse Artillery, (31st July) wrote, 'The Forts ... were very much superior in point of strength to the Fortress of Ciudad Rodrigo, and when we went through them [afterwards] we congratulated ourselves on getting them so cheaply.'

Wellington's 'Means ... to subdue these forts' comprised a measly four iron 18-pounders and three 24-pounder howitzers, with 100, and 200 rounds for each piece respectively; three engineer officers; nine artificers; and entrenching tools for 400 men. This pitiful arsenal had one redeeming feature: the howitzers were (according to Jac Weller) not the brass field piece but iron siege howitzers which could fire solid shot. Which meant, as we shall see, they could fire heated or hot shots, with turf wads placed between the heated balls and the powder.

Fire on the walls of San Vincente opened early on 19 June from two hastily built battery positions, but to little effect apart from consuming half the available ammunition. Next day two more howitzers arrived and part of the convent roof was brought down, but with only a dozen rounds left for each 18-pounder and thirty rounds each for the howitzers, the attack was suspended. This was the day Marmont moved forward to the San Cristobal ridge. On the 21st, when Ferey and Thomières had joined, Wellington had the five howitzers in the town taken forward to join the army on the ridge, and the iron 18-pounders were withdrawn from the city for safety, returning on the 23rd when Marmont marched away. They were placed in a new battery position and fire opened on the rear of Fort Cayetano. That night, without a breach but with a damaged parapet and palisades, it was stormed by escalade. Six light companies of Bowes' and Hulse's brigades in Clinton's 6th Division – new to sieges – ran into withering crossfire. Only two of the twenty ladders were placed. Neither was climbed, 'The undertaking was difficult, and the men seemed to feel it,' as Jones said. The prevailing view was summed up by Lieutenant Ross-Lewin, 32nd, who wrote that 'The result was precisely such as most of the officers anticipated – a failure attended with severe loss of life.' General Bowes was killed whilst encouraging his men, and another five officers and 120 men (a third of the assault party) were killed and wounded. Altogether it was a bloody shambles.

All the round shot having been expended, the next day (24 June) the guns and howitzers were again withdrawn from the batteries until, hearing an ammunition convoy was imminent, they were replaced the following day. Further saps were developed, including one on the 26th which approached along the side of the ravine; fire recommenced that afternoon, the howitzers lobbing hot shot; by sunset the tower of San Vincente and parts of the roof were ablaze. The garrison, however, managed to extinguish every outbreak. The hot shot fire continued during the night, so too the sapping, which approached the rear of Cayetano with a view to laying a mine, should the breaching not progress; and another sap from the side of the bridge came within twenty yards of the cliff, beneath La Merced, also to install a mine.

However, after another four hours hard artillery work during the morning of 27 June, the hot shot eventually created an inferno in San Vincente; at the same time the second storm attempt was ready, lined up in the ravine, to go at the now-practicable breach in the gorge behind Cayetano. The whole area swirling with smoke, the fire spread to the fort's immense store of timbers and gabions, and threatened the powder magazine. A white flag was hoisted on Cayetano's breach, the captain in command requesting a two-hour truce, during which he wished to confer with his colonel in San Vincente. He promised he 'Would anyway surrender at the end of the truce'. Sniffing prevarication, Wellington offered just five minutes to get his men out, or he would send in his stormers which, further haggling ensuing, he did. The garrison threw down their muskets. A similar process of white flag and warnings from and to San Vincente's garrison, saw its capture, with a total of nearly 600 unwounded prisoners (from the three forts).

Since this second attack was almost entirely bloodless, the 6th Division's loss over these ten days, which Oman puts at 430, was not excessive. Add on the fifty-five casualties in the bickering with Marmont around Morisco, and for the equivalent cost of one of his forty-six battalions, Wellington had taken a battalion's worth from Marmont, a major Spanish city and all that that entailed: a massive blow to French morale, delight for the Spanish, cheers in England and plenty of booty – engineers' stores, clothing, rations, powder, three dozen guns etc.

CHAPTER 6

The Affairs at Castrejon and Castillo and Parallel Marching
1–21 July 1812

Once the news of the surrender of the forts reached Marmont, he promptly withdrew north beyond the Douro. This clearance of the French from the whole of southern Leon – for the price of 500 men – could not last. What happened next was that Auguste, Duke of Ragusa, outfoxed Arthur, Earl of Wellington. Both men, however, had much to consider in the meantime.

On his Lordship's side it was all to do with numbers. That is, the chances of Marmont becoming stronger. On the latter's side, it was all to do with reinforcements, if and when and how many. For Marmont sought to spill English blood and the sooner the better. He wrote to King Joseph in Madrid on 1 July 'If only the necessary reinforcements, 1,500 horse and 7,000 foot, come to hand, the army of Portugal could take the offensive and with a certainty of success . . . and Salamanca recovered.' He knew Bonnet was on route, but would be a week or more – and then he would have his numbers up to parity with Wellington – unless, that is, Hill joined; but if only more would come! If men could march in from Caffarelli's army of the North, or from Madrid, or from Soult, or from Suchet he could take the offensive with superiority. For the moment he held a twenty-mile line of the Douro, controlling the fords and bridges between Pollos in the west, Tordesillas in the centre and Simancas to the east. The fords near Pollos belonged to him. Wellington sat opposite with the 3rd Division, Pack's and Bradford's Portuguese brigades, Espana's 3,000 Spanish, and the heavy brigades of Le Marchant and Bock on the left around Pollos. The Light, 4th, 5th and 6th Divisions held from opposite Tordesillas to Puente Duoro opposite Simancas. Alton's cavalry were up on the river line, and Anson's were across to the right. The 1st and 7th Divisions were the reserve, ten miles back around Medina del Campo.

With no way to cross the river bar at Pollos, and hearing on 4 July that Bonnet was but two long marches from Valladolid, Wellington was determined not to fight an action in any disadvantageous situation, especially at a time when he also was catching rumours that Marmont was expecting a division from

Caffarelli. On 9 July he learnt of Bonnet's arrival a couple of days earlier, and four days later that 'The King [is] collecting a large force at Madrid, especially cavalry ... [I am] apprehensive that after all the enemy will be too strong for me'.

On 13 July he wrote to Bathurst:

> It is obvious that we could not cross the Duoro without sustaining great loss, and could not fight a general action under circumstance of greater disadvantage ... The enemy's numbers are equal, if not superior, to ours: they have in their position thrice the amount of artillery that we have, and we are superior in cavalry alone – which arm (it is probable) could not be used in the sort of attack we should have to make.

It was all rather disappointing. He had worked hard to galvanise his Spanish ally into actions which, had they worked in time and with proper effort, would have meant neither Foy nor Bonnet would have marched. The so-called siege of Astorga by the Spanish Army of Galicia under Santocildes, a place held only by three of Thomières' battalions, was conducted in a leisurely way by some 11,000 men and no siege guns, whilst only a detachment of 3,800 had exploited the absence of the French to reach the line of the Esla, and towards Benevente to the south and east. Wellington had hoped for a much greater weight to flood across the northern Leon plain, to force Marmont to guard this flank and his rear. Astorga was to remain intact until the middle of August!

This lack of pressure was in contrast to the 800 Portuguese cavalry under D'Urban, free-running north of the Douro, west and above Toro. Sadly, the Portuguese militia under Silveira, with whom they were meant to be co-operating, was not applying the agreed force against the garrison of Zamora. Only half the militia had even mobilised by 8 June, with little transport.

So when Wellington wrote to London on 9 June, in part explaining why he had not crossed the Douro to challenge Marmont, he said 'It would not answer to cross the river at all in its present [swollen] state, unless we should be certain of having the co-operation of the Galician troops.' He had assumed by the time the river was practicable, Astorga would have been taken and Santoclides would have been well advanced. Well, not for a month and a half yet, your Lordship.

The deadlock continued. On the ground life north of the Douro was altered for the worse for hundreds of French junior infantry officers, doctors, commissaries, sutlers and anyone with a riding horse: they were requisitioned, to mount horseless cavalry troopers. In this move Marmont increased his sabre strength from 2,200 to 3,200. But the price, apart from disgruntling so many junior officers, was that maybe one in four or five of Marmont's cavalry thus would be largely untrained to squadron and regimental drills, and individual close combat.

Also at this time of inaction, with the river Douro drawing small watering parties from both sides, as well as vedettes and picquets, there had developed a degree of fraternisation. William Grattan's 88th participated:

> The French and British lived upon the most amicable terms. If we wanted wood for the construction of huts, our men were allowed to pass without molestation to the French side of the river to cut it. Each day the soldiers of both armies used to bathe together in the same stream, and an exchange of rations, such as biscuit and rum, between the French and our men was by no means uncommon. A stop was, however, soon to be put to this friendly intercourse; and it having been known in both armies that something was about to be attempted by Marmont, on the evening of the 12th of July, we shook hands with our vis-à-vis neighbours and parted the best friends. The French officers said to us on parting, 'We have met, and have been for some time friends. We are about to separate, and may meet as enemies. As "friends" we received each other warmly – as "enemies" we shall do the same.'

The above exchanges were between troops of the French 7th Division (Thomières') and those of the British 3rd Division (Pakenham's). In a fortnight, fifty miles to the south, the latter were effectively to destroy the former.

Kincaid and the 95th were at Rueda, half in the town, and half the battalion bivouacked towards the river. The Light Division obviously continued its light-hearted customs: the town

> Abounded in excellent wines, and our usual evening dances began there to be graced by a superior class of females to what they had hitherto been accustomed. I remember that, in passing the house of the sexton one evening, I saw his daughter baking a loaf of bread; and I fell desperately in love with both her and the loaf.

The deadlock was blown open on 12 July with the late delivery to Marmont of a despatch from Madrid – albeit one which, thanks to the activities of the guerrillas around Segovia, had taken twelve days to travel 150 miles – and in which Jourdan urged Marmont to take the offensive. 'His Majesty would like you to take advantage of the moment, when Wellington has not all his forces in hand,' meaning Hill's 18,000, last heard of advancing against Drouet D'Erlon. The same letter held out no hope of reinforcements, instead concentrating wrongly on reports that Wellington had only 18,000 British troops and 'If this is so, you are strong enough to beat his army'. If Hill rejoined, that would be a different matter and if so 'You must avoid an action as long as possible, in order to pick up the reinforcement that will certainly reach you in the end'. For by 9 July Madrid was suddenly more alert to the situation, and scrambling to create help. On the 13th Wellington had received a captured letter telling

Marmont that Joseph was scraping together 14,000 men. This certainly was news he could do without, and apprehensions grew next day, with considerations of what might or might not come from Caffarelli, or from Drouet D'Erlon, or from Madrid, or from Suchet (having learned to his fury that Bentinck had changed his mind). Napier is right to suppose therefore the Peer's head at this time 'Was filled with care and mortification and all cross and evil circumstances seemed to combine against him.'

Probably with some relief, then, he heard rumours, then positive reports, not only that repair work on the French bridge at Toro begun five days earlier still continued, but that there was growing troop movement towards that place. Foy and Bonnet were there late on 15 July; the divisions in the centre of the French line along the Douro, about the fords at Pollos, shifted towards Toro; and those on their left wing near Tordesillas likewise towards Pollos. Marmont was on the move and no mistake. Next morning Foy and Thomières crossed the river at Toro and set off south down the road towards Salamanca. Marmont was now arguably nearer to that place than his enemy, which meant the allied communications were naked. Wellington learned this about 7pm and promptly confirmed the warning order he had issued at 7am, to move west to a pre-planned defensive line along the river Guarena centred on Canizal and Castrillo. Cotton with the Light, 4th and Anson, however, halted ten miles earlier around the river Trabancos, to act as rearguard in case some French had crossed higher up, at Tordesillas. The marching filled the anxious night hours of 16/17 July.

The morning, however, brought confusing reports. First, that the enemy had halted. Then that they had re-crossed the river and broken the bridge behind them. Then – nothing, throughout the day, until late that evening came astonishing news, brought to Wellington now at Toros: Marmont and his army were four miles from the river Trabancos, Sir Stapleton Cotton and the Light and 4th Divisions! He was at Nava Del Rey, just ten miles south-west of Tordesillas! Lord Wellington had been humbugged!

Forty miles had some French divisions marched in the night, counter-marching from Toros back to Tordesillas and re-crossing the Douro there, or taking a shortcut via the Pollos fords, pushing on to Rueda (which his Lordship's headquarters had quit only fifteen hours earlier) and then sinking exhausted at Nava. It was a remarkable demonstration of French marching power, and nicely repaid Wellington for his own surprise crossing of the same river three years earlier, against Soult. Marmont now could easily cut off Cotton's 5,200 foot and 1,000 horse and destroy them next day, almost at his leisure.

The French feint to Toros had been masterly. To cross there was entirely reasonable and believable, as was Wellington's anticipated reaction, designed to block the Salamanca road and secure his rearward communications. Wellington could do no other. At the mild cost of worn boots Marmont had levered the

British army from the river, creating space to make an unopposed crossing. And, as so often, fortune favoured the bold. For it also created an unplanned windfall opportunity to leap upon two isolated British divisions. If Marmont could move his stiff and footsore men early on 8 July, a great prize lay adjacent, just down the road.

Wellington had to get Cotton back, away from his vulnerable position. As ever, he rode like the wind to get the business done in person. He sent Leith's 5th Division three or so miles forward of his main line on the Guarena, to Torecilla. This was halfway to Castrejon, where lay Cotton on the Trabancos. He took with him the five heavy dragoon regiments, and the two light regiments – of Bock, Le Marchant and Victor Alten, arriving with Cotton at 7am. Cotton's own cavalry, George Anson's three (11th, 12th and 16th) light dragoon regiments, had already clashed with the first probing French patrols before Castrejon. Tomkinson of the 16th rode out with a six-man patrol:

> I had scarcely got beyond our picquets when I met a squadron of the enemy's cavalry. More were coming up, and in half an hour the picquets were driven back on Castrejon, and from the number of squadrons shown by the enemy, it was evident they were in force, and advancing. I joined one of the 11th, and with them retired on the brigade. We were a good deal pressed, and once obliged to turn round and charge. The enemy's cavalry all appeared on the plain in front of Castrejon, and on seeing the brigade, halted their guns and ammunition and commenced a cannonade. Our squadrons were fortunately dispersed over the ground, and at first did not suffer much. Major Bull's and another troop came up and opened against the enemy. Captain Buchanan was absent, which gave me the centre squadron. I was sent with it to cover three guns of Major Bull's troop, and with my own troop moved forward and drove some of the enemy's skirmishers off a small hill, on which the guns were to act; leaving the other troops at the foot of the hill, covered from the enemy's fire ... On the left, two squadrons, one of the 11th and 12th, were supporting two guns from Major Ross's troop. The squadrons were supporting one another, and on the advance of some of the enemy's cavalry (inferior to the two squadrons), the one in front went about. Some of Marshal Beresford's staff seeing this, conceived the guns were in danger, rode up to the retiring squadron, calling 'Threes about!' This of course put the other squadron about in the place of the fronting one already retiring. One person gave one word, one another, and the enemy's cavalry came up to the guns.

And what was Beresford and his staff doing, up the sharp end? The Light Division had picquets forward, beyond Castrejon. Kincaid commanded one of them and explains the reference to Beresford's staff:

There arose all at once behind the rising ground to my left a yell of the most terrific import; and, convinced that it would give instantaneous birth to as hideous a body, it made me look with an eye of lightning at the ground around me; and, seeing a broad deep ditch within a hundred yards, I lost not a moment in placing it between my picquet and the extraordinary sound. I had scarcely effected the movement when Lord Wellington, with his staff and a cloud of French and English dragoons and horse artillery intermixed, came over the hill at full cry, and all hammering at each others' heads in one confused mass over the very ground I had that instant quitted. It appeared that his Lordship had gone there to reconnoitre, covered by two guns and two squadrons of cavalry, who by some accident were surprised and charged by a superior body of the enemy and sent tumbling in upon us in the manner described. A picquet of the forty-third had formed on our right, and we were obliged to remain passive spectators of such an extraordinary scene going on within a few yards of us, as we could not fire without an equal chance of shooting some of our own side. Lord Wellington and his staff, with the two guns, took shelter for the moment behind us, while the cavalry went sweeping along our front, where, I suppose, they picked up some reinforcement, for they returned almost instantly in the same confused mass; but the French were now the flyers; and I must do them the justice to say that they got off in a manner highly creditable to themselves. I saw one in particular defending himself against two of ours, and he would have made his escape from both, but an officer of our dragoons came down the hill and took him in flank at full speed, sending man and horse rolling headlong on the plain.

I was highly interested all this time in observing the distinguished characters which this unlooked-for turn-up had assembled around us. Marshal Beresford and the greater part of the staff remained with their swords drawn and the Duke himself did not look more than half-pleased, while he silently despatched some of them with orders. General Alten and his huge German orderly dragoon, with their swords drawn, cursed the whole time to a very large amount, but, as it was in German, I had not the full benefit of it. He had an opposition swearer in Captain Jenkinson of the artillery, who commanded the two guns and whose oaths were chiefly aimed at himself for his folly, as far as I could understand, in putting so much confidence in his covering party that he had not thought it necessary to unfix the catch which horse-artillerymen, I believe, had to prevent their swords quitting the scabbards when they are not wanted, and which, on this occasion, prevented their jumping forth when they were so unexpectedly called for.

Not far from Kincaid's riflemen were five companies of Napier's 43rd, Lieutenant John Cooke (fortunately for us) being one of his officers. We have been much indebted to Cooke (as indeed was Napier, who used his *Memoirs* as a source) for his animated descriptions of the fighting at both Rodrigo and Badajoz. The following extract presents charming images not only of the Peer 'straight sword drawn ... crossed the ford at full speed ... smiling ... quite alone', but also of Cooke's men showing proper concern for their company mule, and their breakfast tea. More importantly, we get a clear picture of the confusion caused by Marmont's advancing cavalry, and the collective efforts of the Light Division's infantry, cavalry and artillery to stem the tide.

At break of day on the 18th, a few shots were exchanged to our right. The firing increased, and as the sun rose above the horizon, the cheering might be distinctly heard at intervals. Our dragoons became visible while retiring before the enemy's horse and light artillery, which at intervals were blazing away. The scene was sublime and beautiful. An officer said to me 'There will be a row this day; we had better get our breakfast, as God knows when we shall have anything to eat.'

The tea service was laid out and a stubble fire kindled to warm the bottom of the kettle. Suddenly we espied some squadrons of French heavy dragoons in a valley to our right. They were pushing for the main road at full trot. An absurd and ludicrous scene now took place. Into the hampers was thrown the crockery and also the kettle half filled with hot water.

'God bless me!' vociferated another officer, who had come from the rear to have breakfast with us. 'You will not desert my mule and hampers, they are worth 400 dollars!' To get off seemed impossible, but the company formed column of sections and fixed bayonets, fully determined to cover the old mule, who went off with a rare clatter and we after him in double-quick time. The enemy were within 200 yards of us, brandishing their swords and calling out, then they saw some of our cavalry hovering on their right flank and drew up.

A rivulet with steep banks ran parallel with the road, but we soon found a ford where we halted, intending to dispute the passage. The Right [1] Brigade had moved forward and deployed to the succour of our dragoons first engaged, about half a mile to our right. Two squadrons of our light dragoons then formed on a rising ground 200 yards from us, with two pieces of horse artillery on their right. About an equal number of French heavy cavalry, handsomely dressed with large fur caps, made rapidly towards them while our guns threw round shot at them. Within 100 yards of our squadrons, they drew up to get wind; our dragoons remaining stationary.

he victor of Salamanca: Arthur Wellesley, st Duke of Wellington. After Salamanca he vas created Earl Wellington. This image was ainted in 1814 by Sir Thomas Lawrence.

Marshal Auguste de Marmont, defeated by Wellington at Salamanca. He was wounded badly in the course of the battle and the French command passed to Bertrand Clausel.

eneral Bertrand Clausel who took over ommand from the wounded Marmont lthough injured himself. He conducted a kilful withdrawal of the French army from alamanca and was later to knock Wellington ack at Burgos.

General Maximilien Sébastien Foy. A divisional general he covered the retreat of the French army from Salamanca and later in the year at Burgos, when Wellington had raised the siege, he took prisoners and artillery from the British army as it retired to the Douro.

Richard Caton Woodville's depiction of the storming of Badajoz by the 88th Connaught Rangers, the 'Devil's Own'. The defenders were from the French 88th Ligne and the painting is an accurate illustration of the storming of a fortress.

Salamanca. Sir Edward Pakenham's 3rd Division charges General Jean Guillaume Thomières's division in the course of the battle. Thomières was wounded fatally during the battle and is commemorated on the Arc de Triomphe in Paris.

Salamanca. An etching by J. Clarke shows Wellington issuing orders.

A modern image of the central area of the battlefield. This is where the 2nd Battalion of the 44th (East Essex) Regiment captured the Imperial Eagle of the 62^e Ligne.

Looking east to west across the Salamanca battlefield.

Another view of the battlefield.

The Greater Arapile.

Salamanca. The battlefield chapel.

alamanca. The site of the forts.

alamanca. The main bridge.

Salamanca. A view from the British positions across to the French.

François Joseph Heim's image of the siege of Burgos. This was Wellington's only rebuff in 1812 and he raised the siege and withdrew his army across the Douro.

A French officer, the chef d'escadron, to beguile a few moments while his squadron obtained a little breathing time, advanced and invited our people to charge. Holding his sword on high, and crying 'Vive l'Empereur! En avant, Francais!' he rushed on, followed by his men, and overthrew our dragoons. Fortunately, the guns had limbered up, and the horse artillery fought round them with great spirit. The enemy tried to cut the traces, but the drivers held down their heads, and sticking their spurs into the horses' sides, passed the ford under cover of our picquet.

Our company was formed up fronting the right flank of our dragoons, so we had an admirable view of the space between the combatants. The soldiers of the company had made ready, holding their firelocks horizontally at the charging position, but to have fired would have been unchivalrous. It would have destroyed the valiant French officer who, though our enemy, was an honour to his country. The Earl of Wellington was in the thick of it, and escaped with difficulty. His straight sword drawn, he also crossed the ford at full speed, smiling. I did not see his lordship when the charge first took place. When he passed us, he had none of his staff near him; he was quite alone, with a ravine in his rear.

The French squadron commander who so nearly re-arranged the allied command structure, by the way, was warmly admired not only by Cooke, but also by his fellow officers James Fergusson and George Hennell. None of their soldiers would fire either on this French officer or his troopers. 'Our men ... were anxious that these few gallant fellows should escape ... a brave soldier always admires dashing and bold conduct in his opponent.'

If we assume Cotton, as local commander, attended his superior on his flying visit, we can conjure here a nightmare scenario, wherein Wellington, Beresford and Cotton were all killed or taken by the rampaging French squadron. Which prompts the question, just who was the next senior general after Cotton?

Whoever in such chaos took over, the word would have been the same the Peer himself gave: withdraw. Cooke of the 43rd describes the march:

Our Division was obliquely to the rear, in column of quarter distance, with fixed bayonets ready to form square, surrounded by large bodies of our cavalry. Six companies of the 2nd battalion of Rifles, just arrived from England, joined us on the retreat. To avoid an action seemed impossible. The enemy's infantry were almost on the run, and we were marching away from them as hard as we could. While the round shot from a flank fire flew over us, a French division came running to engage and detain us until others came up. They obliged us to abandon the road and trample down a tract of wheat. The heavy German cavalry drew close around us.

The country was open, and a vast sheet of corn enveloped us for many miles. The men became much distressed owing to the rapidity of the movements and the heat of the day. Owing to our numerical superiority of cavalry, which made a curve down a gentle descent, we were able to regain the road. Near Castrillo, the men descried, at a short distance, a dirty meandering stream called the Guarena. A buzz ran through the ranks that water was at hand, and the soldiers were impelled forward, their eyes staring, their mouths open. Within 50 yards of the stream, a general rush was made. I never saw the troops so thirsty. This took place under a cannonade which had continued, at intervals, for more than ten miles.

Napier was commanding the 43rd:

The cavalry were on the flanks and rear, the air was extremely sultry, the dust rose in clouds, and the close order of the troops rendered it very oppressive, but the military spectacle was exceedingly strange and grand. For then were sent the hostile columns of infantry, only half musket-shot from each other, marching impetuously towards a common goal, the officers on each side pointing forwards with their swords, or touching their caps, and waving their hands in courtesy, while the German cavalry, huge men, on huge horses, rode between in a close compact body as if to prevent a collision. At times the loud tones of command, to hasten the march, were heard passing from the front to the rear, and now and then the rushing sound of bullets came sweeping over the columns whose violent pace was continually accelerated.

Thus moving for ten miles, yet keeping the most perfect order, both parties approached the Guarena, and the enemy seeing that the light division, although more in their power than the others, were yet outstripping them in the march, increased the fire of their guns and menaced an attack with infantry. But the German cavalry instantly drew close round, the column plunged suddenly into a hollow dip of ground on the left which offered the means of baffling the enemy's aim, and ten minutes after the head of the division was in the stream of the Guarena between Osmo and Castrillo. The fifth division entered the river at the same time but higher up on the left, and the fourth division passed it on the right. The soldiers of the light division, tormented with thirst, yet long used to their enemy's mode of warfare, drunk as they marched, and the soldiers of the fifth division stopped in the river for only a few moments, but on the instant forty French guns gathered on the heights above sent a tempest of bullets amongst them. So nicely timed was the operation.

The Light and 5th had joined the main army on the heights of Canizal, the 1st and 7th were above the ford at Olmo as the right wing, and the 4th extended the left near Castrillo. The 4th Division was closely followed by Marmont's northern column under Clausel, who tried to bump Cole's men off the hill whilst they were still settling positions. He sent General Carrie with two dragoon regiments (the 15th and 25th) right handed, to cross the Guarena by fords, but which were overseen by Victor Alten's brigade; the French 6th Division under Brigadier Taupin at the same time crossed at Castrillo and put in a frontal attack. The allied infantry were directed personally by his Lordship, as ever on the spot. Faced by three regimental columns, each two companies wide i.e. battalion behind battalion, the 27th and 40th formed one line, each having a Portuguese battalion in close column on their open flank; the allied line being some four times wider than the French, their fire lapped around the deploying columns. In this typical line versus column affair, the exhausted blue coats quickly went about.

> The enemy stood and fired little. They were very firm until within fifty or sixty paces, when our fellows gave them the bayonet with cheers, routed the column and left the French with about eighty dead and one hundred prisoners besides wounded. Our men charged at too great a distance, their ranks were a confusion and they were so breathless and exhausted when they came up with the French, that they could scarcely use the bayonet. (Lieutenant Thomas Browne, 23rd.)

Both Clausel and Carrie were repulsed (the latter being captured) with losses totalling possibly 800 men. Alten had watched and waited for Carrie to cross and form up, before sweeping down the hillside, taking nearly 100 prisoners, and causing another sixty casualties. It was neatly done. His 14th Light Dragoons and 1st Hussars KGL then rode on to herd back more prisoners from the failed infantry attack – six officers and 240 men, and harried Taupin's retreat across the river. Alten lost 138 men, and with a trifling loss in the 3rd Dragoons, who also helped (some say came to their rescue). The same number of casualties applied to the 3rd/27th (Inniskillings) and 1st/40th (Somersets) from Anson's brigade.

In this affair at Castrillo, the lapping of the thin red line around the blue column sounds similar to Solignac's brigade climbing the east hill near Vimiero in 1808, to be met by Ferguson's brigade. (The 1st/40th (Somersets) were present on both occasions.)

It had been a long night and day for both sides, the British being the fresher. Marmont wisely chose to rest his men during the heat of the remains of the day, sensing perhaps that Taupin's regiment had exhibited the plain exhaustion felt by everyone. He had every reason to be pleased, however. Not only had he levered open and crossed a bridge guarded the previous day by four British divisions, he had very nearly cut off two of them. Wellington too showed his accomplishments: forethought in preparing the Guarena line as a fall-back position, and resolution and leadership in extricating the 4th and Light, whose discipline on the march back evoked memories of Fuentes D'Onoro.

At some point during Sunday 19 July, while his tired men rested under the scorching sun, Marmont came to an easy decision: not to attack his enemy. He would again rely upon his swift marching pace, and try his luck on the open plain to the south-west. The river Tormes ran in a right-angled loop through the far side of the plain, and ten miles along the western curve lay the city of Salamanca. Beyond that lay the main road to Ciudad Rodrigo. Since both the city and the road were important to his enemy, his apparently defensive-minded enemy, the more ground Marmont could make, the more likely Lord Wellington might therefore be encouraged to fall back to guard his new posses-sions. He could not possibly allow Marmont to sit on his line of communication, along which flowed sustenance of all natures. That, said Wellington to Earl Bathurst two days later, 'would distress us very materially' especially since 'The wheat harvest in Castille has not yet been reaped, and even if we had the money, we could not now procure anything from the country.' That is, without copy-ing the French and laying waste 'whole districts for a scanty subsistence of unripe wheat'. So Marmont's instincts were surely right. Wellington would not willingly fight, but the road to Rodrigo might force a confrontation on him, to Marmont's advantage.

The blue regiments fell in at 4pm and marched a few miles south near Terazona. On his side of the Guarena, Wellington could only side-step likewise, onto the tableland beyond Vallesa and there he got ready for the night. Napier was able to look down onto the French bivouac fires, and was clearly aghast when earlier the peace had been disturbed by 'Sir Stapleton Cotton coming up ... ordered Captain Ross to turn his battery of six pounders upon a group of French officers ... in a few minutes a reply from twelve eight pounders showed the folly of provoking a useless combat' and which resulted in enough casualties to cause the Light Division to 'withdraw several hundred yards in a mortifying manner'. Cooke tells us it was Marmont himself Cotton had spotted. As the Division withdrew from the counter-fire, the handful of Spanish who had been enlisted only weeks earlier into the British regiments started 'from the left ... I never saw them again ... and the flight in disorder of these patriots was ludicrous'.

The 20th dawned fine and promised a blistering sun. The red regiments stood to, an hour before first light. Like many others, Private Green, 68th

> Expected that in a few minutes we should have been sharply engaged; but instead of this, the enemy broke camp, formed column, and marched to a ridge of hills, their bands and drums playing as though they were going to a general field-day. I saw the head of their column

ascend the hill and march in the direction of Ciudad Rodrigo. We marched in two lines parallel to them.

Lord Wellington apparently agreed with Private Green that Marmont would cross the Guarena and take issue there and then, and every preparation was made for the expected action on the plain of Vallesa. Wellington moved his lines forward to the bank of the Guarena ravine, and even sent a brigade of cavalry halfway up the French ridge opposite to 'entice them to show front and to develop their movements'. (Cooke) But to no avail. The two fighting lines of the allied army were turned smartly to the right and stepped off after Marmont, bands and drums hard at it in musical competition, the wives and other baggage settling into the rear, ahead of them twenty long miles of sun, dust and occasional cannonading. In every soldier's usual search to keep the high ground, Marmont headed south-east initially towards Cantalpiedra, before switching south-west towards Cantalpino, from which ran the good road to the bridge over the Tormes at Huerta.

The allied army's (now) three columns, comprised (nearest the French) the 1st, 4th, 5th and Light Divisions; the centre was the 6th and 7th Divisions together with Pack's and Bradford's Portuguese brigades; the outside column was the 3rd Division and Espana's Spanish. The light cavalry led, the heavies followed at the rear and D'Urban's small Portuguese cavalry brigade shepherded the baggage and stragglers. Across the Guarena the French were marching a mirror image, in two columns, each of four divisions and, like the British, their light cavalry were in the van, all the heavies at the rear. Simply by wheeling left or right, each army could show front and be ready to engage.

As the day wore on the red and blue columns converged slightly following the westerly turn of the French. It was a memorable scene, especially for those in the inner columns – the others probably saw little through the long dust clouds. Marmont's *Memoires* said he had never in all his long service seen such a magnificent spectacle: a parallel march of over 80,000 men, sometimes a few hundred yards apart. 'At times,' said the 88th's Grattan 'the French and British were within musket shot of each other: the soldiers of both in momentary expectation of being engaged, yet not one shot was fired by either.' John Aitchison, 3rd Guards, wrote:

> As the enemy continued to advance on the high ground the British army moved forward on the road in a parallel direction and for the space of three hours there were the most beautiful movements perhaps ever witnessed of two armies of 40,000 men each trying to arrive at a certain point first.

And that really was the object. Marmont was trying – and succeeding – to out-march Wellington, to win a tactical success by manoeuvre without fighting, just as he had on the Douro. He achieved this aim some way past the village of

Cantalpino, where the two columns had looked set to converge. The light cavalry and Henry Campbell's 1st Division had just cleared the village, Cole's 4th Division following closely on, when Marmont brought several batteries into action against the leading battalion. Cole's orders from the Peer were to not respond, but with a swerve to the south-west to skirt the village, away from the cannonading. The entire allied army conforming, and Marmont continuing south and south-west, in effect Wellington had stepped off the dance floor. Marmont was left free to do what he liked. The remaining afternoon passed with the march ceasing to be parallel, widening until contact was lost. Wellington had decided to spend the night on the nearest defensible position which lay around Cabeza Vellosa and Aldea Rubia. Marmont himself had chosen these features when he withdrew from before the San Cristoval ridge, so he knew their strength. But he really wasn't interested in being drawn north or west. His choice for the night was Villa Ruela and Babila Fuente, which latter place was just two miles from the fords over the Tormes at Huerta and Encinas. Thanks to his Lordship's decision, it was a fine end to a tiring day – at least twenty miles at speed, and that following four similar marches. Marmont was now in a position effectively beneath Wellington's southern flank. One more rapid march would surely force a battle, or the abandonment of Salamanca, and put Marmont across Wellington's communications with Portugal.

His Lordship, who believed the French to be much exhausted and unlikely to make the Tormes, was said to be furious. 'Lord Wellington was amazingly angry when he found that the enemy had reached the river, and I believe that if there had been more daylight he would have attacked them then.' (Charles Cathcart to Graham, 21 July.)

He would have been even angrier if he had known that the previous afternoon, the Spanish battalion guarding the bridge in Alba de Tormes had been withdrawn by a nervous Espana; it would be two days before that guilty gentleman deigned to break the news, with what effect we shall see.

Earlier on 21 July the allied army marched to the San Cristoval ridge. We have already quoted part of the letter his Lordship wrote that day to Bathurst, concerning the vital importance pre-harvest of the allied supply lines from Rodrigo. He expressed also the impossibility of turning the tables, since the ability of his foe to live off the land meant he had no supply lines to cut. He also re-iterated that no battle should be fought unless 'The army would be able to maintain the field, while those of the enemy should not.' Thus it seems clear that abandoning Salamanca and withdrawing to Rodrigo was now an active option.

Marmont also was pondering, but his hesitation ceased when news arrived of the abandoned bridge at Alba. His orders were issued at 10am to march south to that place, to cross the Tormes, and to deploy back towards the north. Foy and Clausel persuaded him rather to cross immediately at Huerta, with no time loss and with less chance of interference. At noon the crossings began, a rearguard division left to face Wellington at Babila Fuente, and subsequently a second at Huerta. By last light his cavalry and Foy's light troops reached Calvarrasa de Arriba, on the Alba-Salamanca road, and which lay a little to the east of the chapel of Nuestra Senhora de la Pena. The individual divisions bivouacked in the woods to the south-east. Wellington had received cavalry reports of the gradual build-up west of the river throughout the first part of the day, having remained static that morning, and thus allowing his troops to rest. In the afternoon he crossed in two columns over the fords at Cabrerizos and Santa Marta, leaving Pakenhan's 3rd Division and D'Urban's Portuguese cavalry near Cabrerizos, should any threat appear down the right bank of the Tormes. By nightfall he had his early warning outposts adjacent to the French: British cavalry held Calvarrasa de Abajo and Pelabravo, with light troops up around the Chapel. The mass of infantry was behind the three mile ridge running down from Santa Marta, facing the ravine of a small stream called the Pelagarcia. Below the high ground lay the village of Los Arapiles.

That evening Wellington heard of the passage the previous day from Pollos, up on the Douro, of Marmont's long-awaited reinforcements from Caffarelli's Army of the North – twenty guns and 2,000 horse, it was said (but Wellington believed nearer half). He expected therefore that next day or on the 23rd at the latest, Marmont would have a cavalry advantage over him. Therefore there was no time to be lost. He wrote to Bathurst:

> I determined that, if circumstances should not permit to attack him on the 22nd, I would move towards Ciudad Rodrigo without further loss of time, as the difference of the numbers of cavalry might have made a march of manoeuvre, such as we have had the last four or five days, very difficult and its result doubtful.

Well, that's plain enough. Tomorrow looked like being his last chance. Hence his overheard exclamation next day of 'By God! That will do!' when he saw that chance at last present itself on a plate.

After dark, around 10pm on that Tuesday evening, the sultry heat of the long day resulted in an electrical storm of gigantic strength – neither the first nor last such which the gods of war would fling down before a Wellington victory. Grattan tells us:

> Later in the night a storm arose, and the wind howled in long and bitter gusts. This was succeeded by peals of thunder and flashes of lightning, so loud and vivid that the horses of the cavalry, which were ready saddled, took alarm, and forcing the picquets which held them, ran away affrighted in every direction. The thunder rolled in rattling peals, the lightning darted through the black and almost suffocating atmosphere, and presented to the view of the soldiers of the two armies the horses as they ran about from regiment to regiment, or

allowed themselves to be led back to their bivouac by the troopers to whom they belonged. The vivid flashes of lightning, which seemed to rest upon the grass, for a few moments wholly illuminated the plain, and the succeeding flashes concurred with such rapidity that a constant blaze filled the space occupied by both armies. It was long before the horses could be secured, and some in the confusion ran away amongst the enemy's line and were lost. By midnight the storm began to abate, and towards morning it was evidently going farther: the lightning flashed at a distance through the horizon; the rain fell in torrents, and the soldiers of both armies were drenched to the skin before the hurricane had abated.

Tomkinson tells us that the 5th Dragoon Guards' horses

Ran away over the men sleeping at their heads, by which eighteen in the brigade were wounded, and thirty-one horses not found the following morning ... Colonel and Mrs Dalbiac (that redoubtable lady) of the 4th Dragoons were sitting on the ground in front of the brigade; he had just time to carry her under a gun, which stopped the horses and saved them both.

Next day, some foot-sore French officers, their horses having been commandeered by Marmont, were seen happily mounted on British dragoon horses.

And what of the two commanders that night? Was the storm raging in their heads, as well as outside their tents? Marmont, certainly, slept easy. Had he not run rings round the English for the last week? Was he not within a day's march of the Rodrigo road? Was not the wheat and barley harvest as good as ready? Was not General Chauvel about to arrive with a brigade of horse? Well, he would dine again tonight in Salamanca: Kincaid tells us 'Instructions were sent to his previous landlord in the city, to have the usual dinner ready for 6pm.'

Not so his Lordship. Things had gone wrong ever since the poor intelligence on the strength of the Salamanca forts. Should he after all have seized that fleeting chance on San Cristoval? Could he have stopped Marmont on the Douro or the Guarena? Should he have edged Marmont away from the Huerta road? When would Chauvel arrive? And King Joseph with his 14,000 men? And what about his baggage train – when should it go back? What of Salamanca? At least he knew the men's spirit was one of irritation, not despondency or lack of confidence in themselves (or in him); and that they looked forward keenly to do something about it. Kincaid again:

There was assuredly never an army so anxious as ours was to be brought into action on this occasion. They were a magnificent body of well-tried soldiers, highly equipped, and in the highest health and spirits, with the most devoted confidence in their leader and an invincible confidence in themselves. The retreat of the four preceding days had annoyed us beyond measure, for we believed that we were nearly equal to the enemy in point of numbers; and the idea of retiring before an equal number of any troops in the world was not to be endured with common patience.

Before bed in his headquarters at La Pinilla, some three miles down from the Santa Marta ford, Wellington gave orders for the baggage train to leave at dawn for Rodrigo, escorted by one of D'Urban's three Portuguese dragoon regiments. There were a lot of panicking Spaniards in Salamanca that night, and no doubt some who were quietly rejoicing.

*   *   *

CHAPTER 7

Salamanca – The Early Morning
Wednesday 22 July 1812

Sir Henry Clinton's 6th Division had been the first to cross the Tormes before the heavens opened. Through his covering parties, Sir John Hope's 7th pushed onto the ridge opposite the Chapel, with Pack's Portuguese Brigade to his right and with the other divisions remaining in the dead ground to the west, towards Carbajosa. Victor Alten's light cavalry patrolled up at Calvarrasa de Abajo and Pelabravo, beyond the Pelagarcia brook. Hope had a German Jäger battalion – the Brunswick Oels – across the valley, providing picquets at the Chapel. Six or seven hundred yards away lay Foy's picquets, in front of Calvarrasa de Abajo and, behind his division of 5,000 men, was that of Ferey, slightly larger. Marmont's other six divisions (including Sarrut's, recalled from rearguard duty at Huerta) moved south to join via Machacon, settling down for the night a couple of miles in rear of Foy. The positions are not precisely known, but Bonnet, Maucune and Thomières were the farthest south.

The map shows the two reversed L-shaped features that will concern us and which one must understand: the French one running from Pelabravo in the north via Calvarrasa de Arriba to the turning angle, which is to the east of the Greater Arapile, then running west along the Monte de Azan to the Pico de Miranda (whence it turns right again northwards, on a line to Aldea Tejada, so perhaps more of a horseshoe than an L). The much shorter English L runs from Santa Marta in the north to the Lesser Arapile, then turning briefly west above the village of Arapiles via the nearby feature of the Teso de San Miguel. The down-stroke of the reversed L is covered by what Leith Hay called 'an extensive wood and on the summit of a plateau ... with little variety of altitude, extended from ... the Arapiles ... to the village of Santa Marta'.

The Arapile features are the only prominent objects on this landscape, flat and narrow topped, rocky ridges and 1,000 yards apart. The Greater is some 300 paces long and runs east-west with abrupt, rocky ends and a steep slope to the south, a gentler slope to the north. The Lesser is on the same alignment but is noticeably less long, of much the same height and easier to climb. Both hills stand about 200 feet above Arapiles village, behind which the near-by Teso is perhaps eighty feet higher. From both Arapiles and the Teso you can see great distances, yet the gently rolling undulations, punctuated by minor tributaries which all eventually run to the Tormes, create folds and basins dead to the eye. It is what a later age would term 'good tank country'. Indeed, Salisbury Plain around the village of Imber, after a long hot summer, is a near comparison. The land was mostly grass, with very few trees – the odd stand of cork – except in and around the villages and on the slopes of the Pelagarcia; and extensively south of the French L.

The essence of the two L features is this: if Marmont looked to continue his previous marches around the right flank of the English, the Greater Arapile was as important to him as a doorpost to the door, around which he would turn, whilst retaining the relatively high ground for his march from the north turning then to the west, and which provided observation. Lord Wellington's L, being a minor scale inside the larger French, provided both concealment behind it, and a shorter line for any troop movement needed from one arm to the other. After the days of parallel marching, which had been essentially a sterile tactical occupation, the Arapiles would provide a fruitful, tactical dimension, to the more alert or determined general. It should be stressed that Wellington's ridge, which ended at the Lesser Arapile, entirely hid from the east any troops in rear until the observer's eyes should move south, onto the Greater Arapile – and then only partially.

Before describing the day's opening moves, we should perhaps consider the forces involved. It is proper that your author should acknowledge drawing on Charles Oman's calculations and also those of Rory Muir (whose study of this battle is exhaustive in its detail). Unlike Oman, Muir does not dismiss as a cynical whitewash the official return of French casualties, between 18 July and 8 August, prepared by General Lamartiniere, Marmont's Chief of Staff. However, it is well to repeat the usual point, that all Peninsular strength and casualty figures are as inaccurate as any stated times: both must always be taken as indicative only.

Starting with the relative strengths, the French would appear to field 46,700 all ranks and the allies 50,500, after taking into account the various estimated losses since the last reliable States (15 July on both sides), and adjusting for new arrivals and non-combatants such as gendarmes, engineers and sappers etc.

In terms of tactical fighting units, as a very rough guide, there appeared no great advantage to either side: seventy-three French battalions to sixty-eight allied, ten cavalry regiments to thirteen, seventy-eight guns to sixty-two (if we include the Spanish battery). You could say French cavalry inferiority was balanced by their superiority in guns – possibly more than balanced, given their expertise in the science of artillery. However, around all these nominal figures caveats apply.

Firstly, the cavalry odds were wider than the numbers indicate. Lord Wellington's were in better condition generally, and the mounts of his five heavy dragoon regiments – which Marmont lacked entirely – tended to be markedly stronger and therefore more boisterous cross-country. All were well drilled, which should go without saying, but the French surprisingly were not. A fortnight earlier some 670 hacks, requisitioned from the army's junior officers, had been issued to dismounted dragoons and chasseurs. So perhaps one in four or five of every troop were mounted on novice chargers. Of course, between the knees of experienced horsemen this would matter little in line or column; but when mounted man-to-man hand combat commenced – the prime phase of any charge against other cavalry – a severe disadvantage would arise in individual manoeuvring. A fortnight is not sufficient in which to develop the necessary schooling. And one in four or five troopers would know this, and would not enjoy the prospect.

The infantry were evenly balanced. Working from the States of 15 July, which we know not to be very relevant, but are at least indicative, Marmont's average battalion bayonet strength was 548 and he had seventy-three battalions; Wellington's was 592 and he had sixty-nine battalions. Of these, however, one third (twenty-three) were Portuguese battalions. Fifteen of these had, for some time, been allocated in brigades of three to each of five of Wellington's divisions. Equally absorbed and reliable were the three KGL battalions operating as a brigade in the 1st Division, and two more battalions in the 7th; less so the 'foreign' battalions – the Chasseurs Britannique and the Brunswick Oels; the five Spanish battalions under Espana were independent, although of course like his two lancer regiments under Don Juan de Sanchez they received their orders direct from Wellington's headquarters.

The allies' infantry strength, therefore, is under the possible handicap of differing national characteristics, language and motivation (what Michael Glover delicately called 'the variable fighting qualities of nationalities'); however, the situation was not new, a fair tradition of success having been constructed during the army's previous experiences. One suspects only that a certain amount of crossing of fingers applied, to some of the Portuguese involvement, which in the event proved largely unnecessary. If Lord Wellington gave any thought to the fact that only two thirds of his infantry were British line regiments, Marmont equally might ponder that only two thirds of his had ever faced British volleys. This might be argued as a good thing? Among the innocents who had never faced the British were all eight of Thomières's battalions, and six out of eight of Taupin's. Of course, 'innocents' is relevant only to British volleys, for these were all reliable, old established regiments, who had fought at Wagram (all of Thomières's), Austerlitz (Taupin's 17th Léger), and the 1808 invasion of Portugal (his 22nd and 65th Ligne).

To return to the story. Early that Wednesday morning, which dawned bright, sunny and serene, the intention of both commanders has been clearly enough expressed in their letters. Marmont sought to continue turning Wellington's right flank, in hopes of a fleeting chance to swoop upon any mistake, in any event edging towards the road to Rodrigo; Lord Wellington sought to continue what had become a movement of retreat (not his choice of words), if necessary abandoning Salamanca, while covering Ciudad Rodrigo, and only contemplating action should 'very advantageous circumstances' present themselves. This day, the 22nd, was his best and last chance, before Chauvel joined with his cavalry brigade, to say nothing of King Joseph being on route from Madrid. To be on the safe side, he had sent his baggage away as the light grew stronger.

There is a wooded feature opposite the Chapel near Calvarrasa de Arriba. It is 100 feet higher than the Chapel. From it he could see Foy's Division just over a mile away, and could probably make out other formations behind and to the south, although the wooded terrain made that difficult. At least he knew that Marmont had no troops up around Calvarrasa de Abajo or Pelabravo where his own flank cavalry patrols still stood. It already looked as if Marmont meant to continue his movement south and west.

The Marshal joined Foy somewhere in front of Calvarrasa de Arriba. Foy wrote:

> The position of San Cristoval had been almost stripped of troops: we could see one English Division in a sparsely-planted wood within cannon-shot of Calvarrasa de Arriba, on the Salamanca road: very far behind a thin column was ascending the heights of Tejares: nothing more could be made out of Wellington's army: all the rest was hidden from us by the chain of heights which runs from north to south, and ends in the high and precipitous knolls of the Arapiles. Wellington was on this chain, sufficiently near to us to recognise by means of the staff surrounding him.

So the 7th Division and Pack's Portuguese were all they could see: six divisions were missing, later correctly presumed by Foy to be in the dead ground over the wooded crest. Nearly three miles of crest could hide a whole army. And lifting the eyes, this side of the skyline five miles away, beyond which lay the Salamanca to Rodrigo road, a long dust cloud clearly indicated a large rearwards movement. That skyline comprised wooded heights some 200 feet higher than the present ground. The left of the heights rested on the Tormes, offering Wellington an attractive blocking position covering the Rodrigo road. Marmont was therefore in no doubt about what the dust cloud showed. Writing later to Paris he explained that 'Everything led me to believe that the enemy intended to occupy the position of Tejares (Aldea Tejada) which lay a league behind him, while at present he was a league and a half in front of Salamanca.' Foy confirms this to have been his Marshal's deduction, as they observed beside their horses, telescopes resting on saddles:

> The Marshal had no definite plan: he thought that the English army was already gone off, or at least that it was going off, to take position on the heights of Tajares on the left (or farther) bank of the river

Zurgain. He was tempted to make an attack on the one visible English Division, with which a skirmishing fire had already begun. He was fearing that this Division might get out of his reach! How little did he foresee the hapless lot of his own army that day! The wily Wellington was ready to give battle – the greater part of his host was collected, but masked behind the line of heights: he was showing nothing on the crest, lest his intention should be defined: he was waiting for our movement.

There of course speaks a deal of hindsight. Yes, Wellington was indeed closed up just over a mile away, and hidden; but you could readily understand Marmont's interpretation. He saw what he wanted to see. Wellington was pulling back, and the division across on the immediate slopes was a rearguard. And the temptation to engage was apparently strong. He himself admitted only to the wish to 'concentrate in front of him in order to take advantage of any opportunities' but Foy's diary implies his master thought seriously of attacking the 7th Division and Pack there and then; but deciding against it only after 'much hesitation, as was customary'. He left Foy to visit Bonnet, to look at the scene from a different angle, telling Foy to remove the allied line of picquets from around the Chapel.

The time was variously recorded at 7am when the black-uniformed Bruns-wickers came under attack by Foy's men. Lord Wellington not wanting any chance of French eyes approaching the 7th's crest line, he reinforced the Oels with the 4th Caçadores from Pack's brigade, and Hope's 68th (Durhams). Both battalions, being light infantry, deployed chains of skirmishers, not formed lines. Along the wooded course of the Pelagarcia, towards Pelabravo, two more light battalions of the KGL also became involved in mild skirmishing, while Bock's heavy and Alten's light dragoons held Pelabravo and Calvarrasa de Abajo.

From the low casualty figures it appears that all this business around the Chapel, and to the north, was very low key. It continued, however, throughout the morning and into the early afternoon, whilst of course matters of greater moment were developing elsewhere. Perhaps bickering is a more appropriate word than skirmishing. The scene around the Chapel, sharp initially, turned rather inactive. A flavour is given by Private John Green, 68th:

Early on the morning of the 22nd July, we heard the firing of the advanced guard, and in less than ten minutes our regiment, being light infantry, was ordered forward: having reached the front, we saw the French picquets advancing on ours, and both were sharply engaged. In a moment the left wing was ordered to the front: no sooner did our advanced picquets perceive that they were supported by such a number of light troops, than they advanced on the French picquets, and drove them in confusion to the summit of a high hill; but the enemy receiving strong reinforcements, bore down on my brave comrades, who contested every inch with them. At this period a General came to the front, to see how things were going on: in a fit of passion he enquired, 'Who commands here?' The answer was 'General Hope'. He said, 'Where is he? The whole of the advanced picquets will be taken prisoners.' General Hope came up at the time, but did not appear at all afraid that the men would be taken: he sent one of his aide-de-camps with directions for a squadron of light dragoons to support the skirmishers immediately: they came forward, and had only just taken their stand, when one of them, a youth of about twenty-one years of age, was killed. The enemy now retired to the top of the hill, and brought six pieces of cannon to play on us. About this time the watering parties of the 7th Division came to the valley for a supply of water: the French guns began to play on these unarmed and defenceless men; but not one of them was hurt, although shot and shell fell thickly amongst them; after this the enemy continued firing on us for some hours. We remained in this position until afternoon, but were not allowed to take off our accoutrements. About three o'clock the 95th rifle corps arriving, took our places, and we immediately marched off to join the Division.

The 68th lost twenty men all day, the KGL twenty-five, the Brunwickers and Caçadores rather more, but their records do not allow the answer to be unravelled. It seems that, after the initial flurry, neither local commander thought seriously to contest the ground, presumably knowing the centre of gravity was turning south. The withdrawal of French cavalry from the north, and the non-appearance at the Chapel of a formed French battalion, to strengthen Foy's screen of skirmishers, was confirmation enough.

Major General Victor Alten had tracked the French horse a little too closely at this stage, taking a ball in the knee for his curiosity, thus giving the commander of the KGL's 1st Hussars, Lieutenant Colonel Arentschildt, that also of the 14th Light Dragoons. Both regiments withdrew to behind the 7th Division's ridge, where Lord Wellington told them to rest. He replaced them with the 12th Light Dragoons from George Anson's brigade, who reported continued peace around the two deserted villages. Bock's heavies (the 1st and 2nd Dragoons KGL) remained on the left of the 7th Division. It was about 7.30am.

Within minutes of leaving Foy, Marmont saw the importance of the Greater Arapile hill, two miles south-west of the Chapel. Indeed, his eye would have been drawn to it, and to the lesser feature, while with Foy, since they lay but a few degrees left of his line of observation to the dust cloud made by the allies' baggage train. Unbelievably, he could see no red coats on either Arapile. He immediately ordered Bonnet to seize both, via a covert approach through the woods to the south.

Wellington at much the same time, having quit the 7th Division's observation post, and convinced his left flank had sufficient means of early warning, rode a mile south along the ridge to Cole's 4th Division, where he met one of his Assistant Adjutants General, Lieutenant Colonel John Waters (of scouting officer fame) whom he found concerned at the unoccupied Arapiles sitting slap bang on what was then the right flank of the army. In the previous night's electrical storm, the army having crossed the Tormes to bivouac behind the 7th Division's ridge, the 4th Division as southernmost somehow ceased its deployment without including the Lesser Arapile. There is disagreement as to whether this was a misjudgement made in the poor visual conditions either of the previous dusk, or at first light that very day. That is, that in the gloom the Great Arapile was seen to be farther away and therefore less relevant than it was. But the reference in Napier that 'These hills (plural) were neglected by the English General' is plain enough. A critical letter to Thomas Graham from his old staff officer, Charles Cathcart, also clearly refers to both hills being unoccupied:

> We ought unquestionably to have possessed ourselves of them the very first thing, but through some unaccountable Carelessness, they remained unoccupied. The French saw the importance of these Heights, but did not give us jealousy for them by sending at once a Large Body against them. They sent out some straggling parties in different directions which when they got near the foremost height ran together and got to the summit before a small part of the Portuguese caçadores which had been sent to prevent them could arrive. They were only in time to save the other height which was immediately occupied in Force by the 4th Division.

(Yet Leith Hay categorically states 'the nearest of the Arapiles ... had been occupied by the allies on the preceeding night.')

It was about 8am when the 7th Caçadores from Stubb's Portuguese Brigade in Cole's Division were sent posthaste to claim the Greater. Major John Lillie led them and claimed later not to know they were either in a race, or indeed that there were any French units in the offing. Lillie recounts to Napier a surreal meeting with the French, actually riding with them through the wheat, to confront his own men:

> I received orders through the Duke of Richmond to occupy ... on arriving close to it I found it was too steep to ascend on horseback, and consequently rode round, while my men made the best of their way directly to the top. [It did not seem to occur to him to dismount!] I was not aware of any enemy being in the immediate vicinity, as

some Spaniards had been there a short time previous; thus, when I came suddenly on some troops advancing from the opposite direction, I took them for Spaniards, and questioning them in Spanish, they replied that they were Spanish: they were partly covered by the high corn and the uneven ground, and I rode up in the same direction with them until we met our men at the top of the hill, when all doubts on the subject were removed by their opening fire on us at a few paces distance. We contested the point so long as anything like an equality of numbers permitted us; but as their numbers rapidly increased, and we found that we were encountering the head of a brigade, we were overpowered and closely pursed in the direction of the other Arapiles, for which the enemy made a push, and which they would have succeeded in taking had not the fusilier brigade and the Duke himself been sufficiently near to arrive the first.

The Lesser had the 3rd/27th (Inniskillings) moving to the summit with two 9-pounder guns from Sympher's KGL battery, with the 1st/40th (Somersets) in rear, both battalions from William Anson's brigade. Cole's other brigade, Ellis' Fusilier Brigade of three battalions, was 1,000 yards away to the west, on the Teso de San Miguel (just above the village of Arapiles) with Sympher's other four guns. Stubb's Portuguese Brigade and Pack's Independent Portuguese Brigade filled the gap. Wellington left the Lesser saying to the Inniskillings' Colonel John McClean 'You must defend this position so long as you have a man.'

Over on the Greater Arapile, Bonnet had at least one of the 120th's three battalions on the crest, with the balance in rear, as were Bonnet's other three regiments, totalling another nine battalions. Guns were laboriously manhandled to the crest by Grenadier parties, the barrels detached – four or six pieces but probably not more. It offered a superb artillery platform, safe from cavalry, and just about within effective range of the Lesser and its wide-open surrounding country. The two snags were the dead ground immediately beneath the guns' maximum depression angle – but attacking infantry would have to make it through a killing zone first – and the impossibility of affecting a quick exit off the hill in case of need.

That the one-eyed Bonnet, twenty-six years a soldier, had eleven battalions formed up behind the French Arapile is worth contemplating. That is all of 6,000 men, a positive blue host stretching in neat battalion columns across the slopes in rear, and largely visible from the British Arapile and from the Teso, a mile away. At that range a decent telescope will pick out individuals and make head counts entirely accurate. Thus Wellington would deduce the importance placed on continued possession of this hill – it was worth an eighth of his enemy's infantry. Or, assuming he meant to maintain the two divisions in rear of the Chapel, a sixth. So he now had five divisions free for other purposes.

Which were now on the move. Around 9am Marmont ordered Maucune, Clausel, Taupin (Brennier's) and (possibly) Sarrut to move west into the long line of woods to the south-east of their Arapile, and Thomières to a modest height at the edge of the woods, due south (presumably points 912 and 913 on current Spanish maps).

His Lordship reacted, though whether on catching sight of this movement or of Bonnet's, is unclear. Either or both obviously indicated a continuation of Marmont's flank marches of previous days, the object of which was plain and undesirable. To re-balance his north-south army was therefore necessary and, thanks to his interior lines behind his Arapile, could be done without committing to any assumptions which might still prove wrong. He brought Leith's 5th, Clinton's 6th, Espana's Spanish and Bradford's Portuguese down around the village of Las Torres, behind the Arapile village. He replaced the 7th by the Light, the former also going into reserve, and took the two light companies from Campbell's Guards to deploy on the forward edge of the Arapile village. The rest of the 1st Division were in support of the Light. Alton, Anson and Le Marchant moved from the left flank into reserve near the 6th Division, leaving Bock's two KGL dragoon regiments and two squadrons of Alton's 14th Light Dragoons to cover Boyer's dragoons, on the original left, above the Chapel.

Most of these adjustments were finalised by mid-morning – say 10.30am. At about the same time Edward Pakenhan's 3rd Division got underway from Cabrerizos, having been instructed to cross the Tormes and form around Aldea Tejada. Pakenham had been left on the north bank should any threat develop there, but it was clear now to Wellington that he could re-join. With Pakenhan went D'Urban's two remaining Portuguese dragoon regiments (1st and 7th), the 12th absent of course escorting the baggage. It is thought Pakenham chose not to cross entirely by the old Salamanca bridge, but also by the ford, and then marched across country. According to John Cooke, raising 'clouds of dust as they passed along the rear of our army ... near 1pm the 3rd Division were passing within a mile in rear of us (the Light Division)'. They would reach their destination about 2pm and then be some three miles north-west of Arapiles village. Pakenham and D'Urban rested along the mile-long road between Aldea Tejada and La Pinilla, and which was screened to the south-east by trees and hill slopes. There is a prominent long box-shaped feature just east of the former village.

His Lordship needed Pakenham there or thereabouts, just as he needed the Light Division on his extreme left: if the worst transpired, the latter would become – not for the first time – the army's rearguard, and the former a support position to fall back on en route to the Rodrigo road. Whether any more optimistic use was in Wellington's mind at this stage is impossible to know. It would take an hour to close the 3rd Division on the Arapiles, should he wish it. But then he already had a mass of unengaged troops under his hand,

and an enemy who, at the Chapel, had shown no determined forward signs. It was quite hard to know what the French meant for in this first half of the morning there stood two full divisions all on their own, at the Chapel and on the Arapile, in isolation. That could not be the sum total of his enemy's plans. The optical advantage lay with Marmont, whose troops Wellington in the main could scarcely see, whereas Marmont from his Arapile could see red coats only too well. Apart from those in dead ground immediately behind the Lesser (Anson's 1st/40th), Marmont's telescope gave him the red guardsmen in Arapile village, Ellis' red fusiliers, Pack's and Stubb's brown Portuguese this side of the Teso, together with much of the 5th and 6th Divisions between there and Las Torres – and perhaps even the Spanish the other side, some two miles away.

Halfway through the morning, with no sign of any French movement, and with no activity bar the occasional shot by marksmen around the Chapel, and the odd random cannon fire between the Arapiles, Wellington now gave in to uncharacteristic temptation. Not surprisingly, his *Despatch* is silent on this lapse to human frailty – albeit a brief one. We cannot know whether it was to be a limited action, or the pre-cursor to a general action. No doubt he would not have known either.

He was going to attack Bonnet on the Greater Arapile.

CHAPTER 8

Salamanca – The Middle of the Day
Wednesday 22 July 1812

Henry Campbell, commanding the 1st Division, three days after the battle
wrote:

> The French had got on a very commanding hill close to our front,
> from which they could see all that we did, and behind which they
> were playing the old game again and stretching away to turn our
> right. Lord Wellington at one time determined to attack them, and
> sent for me, and told me to move forward in two columns up the hill
> in front of our right, where this Division then was, and attack their
> left, while the 4th Division was to attack them in front; but I had
> hardly put the columns in motion before I received a counter-order
> and moved back to the ground I had quitted.

One of his officers, John Aitchinson, 1st/3rd Guards, wrote:

> Lord Wellington immediately issued orders for the 1st Division to
> attack. We moved therefore into the village of Arapiles, but had
> hardly entered it when the order was countermanded ... It was now
> noon and the enemy were seen moving large bodies under cover of a
> distant wood upon our right, and they occupied with artillery all the
> eminences on our front.

John Mills, 1st Coldstream: 'At 11 o'clock the 1st Division was moved from
the left of the line to the village, being ordered to attack the height the enemy
occupied. They were, however, countermanded.'

So it did nearly happen. There are two obvious curiosities here: why the
order, and why the counter-order? Given Wellington's stipulation that any
action would require 'very advantageous circumstances', one wonders quite
what these were. The 1st and 4th Divisions between them, less the 27th and
40th who secured the home Arapile, comprised twelve battalions, but then
so did Bonnet. Granted the 1st's were well above-average in strength, yet a
thousand-man superiority was hardly a sure-fire guarantee of a successful outcome of whatever the Peer had in mind. And unless Bonnet could be overcome

quickly, other French Divisions would soon join the fray, the action becoming general.

Tomkinson of the 16th Light Dragoons says the Light Division were also ordered to the attack, along with the 1st (no mention of the 4th). However, none of the 95th's scribbling diarists left any such record, bar possibly a tangential reference by Kincaid: 'We were kept the whole of the forenoon in the most torturing state of suspense through contradictory reports, one passing officer telling us that he had just heard the order given to attack, and the next asserting with equal confidence that he had just heard the order to retreat.' One must assume Henry Campbell, having been told he would have one role and the 4th another, would have mentioned in his letter if his Lordship had allocated a third to the Light. So it was to be just the 1st and 4th.

It would perhaps seem Wellington saw Bonnet as a fleeting chance to bloody Marmont's nose, to pinch him off the landscape and to gain the Greater Arapile; but no more than that. Yet Marmont could still march around it. Had his ambitions been wider, the order to Campbell would surely have been followed immediately by others to the cavalry, and to other adjacent divisional commanders. And in his shoes, after so many days of backwards manoeuvring and parallel marching, most soldiers' red blood would have pounded a little at such temptation, however fleeting. A rare show of normality by the Peer? For he was on the verge of surrendering Salamanca back to Marmont, and without a fight at that: a frustrating position.

By general report it was Beresford who persuaded him otherwise. Indeed, Wellington himself said so, in conversation with Marmont years later, according to Oman, that the attack 'was put off in consequence of the representation of Beresford, who had counselled delay'. We have earlier commented on Beresford's post-Albuera caution – on the San Cristobal position. It has been suggested that on the Arapile his latest caution may have been seconded by Cotton, and in all fairness in this case it was probably a very appropriate caution. Yet that his Lordship paid attention and gave in, remains a puzzle, since if ever there was a general absolutely not given to consultation, nor to welcoming the tactical opinion of others, it was the very self-contained Arthur Wellesley. As Tomkinson commented, 'His attending to the Marshal was considered singular' and it remains so today.

While the 1st Division marched to, then fro, and Marmont watched no doubt with staring eyes as the red-coated company columns halted en route to the attack and then turned about, two other large bodies of troops were continuing their movements. Firstly there were his own divisions now emerging from the wood line up on the Sierro, having at last come around to the far south of his Arapile. Secondly, there was Edward Pakenham's 3rd Division, some 3,500 bayonets, as they too crossed in rear of their army in another long cloud of dust which, just like that of the baggage train, was heading generally west beneath Salamanca.

This movement, together with the aborted attack, convinced Marmont his enemy was now in the process of retreat. He explained the various factors, together with what seemed to him the logical deduction, in his self-serving *Memoires*. With the change of mind on Bonnet, he wrote:

> Wellington renounced his intention of fighting, and from that moment he had to prepare to draw away, for if he had remained in his present position I should from the next day have threatened his communications, by marching on to my left. His withdrawal commenced at midday ... He had to retreat by his right, and consequently he had to begin by strengthening his right. He therefore weakened his left, and accumulated troops on his right. Then his more distant units and his reserves commenced to move, and in succession drew off towards Tejares (Aldea Tejada). His intention was easy to discern ... The enemy having carried off the bulk of his force to his right, I had to reinforce my left, so as to be able to act with promptness and vigour, without having to make new arrangements, when the moment should arrive for falling upon the English rearguard.

Now from Marmont's viewpoint one cannot argue with all this. It's what he thought he saw. His Lordship was indeed all set to go backwards. He had been all morning. Or forwards, given a chance. Earlier, after the greater Arapile was lost, with common prudence he had caused his acting Quartermaster General the American-born Lieutenant Colonel William de Lancey, to prepare the route orders for the divisions to withdraw, when necessary, to the heights of Aldea Tejada. These included instructions for the prior movement of the commissariat and baggage. Commissary J. E. Daniels received his copy at 10am. Needless to say, that news quickly got around the divisions, adding to earlier disappointments. Being ready to withdraw, however, was no more than a prudent act of good generalship. The French would have to make further progress around the allied right before such a move became necessary. The order had not been given. What Marmont misinterpreted as a movement of withdrawal was actually part re-balancing (including the 3rd Division's approach) and part misidentification of the baggage train.

The country the French would cross was perfectly open and without impediments. There were then no walls, fences or real ditches, bar those cut by the rains. These in places were 'so deep and broad that it took a good spring to leap over' (Corporal Douglas, 1st (Royals)). So basically we are concerned with an area of grassland nearly three miles east-west and a mile and a half going away from the village of Arapiles. This was the Monte de Azan. As the 4th and 5th Divisions looked to their front, the land rose gently to a convex crest, beyond which lay an upper flattish plateau ending, a mile from the village, in another rising slope, edging into extensive woodland. The western half of the Monte de Azan is a mile and a half of open slopes, narrowing gradually into something resembling a vague ridge, and which eventually becomes a flat-topped sixty-yard-wide feature with steepish slopes. This is the Pico de Miranda, taking the name of the hamlet Miranda de Azan which lay 100 feet or so beneath its south-western end. Finally, one should mention a low ridge running north at a right angle for over a mile beside, and in front of, the track from Aldea Tejada.

Clearly the Monte de Azan proffered Marmont an ideal route to continue turning the allies right: three miles and he would then be just four miles from the heights beyond Aldea Tejada and the Rodrigo road. He could almost feel the end of the turning journey, begun so many days before. And each day had shown that the British did not mean to fight. This Wellington was indeed a man for defensive actions. Apart from at Roliça, four years previously, he had never yet been known to attack. He had even aborted one that very morning! So let's get on with it, with due prudence, of course. Let's progress along the Monte de Azan in considered steps, fixing the British as we go. At some point Foy and Ferey must close up as we sidestep westwards, for it is all of six miles from their location to Miranda de Azan, and that's way too much front to cover. Let's start by seizing the nearer end of the plateau, opposite Arapiles village and alongside Bonnet, before Wellington regains his courage and has a second bite at that cherry.

Marmont's despatch to Paris:

> It was indispensable to occupy it, seeing that the enemy had just strengthened his centre, from whence he could push out en masse on to this plateau, and commence an attack by taking a possession of this important ground. Accordingly I ordered the 5th Division (Maucune) to move out and form up on the right end of the plateau, where his fire would link on perfectly with that from the (Great) Arapile: the 7th Division (Thomières) was to place itself in second line as a support, the 2nd Division (Clausel) to act as a reserve to the 7th. The 6th Division (Brennier) was to occupy the high ground in front of the wood, where a large number of my guns were still stationed. I ordered General Bonnet at the same time to occupy with the 122nd regiment a knoll intermediate between the plateau and the hill of the (Great) Arapile, which blocks the exit from the village of the same name. Finally, I directed General Boyer to leave only one regiment of his dragoons to watch Foy's right, and to come round with the other three to the front of the wood, beside the 2nd Division. The object of this was that, supposing the enemy should attack the plateau, Boyer could charge in on their right flank, while my light cavalry could charge in on their left flank.

As we know, Marmont had every right subsequently to feel aggrieved, these orders not being obeyed and catastrophe following. Since any despatch by a defeated General must traditionally make plain who the culprit was, Marmont's is a fair effort to shift the blame onto Maucune and the dead Thomières whilst carefully not addressing his own involvement, or rather lack of involvement. As his Emperor commented when the above despatch reached him in Russia, Marmont's situation had as 'much complicated stuffing as the inside of a clock, and not a word of truth as to the real state of things'.

These orders were issued sometime after 1pm. The moment Maucune's columns were seen deploying up on the plateau, with guns to the flank, a now happy Peer hastened to adjust his positions, in anticipation of his long wished for defensive battle. Leith's 5th Division was brought forward at double quick, to the right of the 4th on the line of the Teso, behind and to the right of the village; Clinton's 6th was placed in rear of the 4th; Hope's 7th similarly went into the second line in rear of the 5th. The Light and 1st remained the left wing, together with Bock's Dragoons. Wellington's reserve of Bradford's three Portuguese battalions and Espana's five Spanish were around Las Torres, so too the eight cavalry regiments of Le Marchant, Anson and Arentschildt.

But his Lordship was to be disappointed. The French were not about to attack. The words 'occupy' and 'form up' occur in Marmont's orders, according to his later despatch, not 'attack' or 'advance'. As he makes plain, it is to seize important, unoccupied ground in case his enemy had the same idea; yet at odds with this, he later quite categorically stated Wellington had already commenced his retreat. So quite what was in his mind, and what his actual orders were, rather than what he said they were, is another puzzle.

For now, Maucune's 5th Division with nine battalions – some 5,000 bayonets – advanced on to the plateau. It is easy to see why Maucune did more than occupy the heights, finishing up near the village, but not easy to understand his attempt to seize it. As Foy noted 'The elevations which dominate the plain . . . swell up one after another. The occupation of one led to the temptation to seize the next, and so by advance after advance the village of Arapiles was at last reached.' (The heights Foy meant are points 889 and 898, followed half a mile later by points 876 and 877 on current maps.) The latter heights are but 700 yards from the village and there at last in full view Maucune halted, his voltigeurs running forward down the slope. Away to their left squadrons of Curto's Light Cavalry Division covered the movement, to be engaged by Alten's 14th Light Dragoons and the German 1st Hussars, who being outnumbered had rather the worst of the skirmishing, for it was no more than that. Guns exchanged fire on both sides, of course. Maucune's own divisional battery was reinforced by two more from Marmont's reserve, opening on both the village and the Lesser Arapile. Wellington brought forward Lawson's 6-pounder battery from the 5th Division to support Sympher's German 9-pounders, and later the 6-pounders of E Troop (Macdonald's) RHA from the 7th Division; gun positions were established on the slopes held by Anson's 1st/40th, on the crest of the Arapile itself, and on the slopes of the Teso. Generally, French firepower was superior. Wellington's three deployed batteries were simply outgunned for, according to Oman, they were eventually opposed by six French. The effect of the French fire was as always in the nature of a lottery. Private John Green, 68th experienced it as the 7th Division came forward to its position behind the 5th:

> About this time the cannonading commenced: the French had nearly one hundred pieces of cannon firing on our army ... We had about sixty pieces; and the thunder of these one hundred and sixty guns was terrible, and beggars description. Having joined the division (the Seventh), and taken our place on the left of the first brigade; we halted a few minutes, and then advanced to the spot where our artillery were stationed. We now came into an open plain, and were completely exposed to the fire of the enemy's artillery. Along this plain a division of the army was stationed: I think it was the 4th division: the men laid down in order to escape the shot and shells, the army not yet being ready to advance. As our regiment was marching along the rear of this division, I saw a shell fall on one of the men, which killed him on the spot; a part of the shell tore his knapsack to pieces, and I saw it flying in the air after the shell had burst.
>
> The shot of the foe now began to take effect on us. As we were marching in open column to take our position, one of the supernumerary sergeants, whose name was Dunn, had both his legs shot from under him, and died in a few minutes. Shortly after, a shot came and took away the leg and thigh, with part of the body, of a young officer named Finukin: to have seen him, and heard the screams of his servant, would have almost rendered a heart of stone: he was a good master, an excellent officer, and was lamented by all who knew him. The next thing I have to relate is of the company which was directly in our front, commanded by Captain Gough: a cannon-ball came, and striking the right of the company, made the arms gingle and fly in pieces like broken glass. One of the bayonets was broken off, and sent through a man's neck with as much force as though it had been done by a strong and powerful hand. I saw the man pull it out, and singular to relate, he recovered: three others were also wounded. About this time I had a narrow escape from a cannon-ball, which passed within a few inches of me: although it was nearly spent, yet, had it struck me, I should have been either killed or wounded by it.
>
> After this, we formed column of quarter distance; and several shells fell into our column, and did execution: one shell I shall ever remember: we were in the act of lying down, that it might burst, and do no mischief: the colonel cried out, 'It is a shot!' and we stood up

immediately; but while in the act of rising, the shell burst in the midst of the regimental column, and, astonishing to relate, not a man received an injury by it.

The Colonel would feel pretty stupid.

Private William Wheeler, 51st, also commented on the cannonading as the 7th Division moved double quick to the right of the line 'The fire at length became so furious that it was expedient to form grand Divisions, thus leaving an interval of double the space for their shot to pass through'.

The village was defended by the two light companies from the Guards, the three from Ellis's Fusilier brigade (1st/7th Royal Fusiliers, 1st/23rd Welsh Fusiliers and 1st/48th Northamptons), and the company of Brunswick Oels. Maucune's voltigeurs actually twice penetrated the village, seizing the houses on the outskirts. Only a company's worth came first and were held; reinforcements however then joined and with artillery covering fire they drove the light companies back into the village; a counter-attack by two companies of the 7th under Captain Crowder pushed them back but, more reinforcements joining, again the French reached the buildings. A second counter-attack restored the position and that really was that. The Brunswickers suffered ten men hit, the Coldstream thirty-five and the 3rd Guards twenty-four. Ellis's casualties are not known. Taking the Guards' company strengths at, say, ninety each, however, these were particularly heavy losses.

There was some puzzlement among onlookers that the voltiguers' gallantry was not followed up. William Warre:

> The enemy opened a most tremendous cannonade upon our whole line from, I should guess, upwards of 50 pieces of cannon, and soon after pushed forward a crowd of sharpshooters, it should appear, however, only to insult our army, as they were not supported, and the heavy columns they had on the hills did not move forward. I suppose that Monr Marmont, with French insolence, thought, because we had not attacked him before, and had moved back to counter manoeuvre him and to avoid being turned, that we were afraid of him, and that he could thus insult us with impunity.

It certainly appears strange, in view of his apparent orders merely to form up on the right end of the plateau, that Maucune should actively unleash several waves of voltigeurs at the village. Or was he encouraged by Marmont to try it on, to try to provoke Wellington? Into attacking, or into withdrawing? His Lordship later was reported to have used the phrase 'We will show them we are not to be bullied', so perhaps Maucune did, after all, provoke an element of reaction. However, there came nothing further from him, bar a continuation of the artillery duel, the infantry on both sides lying down to escape the worst of it. The hard open ground saw the shot grazing for long distances.

During this affair of the light troops before Arapiles, which was over by about 2.30pm, the divisions earmarked to support Maucune (Thomières) and to be his reserve (Clausel) began slowly to emerge from the woods to the south, and move forward on to the plateau. After his voltigeurs' foray ceased, it is said Maucune moved his division perhaps half a mile farther west, to face Las Torres. Thomières went off at a tangent, not halting in rear of Maucune as one would suppose, but marching west along the heights, passing Maucune's rear. Clausel still had to clear the line of woods, so with him yet to reach the plateau, nor with Taupin on his designated high ground, neither Maucune or Thomières had support behind them or to either flank.

Curto's chasseurs on the Monte de Azan ranged ahead of Thomières's 7th Division, some four miles distant now from Foy's 1st Division, back at the Chapel. Such an attenuated arc, of length but little depth, wrapped as it was around a much tighter allied concentration, invited the latter to make full use of its interior lines. Wellington with five divisions at his immediate beck and call had just Bonnet and Maucune to his front, with a gap between them of nearly a mile, and with a further three divisions in full view: Foy and Ferey up north, and Thomières heading west.

Now contrary to some views, time and space on the Monte de Azan indicate the latter's progress was neither continuous nor rapid. It is generally accepted that he met his fate above Miranda de Azan shortly before 5pm, having covered some three and a quarter miles along the Monte from the woods south of the French Arapile. It is not credible that this distance, even allowing for the mid-day heat, could take two or more hours. This rather weakens the idea that he was trying, contrary to what Marmont said his orders were, by forced march to get around the allies' flank. For whatever reason, it seems his division was at times static. This nicely introduces the next critical development in the story, which is Lord Wellington's apparently sudden, indeed dramatic, intention to attack. There are a great many descriptions left to us, the details naturally varying, but not in two particulars: that the decision to attack was taken instantly, and was as instantly acted upon. For such to occur, a plan would already have been formed in the Peer's mind (as no doubt he had several others) and it would have been predicated on the development of events. 'That will do' appropriately summed up the moment he recognised the arrival of the catalyst. Indeed, since it revolves around the curious progress, all by itself, of Marmont's left flank division gradually going further out on a limb, Wellington would previously have settled on some physical point on the crest opposite at which, if reached by Thomières, he would swing into action.

Charles Greville in his *Memoires* gives Wellington's own account as recorded in early 1838:

> He was dining in a farm-yard with his officers, where (he had done dinner) everybody else came and dined as they could. The whole

French army was in sight, moving, and the enemy firing upon the farm-yard in which he was dining. 'I got up,' he said, 'and was looking over a wall round the farm-yard, just such a wall as that' (pointing to a low stone wall bounding the covert), 'and I saw the movement of the French left through my glass'. 'By God,' said I, 'that will do, and I'll attack them directly.' I had moved up the Sixth [sic: Third] Division through Salamanca, which the French were not aware of, and I ordered them to attack, and the whole line to advance. I had got my army so completely in hand that I could do this with ease.

Ten months later Greville recorded the account by Fitzroy Somerset.

They were going to dine in a farm-yard, but the shot fell so thick there that the mules carrying the dinner were ordered to go to another place. There the Duke dined, walking about the whole time munching, with his field-glass in his hand, and constantly looking through it. On a sudden he exclaimed, 'By G—, they are extending their line; order my horses.' The horses were brought and he was off in an instant, followed only by his old German dragoon, who went with him everywhere. The aides-de-camp followed as quickly as they could. He galloped straight to Pakenham's division and desired him immediately to begin the attack.

Many other versions of the story exist but all contain the excitement of the moment of Wellington's sudden decision, and its immediate translation into action. His army was balanced near to hand, ready either to withdraw, defend or attack, and had been moved into that posture with a proper and admirable forethought for all contingencies. Here indeed is a great General at work, for the first time on the brink of allowing himself, and his patient, frustrated soldiers, a chance for real glory. Therein lay his one fear, for the men were unaccustomed to making ground rather than to holding it. The excessive enthusiasm of the Guards at Talavera, the mounted version repeatedly performed by his forward-going cavalry, and the anarchy at Badajoz, must all give some pause as to their discipline when off the leash. Well, there was one way to find out, and he had now made his decision.

The plan was for Foy and Ferey at the Chapel to be fixed by the Light Division and by Bock's dragoons; for Bonnet on the French Arapile to be likewise masked by Pack's Portuguese brigade; for Cole's 4th on Pack's right, supported by Clinton's 6th, to make for the gap still existing between Bonnet and Maucune; for Leith's 5th supported by Hope's 7th, the Spanish and Bradford's Portuguese brigade, to attack Maucune and Thomières (and who would also be assaulted by Le Marchant and Anson's six cavalry regiments.) Henry Campbell's 1st Division would be the reserve, tucked behind the Lesser Arapile.

But first, Pakenham's 3rd Division supported by D'Urban's two regiments of Portuguese horse and Arentchildt with his five squadrons, were to hook round to the western end of the Monte de Azan, and roll up Thomières from that direction. Speed of contact now mattered: the quicker the closure upon, and engagement of, the ill-supported Maucune and Thomières, the better the chance of overwhelming them before support could arrive. In essence his Lordship was putting the equivalent of four infantry divisions of thirty-one battalions (twenty British, six Portuguese, five Spanish) and four cavalry brigades of 3,200 sabres against two infantry divisions of seventeen battalions and two cavalry brigades of 1,900 sabres. That is, if we exclude Bonnet, which of course is arguable. In theory, Marmont should be in all sorts of trouble. The question was, however, could Wellington apply his battalions' firepower before Marmont could strengthen his?

So sometime around 3pm his Lordship hopped on his thoroughbred horse, and set off hell for leather for Aldea Tejada and his brother-in-law Edward Pakenham. He faced a good three mile point. At a 15mph canter he would use up a valuable twelve minutes. There was no question of merely sending a message! In any event, during the time it would take the 3rd Division to come into contact he would be back, to brief his other Divisional Commanders. He would be absent perhaps half an hour. His faithful German dragoon bodyguard went with him, while the rest of his escort, and his staff, followed his dust as best they could on their slower chargers.

CHAPTER 9

Salamanca
The 3rd Division's Attack

About the time of Wellington's urgent rush to the 3rd Division, his opposite number was hit by shrapnel from one of Captain Dyneley's two 6-pounders, up on the Lesser Arapile. He suffered a badly lacerated right arm and two broken ribs – not life threatening, but serious enough for his surgeon to wish to amputate the arm (permission refused). It was said, perhaps conveniently, to have happened as he descended the Greater Arapile prior to galloping to stop Thomières's westwards progress, and to refuse Maucune's request to make a proper divisional attack on Arapiles village. His *Memoires* omit explaining why Thomières was not stopped earlier.

The command fell to Clausel as senior divisional commander. But when news of Marmont's incapacity was carried to the 2nd Division's headquarters, Clausel had been removed to the rear. His own injury – a heel injured by shell fragments – needed dressing. Without Clausel, therefore, Bonnet as next senior assumed the command. He had been present with the injured Marshal in rear of the Arapile. He also soon afterwards was seriously wounded in the leg. Clausel eventually arrived, but it can be seen that for an hour or so the French army was effectively headless. There was now no question of averting catastrophe, for Brigadier Jean-Guillaume-Barthelemy, Baron Thomières, with less than two hours to live, was not to be recalled from his appointment with the Hon. Edward Pakenham.

The latter stood dismounted among his officers, two miles from the Pico de Miranda. He watched a pair of horsemen close rapidly from the east. His wife's brother had already passed Brigadier D'Urban, ordering him to cover the right flank of the 3rd Division, who were, he said, about to march to the west end of the plateau and upon Thomières. D'Urban's Journal noted:

> Lord Wellington came down from the neighbourhood where he had been examining the enemy's left, at a rapid gallop accompanied only by Colonel de Lancey (but followed immediately afterwards by Colonel Sturgeon) and gave us orders for the attack verbally – first to me (whom he had first met with) and then to General Pakenham.

D'Urban of course had Arentschildt's 1st Hussars KGL and the 14th Light Dragoons, as well as his own 1st and 11th (Portuguese) Dragoons – some 1,200 sabres.

William Grattan of the 88th, in Wallace's brigade, recounts his version of the meeting:

> As Lord Wellington rode up to Pakenham every eye was turned towards him. He looked paler than usual; but, notwithstanding the sudden change he had just made in the disposition of his army, he was quite unruffled in his manner, as if the battle to be fought was nothing but a field-day. His words were few and his orders brief. Tapping Pakenham on the shoulder, he said, 'Edward, move on with the 3rd Division, take those heights in your front – and drive everything before you.' 'I will, my Lord,' was the laconic reply of the gallant Sir Edward. A moment after, Lord Wellington was galloping on to the next Division, to give (I suppose) orders to the same effect.

His Lordship doubtless added to this dramatic version, short as it is on the practicalities of generalship, that D'Urban was to be on his right, and that Leith and Le Marchant were to attack from the north. Grattan's words, of course, were hearsay, since he would not have been among those officers present at the head of the column, the 88th not being the front regiment but the second. Someone who *was* at the head of the column with the leading regiment (the 45th) and who, therefore, might actually have heard the words, was Captain Thomas Lightfoot:

> His Lordship's orders to General Pakenham in our hearing were: 'Pakenham, you will carry that height where the enemy's left is posted by storm, and when you have gained it, go at them hard and fast with the bayonet.' 'Yes my Lord' said Pakenham 'That I will by God' and galloping off, placed himself at our head.

(Lightfoot wrote this eight weeks later.) The Division had only just halted, the men looking to get a meal going at last – on the march since 11am, and before that an early breakfast – but 'our camp kettles were in a moment overturned, and mounted on the mules. Many men looked blank at having to go without their meal' (94th's Regimental History). The country being passable every-where, the Division was not confined to any road. It formed in four columns. The eastern-most was Wallace's Brigade of the 1st/45th (Nottinghamshire), the 74th (Highlanders) and the 1st/88th (Connaughts); the next being Lieutenant Colonel James Campbell's Brigade of the 1st and 2nd/5th (Northumberland), his own 94th (Scotch Brigade) and the 2nd/83rd; the outside (westernmost) column was Power's Portuguese Brigade of the 9th and 21st Line and the 12th Caçadores; and outside of all was D'Urban's and Arentschildt's horse. Two artillery batteries were present: Bull's 6-pounder RHA and Douglas' 9-pounder battery. The advance and left flank guards comprised all seven light companies, three companies of the 5th/60th and the 7th Caçadores – around 1,000 men. There is a track running south from Aldea Tejada for about a mile, which then turns south to Miranda de Azan, with a low feature to its east running down to join the Pico de Miranda.

Wallace's Brigade Major, Captain James Campbell wrote:

> To me, as Brigade Major of the right brigade (i.e. senior) Sir Edward Pakenham, in his quick decided manner, pointed out the direction we were to take, and desired me to tell Colonel Wallace, 88th regiment, the officer in temporary command of the brigade, to move on with as much rapidity as possible, but without blowing the men too much. The division was soon under arms, and moved off rapidly in open column, right in front, the 45th regiment leading ... We soon descended into a kind of valley, or rather hollow, and having brought up our left shoulders a little, we pushed on at a quick pace, but in excellent order, to the right; the side of the hollow towards the enemy concealing our movements from their sight. The whole scene was now highly animating. The left brigade, headed by the 5th regiment, was, I saw, marching parallel to the right, so as to be ready to form a second line. The Portuguese brigade followed the right, and the whole of the left flank of the columns was covered by a cloud of sharpshooters, composed of light infantry companies, and riflemen of the 5th battalion, 60th regiment.

The battalions moved briskly, company behind company, each in two lines, some twenty men broad (the average bayonet strength of Pakenham's battalions, excluding the large 1st/5th, was only 400 men), with sufficient space that each, given the simple order 'Left Form', would pivot left into a battalion line. The uncased Colours moved between the two centre companies. Thus if all three columns formed left Pakenham would have his 2 Brigade immediately supporting 1, with the Portuguese in rear. Brigadier D'Urban rode ahead of his squadrons, to the right of the 3rd Division.

> The enemy was marching by his left along the wooded heights, which form the southern boundary of the valley of the Arapiles, and the western extremity of which closes in a lower fall, which descends upon the little stream of the Azan, near the village of Miranda. As the head of our column approached this lower fall, or hill, skirting it near its base, and having it on our left, we became aware that we were close to the enemy, though we could not see them owing to the trees, the dust, and the peculiar configuration of the ground. Anxious, there-fore, to ascertain their exact whereabouts I had ridden out a little in front, having with me, I think, only my brigade-major Flangini and

Da Camara, when upon clearing the verge of a small clump of trees, a short way up the slope, I came suddenly upon the head of a French column of infantry, having about a company in front, and marching very fast by its left. It was at once obvious that, as the columns of the 3rd Division were marching on our left, the French must be already beyond their right, and consequently I ought to attack at once.

Curto, commanding Marmont's Light Cavalry Division, and who was tasked to look after Thomières, does seem to have been entirely absent from this northern flank; why he should think the southern to be his prime care, no-one knows. His choice allowed D'Urban a free run at Thomières's point battalion from the 101st Ligne. The only description we have is in Charles Oman, who had privileged access to D'Urban's unpublished diary:

> This was apparently the leading battalion of the French 101st, march-ing with its front absolutely uncovered by either cavalry vedettes or any exploring parties of its own. D'Urban galloped back, unseen by the enemy, and wheeled his leading regiment, the 1st Portuguese dragoons – three weak squadrons of little over 200 sabres – into line, with orders to charge the French battalion, before it should take alarm and form square. The 1st Portuguese, and two squadrons of the British 14th Light Dragoons, which had only just arrived on the ground, being the foremost part of Arentschildt's brigade, followed in support. The charge was successful – the French were so much taken by surprise that the only manoeuvre they were able to perform was to close their second company upon the first, so that their front was six deep. The two squadrons of the Portuguese which attacked frontally suffered severe loss, their colonel, Watson, falling severely wounded among the French bayonets. But the right-handed squadron, which overlapped the French left, broke in almost unopposed on the unformed flank of the battalion, which then went to pieces, and was chased uphill by the whole of the Portuguese horsemen, losing many prisoners.

Notwithstanding the above, other accounts vary on the formation of the 101st when its leading battalion was caught by the 1st (Portuguese) Dragoons: square or line. They are even at odds on the immediate success or otherwise of D'Urban's charge. Oman's narrative therefore seems to be an attempt at com-promise. Where no doubt exists, however, is that D'Urban's ultimate success removed, as a formed body, one fifth of Thomières's force, which in any event was already heavily outnumbered. He now would have four battalions to hold Pakenham's approaching ten battalions. For the 1st Ligne seems to have been halted earlier by Thomières, farther back on the Monte de Azan, possibly to form a link with Maucune. His now 2,000 bayonets faced the 3rd's 5,600. Still, he had the high ground, which always counts a lot, and he had (somewhere) Curto's 1,800 sabres.

While Pakenham made best speed behind D'Urban's horse, Lord Wellington made straight for the low ridge in front of Las Torres, behind which his heavy cavalry lay. There the 1,000 dragoons of Le Marchant's Brigade were halted, dismounted and awaiting orders, with Anson's Brigade nearby. According to Le Marchant's biographer son, he was told

> That the success of the movement to be made by the Third Division would greatly depend on the assistance they received from the cavalry; and that he must therefore be prepared to take advantage of the first favourable opportunity to charge the enemy's infantry. 'You must then charge,' said Lord Wellington, 'at all hazards.' After some brief remarks on the chances of the day, Lord Wellington rode towards the centre, having desired the Dragoons to remain in the same position until the time of action was come.

He went next to Sir James Leith, at forty-nine his oldest general with the largest Division. The 5th comprised eight British and three Portuguese battalions, some 6,300 bayonets, in rear of Arapiles village on Cole's right. The Division was deployed in two lines, Greville's Brigade in front. To equalise the lines, Pringle's 1st /4th (King's Own) had been placed with Greville. Pringle's other battalions and Spry's Portuguese formed the second line. Greville had forty-five battalion companies (his five light companies being forward) with a first line of some 1,300 men, who thus stretched perhaps 900 or 1,000 paces behind the village. Those on the right were rather more exposed to the French artillery. The men were lying down under the continuous fire from Bonnet's and Maucune's guns described as the 'heaviest cannonade I have ever been exposed to' by Leith's DAQMG Major (later Field Marshal) William Gomm. Corporal John Douglas, 3rd/1st (Royal Scots) wrote:

> Down we lay on the slope of the hill for the purpose of letting the round shot pass over us as quickly as possible. In this position we loaded. The 2nd Brigade formed in our rear. The 3rd Brigade on coming down did not please Sir James. He marched them back under the whole fire in ordinary time and back again to make them do it in a soldier-like manner. The Brigade, on coming to its ground, the centre sub-division of the 15th Portuguese was struck with a shot (I mean cannon shot) which did fearful execution. It scarcely left a man standing. On the 2nd Brigade forming a man of the 44th was killed and lay for a few minutes, when a shell fell under him and exploding drove him into the air. His knapsack, coat, shirt body and all flew in every direction. A Dublin lad lying on my right looks up and exclaims with the greatest gravity, 'There's an inspection of necessaries.'

The Division had been lying beneath the ricochets for about an hour, with General Leith riding up and down his line to calm the men, when Lord Wellington and his staff officers, who had now caught up with him, arrived from Las Torres. He gave his orders, according to Leith's ADC Andrew Leith Hay 'in a clear, concise, and spirited manner, there was no appearance of contemplating a doubtful result.' Leith was to await General Bradford's Portuguese Brigade coming in from the rear to his right, so as to provide a line with Pakenham, and then he was to attack Maucune. By then Pakenham would be up on the ridge, threatening Maucune's flank. Cole would advance on his left. Espana's 3,000 and Le Marchant and Anson would be behind his right shoulder, and the 7th Division would be in support in rear. 'His instructions,' says Leith Hay 'concluded with commands that the enemy should be overthrown and driven from the field.'

Edward Pakenham's men now emerged from their covered approach. Wallace's Brigade Major, James Campbell:

> Having moved a considerable distance in this order, (field officers and adjutants prolonging the line of march,) the head of the column, by bringing up the right shoulder, began gradually to ascend the hill, on the top of which we expected to find the enemy still extending to their left. At length, having fairly outflanked the French left, the whole formed line, and with Sir Edward Pakenham in front, hat in hand, the brigades advanced in beautiful style, covered by our sharpshooters, the right of the first line admirably supported by the left brigade.

Thomières' men were caught in column, two battalions of the 101st Ligne leading, the survivors of their 3rd battalion now being chased back by D'Urban; then came two battalions of the 62nd with quite a gap to the 1st Ligne. There was probably time for Thomières to send forward the voltigeurs of the 101st – say 150 men – but these were heavily outnumbered. Even so, a contemptuous comment by William Grattan, a man with little time for his Portuguese allies, indicates it didn't go without incident:

> A number of Caçadores commanded by Major Haddock were in advance of us. The moment the French fire opened, these troops, which had been placed to cover our advance, lay down on their faces, not for the purpose of taking aim with more accuracy, but in order to save their own sconce from the French fire. Haddock dismounted from his horse and began belabouring with the flat side of his sabre the dastardly troops he had the misfortune to command, but in vain; all sense of shame had fled after the first discharge of grape and musketry, and poor Haddock might as well have attempted to move

the great cathedral of Salamanca as the soldiers of his Majesty the
King of Portugal.

Grattan's account of the attack, somewhat over-blown in places, very much
catches the smell of it. Nor should we forget that his regiment, his beloved
Connaughts, were the centre regiment and because of their strength it comprised nearly half of Wallace's line.

All were impatient to engage, and the calm but stern advance of
Pakenham's right brigade was received with beating of drums and
loud cheers from the French, whose light troops ... [ran] down the
face of the hill in a state of great excitement ... [and] commenced an
irregular and hurried fire ... Regardless of the fire of the riflemen,
and the showers of grape and canister, Pakenham continued to press
onward; his centre suffered, but still advanced; his left and right
being less oppressed by the weight of the fire, continued to advance
at a more rapid pace, and as his wings inclined forward and out-
stripped the centre, his right brigade assumed the form of a crescent
... it so happened that all the British officers were in front of their
men – a rare occurrence. The French officers were also in front;
but their relative duties were widely different: the latter, encouraging
their men into the heat of battle; the former, keeping their devoted
soldiers back! ... the soldiers, with their firelocks on the rest, followed
close upon the heels of their officers, like troops accustomed to
conquer. They speedily got footing upon the brow of the hill, but
before they had time to take breath, Thomières's entire division,
with drums beating and uttering loud shouts, ran forward to meet
them, and belching forth a torrent of bullets from five thousand
muskets, brought down almost the entire of Wallace's first rank, and
more than half of his officers. The brigade staggered back from the
force of the shock, but before the smoke had altogether cleared away,
Wallace, looking full in the faces of his soldiers, pointed to the French
columns, and leading the shattered brigade up the hill, without a
moment's hesitation, brought them face to face before the French had
time to witness the terrible effect of their murderous fire.
Astounded by the unshaken determination of Wallace's soldiers,
Thomières's division wavered; nevertheless they opened a heavy
discharge of musketry, but it was unlike the former, – it was irregular
and ill-directed, the men acted without concert or method, and
many fired in the air. At length their fire ceased altogether, and the
three regiments, for the first time, cheered! The effect was electric;
Thomières's troops were seized with a panic ... The French officers
did all that was possible, by voice, gesture, and example, to rouse

their men to a proper sense of their situation, but in vain. One, the colonel of the leading regiment . . . seizing a firelock, and beckoning to his men to follow, ran forward a few paces and shot Major Murphy dead at the head of the 88th, however, his career soon closed: a bullet, the first that had been fired from our ranks, pierced his head; he flung up his arms, fell forward, and expired.

The brigade, which till this time cheerfully bore up against the heavy fire they had been exposed to without returning a shot, were now impatient, and the 88th greatly excited: for Murphy, dead and bleeding, with one foot hanging in the stirrup-iron, was dragged by his affrighted horse along the front of his regiment; the soldiers became exasperated, and asked to be let forward. Pakenham, seeing that the proper moment had arrived, called out to Wallace 'to let them loose'. The three regiments ran onward, and the mighty phalanx, which but a moment before was so formidable, loosened and fell in pieces before fifteen hundred invincible British soldiers fighting in a line of only two deep.

Two items in Grattan's account were totally inaccurate, of course: the number of Frenchmen and Wallace's casualties, both exaggerations. Yet we are left with a clear picture of the three battalions climbing the Pico de Azan and curling round the French. The British line might be 600 yards wide, the Pico half of that, still less the ridge's top. The angle of slope would make for slightly awkward progress on the flanks. Not surprisingly, we don't know how Thomières's battalions were formed. One strong possibility, given the ground, is that the four battalions were one behind the other, each in column of Divisions i.e. two companies wide i.e. twelve companies deep among the top of the Pico. If so their frontage could be no more than eighty yards wide (assuming eighty men per company), although it is possible that, at the last minute, Thomières brought up a second battalion, so that the 101st fought four companies wide over say 150 yards. Grattan refers not to a line but to 'the French column', as does William Brown, 45th.

The former's regiment, in the centre, suffered double the casualties of the 45th and 74th on the flanks, but of course the outcome could scarcely be doubted. Wallace commanded some 1,500 muskets, even excluding his three companies of riflemen of the 5th/60th, and all these pieces could be brought to bear. If Grattan was right and Thomières did not present a line – and in the swiftness of the circumstances it seems most unlikely – but was on a width of four companies, he could not volley fire with more than about 300 muskets. That, however was academic. Wallace's men fired but one shot – to revenge Major Murphy – and it was their electrifying cheer which seemed enough to panic the 101st, together with the lowered bayonets and, doubtless, the Connaughts' scream. That no ball was expended is confirmed by Wallace's Brigade Major, Captain James Campbell:

> The enemy's skirmishers and ours now set to work, yet we did not wait for their indecisive long shots; but advancing still rapidly and steadily, our right soon came into contact with their left, which had opened a very heavy and destructive fire upon us, and which would have lasted long enough had the brigade been halted to return it, but it was instantly charged and overthrown. It was now evidence to us all that Sir Edward Pakenham knew how to handle Picton's division.

The French colonel who shot Major Murphy as he rode up the slope in front of his Colours, was thought by Murphy's two subalterns, carrying those Colours, that they themselves were the colonel's target. Lieutenant Thomas Moriaty, with the Regimental Colour, remarked 'That fellow is aiming at me!' 'I hope so,' said his fellow, Lieutenant John D'Arcy, under the King's Colour, 'for I thought he had *me* covered!' And as Major Murphy slumped in his saddle, another ball took off D'Arcy's epaulette and cut the Colour pole in two.

Just shy of the summit, but before the cheer and charge, the leading ranks opened to allow riflemen from the 5th/60th, whose job was now done, to filter back. They came in with a special urgency on the right, crying 'Dere Deivel, French horse coming!' The 45th promptly made a flank with the Grenadier and Nos 1 and 2 Companies – a tricky drill in the circumstances – as squadrons of Curto's chasseurs thundered round the slopes from the east. Not being in square the 45th, and the 1st/5th in second line behind them, and who had not even a timely warning to wheel back the end of their line, were both badly mauled. Private William Brown, 45th:

> As our brigade was marching up to attack a strongly posted column of infantry, a furious charge was made by a body of cavalry upon our Regiment, and, not having time to form square, we suffered severely. Several times the enemy rode through us, cutting down with their sabres all that opposed them. Our ranks were broken and thrown into the utmost confusion. Repeatedly our men attempted to reform, but all in vain – they were as often cut down and trampled upon by their antagonists ... Numerous and severe were the wounds received on this occasion. Several had their arms dashed from their shoulders, and I saw more than one with their heads completely cloven. Among the rest I received a wound, but comparatively slight, although well aimed. Coming in contact with one of the enemy he brandished his sword over me, and standing in his stirrup–irons, prepared to strike; but, pricking his horse with my bayonet, it reared and pranced, when the sword fell, the point striking my forehead. He was, however, immediately brought down, falling with a groan to rise no more.

Oman cannot have read Brown's account, saying only that the 45th were 'Feebly attacked ... [and] beat off their assailants easily'. Not so, according to Brown. On the other hand, he has the chasseurs make better progress against the 5th, who are in effect routed, and quotes Sergeant Morley, 1st/5th:

> There was a pause – a hesitation. Here I blush – but I should blush more if I were guilty of a falsehood. We retired – slowly, in good order, not far, not 100 paces. General Pakenham approached, and very good-naturedly said 'reform,' and after a moment 'advance – there they are, my lads – let them feel the temper of your bayonets.' We advanced – rather slowly at first, a regiment of dragoons which had retired with us again accompanying ... and took our retribution for our repulse.

Of course, Morley makes no actual mention of French cavalry. But the 5th, in second line, could not possibly have retired that 100 paces because of an advance by French infantry – through the 45th? The casualty figures perhaps help a little. The 45th's losses during the entire battle (fifty-five men or twelve per cent) were nearly identical to the 74th's on the other flank (forty-nine men or eleven per cent). In the middle not surprisingly the 88th lost 135 men or twenty per cent. The 1st/5th, however, lost 126 men or fourteen per cent, whereas the other three battalions in Campbell's Brigade averaged nine per cent. So maybe a fair conclusion is firstly, that part of the 5th did run; and secondly, that Brown's account could be a little exaggerated. After all, the 45th's Regimental History claims Pakenham called out 'Well done, 45th', presumably, en route to steady the 5th.

The chasseurs were driven off by D'Urban's dragoons. It is thought Curto had forward only one of his brigades at this stage, of eight or nine squadrons, and that two or three of these had tried their luck against the 45th and the 5th, the rest clashing on the southern flank with Arentschildt's five squadrons of the 1st Hussars KGL and the 14th Light dragoons. The former under Major Gruben charged and broke the front French squadrons, but were then held until the 14th came up to add their weight.

At this point, as Pakenham led his men forward on to the Monte de Azan, driving the pitiful remnants of the 101st and 62nd pell mell backwards, General Thomières was killed. The French outran the British. 'The enemy's infantry was quickly pursued, chiefly by Colonel Wallace at the head of the 88th, whose impetuosity was found most difficult to restrain ... another charge was intended; the French would not stand however, and retired in tolerable order,' said Wallace's Brigade Major. The death of Thomières had come most untimely for his one remaining colonel, utterly involved in trying to form a line, then failing that, getting the men back in one piece to shelter behind the 1st Ligne.

French casualty figures cover the whole day, and clearly many listed for the 101st and 62nd were not caused by Pakenham's 3rd Division, but subsequently by Le Marchant's dragoons. We cannot say what was caused by sabre, what by firelock. By the end of the day the 101st Ligne had 263 fit for duty out of 1,449 i.e. losses of 1,186 or a wipe-out, eighty-two per cent; the 62nd Ligne had just 255 men fit out of 1,123 i.e. losses of 868 or an equally staggering seventy-seven per cent; and the 1st Ligne 1,533 fit out of 1,743 i.e. losses of just 230 men or thirteen per cent. The 62nd and 101st effectively ceased to exist this day. Their General was dead, their divisional battery of six guns was captured, the 101st's Colonel and their Eagle (possibly – or the 62nd's) were taken, and the Division had lost half its strength. Having inflicted 2,284 casualties, for its own losses of 560, the 3rd Division had triumphed. Yet they were now nudging into a further mass of blue coats, with cavalry milling around to their right. Grattan caught the mood:

> We found ourselves in an open plain, intersected with cork trees, opposed by a multitude who, reinforced, again rallied and turned upon us with fury . . . the attitude of the French cavalry in our front and upon our right flank caused some uneasiness . . . the peels of musketry along the centre still continued without intermission; the smoke was so thick that nothing to our left was distinguishable.

Wallace was coming up against the 1st Ligne, formed in good order across the Monte, and behind which the remnants of the 62nd and the 101st were trying to regroup. Down the slopes to their left, although Pakenham's men could not see through the smoke, Cotton's cavalry were approaching and, beyond them, Leith's 5th Division, to whose Colours we will now hurry, at about a quarter to 5pm.

CHAPTER 10

Salamanca
The 5th Division's Attack

Sometime before 5pm, with the French command increasingly in chaos, Marmont struck down, Bonnet and Clausel attempting control whilst wounded by turn in leg and heel, all British eyes were divided between the progress far right of Pakenham, and near right of Bradford's Portuguese. Leith needed the latter on his flank, unless the former engaged Thomières first, when the Portuguese would have to go hang. Whilst waiting, Leith kept busy by setting the calm example under shellfire expected of him, riding his line and talking to his recumbent regiments. Two of his eight British battalions were new – the 2nd/4th (King's Own) had been out only eight weeks, the large (800 strong) 1st/38th (Staffords) only one day; the former had experienced the fetid airs of Walcheren but little else of relevance, the latter survived the Corunna march three and a half years earlier. Leith's other six had all climbed the San Vincente walls at Badajoz, the three of Walker's Brigade suffering substantially (1st/4th, 2nd/30th Cambridgeshire and 2nd/44th Essex, the other three very lightly (3rd/1st Royal Scots, 2nd/38th and 1st/9th Norfolks). In addition, six of the battalions had been at Fuentes, three at Busaco and four at Corunna, so there was fair Peninsular experience, except for the 2nd/4th who had none. Spry's Portuguese (3rd and 5th Line, 8th Caçadores) had all been present at Badajoz, Fuentes and Busaco, but with little fighting.

John Douglas, 3rd/1st, recalls Leith turning in the saddle and saying:

> 'Royals,' on which we all sprang up. 'Lie down men,' said he, though he sat on horseback, exposed to the fire as calm as possible. 'This shall be a glorious day for Old England, if these bragadocian rascals dare but stand their ground, we will display the point of the British bayonet, and where it is properly displayed no power is able to with-stand it. All I request of you is to be steady and obey your officers.'

And then, passing to the 38th next in line 'As for you, 38th, I have only to say, behave as you have always done.'

At the end of a very long and tiresome hour under fire, he got his Division on their feet, perhaps hearing Pakenham's battle commence and seeing a staff

officer approach at the gallop. Captain Philip Bainbrigge, DAQMG, had been
sent by Lord Wellington to move the 5th Division forward at last, even though
Bradford was still not up with them.

> I galloped up to General Sir James Leith, who was riding backwards
> and forwards along the front of his men, with two or three staff
> officers; the round shot were ricocheting into and over his line, and
> as I was about to deliver the order, a shot knocked up the earth close
> to his horse's nose. He took off his hat to it, and said, 'I will allow you
> to pass, Sir!' The men heard him, and said, 'Hurra for the General.'
> They were at ordered arms, standing at ease. I delivered my order,
> and the General replied, 'Thank you, Sir! That is the best news I
> have heard today,' and turning to his men he said, taking off his hat
> and waving it in the air in a theatrical manner, and in a tone of voice
> which was grand in the extreme, said, 'Now boys! We'll at them.'

An anonymous soldier of the 1st/38th wrote 'General Leith came up,
waving his hat and shouting "Now my lads, this is the day for England. They
would play at long ball with us from morning til night, but we will soon give
them something else." ' Douglas says that when Leith reached the Royal Scots
he heard him say 'Stand up men! Then taking off his cocked hat and winding it
around his head he gives the words "March!" ' And very welcome that word
was, to get the blood moving – and also for the light troops, who all this time
had been out front. Leith had Major Alured Faunce, 1st/4th, in command
of the light companies from his British battalions, two companies of the
Brunswickers, and all of the 8th Caçadores – a covering party of possibly
1,000 men. They had not been actively skirmishing, since no forward movement had yet been required; their job was to keep their opposite numbers from
harassing the Division at close range. Now they could move up the slope, and
readily did so. Behind them the 9th (Norfolks) and probably the left wing of
the 2nd/38th (Staffords) necessarily broke their line while filing through the
western end of the Arapiles village. Once in the clear, their neat dressing 'as if
it had been a common field day' impressed John Douglas's Company commander Captain Stewart. '(He) Stepping out of the ranks to the front, lays hold
of Captain Glover and cries, "Glover, did you ever see such a line?" Douglas
avers "That in the regiments which composed our lines there was not a man
six inches out of his place." '

And what a sight it must have been. Five battalions all in red, from right to
left the 1st/4th, 3rd/1st, 1st/38th, 2nd/38th and the 1st/9th, two ranks each
1,300 men long or say 1,000 yards, well over half a mile of red, five sets of
Colours and in front of those belonging to the 1st/38th (the new boys), in the
middle rode General Leith and his gilded staff. A hundred yards in rear came
the Division's second line of Pringle's and Spry's five battalions, half red, half

in brown, and ahead of the 2nd/44th (Essex) Colour party, or thereabouts, rode his Lordship and staff, for a brief spell.

One of Leith's ADCs was his nephew Lieutenant Andrew Leith Hay, 29th. In his *Narrative* he makes no mention of the arrival of Captain Bainbrigge with Wellington's order to move out, but predicates that act on the arrival of Bradford's Portuguese: 'The moment he (Bradford) was in line, General Leith gave the signal'.

Previously to this movement, Leith had despatched his other aides-de-camp, Captains Belshes and Dowson, to different parts of the line 'to help restrain over-keenness.' For the business of advancing a long thin line over a mile of broken ground is quite fraught, yet quite essential to the delivery at the end of it, of either a disciplined volley or a meaningful cheer to precede the charge. Anyone whose battalion has sweated in the arcane parade ground drill known as the 'Advance in Review Order', or tried to present his company with a straight front while marching past some visiting Royal, eyes right, sword just so, will know the practicalities. On rough ground, there is a human but infuriating guarantee of over-compensation: any section of the line lagging because of obstacles, however minor, would not immediately be followed on the flanks by a reduction in speed, only after a little time has passed and the need becomes obvious. By then the lagging section has speeded up, to catch up. Thus flows a line with alternate bulges, with all the sergeants in rear screaming 'Get up, Get up on the right!' or 'Steady on the left, Steady!' or 'Hold back in the Centre'.

Neither a level line nor calm lungs – essential to all volleys and cheers – can result from too fast or too harassed a march. It was upwards of a mile to the crest behind which Maucune's Division, out of sight, lay in wait. Many soldiers, and all Frenchmen, would have made this approach in column, like Cole's 4th Division at Albuera. 'March in column, fight in line', however, is all very well as a dictum – fastest, most accurate approach, total control etc. – but it is also horribly vulnerable to artillery, and demands a nicety of timing not to leave it too late (as the French always found) to change into line. So Leith Hay's reference to 'That beautiful line ... admirable dressing ... orderly steadiness' in the following account indicates his uncle's troops were indeed highly disciplined. In particular, since the 1st/38th comprised nearly a third of his front, his new boys were making an impressive start.

Leith needed to clear the front of Maucune's skirmish line. His nephew was given the job:

> In ascending the height on which the French army was placed, the division continued to be annoyed by the artillery fire from its summit; the ground between the advancing force and that to be assailed was also crowded with light troops in extended order, carrying on a very incessant tiraillade. The general desired me to ride forward, making

the light infantry press up the heights to clear his line of march, and if practicable make a rush at the enemy's cannon. In the execution of this service, I had to traverse the whole extent of surface directly in front of the 5th division: the light troops soon drove back those opposed; the cannon were removed to the rear; every obstruction to the regular advance of the line had vanished. In front of the centre of that beautiful line rode General Leith, directing its movements, and regulating its advance. Occasionally every soldier was visible, the sun shining bright upon their arms, while at intervals all were enveloped in a dense cloud of dust, from whence, at times, issued the animating cheer of British infantry.

It took twenty minutes to close on the French, under a galling fire from Maucune's and Bonnet's batteries. The 4th Division on Leith's left were a little delayed – as was Bradford's Portuguese on the right – but Leith had the comfort of knowing his flanks were secure, or would be very soon, with the addition of the whole of Hope's 7th Division in rear. He could see the smoke of Edward Pakenham's men working in from the near horizon on the right, and behind his right shoulder he could see the Heavy Brigade of the 3rd and 4th Dragoons, and the 5th Dragoon Guards, and Anson's three regiments of Light dragoons – some 1,500 horsemen. The same sight had been not quite so enjoyed by Maucune a little earlier from his elevated position, and caused him – or some of his colonels – to make the fatal error of attempting to form square from their battalion columns. Though why, under the imminent threat of the British line coming over the convex crest, they were still in column, is beyond understanding. They were only a fair musket shot back. Leith Hay:

> His columns, retired from the crest of the height, were formed in squares, about fifty yards removed from the ground, on which, when arrived, the British regiments would become visible. The French artillery, although placed more to the rear, still poured its fire on the advancing troops. In the act of urging forward the light infantry, a ball struck the horse I rode, and passing through his body, laid him dead on the spot. In this dilemma I waited until the line approached, and having dismounted an orderly dragoon, proceeded with the general, who continued in the same situation he had occupied when the division commenced its advance; namely, in front of the Colours of the 1st battalion of the 38th regiment. We were now near the summit of the ridge. The men marched with the same orderly steadiness as at first: no advance in line at a review was ever more correctly executed: the dressing was admirable, and spaces were no sooner formed by casualties then closed up with the most perfect regularity, and without the slightest deviation from the order of march.

General Leith, and the officers of his staff, being on horseback, first perceived the enemy, and had time to observe his formation, previous to the infantry line becoming so visible, as to induce him to commence firing. He was drawn up in contiguous squares, the front rank kneeling, and prepared to fire when the drum beat for its commencement.

The Light companies pressed closer and closer 'To within a few yards of their lines' says Douglas, 1st/3rd. The Royal Scots were towards the right of the line. He was impressed by the Portuguese, who advanced crying out 'Fogo ma felias' or 'Away my sons.' He went on:

> At this moment a French officer mounted on a white horse seemed to be very busy endeavouring to keep his men to their work, when a Corporal of the name of Joffrey and I got leave to try if he was ball proof; and running out a few yards in front kneeled down and fired together, but which of us struck him must still remain a mystery, but down he went. Poor Joffrey, while in the act of rising off his knee, received a ball in the breast which numbered him with the dead also.

It is thought Maucune had deployed in two regimental lines of columns: the three battalions of the 15th Ligne left and the two battalions of the 82nd Ligne right; in second line were two battalions 66th Ligne left and two of the 86th Ligne right i.e. five battalions up front and four in support. Accounts vary in the description of the formation, with phrases including 'Contiguous squares', 'square', 'columns and squares', 'solid columns', 'parts of squares and parts of lines' and 'ill-arranged column(s)'.

The French fired first, but were as promptly hit by a far greater weight of lead from Greville's Brigade. Leith Hay:

> All was still and quiet in these squares; not a musket was discharged until the whole opened. Nearly at the same moment General Leith ordered the line to fire, and charge: the roll of musketry was succeeded by that proud cheer that has become habitual to British soldiers on similar occasions – that to an enemy a tremendous sound, which may without exaggeration be termed the note of victory. At this moment, the last thing I saw through the smoke was the plunge of Colonel Greville's horse, who, shot through the head, reared, and fell back on his rider. In an instant every individual present was enveloped in smoke and obscurity.

John Douglas takes up the story:

> Our murderous fire opened, which swept all before it. Their first line we fairly ran over, and saw our men jumping over huge grenadiers, who lay down exhausted through heat and fatigue, unhurt, in the

hope of escaping. Of course we left them uninjured, but they did not behave honourably, for as soon as they found us at a little distance they resumed the posture of the enemy and commenced to fire on our rear; but nearly the whole of them paid the price of their treachery with their lives.

The first line of the enemy being broken and falling back in confusion, the second lined the side of a deep trench cut by the torrents of water which roll down from the hills near the village of Arapiles, and so deep and broad that it took a good spring to leap over it. Here the second line kept up a heavy fire of musketry, which checked our centre for a few minutes, while our poor fellows fell fast. To remain long in this way was too much to be borne. The cheer was raised for the charge, a general bound was made at the chasm, and over we went like so many beagles, while the enemy gave way in confusion.

Sergeant James Hale, 1st/9th, was in the left flank battalion of the first line, which being wider than Maucune's, the Norfolks to a degree were lapping around the French right, to the obvious disadvantage of the 82nd Ligne: 'We showed them the point of the bayonet, and gave them a grand charge, by which we obliged them to leave three pieces of cannon in our possession in a short time: this part of the enemy's line continued retreating for some considerable distance, and we continued firing advancing.'

There is now a converging of blue on blue, red on red, as from the west the shattered remnants of Thomières 101st and 62nd Ligne attempted to move back while rallying behind his 1st Ligne, with Wallace's Brigade pushing along the ridge. Suddenly, Wallace's men were warned to prepare to form square! Grattan was with the centre battalion:

The smoke was so thick that nothing to our left was distinguishable; some men of the 5th Division got intermingled with ours; the dry grass was set on fire by the numerous cartridge-papers that strewed the field of battle; the air was scorching; and the smoke, rolling onward in huge volumes, nearly suffocated us. A loud cheering was heard in our rear; the brigade half turned round, supposing themselves about to be attacked by the French cavalry. Wallace called out to his men to mind the tellings off for square. A few seconds passed, the tramping of horses was heard, the smoke cleared away, and the heavy brigade of Le Marchant was seen coming forward in line at a canter. 'Open right and left' was an order quickly obeyed; the line opened, the cavalry passed through the intervals, and, forming rapidly in our front, prepared for their work. The French column, which a moment before held so imposing an attitude, became startled at this unexpected sight. A victorious and highly-excited infantry pressing close upon them, a splendid brigade of three regiments of cavalry ready to burst through their ill-arranged and beaten column, while no appearance of succour was at hand to protect them, was enough to appal the boldest intrepidity. The plain was filled with the vast multitude.

Grattan suggests 'Some men of the 5th' were now very close, (presumably their light troops) the cavalry moving forward through Wallace's ranks. Certainly John Douglas noted them on his right: 'The 1st Royal Dragoons, the 5th Green Horse (5th Dragoon Guards) and a Regiment of Heavy Germans advanced with us on our right. Some of the Greens sung out "Now boys, lather them, and we'll shave them".' These early sightings of Cotton's cavalry will lead us into the next chapter. But first we should consider the butcher's bill for Leith's work. Maucune's casualty figures, of course, are rather irrelevant at this stage, since Le Marchant's dragoons are about to make them much, much worse.

Whilst as we have seen there is no certainty quite how Maucune's battalions were formed and, therefore, we cannot calculate the frontage upon which he stood, Leith's casualty figures (like Wallace's) indicate the British line over-lapped the French front, and would therefore tend to bend into a crescent. This explains the lighter losses in Greville's brigade by the 1st/4th (four per cent) and 1st/9th (seven per cent) on the right and left flanks, and the heavier losses in the centre by the 3rd/1st (twenty-one per cent), 1st/38th (eighteen per cent) and 2nd/38th (seventeen per cent). In fact, there is greater disparity here than in Wallace's (who averaged eleven per cent on the flanks to twenty per cent in the centre of the line). As to the Royal Scots' twenty-one per cent losses, John Douglas's reference to the ditch behind which the French second line were located and which 'Checked our centre for a few minutes, while our poor fellows fell fast,' is perhaps reason enough; although some say they also suffered losses earlier in the day, when Wellington chose them to tempt a French attack.

Greville's Brigade's casualties totalled 400 with fifty-one killed (two officers) and 349 wounded (twenty-three officers). Pringle, on the other hand, was but a quarter of that, at 105 all ranks with eleven killed (two officers) and ninety-four wounded (again just two officers). Pringle's overall casualty rate was five per cent, compared with 15.9 per cent for Greville's. One can but speculate, there-fore, at the extent to which Pringle's Brigade was properly involved in Leith's attack. That is, actually fighting, other than providing the necessary second line. To lose but four officers out of 103 officers surely, in the Peninsular context, indicates minimal engagement, with losses mostly attributable there-fore to gunfire both whilst waiting to attack and during the approach march. There were reported to be at least four batteries in position on Maucune's right.

The same remarks apply to Spry's Portuguese, on Pringle's left (their casualty rate was a similar 5.3 per cent) a total of 123 all ranks with a mere seven officer casualties out of 156 officers. It is possible therefore the 2nd King's Own, the 2nd Cambridgeshires, the 2nd Essex and the Portuguese took little active part in Leith's attack. Which, therefore, is at odds with the regimental histories of the 30th and 44th by Bannatyne and Carter respectively, who both have Greville's and Pringle's positions reversed. That is, that Pringle was the first-line brigade. The eyewitness accounts quoted and the above casualty figures make this assertion untenable. It does not, of course, deny the splendid capture of an Eagle by Lieutenant Pearce, 44th, which we will describe in all its glory in later pages.

As to Leith's overall divisional losses, because the casualties amongst his two companies of Brunswickers are not known, we can only estimate a total of 640–660 all ranks, out of 6,691 men – say nine per cent overall. These are modest, but sadly they included himself and two ADCs – Leith Hay and William Dowson. We have noted before the custom, in the Peninsula, for senior officers to lead from the front, and whilst no doubt it did much for the men's morale to see Lieutenant General Sir James Leith and six of his operational staff some ten or twenty yards in front of their own Colonel and their own Colours, it brought equal joy to numerous French gun captains peering greedily down their sights. Their presence alone guaranteed the poor old 38th, especially Nos 3, 4 and 5 Companies, caught it in the neck. But it was a small matter of honour, and Leith could do no other. He received a 'most severe contusion on the breast, and his left arm broken' from a musket ball. His nephew had two horses killed under him, the ball in the second instance perforating his calf muscle. Dowson, the extra ADC, suffered a mangled foot and died two years later. Colonel Greville, 38th, had his dead horse fall on him but was not himself wounded. The commanding officer of the 3rd/1st was killed and Colonel Miles of the 38th severely wounded.

It is plain from all this that the forty-year old General Antoine-Louis Popon, Baron de Maucune, twenty-six years a soldier and a much wounded veteran of many battles – most recently at Busaco and Fuentes – did nothing this day to add to his reputation. He and his men have yet to be hit by the tempest of rampaging dragoons, but his infantry defeat deserves comment. Of course Leith had more men – we have taken Oman's 6,691 all ranks, to Maucune's 5,079 – which superiority of 1,612 men could be described as another three battalions, or an advantage of a third. But that fails to acknowledge that Pringle and Spry were scarcely involved. If we are being fair in this view, it means 5,079 Frenchmen in nine battalions, at the top of a slight hill, in the dead ground behind the false crest, with between four and six batteries in support, were bested by 2,600 British in five battalions fronted by say 1,000 light troops. How could that be? Was not Maucune advantageously in the classic Wellington defensive posture? Who can doubt our 'Atty would have merely reprised, say,

Vimiero? Wherein lay Maucune's problem? Of course we know now it was to be the cavalry that turned defeat into rout, but it is a puzzle to understand the prior infantry defeat. Pakenham's business with Thomières off to their left was certainly audible, and possibly some early 'runners' could have passed through, spreading alarm and despondency. But while good soldiers look to their front when cowards pass by in rear, an element of uncertainty would inevitably be introduced; still more the sight and sound of 1,500 horse off to the left front; still more uncertainty at their commander's response. It is surely certain Maucune's battalions were not at any time in square prior to Cotton's initial forward movement. The lengthy light troop bickering, if anything, would indicate the approaching need for line; unless, that is, Maucune had decided he was going to meet Leith's line by a downhill charge in column. Whatever, line or column, his battalions were probably caught by Leith in a last minute process of change, towards squares. While Leith Hay saw some squares – presumably on the French left – with 'the front rank kneeling and prepared to fire when the drum beat', Maucune's second line of the 66th and 86th may well still have been in column. We know John Douglas heard an exchange of words with the 5th Dragoon Guards before Greville's Brigade made final contact. He states, 'The French seemed to be taken by surprise as ... [British cavalry] advanced with us on our right ... The enemy seemed to be rather in confusion ... The cavalry was to them a puzzle. [They] seemed to have formed parts of squares, and parts of lines.' Into such unfinished chaos Leith unleashed his volley. Let us not forget he presented some 2,500 muskets, not counting light troops. This was infinitely more than Maucune's men could bring to bear. The French fired first, but Leith's volley must have come as a massive hammer blow and immediately, whilst reeling and looking about to see who still stood, individual Frenchmen would hear the British raise their cheer from behind the bank of smoke, emerging with bayonets down, a red crescent all across their front.

At this stage Maucune's second line should have been the rock behind which the 15th and 82nd Ligne could shelter, or else provide the counter-attack to catch the British at their most disordered. Throughout history, the prime requirement for any counter-attack has been to provide an immediate reaction. The Guards and KGL at Talavera broke and chased four of Sebastiani's regiments, only in turn to be routed back by his second line. As Leith Hay said after that battle, 'Who has ever seen an unbroken line preserved in following up a successful bayonet charge?' Half the men are invariably busy looting through French knapsacks. But Maucune's second line also crumbled, and we can be sure that was due to the utter confusion and panic caused both by Thomières's men coming back from the left, and Le Marchant's horses now pounding up through the smoke from their left front. So let us hop into a saddle and join the dragoons.

CHAPTER 11

Salamanca
The Cavalry Charges

The historian who approaches this chapter without trepidation was either present at the battle in a helicopter, or is an arrogant fellow without shame. The difficulties of arranging people in their proper place and time daunt casual interpretations. Your present author claims no certainty for his version of events. We can but hope that one day more diaries (preferably in French) will be discovered which confirm our deductions. To say that multiple scenarios exist understates the position. What follows is one understanding, and we shall try to resist the temptation to set out others, which, ultimately, will only confuse and mar a very fine tale.

Firstly, however, it is well to remind ourselves that this equestrian chapter of the story took place – literally – alongside what is not yet touched on: the unsuccessful actions on the left of the 5th Division by the 4th Division and others. We will turn to them in due course, but do bear in mind that to our left some 8,000 Allied troops under Cole and Pack had been launched against some 13,000 men in two French divisions under Clausel and Bonnet. It was not going well, as we shall see. Somewhere behind Clausel and Bonnet were Boyer's 1,700 dragoons, and behind them in the woods of the Sierra, Ferey's 3rd Division of 5,700 men. And coming up fast behind Maucune's now broken – but not defeated – 5,200 men, were the 6th Division under Taupin, with another 4,500, not to mention (somewhere) Curto's 1,900 chasseurs. So there were many formed French bodies whose location Lord Wellington could not possibly know and take into account. However, one essential of any successful attack is the provision of adequate reserves to allow for the unexpected. In this regard when he launched the cavalry he had Clinton's 6th Division behind Arapiles village, and Hope's 7th and Bradford's Portuguese to their right (all totalling nearly 13,000 men), with the unengaged 1st and Light Divisions up above the Lesser Arapile. It was a masterly set of dispositions, setting prudence behind audacity.

Immediately he received orders from his Lordship, Major General John Gaspard Le Marchant sent a small mounted party forward, under Lieutenant Colonel Charles Dalbiac (second Lieutenant Colonel of the 4th Dragoons, who were commanded by Lieutenant Colonel Lord Edward Somerset), and Lieutenant William Light, to check the Heavy Brigade's route to the attack on the plateau, posting vedettes at any difficult places. Le Marchant having formed his three regiments, the lines dismounted whilst waiting what would be a long hour before the next order came. He had eight squadrons (Major Onslow's of the 4th Dragoons had been detached around midday). Dalbiac put the strength at 750, but that probably excluded officers, orderlies, farriers etc. Taking the 15 July States, which is all we can go on, and allowing for Onslow's absence, Le Marchant's first line was of six squadrons (he had a squadron each from the 3rd Dragoons and 5th Dragoon Guards in rear in support) and would have comprised 650 sabres, with another 200 in support. Those 650 were in two lines, so each squadron would have drawn up a little in excess of fifty men wide. Allowing two paces per horse that is a line of 600 yards; if closed stirrup to stirrup, half that. The 5th Dragoon Guards (Douglas's 'Green Horse') were almost certainly on the left of the line.

Wellington's order to move was eventually sent, quite properly, to Sir Stapleton Cotton, as commander of the cavalry. The axis for Le Marchant ran obliquely south-east into the gap which at that stage still existed, between the 3rd Division on the right, and Maucune's as-yet unengaged Division, in front of Leith. The latter was well on his way. His Lordship's timing was exactly right.

It is said Dalbiac had found a route offering partial concealment. The country was, of course, entirely open, but in the nature of convex slopes, however mild, lines of observation for those above cannot always fully cover those below. Cotton was probably in rear of the dragoons, and possibly with George Anson's 11th and 16th Light Dragoons behind him in their turn. Le Marchant's orders were to charge at all hazards, at the first favourable opportunity following release by the Peer, and judging that moment was clearly to be his make-or-break decision. Or was it Cotton's? Go too soon, or go too late, would not do. Right now the French on his right shoulder were trickling back in increasing numbers from Pakenham's men. They were making their way along the ridge to Thomières' 1st Ligne, three battalions formed in good order across the Monte de Azan, some 1,700 men. Wallace's Brigade was pushing forward, on to Grattan's 'open plain intersected with cork trees, opposed by a multitude who again rallied'. Pakenham's second line battalions had not kept up with the thrusting 88th, there having been the small matter of the 5th's temporary reverse; and Wallace was concerned by 'the attitude of the French cavalry to our front and to our right flank'. Therefore, while waiting for the other six regiments to close, he was busy ensuring the men could form square without confusion.

During this pause on the Monte, the survivors of Thomières' 62nd and 101st did their best to rally between the right rear of the 1st Ligne (who faced west) and the left rear of the 66th (Maucune's left flank, second line regiment) and who faced north. Towards them, although yet quite distant, came the point regiment of Taupin's 6th Division: two battalions from 22nd Ligne of some 1,000 men.

About this time Leith came over the crest and into the view of the 15th and 82nd Ligne, who fired their defensive volley from their squares and half-formed squares, but of course without great effect; they were immediately out-volleyed, cheered and charged and, seemingly without any prolonged firefight, breaking to flee back to and through their second line of the 66th and 86th Ligne. Thus, in effect the 66th's two battalions now became Maucune's left wing, and the 86th's two battalions his right. So four French regiments – Thomières' 62nd and 101st and Maucune's 15th and 82nd – the much reduced rump of ten battalions, were attempting in great confusion to rally in rear of their comrades, and with the regularly formed 22nd Ligne from Taupin coming to their aid.

This surely was Le Marchant's moment. Some 4,000 blue coats were now entirely vulnerable, loosely forming or running to the rear. Yet it appears Stapleton Cotton, having moved forward, decided at this point to exercise his rights of command. His widow, Mary Viscountess Combermere, in her *Memoire* relates a brief quarrel wherein Cotton orders Le Marchant to attack, and being coldly asked (for there was no love lost) in which direction, lost his temper and snapped 'To the enemy, sir'. An exchange of 'high words' is hinted at in other sources. One imagines Le Marchant rode off in a foul humour which, since he rode to his death, is indeed a sad thought.

We have already noted reports of thick smoke billowing across the plateau, the scorching air, the dry grass in places blazing from scattered cartridge wads (the light breeze took the smoke directly at the French); and Grattan noted the noise of approaching horses to the 88th's left rear. Through the smoke emerged the Heavy Brigade in line at canter: 'Open right and left ... and they passed through the intervals, forming rapidly in our front, prepared for their work.' A quarter mile to the left we have noted Douglas's exchange with the Green Horse (the 5th) as they flanked Greville's light troops, just before Leith volleyed and charged Maucune: 'Now boys, lather them and we'll shave them'. So just as the sudden noise of massed horse threw Wallace's men briefly into a worry over forming square, a similar cringe would sweep Thomières's 62nd and 101st. Grattan paid them the compliment that at least 'all things considered they attempted to get into square with much regularity ... but before the evolution was half completed' they were hit by the double dragoon line. For Le Marchant had put his squadrons straight into them, the right squadrons seemingly at the 62nd and 101st, the left at the 66th who were now being broken and swept back by Greville's brigade.

One eyewitness ('AZ' writing in the *United Services Journal* in 1833) described the 66th's formation as 'A sort of column of half battalions'. That would be three companies wide, therefore, with four such lines for the two battalions present. If the companies were formed in three ranks the half battalion column would have stretched some 100 yards wide – about the same width of one of Le Marchant's squadrons, which now descended upon them.

'AZ' says the 66th's fire (they had previously been engaging Leith's men)

> was so ill-directed, that it is believed scarcely a single dragoon fell from its effects; and no check taking place, the cavalry bore vigorously forward at a gallop penetrating their columns, nearly the whole of which were killed, wounded or taken, leaving the broken infantry to be made prisoners by the 3rd Division as they cleared the ground before then, to assist in which one squadron of the 4th Dragoons was for the moment detached.

It is probable the 66th was knocked over by the two squadrons of the 5th Dragoon Guards on the left of Le Marchant's line; on the right it is probable the two squadrons each of the 3rd and 4th Dragoons at the same time ploughed through Thomières's 62nd and 101st Ligne. The French casualties as we shall see were dreadful.

The 5th Dragoon Guards continued until they came 'upon another column, of about 600 men, who brought down some men and horse by their fire, but attempted no stand of any consequence and, falling into confusion, were left as before to be captured by the advancing infantry.' This second grouping are thought to be the survivors of Maucune's broken 15th Ligne, his original first line, who had now fled through the 66th and were attempting to rally.

By now the squadrons had become a little mixed, the original line not helped by having to negotiate increasing numbers of evergreen oaks, and of course all the individual confrontations after which, spurring to catch up, the line was re-joined where convenient. Gaps between squadrons disappeared; by the same token, and in that excitable spirit of the hunting field which all too often bedevilled British cavalry, it may be the two squadrons in the second or support line also joined in. No source suggests this, but such widespread destruction of the entire French left wing now being apparent to the most hesitant observer, the temptation to reinforce success must have called strongly. The surging dragoon line thundered on, blowing by now, sighting a third

> French brigade, which, taking advantage of the trees, had formed a colonne serree, and stood awaiting their charge. These men reserved their fire with much coolness till the Cavalry came within twenty yards, when they poured it in upon the concentrated mass of men and horses with a deadly and tremendous effect. It is thought that nearly one third of the dragoons came to the ground; but as the remainder retained sufficient command of their horses to dash forward, they succeeded in breaking the French ranks, and dispersing them in utter confusion over the field. At this moment Colonel Lord Edward

Somerset, discovering five guns upon the left, separated from the brigade with one squadron, charged, and took them all.

There was now complete chaos, with many hundreds of Frenchmen throwing down their muskets, and standing still with arms raised waiting to be taken; others still attempting to load and fight, still more running to the rear, the dragoons in amongst the 22nd 'excited by the struggle, vied with each other in the pursuit, and galloped recklessly into the crowd of fugitives, sabreing those who came within their reach. To restrain them at such a moment was very difficult.' Le Marchant 'fought like a private soldier, and as many as six men fell by his hand'. Sensing their vulnerability to a counter-attack, he sent his ADC son back to Cotton, hopefully now bringing up Anson's squadrons, while he joined a half squadron of the 4th, under Lieutenant Gregory, about to charge a square. Taking the lead, he was shot in the stomach and fell to the ground mortally wounded. 'The ball . . . passed through his sash into the abdomen, and he breathed his last a few moments after the surgeon found him. He was lying a few yards to our left, his sword was firmly grasped in his right hand, the knot round his wrist, and the edge very much hacked.' (Lieutenant Colonel John Cameron, 9th, to Napier in 1827.) His son, no doubt full of excitement, pride and glory, returned only to see his father's body on a stretcher being carried by two dragoons. 'Over powered by this unexpected calamity he threw himself upon his father's body in an agony of grief.' It is thought Le Marchant and Gregory had run into some of Taupin's main body. A sergeant major of the 65th did later claim to have shot a British general.

Le Marchant's death occurred at the very end of his brigade's endeavour. For there were troopers sufficient only to form three squadrons or so, according to 'AZ'. Prudence for once asserted itself, aided by temporary exhaustion and, presumably, the spreading news that the General was down. The final, and most bloody massacre, had been of Taupin's 22nd Ligne, two battalions (the 3rd not being present) of about 1,000 bayonets. The memoirs of Lieutenant Colonel Castel, who was one of Clausel's ADCs, says he was sent by Marmont, shortly before the latter's wounding, to bring up Taupin in rear of Maucune; and that in Taupin's absence he was only able to move up the 22nd. It is said that the two battalions mustered forty-seven men at the end of the day. Such an annihilation is, however, quite difficult to understand, since they must surely have had adequate warning to form squares. Perhaps they had advanced rather too far forward into the smoke.

Le Marchant's charge with the Heavy Brigade lasted forty minutes, and the distance must have been a little under two miles, with a mile first at walk and trot to get onto the plateau. At that average speed, a running man could easily have kept up with them. Clearly far less time was spent in headlong, glorious canter, than in steady walk and disciplined trot, allowing much static time for belabouring blue coats. At the end, however, the dragoons' vulnerability was obvious, in their lack of formation, horse power and numbers: a counter-attack by Boyer's eight squadrons of heavy dragoons and even some small part of Curto's seventeen squadrons of chasseurs must have brought a full revenge. Several accounts refer to the presence among the French infantry of 'a few chasseurs and dragoons' or of 'a chasseur of the 20th being closely pursued' but there are no references to formed mounted bodies: perhaps 'their cavalry ran away' was an accurate statement. In any event, a formed counter-attack would not have altered the day's outcome. Le Marchant had now completed the devastation of twelve of sixteen infantry battalions begun by Pakenham and Leith – a fifth of the Army of Portugal.

Such was the terror induced by the points and sword edges wielded by the dragoons with such vigour, that there was the rare sight of Frenchmen actually running for shelter, inside British lines (having necessarily first dropped their muskets). Their trust was not misplaced.

> Such as got away from the sabres of the horsemen sought safety amongst the ranks of our infantry, and scrambling under the horses, ran to us for protection – like men who, having escaped the first shock of a wreck, will cling to any broken spar, no matter how little to be depended upon. Hundreds of beings, frightfully disfigured, in whom the human face and form were almost obliterated – black with dust, worn down with fatigue, and covered with sabre-cuts and blood – threw themselves amongst us for safety. Not a man was bayoneted – not one even molested or plundered.

We may, however, take Grattan's last point as mere pious cover for his genteel Victorian readers. It is inconceivable the Connaughts would not rob blind every French knapsack thus presented on a plate – and in return for their lives, Johnny Crapaud no doubt was quick to hand them over.

The charge of the Heavy Brigade was naturally noted in letters home and later memoirs, and these well illustrate the confusion, and narrowed vision, experienced by individuals. Success or failure overall was the sum of these individual actions. It is hoped the following give a fair flavour of the action. We start with a Frenchman: Captain Parquin, of Marmont's escort:

> I saw a chasseur of the 20th who was being closely pursued by two English horsemen. 'Turn and face them!' I cried, going to his help. But he did not stop and one of the Englishmen, whose horse was obviously out of control, cannoned into me and we both went down. Then the second Englishman galloped up and shouted: 'You are my prisoner!' With his sabre he gestured me to walk ahead of him. The memory of my captivity in Russia flashed through my mind. I noticed that my would-be captor had not drawn his pistol; if he had done so, I would have been forced to obey him. Instead, I parried the blows

which he aimed at me with his sabre for I had quickly risen from beneath my horse which made off towards the escort. I endeavoured to strike the legs of his horse so as to unhorse him. When my horse returned without me the other members of the escort became alarmed and two of them came to look for me and to bring me my horse. As soon as they saw me they rode towards us at full speed and the Englishman, when he saw them, retired immediatcly.

Then William Bragge, 3rd Dragoons, writing home three days later:

My Dear Father, Knowing the Anxiety you and my Mother will feel upon hearing of a great and sanguinary Battle, in which the Third Dragoons bore no inconsiderable share, I take the earliest possible opportunity of informing you that I escaped perfectly sound, Wind and Limb, together with the Little Bay Mare who carried me through the Day delightfully and I believe to her Speed and Activity I may in a great measure attribute my marvellous escape, as I at one Time had to gallop along the whole Front of a French Brigade retreating in double quick step ... the Cavalry advanced upon the Backs of the Infantry. Our Brigade literally rode over the Regiments in their front and dashed through the Wood at a Gallop, the Infantry cheering us in all Directions. We quickly came up with the French Columns and charged their Rear. Hundreds threw down their Arms, their cavalry ran away, and most of the Artillery jumped upon the Horses and followed the Cavalry. One or two charges mixed up the whole Brigade, it being impossible to see for Dust and Smoak.

Another officer of the 3rd Dragoons, Lieutenant John Massey, wrote to his brother a week later that: 'Our loss in men was trifling all things considered for we charged infantry which is a thing very rarely done. I can't tell you of any hairbreadth escapes that I had for I don't know of any, but the balls were thick and near enough to be unpleasant.' And then there was the infantry officer who yearned for mounted glory:

When the cavalry of Le Marchant passed through Wallace's brigade Captain William Mackie of the 88th was missing. In the confusion that prevailed it was thought he had fallen. No one could give any account of him; but in a short lapse of time, after the cavalry had charged, he returned covered with dust and blood, his horse tottering from fatigue, and nothing left of his sabre – but the hilt! He joined the cavalry so soon as the fighting amongst the infantry had ceased. (Grattan)

John Luard, 4th Dragoons, discovered a French gun team all hooked in and about to escape: 'I cut down their leader, turned the horses heads towards our side, and then galloped on.' A brother officer of Luard was the sole 4th Dragoon officer to be wounded that day, and had a gruelling experience as a temporary prisoner. He escaped after very honourable treatment by Taupin's 65th, and wrote home three weeks later. He had the memorable name of Lieutenant Norcliffe Norcliffe:

> My Beloved Father, Thanks to the Almighty, and the very great care of my surgeon, I am quite out of danger from the severe wound I received, but it was perhaps the most hairbreadth escape that ever was heard of, the skull was just injured, and the tenth part of an inch more must have consigned me to an eternal rest. We were pursuing the French Infantry, which were broken and running in all directions. I was cutting them down as well as I could, when in the hurry and confusion I lost my regiment and got with some soldiers of the 5th Dragoon Guards; on looking behind me, I could only see a few of the 5th, and we were in the centre of the enemy's infantry, amongst whom were a few Chasseurs and Dragoons. Nothing now remained but to go on, as we were in as much danger as by going any other way.
>
> I rode up to a French officer, who was, like the rest, taking to his heels, and cut him just behind the neck; I saw the blood flow, and he lost his balance, and fell from his horse. I perceived my sword was giving way in the handle, so I said to the officer who lay on the ground: 'Donnez-moi votre épée' – I really believed he was more frightened than hurt; I sheathed my sword and went on with his. I had not gone 10 yards further before my horse was wounded in the ear by a gunshot; he turned sharp round, and at the same instant I was shot in the head. I turned giddy, and fell off. I can recollect a French Dragoon taking away my horse. I was senseless a few seconds, and when I recovered, I saw the French Dragoons stripping me of everything; they began by turning my pockets inside out, to look for money which they stole; my sword and sash, hat, boots, and spurs off my feet, dragging me along the ground in the most barbarous manner, saying: 'Eh ... Anglais, vous n'etes pas a cheval.' Another said: 'Eh, je sais [sic] bien le garçon, il m'a poursuivi ...', in fact I never saw such usage in my life. 'Allons donc, enlève-toi,' said another; I shook my head as much as to say 'I am unable to rise,' when he held a sabre over me, crying out: 'je vous mettrai a coup de sabre'. At last I was left by the cavalry, and the French infantry came all round me, and I expected the same treatment. Judge of my surprise, when I experienced quite the contrary: 'Courage mon ami'. I asked for water, being very faint from loss of blood, 'Ma foi! Je n'ai point de l'eau, pauvre garçon,' and another 'Etes-vous officier?' I stammered out: 'Oui, Lieutenant de Quatrième Regiment de Dragoons.' Presently

an officer came up with five; each took a leg and an arm, and the fifth supported my head, which was bleeding profusely, and I will say I never saw men more careful; if ever I groaned, owing to the pain of being carried, they said to each other: 'Gardez-vous, gardez-vous, camarade.' They carried me into the very centre of the French column, close to a very fine battalion of Grenadiers, with great bear-skin caps. I rested here a little, for I was very weak, and a great number of French officers came round me and were most particularly civil. One, Colonel of Grenadiers, poured some brandy into a cup and wanted me to drink it; I just wet my lips. He then ordered five Grenadiers to fall out, and carry me further into the wood. I made a sign that I had rather be carried by the men who brought me there, fearful of falling into fresh hands. Our infantry was at the time advancing again to the attack; the five men who carried me were desired by all the French officers to take particular care that no-one ill-used me, and that if I could not get away, I was to be laid under a tree. The 5 men seeing our infantry advance, laid me down very carefully under an olive tree, and each of them shook hands with me before they left me, and said: 'Je vous souhaite bien, Monsieur,' and they also desired that I would remember they belonged to the 65th Regiment. Our Infantry I could now see (though it was getting dark) were bayonet to bayonet and I had at last the pleasure of seeing the enemy running in every direction. I had the presence of mind to take off my jacket and cram it into a bush, and as my boots were off I lay as if I was dead, and when they were running away they all passed my tree and took me for a Frenchman. Several of the musket shots from our men struck the back of the tree where I was, but I lay very close to the root. Drums, muskets and everything they could not easily carry, were thrown away by the enemy. One Frenchman was wounded by a musket ball in the side, and fell close to me. I waited till the French had all passed me, and then ran as far as my strength would let me towards our Riflemen. I was so delighted at getting back, I actually threw my arms around the necks of our infantry. They led me up to where the 6th Division was, and I fell down quite exhausted at the feet of the Grenadier Company of the 32nd Regiment ...

This is the second horse I have lost in action, as also my saddle, bridle, collar, sword, sash, musket, boots and spurs, and pouch. My beloved Father will see I have been obliged to draw largely on the agent owing to these losses. It was a glorious day for our Brigade. They behaved nobly; 4 men killed of the troop I commanded, and several men and horses wounded. It was a fine sight to see the fellows running, and as we held our swords over their heads, fall down on

their knees, drop their muskets, and cry: 'Prisonnier, Monsieur.'
You see I am not born to be a prisoner. Love to my Mother.

As we have seen, Norcliffe's 65th captors also have some claim to have killed
Le Marchant, when he charged with Lieutenant Gregory's half squadron of
the 4th Dragoons. As ever with this battle, we need constantly to be alert to the
different phases, as they relate one to another in time – or as we think they
relate. Thus between Le Marchant's death charge and Norcliffe's capture,
which presumably took place very much together, and his eventual rescue by
the 32nd, we must picture the unsuccessful divisional attack by Lowry Cole's
4th Division upon Clausel and their retreat before Clausel's counter-attack;
and the successful divisional counter-counter-attack by Clinton's 6th Division,
whose 32nd were in Hinde's Brigade on the right. These events are yet to be
described, but the delay ascribed to Clinton's wait in front of Ferey's ridge,
put variously as 'about an hour and a half' (Thomas Hamilton) 'a long time'
(Napier) and 'for near three quarters of an hour' (61st's *Digest*), would indicate
poor Norcliffe, stripped, bootless and bleeding, was to enjoy French hospitality
for perhaps two hours.

During this time, two Eagles were taken. This account of the 44th Essex's
capture is taken from Edward Fraser's *The War Drama of the Eagles* (1912):

> The first Eagle – that of the hapless French 62nd, whose fate has
> been told – fell to Lieutenant Pearce of the 44th, a regiment in the
> Fifth Division. He came on the Eagle-bearer while in the act of
> unscrewing the Eagle from its pole in order to hide it under his long
> overcoat and get away with it. Pearce sprang on the Frenchman, and
> tussled with him for the Eagle. The second Port-Aigle joined in the
> fight, whereupon three men of the 44th ran to their officer's assist-
> ance. A third Frenchman, a private, added himself to the combatants,
> and was in the act of bayoneting the British lieutenant, when one of
> the men of the 44th, Private Finlay, shot him through the head and
> saved the officer's life. Both the Port-Aigles were killed a moment
> later – one by Lieutenant Pearce, who snatched the Eagle from its
> dead bearer's hands. In his excitement over the prize Pearce rewarded
> the privates who had helped him by emptying his pockets on the spot,
> and dividing what money he had on him amongst them – twenty
> dollars. A sergeant's halberd was then procured, on which the Eagle
> was stuck and carried triumphantly through the remainder of the
> battle. Lieutenant Pearce presented it next morning to general Leith,
> the Commander of the Fifth Division, who directed him to carry it
> to Wellington. In honour of the exploit the 44th, now the Essex
> Regiment, bear the badge of the Napoleonic Eagle on the regimental
> colour, and the officers wear a similar badge on their mess-jackets.

Not all historians accept that Pearce's Eagle was that of the French 62nd, for there is a case to be made for the 101st. Either way, it is a stirring tale, and presumably came about as the 44th, being in second line, had moved forward to assist in rounding up surrendered prisoners.

The second Eagle taken was that of Taupin's 22nd Regiment. John Douglas tells us:

> A little before sunset a Portuguese soldier of our Division picked up an eagle and brought it safe into the lines, to the astonishment of all as you would imagine that a sparrow could not escape between the two fires. This Eagle was the subject of an account in a book of anecdotes a few years ago, when it was stated to have been captured by an officer of the British. The statement was false. It was taken as I have mentioned. It lay on the ground along with a number of the Regiment to which it belonged, having fallen by our fire, and was free to be picked up by anyone, but it was first discovered among the dead by the Portuguese soldier. But what became of it afterwards I cannot say ...

The lucky Portuguese was one of Powers' 12th Caçadores, so one Eagle to the 5th Division, one to the 3rd. According to Edward Pakenham, the latter's capture was accompanied by two flags. Since the 22nd had two battalions present and knocked over, it would appear they lost both their battalion's fannions or Colours, *and* the regimental Eagle, a black day indeed.

Tempting though it is now to take note of the battle raging to the left of Leith's 5th and Le Marchant's cavalry, for our story is otherwise getting out of step, we must make room to record the casualty figures for Le Marchant, and for Maucune's Division. Leith, as we saw in the previous chapter, suffered a total somewhere around 650 all ranks killed and wounded (just eight men were taken, six of whom were in the 2nd/4th in the second line, which is very strange), or say nine per cent overall. Pakenham's had been very similar at 560 or ten per cent. Thomières, on the other hand, totalled 2,284 men or fifty-three per cent and Maucune 1,737 men or thirty-five per cent. The worst unit rate was Taupin's two battalions of the 22nd Ligne who, according to French sources, ended the day with just forty-seven men (meaning losses of nearly 1,000) – effectively wiped out, and entirely by the Heavy Brigade; the next worst were Thomières's 101st and 62nd Ligne, with casualties at eighty-two and seventy-seven per cent respectively; then the two regiments of Maucune's who, being on his left flank, also caught the Heavies: the 66th and 15th Ligne (fifty per cent and thirty-six per cent respectively). Maucune's other two regiments, the 82nd and 86th who probably escaped the main cavalry charges, had rate of twenty-seven and twenty-three per cent respectively. Thomières's 1st Ligne escaped lightly, and for no reason that one can understand. Their loss of 230 men or a mere thirteen per cent indicates that they somehow not only disengaged from Wallace's Brigade, but threaded their way back through the British cavalry (possibly making a swing to the south).

So the three French regiments closest to Le Marchant's axis, the 62nd, 66th and 101st, suffered so severely that they were effectively destroyed; that which stood directly in his path, the two battalions of the 22nd, was annihilated.

And what of the cost to Le Marchant, apart from the small matter of his own life? One other of his sixty-one officers was killed, and five wounded; twenty-two troopers were killed and seventy-four wounded, with five taken: a total of 108 casualties or 10.6 per cent; that is less than one squadron's worth. So we can summarise: Pakenham, Leith and Le Marchant with 1,318 casualties altogether, Thomières, Maucune and Taupin's 22nd in excess of 5,000. We know not the figures for sabre cuts or musketry, but as a combined operation, it was a famous hour, a brilliant deed; all the better too for the cavalry. An unusual control of the men had been somehow exercised by their officers. To ride down one confused but not incoherent body of the enemy is one thing; three such cannot be done without tight maintenance of due form as to direction, pace and line.

It is tragic that such a day of high endeavour was to be marred by a death which, like that of Robert Crauford at Rodrigo, was to deprive the British Army of a leader of the highest potential. Le Marchant's earlier contribution at his Military College to the education of young officers, his field training of cavalry regiments in Suffolk, and his important work on cavalry weapons and drills, marked him out as a great innovator. He had shown this day that he could command cavalry in the field, enough for us to wonder, how he might have led the Heavy Cavalry at Waterloo, had he lived another three years?

CHAPTER 12

Salamanca
Cole and Pack's Attacks

We now have some 34,000 men actively engaged in battle, one against another on foot and horse, with many already hors de combat. We are about to add a further 26,000 men, and all will be conscious that the day is wearing on. The sun is lower behind the Allies and another two hours will see the day begin to lose its light. Many will look forward to that. On the Monte de Azan, the 3rd and 5th Divisions are joining in one long line, the 7th Division, Bradford's Portuguese and Espana's Spanish in the rear. Taupin's 65th Ligne and 17th Léger immediately face Pakenham and Leith, with Boyer's dragoons close by, and the divisions of Clausel and Sarrut over their shoulders.

The previous chapter omitted mention of George Anson's two light dragoon regiments (the 11th and 16th), and also of the 1st Hussars KGL and 14th Light Dragoons inherited from Victor Alten by Colonel Frederick Arentschildt. We assume they were brought forward by Cotton as a support in rear of Le Marchant. At some point, however, they were sent around the right, and what they eventually found points out the difficulties under which Lord Wellington was operating at this stage: the usual 'other side of the hill' problem, which must be met by a margin of caution. For what was about to happen to Cole's unhappy 4th Division shows us (with our comfortable hindsight) possibly a rare lapse of generalship on his Lordship's part. Not a terminal lapse, thanks to his earlier provision of substantial reserves, but certainly something of a blot on the day's brilliance. For the regiments involved (including your author's) it meant further destruction. In our case, adding Albuera, Badajoz and now Salamanca together the 48th's total casualties were to be 875 all ranks – the equivalent of two battalions.

First as to Anson and Arentschildt, the latter wrote:

> About this time our heavy cavalry fell upon the French infantry from the other side, and I ordered the hussars to keep to the extremity of the left wing of the enemy's infantry, and cut off whatever they could, following myself with the 14th in close order. The hussars were then a great way in front, doing great execution among the enemy's infantry, and according to the nature of the service and ground

very much dispersed – when about two squadrons of the 3rd Hussars (Curto's division) came up to attack them. But Major Gruben, Kauchenberg and other officers rallied by great exertion a body strong enough to oppose the enemy though they were all mixed; some hussars some 14th and even some Portuguese. They then fell upon the enemy and drove them back, on which occasion some French officers were cut down, and from that moment the French officers never showed their faces again on that side. The pursuit of the infantry was then renewed together with some advanced parties of General Le Marchant's brigade until they came close to the large hill under the French batteries where you have seen them four guns have been sent back by the Hussars. I annex a receipt for two; the men who brought back the other two forgot to ask for receipts. Two colours have been taken likewise.

Pushing on further, Arentschildt emerged from a bank of smoke to find column upon column of undisturbed Frenchmen to his front. A similar description is given by an officer in Anson's brigade called Money:

To gallop, and the third division pressing them (the French), they run into the wood, which separated them from the army; we (Anson's light cavalry) charged them under a heavy fire of musketry and artillery from another height; near two thousand threw down their arms in different parts of the wood, and we continued our charge through the wood until our brigade came into an open plain of ploughed fields, where the dust was so great we could see nothing and halted; when it cleared away, we found ourselves within three hundred yards of a large body of French infantry and artillery, formed on the declivity of a hill. A tremendous battle was heard on the other side, which prevented the enemy from perceiving us. At last they opened a fire of musketry and grapeshot, and we retired in good order and without any loss.

Arentschildt sensibly back-pedalled away from this new foe, who we can probably take to be Sarrut's 4th Division of 5,000 men, since Clausel's 2nd Division by now must be farther forward. Clausel numbered 6,500 men, and thus with Sarrut within call, the gap between Bonnet and Maucune was about to fill with a total force over twice the size of that which Wellington was to send from his side. We need to think back to that earlier spell between 3pm and 4pm, when he was dashing from one divisional commander to the next. At that stage, we can summarise: across to the right was Thomières, in front is Maucune, half left an empty space part-filled by Bonnet's 122nd, then the latter on and behind the Greater Arapile with his other nine battalions. Cole was conveniently adjacent to the Lesser Arapile and therefore already on Leith's left flank, as was Pack's Portuguese Brigade. So Cole and Pack got the job. But equally adjacent were Clinton's 6th Division and Hope's 7th, neither of whom, nine weeks earlier, had been utterly shattered in the breach at Badajoz – they were away to the south with Graham's covering force.

The 4th Division's losses on 6 April, especially among the officers, had substantially weakened the effectiveness of Cole's five British battalions. Of an officer strength of about 125, two thirds (eighty-three) were knocked over in front of Trinidad (sixteen killed and sixty-seven wounded), and while those not severely wounded in due course would live to fight another day, the settled leadership of these battalions was totally disrupted. Three of Cole's five battalions acquired new commanding officers overnight, and at least eighteen of the fifty companies acquired new officers commanding. That is, eighteen captain vacancies; however, many companies were taken forward to Trinidad by senior lieutenants, and sixty-five of the killed and wounded officers were subalterns, of whom we may suppose ten or so might well have been in command. It is therefore reasonable to suppose that over half of the companies now going against Clausel were under new management. The same consideration applied to the all-important senior other ranks. New captains, new sergeants, new corporals, just nine weeks in post. We should bear this in mind when describing Cole's Fusilier Brigade, turning and running away. It is impossible not to speculate that any other division, less damaged, might have done better. Leadership is all.

Equally questionable was ordering Brigadier Sir Dennis Pack, without close support, to capture the Greater Arapile with his independent Portuguese Brigade. The hill and the ground in rear was held by Bonnet with 4,600 men in nine battalions, and with another three battalions of 1,600 men only 700 or 800 yards away. Pack had 2,600 men altogether. No wonder he wrote later 'No one admires Lord Wellington more than myself, but I fear he expected over much from my "Hidalgos", whose courage is of a vastly changeable nature.' This extraordinarily candid comment from the man who also said of his men 'standing well' at Busaco and at Ciudad Rodrigo, that it was 'Much to my wonderment'. He had commanded them over the previous two years, so his apparent lack of trust in his men and in his own ability to use them successfully against the Great Arapile, presumably was well founded. Again, as with his battered 4th Division, Wellington maybe snatched too easily at the convenient but understrength Pack. It is true that the dead ground immediately in rear of the Greater Arapile would have contained men in blue not visible to Wellington's telescope, whether he was on the Lesser Arapile or on the Teso. But that dead ground would not adequately hide the mass of Bonnet's eight reserve battalions, who must surely have been visible. A nut was sent to crack a sledgehammer.

One of Pack's ADCs, Lieutenant Charles Synge, has left us a splendid account of the attack on the Greater Arapile, and which we shall quote at length in due course. He does, however, put the cat among the historical pigeons by maintaining his master's orders were discretionary. That is that he was to exercise his own judgement in the matter, and attack Bonnet only if he saw a favourable opportunity. Pack himself however clearly states 'When I received the order to attack the hill ... It is the duty of the soldier to obey ... Hence we advanced up the hill', which is plain enough. Since Bonnet quite obviously must pose a brooding and massive threat to Cole's left flank, the more so the farther he advanced, it is inconceivable the Peer would leave the protection of that flank to the discretion of a brigadier. In any event, he was absolutely not in the habit of giving discretionary orders to any of his officers, beyond Hill, Beresford and Graham. Our narrative therefore assumes Cole and Pack set off together, and we will start with the latter.

Dennis Pack was positioned a little to the west of the Lesser Arapile. He had command of the 1st and 16th Portuguese Line, each of two battalions, and the 4th Caçadores. The latter had started their day skirmishing around the Chapel. These five battalions Pack decided to use in an interesting way. As if regarding the long slope to the crest of the ridge as some huge breach into a walled town, he deployed with a firing party, a storming party/forlorn hope backed by a grenadier force, and then his main force in two columns. All that was lacking was a ladder party! The storming party comprised 100 men of the 4th Caçadores led by Major Peter Fearon, with orders to gain the top of the slope if he could 'And then lie down', with the other 400 or so Caçadores to go forward on either flank with a view, presumably, of providing a firebase when the Brigade's four grenadier companies – say 200 men – under Lieutenant Neil Campbell went through to the assault. In two columns in rear were to be (on the right) the two battalions 1st Line under Lieutenant Colonel Noel Hill, and two of the 16th under Colonel Pizarro, on the left.

Bonnet held the ridge with the 120th Ligne, three battalions some 1,800 men strong, and a battery of eight guns. That's an awful lot of men for a feature 300 or so paces long. The infantry could remain hidden until required, as would some at least of the guns, firing from defilade positions from either flank. Those guns firing forward inevitably had safe ground (for the attackers) immediately beneath their lowest trajectories. But set against that the attackers were faced with a rocky scarp or ledge around four feet high, which ran along parts of the front top of the final slope. On the western edge of the ridge there was a larger rocky outcrop. Dennis Pack decided to assault with muskets not loaded, apart from the 400 men of his firing party. This was a mistake, although understandable. He clearly felt the necessary final impetus, so vital in an uphill attack, would be lost if men stopped to fire. But his words again imply some lack of trust: 'Once such troops as we had began firing, they would never get to the top.' Which may be so, but it's not terribly good for morale to send men forward in such naked fashion, nor does it allow either for an opponent who won't fret at the sight of your bayonet, nor if his cavalry should suddenly appear. Neither it is the time calmly to set about the loading drill, and certainly not if your 'courage is of a vastly changeable nature'. However, Pack obviously felt the enormity of his task required this rather sad do-or-die measure.

The attack is well described by Charles Synge:

> In a moment all the commanding officers were under way. As the General and I were riding to Major Fearon's storming party, he remarked that both on the right and left of the point of direction which the storming party were taking there appeared better openings to get to the top, and he added, 'I wish I had divided Fearon's party into two and sent half towards each of the openings, but it is too late now.' I said, 'Not if you choose to let me gallop at once and give him the order, and allow me to take command of one.' He hesitated for a second, but on my repeating the offer and urging the necessity of my being off or it would be too late, he consented. I was soon up with Major Fearon. He took fifty to the left, and I the same number (not that we stopped to count) to the right. Immediately after this change, my direction led through a patch of standing rye, where several of my little party fell, at first I supposed killed, for the enemy opened their guns as soon as they saw what we were about; but one man near my horse fell in such a manner that it struck me it was sham, and as he lay on his face I gave him rather a sharp prod with my sword – there was no time for any other appeal to his 'honour' – on which he turned up perfectly unhurt! What became of him afterwards I know not; I had other matters to think of ... While I was appealing to feelings of all sorts and had just got through the last of the rye, Pack overtook me, and said in a whisper, 'Synge! I think those fellows won't carry it for you.' I said 'Oh! Yes, they will, we are over the worst of it.' I meant the ground. The roar of the enemy's guns was tremendous as we approached the top, and somewhat unusual in its sound, for they tried to depress the muzzles of their guns as much as possible, and though they could not do so much harm, so steep was it, it sounded as if it all but touched the top of our heads. I have never heard the like before. Those following in support fared worse.
>
> The last part of the ascent was so steep that it was almost impossible for a horse to climb it; even the men did so with difficulty – but I had a horse that would do what scarcely any horse would attempt. It was not until I was close upon the summit that I knew what we had to contend with, for I found the ground, which had at a little distance the appearance of a gentle slope, formed a natural wall of I suppose between three and four feet high, at the top of which it spread out into a level table-land, on which the enemy were drawn up in line about ten yards from me. We looked at each other

for a moment. I saw immediately that what we had undertaken was impracticable, as the men could not mount the scarped ground without first laying their arms upon the top, and even then in such small numbers that it would be absurd – but I also saw that we were so easily covered by 'the wall', and the enemy so exposed from head to foot, that if we fired they could not remain an instant. At this critical moment the head of Sir Noel Hill's column, which had followed me in support, was close up, and Hill himself called to me to ask what to do and what was before us (he could not see). I said, 'Be quick, and let your leading company close up to this bank and fire away while the others deploy as fast as they can and fire as they get up – the enemy are exposed and we are protected by this parapet.' To my horror Hill replied, 'You forget we are not loaded!' 'Well,' said I, 'we have no other chance. Load away as fast as you can.' He gave the word of command, and the men were in the act – I was addressing some few words of encouragement as well as the breathless state of anxiety I was in permitted (my poor old Ronald with great difficulty keeping his position on the steep), and two or three of the storming party were trying to scramble up the scarp, when the whole line opposed to us fired, knocked me over and literally cut to pieces the few that had climbed the 'wall'. My thigh was broken, and in falling, having no hold of the saddle, I could not in any manner save myself. Ronald made a couple of springs down the hill while I was falling, and this, together with the mangled bodies of those who fell back off the scarp on the head of Hill's column, which in the confusion of loading was unable to see what was happening above, caused a sensation of panic which was complete.

The French line followed up their volley by charging up the edge of the scarp, down which they leapt when they saw our confusion. Sir Neil Campbell's Grenadiers, the left column and all, went! – the disaster was complete. I had fallen to the ground on the near side of my horse, it being the left thigh that was broken, and was in great agony owing to a sort of instinctive effort to use the broken limb in which the marrow also seemed to be breaking. A gallant little fellow, an ensign, who was adjutant of Hill's Regiment, ran up to me and put his arms under mine to try to raise me, and if his strength had equalled his courage and goodwill he would have carried me off, but he was of the smallest stature. I told him that my thigh was broken, and that it was of no use. The bayonets of the charging army were all but touching him before I could persuade him to save himself, and I actually pushed him away. A lot of the French ran over where I was, and amongst them an officer, cheering them on. As he passed over me, seeing me twirling about in frightful agony owing to the position in which I had fallen, he called out at the appalling spectacle my state exhibited. 'Oh! Mon Dieu!' and then asked, 'Est-ce-que vous etes Anglais?' I said, 'Yes,' and he pointed to a man by his side as he ran by and told him to save me. The man, who I suppose was a non-commissioned officer, did stop for a second or two, which perhaps saved my life. Some of the enemy then began to plunder those who had fallen, wounded, dying or dead, and several began at me. I was in Hussar uniform, and worse all my riches about me, with some smart things about my neck, which there was a scramble for. Most foreign soldiers, at least such as I have known, conceal their money in the waistband of the dress or inside the leg of the boot. To see if I had any such store some began cutting my clothes off, as you might have seen a sheep in the act of being shorn, and one began to pull off my boots. This was horrid, for my overalls were fastened down by curb-chain piping, and the attempt to get the boot off the broken limb was intolerable. I was soon left to go out of the world nearly as naked as I had first entered it.

Just then my attention was called from my own state to a fine young fellow of the 1st Grenadiers, who was defending himself with his musket against four or five men who surrounded him, and who were all trying to bayonet him. I called to them to spare him as he was now their prisoner. Someone, who I believe was in authority, thought I wanted something for myself, and seemed disposed to ascertain what I stood in need of, but when he learnt I was appealing for the young Portuguese sergeant, he turned away. 'Oh! As for these canaille!' was all I heard, and how it ended I do not know, for I myself became an object of the same sort of extinguishers. Suddenly they were called off to re-form on their original position on the top of the Arapiles, and I and the bodies of my comrades were left to our fate.

Of course, where French infantry would generally spare a *Rosbif*, if that were not inconvenient to themselves in stripping him naked, few Portuguese would receive the same courtesy (and absolutely no Spaniards). For disrobed you would be, dead or alive, as Captain Thomas Dyneley observed from his guns on the Lesser Arapile 'The enemy had a party without arms in their rear for the purpose of stripping and plundering our wounded, which I saw them do; for they had the poor fellows naked before they had been down two minutes.' Which made scrimshanking, of the sort which Synge reports, a high risk gamble and a lottery if your coat was not red; a dagger in your Iberian heart was to be expected, if you chose to sham for too long.

So Pack was repulsed. It should be noted his five battalions failed not against Bonnet's nine battalions on and in rear of the ridge, but against just the three of his 120th Ligne actually holding it; 2,600 Portuguese were beaten off by 1,800 French. It was not well done. Essentially, it was a prime example of what a later generation of soldier would describe as 'Hey diddle diddle, straight up the middle', bordering on the reckless in its light-hearted contempt for the enemy. But whose contempt? Surely not Pack's, who later was to write 'It is the duty of soldiers to obey and not to question.'

We must now turn our eyes westwards into the sun, Pack's failure to be held in our memory, whilst we watch the 4th Division's progress against Clausel; and recall that beyond Cole, Leith and Pakenham had likely joined hands, with Le Marchant alive and running riot through battalion after battalion of French.

The 4th Division advanced in one line of two ranks. Unlike Leith on his right, Cole was too weak to afford a second line. He stretched perhaps 1,000 yards, seven sets of Colours, a very thin red and brown line indeed. From right to left were placed the 1st/7th Royal Fusiliers, the 1st/23rd Royal Welch Fusiliers and the 1st/48th Northamptons; then came the four battalions of Stubb's Portuguese, the 11th and 23rd Line. The three British light companies, the Brunswickers and the 7th Caçadores were out front, perhaps 900 strong. Cole's other British brigade, William Anson's of the 3rd/27th (Inniskilling) and the 1st/40th (Somerset), remained holding the Lesser Arapile, with the guns of Dyneley, Sympher and Lawson on and around that feature and the Teso.

When the Division set off, Pack's Portuguese being immediately on their left adjacent to the Lesser Arapile, Cole's British battalions necessarily had to file from the Teso through the alleys of the village, the companies reforming on their rightmarkers placed ready the other side, before the whole cumbersome line could proceed. This was no quick job, with some 3,300 rank and file to chivvy into position, and partly accounts for the 4th's advance lagging that of the 5th, who had made a cleaner getaway. Guns on the Greater Arapile and on the high ground in front immediately opened up. The French artillery were presented with a human skittle alley: 1,000 yards long, the width of two lines of men. The prize was huge for any accurate ball, to bound and bounce (and preferably roll) along the length of the skittles: mayhem. None managed it, but the fire was severe.

It is thought Clausel's Division was not yet settled on its ground. Bonnet's 122nd Ligne however was drawn up to Cole's left front, and he detached the 7th Caçadores to mask it. Surprisingly, since they outnumbered the Portuguese three-to-one, the three French battalions withdrew without any great fire-fight. Cole's line continued upwards beyond the plateau; over the crest he met Clausel's front line of the 50th and 59th Ligne, five battalions totalling some 3,000 bayonets – very much Cole's equivalent, now that the 7th Caçadores were away to the left. Opinions differ on whether the French stood in line or in a line of columns. A fire was commenced from both sides, and which continued without the usual early charge. Cole was himself hit about now and which may have been why the exchange dragged on. His wound was a ball 'A little below the left shoulder (which) broke the rib and passed out through the breast bone – the lungs were very slightly touched.' So he was out of it, and at a most unfortunate time. Ellis we think took over, with his Fusilier Brigade in turn going to the 48th's Lieutenant Colonel James Wilson — he who had captured Fort Picurina at Badajoz.

Clausel's line withdrew from the crest in some confusion, back down their slope to their supports, but without pressure from the Allies, who were also shaken and ill-formed. Memories of Albuera would be re-awakened for the older soldiers amid the continuing fire of canister from Clausel's guns, set just in front of them in what had been his intervals. They were not alone for long, however, as his second line, another five battalions or 3,000 men of the 25th Léger and 27th Ligne, as well as the now-reformed first line battalions marched briskly forward in columns, perhaps 200 yards in a well-timed and resolute counter-attack. The drums beat the pas de charge, the men with-holding their fire, ten battalions now against five. In fact, it is not clear that the French ever did open fire – or needed to. It sounds from the following accounts as if the officers and NCOs – so many newly promoted since Badajoz – had lost control of forming, loading and firing; the veterans among the men would have known they had been caught on the hop, unable now to produce the devastating volleys their situation demanded.

Lieutenant Colonel John Burgoyne (he got his brevet after Badajoz) wrote three days later:

> Our troops had but just gained (the height), and had not had time to form again in order, but even then they did not give it up, although ours was a much smaller regiment, until the enemy's column was close to them. The French regiment came up the hill with a brisk and regular step, and their drums beating the pas de charge, our men fired wildly and at random among them; the French never returned a shot, but continued their steady advance. The English fired again, but still without return they stood their ground however with great courage. But men in such confusion had no chance against the perfect order of the enemy, and when the French were close upon them, they wavered and gave way. The officers all advanced in a line in front, waving their swords, and cheering their men to come on, but the confusion became a panic, and there was a regular sauve qui peut down the hill.

Extra detail is added by an anonymous Fusilier officer, who wrote five days later:

> The Fuzileers on the left (sic) of the 4th Division had gain'd the most commanding point of the position where they immediately found

themselves exposed to a heavy fire from the ground mark'd as the 2nd Position & a French Regt. Of 4 Battalions (about 12000 (sic) men) below at a very short distance & regularly formed. The Fuzileers in this situation unsupported at the moment commenced firing without forming after its first attack. The French regiment form'd close column with the Grenadiers in front and closed the Battalions. (I was very close on the right flank of the Fuzileers, & witnessed the whole proceeding.) They then advanced up the hill in the most beautiful order without firing a shot except a few individuals in the rear of the column. When about 30 paces distant our men began to waver, being still firing not properly formed. The Ensigns advanced two paces in front & planted the colours on the edge of the hill & Officers stept out to encourage the men to meet them. They stopt with an apparent determination to stand firm, the enemy continued to advance at a steady pace & when quite close the Fuzileers gave way: – The French followed down the hill on our side.

There are two further accounts, which not only add to the overall impression of confusion along Cole's line but also introduce the possibility that Clausel's counter-stroke was a combined operation. That is, that Boyer's dragoons were already loose on Cole's flanks. Lieutenant Thomas Browne, 23rd, talks of cavalry operating against the Portuguese on the left.

The 4th Division after driving the enemy from a hill, which he had warmly contested, were in their turn charged by the five Battalions of Infantry drawn up six deep & probably would have withstood even this tremendous fresh formation, had not some Squadrons of French dragoons charged the Portuguese in flank, & broke them, which also for a moment, disordered the Fusileers & the five French Battalions succeeded in retaking the hill.

Then Lieutenant Donald Cameron, 7th, who was on the right of the line, talks of cavalry there also:

We were at this moment ordered by Colonel Beatty to retire and form square, a most hazardous movement when the enemy's Infantry were advancing, and within thirty yards of us. The order was only partially heard and obeyed on the right, while on the left we kept up a hot fire on the enemy, who were advancing uphill, and within a few yards of us. The Companies on our right having retired in succession we found ourselves alone, but the ground the enemy were ascending was so steep that we got off without loss and joined the rest. Luckily while we were forming square to receive the cavalry, the 6th Division came up and received the charge intended for us.

Apart from expressing some ungrudged admiration for the enemy, these accounts are quite open about the poor conduct of Ellis's Fusilier Brigade. Not, that is, in the irregular sauve qui peut – that merely acknowledged their plight and was the only sensible course with a future; no, the poor conduct which put them into trouble was the apparent lack of the normal disciplines: 'Our men fired wildly and at random' ... 'in such confusion' ... 'And not properly formed.' The eyewitnesses are at pains to compare the French: 'In the most beautiful order ... at a steady pace' ... 'A brisk and regular step ... A steady advance', and stress the French not firing a shot. Men who had stood at Albuera would know only too well what happens next, at around ten yards. This unusual lack of cohesion we can almost certainly put down to a lack of proper leadership from far too many newly promoted. Napier's 'the soldiers were breathless and disordered by the previous fighting' still begs the question 'Why?'

The final straw came, however, from their left flank, where the Portuguese had begun to run first, for by now Pack had been chased away from the Greater Arapile, and Bonnet could safely erupt from its rear with the nine battalions of the 118th, 119th and 122nd Ligne – over 4,000 men – into Cole's left. The 500 men of the 7th Caçadores were simply overwhelmed. Next to be charged was the Portuguese 23rd Line. Captain Philip Bainbrigge, DAQMG of the Division wrote:

> A column of French Grenadiers with hairy caps from the right of their line came on at a run with drums beating, and charged the left of the Portuguese, taking them obliquely in the flank. Nothing could be better done on the part of the French. The Portuguese gave way like a wave of the sea, first on their left, then by degrees all the way to the right. It then became a question of whether the Fusiliers would stand it, but, finding their friends on the left gone, a tremendous fire directed upon them in front, and the victorious French column coming on with shouts on their left flank, taking them also in flank, and perceiving that their own fire did not bear upon these fellows close to them, they, in like manner, gave way.

Help, however, was on its way. The speed with which Clinton's 6th Division got up can only be accounted for by Wellington's ordering him forward *before* the disasters of Cole and Pack became visible. This is confirmed in the 61st's *Digest of Service*. Rather like his anticipatory genius at Talavera, when the 48th were ordered down off the Medellin to plug the gap about to be left by the over-keen Guards, this gift of near-second sight was priceless. For Clausel, now of course commanding the French army, was suddenly presented with an opportunity. It would not even the score, still less could it turn a partial defeat into an overall victory, but limited glory of a splendidly Napoleonic nature beckoned. Not for him the careful extraction of his mauled divisions during this pause, with 6,000 red and brown coats turning their backs on him, he was not going to slip away into the woods. He was like the boxer whose left arm, having been shattered, hangs loose. Yet his right flashes an upper cut of precise accuracy, and forces his opponent to step back. Does he take the opportunity to seek his corner, and a breather? Or does he follow the upper cut with more right arm jabs, and hope for the best? He is a French General! He goes forward!

So he calls for Sarrut to shield the broken divisions of Thomières and Maucune; he calls forward Ferey to his own support in rear; he calls forward Boyer's Dragoons to support the right of Bonnet, and he and Bonnet set off down the slopes in pursuit of Pack and Cole, 11,000 men and 1,200 horse.

> Colonel Delancey said to me 'For God's sake bring up the 6th Division as fast as possible', then dashed in amongst the Portuguese, seized the colour of one of the regiments and endeavoured to rally them. I galloped off to the rear, as to restoring order and reforming the regiment it required some time and the work of regimental officers.

Phillip Bainbrigge and the acting QMG were behind the 4th Division when they ran: 'They gave way like a wave of the sea; I can compare it to nothing else. My heart was in my mouth, and they all came down into the hollow in the rear, where they halted.' A thousand or more troopers of Boyer's 6th, 11th and 25th Dragoons quickly got in among the tail end of Cole's men, those slow to reach the advancing 6th Division, and were ahead of Bonnet's 118th, 119th and 122nd Ligne. Going in the other direction, the 6th Division passed through in two lines of columns, Hinde's Brigade of the 2nd (Queen's Royals), 1st/32nd (Cornwall) and 1st/36th (Herefords) on the right, with Hulse's Brigade of the 1st/11th (Devons), 2nd/53rd (Shropshires) and 1st/61st (Gloucesters) on the left, with the 2nd/53rd the flank battalion. The Portuguese Brigade under Rezende were in rear. The Division was in the process of forming line from their columns when the fugitives, mixed up with their pursuers, arrived. Major Frederick Newman of the 11th:

> Our brigade advanced in contiguous columns ascending a rising ground, you may recollect that, just before we reached the top, the 4th Division came over in a state of disorder, the enemy close upon them, the French officers in advance, and actually making use of their swords against our retreating men: our brigade was immediately halted and began to deploy. By the time three companies had formed, the portion of the 4th Division opposite to the 11th passed round the right flank; these companies at once opened their fire and swept away nearly the whole of those officers; this checked them, and after some firing they turned about and fled ... The brigade now advanced in line, and when we rose the hill a body of French cavalry was coming up at a hand canter, either to cover their retreating infantry, or to put

a finishing hand to the 4th Division; we at once halted and gave them a volley which sent these cavaliers to the rightabout in much quicker time than they came, leaving several horses and men on the ground.

The French dragoons were much luckier to the left of the 11th, with the 2nd/53rd, whose adjutant Lieutenant John Carss wrote three days later that they were:

> A little from the division, to support a pass in order to prevent the enemy from flanking us. We had fired about 10 rounds ... when about two or three hundred of the enemy's cavalry supported by infantry made a charge and totally surrounded us. They called out 'Surrender'. We answered 'No'. Our brave fellows kept up such a blaze on them that in about five minutes we drove them off after killing and wounding nearly one half; in this charge we had about five officers wounded and about 40 rank and file killed and wounded. We formed line and advanced.

One does not, from this brief description of what is, after all, an exceedingly rare event – that of being surrounded – quite grasp the near disaster he experienced.

Carss' commanding officer, Lieutenant Colonel George Bingham, paints a more chaotic picture, including his own heroic if extremely desperate attempt to rally part of his battalion. It seemed to involve riding through Boyer's dragoons while carrying his Regimental Colour:

> We were attacked by the enemy's Heavy Dragoons; we retired in good order, in line, and twice stopped their advance by halting and firing. At last a circular rocky hill, about two hundred yards in the rear, offered an advantage; I determined to profit by it; the Dragoons being too near, and the ranks too much thinned to attempt a square, we made a dash for the hill. The Dragoons came thundering on the rear, and reached the hill just as our people faced about. The fire checked them and it was soon obvious that they would make no impression. At this moment I saw a part of the Regiment which had not reached the rock, running down the hill in great confusion, without however being pursued by the Dragoons. Giving the charge of the hill to Mansell, I dashed through the Dragoons, who made way for me, and succeeded in rallying the men round the Regimental Colour that I had with me. The several attacks of the Dragoons on the mass failed, although at one time they seized the end of the King's Colour, and there was a struggle who should have it; when a sergeant of grenadiers wrested it from the Dragoon who held it, or rather tore the silk from the pole, while I rather think remained with

the enemy; at the same time our people gained ground on the right, and the Dragoons retired in confusion.

Bingham chose the Regimental Colour to take so hazardously to his stragglers since, (apart from the small Union flag in the corner and a wreath with the regimental number) it comprised just their facing colour, that is a large six feet by six and a half feet of solid red. There was no other red Regimental Colour in the 6th Division, so his men would know it from afar, and close upon it. There would be no point his taking the King's Colour which, of course, was the Union flag common to all regiments. If Bingham did indeed use the Regimental Colour in this way, and had first to take it to his men through the enemy, it was a remarkable and surely unique return to the medieval purpose of coloured standards. Bingham presumably succeeded in concentrating his battalion on the rocky hill, and that would be where the pole and some silk of the King's Colour was lost. Surrounded by cavalry, it really does sound a bit like Custer's Last Stand. His regiment suffered forty per cent casualties. The Shropshires would remember Salamanca.

Another battalion which seemed semi–independent in the chaos on the left was William Anson's 1st/40th. Kept back originally to assist its fellow battalion 3rd/27th in holding the Lesser Arapile, like the 7th Caçadores it was apparently sent forward into the space between Pack and Cole, possibly to extricate the former. Isolated, it was caught by Bonnet. John Scott Lillie of the Caçadores wrote:

> I happened to be at the time with some companies of the Caçadores and the 40th Regiment ... This was one of the few occasions on which I saw the bayonet used; the 40th under the late Colonel Archdall, having come into close contact with Bonnet's French brigade in consequence of this movement, which was directed by General William Anson in person; he was moving on with the 40th, leaving the [Greater Arapiles] on his left and in his rear, on which a corps moved from behind the hill in rear of the 40th for the purpose of attacking it, the regiment being at the time engaged in front. I happened to be between the 40th and the enemy, and rode after the former to tell Colonel Archdall of his situation, on which he wheeled round and charged the enemy's column with the bayonet and this terminated the contest at that point.

This is a snapshot, typical of a confused situation, in seemingly describing a battalion 'being ... engaged in front' which yet successfully charged to its rear. Another source later has the 40th back with the 27th, having suffered 132 casualties.

Quite who threw back Bonnet's nine battalions and Boyer's dragoons remains unclear. It can scarcely have been just Hinde and Hulse's five British battalions (the 2nd/53rd were effectively out of action). One possibility is that Coles's remnants rallied and reformed, once Clinton had passed through. John Burgogne certainly thinks so:

> No sooner had they arrived at the bottom, than they came to their senses, and were furious with themselves for having allowed the enemy to gain the advantage. In about five minutes, they were formed in perfect order at a short distance below, and they then re-ascended the hill most gallantly, and drove the French down the other side as quickly as they themselves had been driven before.

But as we shall see it was again Clausel that they returned, not against Bonnet. Another officer with the 7th confirms that 'When we reached the valley, the shouting of the officers began to have an effect, particularly as everyone was out of breath.' They were mixed up, different regiments, red and brown coats, and hastily formed joint squares as the dragoons swept down towards them – that's when, the 6th Division passing forward, they were taunted with cries of 'Be ashamed, Fusiliers!' But while Bonnet's supporting dragoons, like Le Marchant's, had a clear run at retreating infantry, largely unformed, they had nothing like the same effectiveness. Perhaps this should be no surprise, considering the number of ill-drilled riding horses so recently pressed into service as chargers.

William Grattan's pen as ever catches the scene.

> It was nearly dark; and the great glare of light caused by the thunder of the artillery, the continued blaze of the musketry, and the burning grass, gave to the face of the hill a novel and terrific appearance: it was one vast sheet of flame, and Clinton's men looked as if they were attacking a burning mountain, the crater of which was defended by a barrier of shining steel. But nothing could stop the intrepid valour of the 6th Division, as they advanced with a desperate resolution to carry the ill. The troops posted on the face of it to arrest their advance were trampled down and destroyed at the first charge, and each reserve sent forward to extricate them met with the same fate. Still Bonnet's reserves, having attained their place in the fight, and the fugitives from Thomières's division, joining them at the moment, prolonged the battle until dark. Those men, besmeared with blood, dust, and clay, half-naked, and some carrying only broken weapons, fought with a fury not to be surpassed; but their impetuosity was at length calmed by the bayonets of Clinton's troops, and they no longer fought for victory but for safety. After a frightful struggle, they were driven from their last hold in confusion; and a general and overwhelming charge, which the nature of the ground enabled Clinton to make, carried this ill-formed mass of desperate soldiers

before him, as a shattered wreck borne along by the force of some mighty current.

Bonnet's casualties were heavy, perhaps a third of his force or some 2,200 men, and in themselves easily enough for their commander to feel he had done his duty. He would see his neighbour – and now commander – Clausel had not seemingly kept pace on his left, having been headed by Marshal Beresford, who was fortuitously in rear of Leith's 5th Division, and seized Spry's Portuguese from the second line, turning them to face east and putting them at Clausel. Two oblique references, however, exist of what we might call difficulties, in inspiring an aggressive spirit in the Portuguese, possibly proven by their minimal casualties for the day's work (6.7 per cent). It does not seem likely that it was the Portuguese who drove Clausel off. First, William Warre:

> It was near sunset, and in endeavouring to make a Portuguese Brigade charge the enemy, (who were driving the 4th Division back to 5 Battalions) in flank, that our excellent Marshal was wounded, while exerting himself, as he always does with the greatest zeal and gallantry, and by his noble example, to cover the 4th Division by this flank charge. But they soon rallied and regained the ground they had lost by the sudden attack of the enemy, and the heights were retaken just as the Marshal was hit.

Then Lieutenant Thomas Browne, 23rd, who also confirms his Division had got back into the action, keen no doubt to make amends:

> The Portuguese Brigade of the 5th Division from being on the left took these Battalions of the enemy completely in flank; but there was so much hallooing that instead of charging they began firing which was as dangerous to the British as to the French. Marshal Beresford & his staff put a stop to this firing, and he was making a disposition to charge the enemy in flank, which these Regiments, the 3rd and 15th Portuguese were not very willing to try – a few companies made a sort of shabby charge which these French troops would scarcely have regarded but that the 4th Division again attacked & the 5th took them in rear. They then moved off & the greater part were killed or taken prisoners.

Yet it is hard to see how the 2,000 or so British and 2,000 Portuguese of the 4th Division, having been chased three quarters of a mile back to their starting point, could then return up a hill, re-engage and beat nearly 5,000 Frenchmen, unassailed other than by another 2,000 apparently rather shy Portuguese on their flank. There is, however, a French description of British cavalry being involved and which, if true, provides the answer. Unfortunately, no other source confirms their presence. Yet why should old General Marquis Alphonse d'Hautpoul, ex-captain of the 59th Ligne fabricate?

> General Clausel, who was pursuing General Hill, [sic – Cole] seeing that his left was outflanked by numerous cavalry, halted his line and tried to form it in squares, but he lacked time, and his regiments, taken by surprise, were broken. General Hill, reinforced by a corps of Portuguese, resumed the offensives and a frightful melee ensued. At this moment I received from a Scottish sergeant – whom I'd just dealt a sabre blow – a musket ball in the hip and at the same time a bayonet which pierced my right arm. I fell covered in blood. A few moments after I received my two wounds the English cavalry rode over our line, taking it in the rear. Monsieur de Loverdo, my colonel, who had succeeded Colonel Caste, saved the regiment's Eagle by carrying it at a gallop into the squares of Ferey's division, behind which the debris of Clausel's division tried to rally. Stretched on the ground I lay at the mercy of the enemy. During the charge, two squadrons passed over but the horses instinctively leapt over me. I saw their feet almost crush me: my position was critical, but I was powerless to do anything and had to resign myself.

Never has the Peninsular historian lacked eyewitness accounts more painfully in this, the repulse of Bonnet and Clausel's counter-attacks, the failure of which leads us to the closing stages of this remarkable battle, with a sense of frustration that all is not quite understood. The previous phases of Pakenham, Leith and Le Marchant, and indeed the earlier phases of Pack and Cole, are all reasonably intelligible; not so the French retrograde movements and what caused them. Yet maybe there was no one cause, any more than the counter-attack itself had a cause: commanders sometimes do just go with the flow of events. Opportunities present themselves, local commanders seize them. Bonnet and Boyer were not even necessarily ordered by Clausel to take the offensive movements that they made – we assume they were acting under orders, but perhaps they just did what seemed obvious. Similarly, there need not have been any one tactical success by the Allies on the lower slopes, whether occasioned by the 4th Division or the 6th or Beresford's Portuguese or the British cavalry. Just the rising French casualty levels might have been sufficient message: we've had a go, done our best, it hasn't worked, there's chaos to our left, it'll be dark soon, let's call it a day.

As to casualty figures, Bonnet's and Clausel's casualties were researched by Sir Charles Oman with the greatest care, but with a partially incomplete result: the following can best be described as his considered opinion, and the nearest anyone will ever get. Bonnet's three regiments which sallied forth from the Greater Arapile each lost more than 500 men – a third of their strength. The 120th Ligne lost a similar proportion during their sojourn on the hill itself.

Presumably the majority of their casualties were caused by allied gunfire, for apart from the brief trouncing of Pack's Portuguese they are not thought to have stood in line musket-to-musket elsewhere; although when chasing the Portuguese down the northern slope they were engaged by Dyneley's canister. Oman comments on the unusually low officer casualty figure for the 120th Ligne (eight out of sixty-three) which he describes as 'inexplicable disproportion' to the 580 other ranks. Possibly the unusual feature was not being required to stand in the open in front of their men. He put Bonnet's total loss at 2,200 men out of a starting strength of 238 officers and 6,283 other ranks. Clausel he thought totalled over 1,200 men, which is around nineteen per cent of his original 200 officers and 6,362 men.

So Bonnet, Clausel and Boyer all seized their opportunities and delivered a nasty fright to Cole and Pack. Doubtless his Lordship was unperturbed by their bloody noses, with Clinton to hand and Hope's 5,000 in the wings; but the French had shown again their aggressive spirit, and a typically robust attitude. Neither French division was broken. Their losses were severe, but if they could draw away, they would undoubtedly be able to reform and fight again, with three quarters of their own strength retained. French honour was largely restored. British honour, however, was now about to be tested again, with Cole and Clinton faced with yet another French division on a hill, fresh and ready.

It is not the time to list British casualties, for there are many more to come.

CHAPTER 13

Salamanca
Ferey's Rearguard

Poor Bertrand Clausel, ten years a general but never before an army commander; yet he knew enough to prepare for retreat. What a deep end to be plunged into, and with a wounded foot to boot. Of Marmont's eight infantry divisions, three now remained to him, formed and intact: Foy, Ferey and Sarrut. He had perhaps an hour's daylight left in which to reach the woods behind him, and the seven mile road to the bridge at Alba de Tormes. That lay to the south-east. The alternative road to the fords at Huerta and Encinas, to the north-east, meant leaving the woods and somehow edging past Wellington's Light Division. So once it was apparent his own and Bonnet's divisions could achieve no more – it would be around 7pm – he ordered Foy to quit Calvarrasa de Ariba. He was to close in to the northerly flank of the broken divisions, fending off the Light Division who were sure to follow, and eventually to become the Army's rearguard. At this stage Sarrut and Ferey were behind the defeated divisions, the former on the left, the centre of a retreating resistance; the latter now ordered to hold the El Sierro ridge. Behind that lay the woods, darkness and a two hour march to the Tormes bridge. It was imperative that Sarrut, Ferey and Foy held a perimeter behind which the scattered remains of the Army of Portugal could regain some cohesion as they force-marched to relative safety.

In front of the woods a ridge ran across the Alba road, lying north-east to south-west. It was slightly higher at its peak than the Greater Arapile itself, and the approach slopes were quite open and in places the ridge rose steeply, with excellent fields of fire. Ferey had fifteen guns. He was to sit on the ridge, to block access to the Alba road and this he did in a long three-rank line with all his nine battalions, the flank battalions being in square. He kept no second line or support. With light companies forward, his 5,000 bayonets stretched nearly a mile, and somewhere to his left lay Sarrut, presumably trying to tie in; somewhere also to the left lay Taupin's 17th Léger and 65th Ligne, five battalions no doubt harbouring the few strays of their dismembered 22nd Ligne. However, it has been argued that the 17th were but lightly engaged this day and probably ran, while from their casualties the 65th took a much fuller part in the fighting withdrawal. Norcliffe Norcliffe, it will be recalled, was well treated by the 65th, then in column at the edge of the woods before it was attacked by the 32nd, so Ferey was not alone.

Sarrut earlier advanced onto the Monte de Azan with the six battalions of the 2nd Léger and 36th Ligne deployed in line – possibly 1,000 yards from end to end – with the three battalions of the 4th Léger in column towards the left as a cavalry screen. But we have no anecdotal evidence of their involvement in the fighting, and judging by the casualty figures for the day it was minimal: 384 all told or eight per cent. This is scarcely forty men per battalion, or less than half a company's worth. Sarrut seems to have got his men away scot-free, an almost shamingly light butcher's bill, and one wonders if questions were later asked by his fellow divisional commanders – those who survived intact. But it may be that Sarrut's very presence in front of the 3rd and 5th Divisions, for a while, was enough. Pakenham's men had marched a good fifteen miles from the other side of the Tormes in great heat, dust and at times in great haste. They were tired. They were also busy rounding up prisoners, by now a couple of thousand or so, the escort parties for which much weakened the ranks – even if the contents of French knapsacks much strengthened the inner man. So the 3rd Division would not have pressed Sarrut's line too fiercely, and were doubtless looking for help from the 5th on their left. Wellington's orders for the attack now imminent made plain that, to the front, it was to be the job of the 6th Division 'supported by the 3rd and the 5th'. After that order was sent to Edward Pakenham and Leith's successor, Major General William Pringle, they would relax the harassment of Sarrut, who may well then have pulled back behind Ferey's left wing. But we can only conjecture.

Across to the right, Clausel and Bonnet's reversal meant Colonel Bouthmy and his 120th Ligne on the Great Arapile were exposed and doing no good. Clinton's 6th Division passed them on their left, and some forward movement menaced their right. This was the arrival of Sir Henry Campbell's 1st Division, ordered by his Lordship to get between Foy at the Chapel and the French main body. He knew Foy held the key to any successful withdrawal. But Campbell's Division, which (said by Tomkinson), 'seemed as peaceably inclined as the enemy's right', advanced in too leisurely a fashion to cut off Foy. The light companies of the KGL in Lowe's brigade – 200 men at most – were in the circumstances enough to persuade Bouthmy to quit, although he was unable to extricate his guns.

Clausel and Bonnet having removed themselves, Clinton's 6th Division on moving up the slopes to the south came upon the horizon-length line of Ferey's Division, guns in the intervals, and at that sight they halted – or were halted by Lord Wellington, who had need to arrange matters for the best. They stood in plain range of the guns and suffered accordingly. Major Newman, 11th, (Hulse's Brigade):

During this time their artillery played incessantly on us with shot and shell by which I lost about forty men; and the loss increased so fast by their getting the range, that I told Hulse something should be done, either in retiring or by the line lying down. The latter he agreed to, and we hardly had a casualty after.

Cole's Fusilier Brigade came up to extend Clinton's line to the left, with his Portuguese (Stubbs) and William Anson's 3rd/27th and 1st/40th directed to turn Ferey's right. In this they were to be supported by the 1st Division's battery of five 9-pounders under Major Gardiner (and presumably Clinton's own five 6-pounders under Captain Greene) all to get into an enfilade position from the north-east. As we have seen, the 3rd and 5th Divisions were to support the 6th, that is in rear. We cannot be sure of the time when Clinton was ordered forward (Ross-Lewin, 32nd says 7.30pm) but the sun was setting behind the Monte de Azan. Clinton's three brigades were all in line, Hulse left, Hinde right, Rezende's Portuguese between. The following account rather implies Cole's 4th Division was not to Hulse's left, but in rear. Major Newman gives a clear picture, and again we must note the Portuguese seem in need of help.

The next advance of the 6th Division was to the attack of the French position. As soon as the French saw this, a cloud of their skirmishers came down to the foot of the hills forming their position, and as we neared them opened their fire, supported with terrible effect by their artillery with grape; however, the brigade kept moving on, and in spite of every obstacle carried the position. Not a shot was fired by the 11th until we reached the top, when we gave them a farewell discharge. By this time the loss of the 61st and 11th was most severe: the Portuguese brigade in attacking their portion of the position found the ground steeper and more difficult of access, which enabled the enemy to retain that part, and eventually the French came down and attacked them in turn. I saw this and proposed to Hulse to wheel up the 11th to their right and attack them in flank, but for the present he declined, thinking we were too much reduced. After a while poor Bradford, the assistance adjutant-general, came up, and instantly went to the rear and brought up our support a brigade of the 4th Division which had been reformed; the 61st and 11th then changed their front to the right, and attacked this hill and carried it. This was the last of the engagement, and at this period the 61st and 11th had about five officers and eighty men each left.

(Note there is no mention in this or any account of the 2nd/53rd being in its proper place between the 1st/11th and the 1st/61st, which absence confirms its earlier drubbing.)

It sounds as if, unfortunately, the Portuguese struck the centre of Ferey's line, placed on the most commanding height with corresponding difficulties for them. The decision by Clinton to support them by a flank attack by the 11th and 61st, once the Fusiliers had come up as stated by Newman, is effectively confirmed by the 61st's *Digest of Service*. Note that the French battalions concerned changed from line to column:

> The Major General finding that the brigade was losing many men from the fire of the enemy called the COs of the Regiments to him to intimate his intention of attacking the hill in front . . . [and told] them to make the same known to their respective corps. The communication was received by the two corps with an instantaneous shout of 'Yes, we will!' and three cheers. This was followed by an immediate advance unchecked by the destructive fire from the French artillery and numerous sharpshooters. The movement was performed by the Regiments with sloped arms, by order, until the hill was crossed.
>
> On the arrival of the brigade at the summit of the hill, the enemy again formed their troops into column and faced a proportion of their files outward to receive the attack of the 11th and 61st who threatened their flank. The two Regiments formed to the right, on the right file of the 11th and then opened their fire upon the column . . . and soon compelled it to retire.

Over the other side of the Portuguese, Hinde's Brigade also had a hard fight. Captain Harry Ross-Lewin, 32nd:

> It was half-past seven when the sixth division, under General Clinton, was ordered to advance a second time and attack the enemy's line in front, supported by the third and fifth divisions. The ground over which we had to pass was a remarkably clear slope, like the glacis of a fortification – most favourable for the defensive fire of the enemy, and disadvantageous to the assailants, but the division advanced towards the position with perfect steadiness and confidence. A craggy ridge, on which the French infantry was drawn up, rose so abruptly that they could fire four or five deep; but we had approached within two hundred yards of them before the fire of musketry began, which was by far the heaviest that I have ever witnessed, and was accompanied by constant discharges of grape. An uninterrupted blaze was then maintained, so that the crest of the hill seemed to be one long streak of flame. Our men came down to the charging position, and commenced firing from that level, at the same time keeping their touch to the right, so that the gaps opened by the enemy's fire were instantly filled up. At the very first volley that we received, about eighty men of the right wing of my regiment fell to the rear in one group;

the commanding officer immediately rode up to know the cause, and found that they were all wounded.

Previously to the advance of the sixth division, the light companies of the right brigade were formed on the right of the line, and, as we moved on, one of the enemy's howitzers was captured by the light company of the 32nd regiment. It had been discharged once, but before the gunners could load it again, it was taken by a rush.

We may note that the above account of the 32nd's attack on the right makes no mention (not surprisingly) of the rescue of the Dragoon officer Lieutenant Norcliffe Norcliffe, from Taupin's 65th; nor indeed mention of that regiment, nor of British cavalry besetting them. However, there is a French account which does categorically state that the reason Ferey's line disintegrated from the left was that the 70th Ligne was turned by cavalry. An officer of Ferey's 31st Léger, Captain Lemonnier-Delafosse, wrote in his memoires:

The cruel fire cost us many lives. Then, slowly, having gained almost an hour's respite for the army, we retired, still protected by the squares, to the edge of the wood which stretched away to Alba de Tormes. Here Ferey halted his half-destroyed division, and formed in line it still presented a respectable front to the enemy. Here he made his stand despite the enfilading fire of the English batteries; here he found the death most desired by a soldier, that caused by a cannon-ball.

The 3rd Division thus formed on the edge of the wood, deprived of its artillery, saw the enemy advance on it in two lines, the fire composed of the Portuguese, the second of the English. Left alone to fight, its position was critical, but it awaited the shock. The two lines marched on the division; their order was so regular that we could see the officers in the Portuguese lines maintain company intervals by striking their men with their swords or canes.

We opened fire on the enemy as soon as they came within range, and the fire of our front two ranks was so effective that it halted their advance, and although they tried to return our fire, they melted away completely – but they were Portuguese. The second line, composed of English soldiers, now advanced upon us; we should have tried to receive it like the first, without yielding an inch, despite the fire of the enemy's batteries, but a sudden blow on our left was too much. The 70th Ligne was turned and broken by cavalry and their flight carried away the 26th and 77th [sic – 47th] regiments. My own 31st Léger, although only two battalions strong, held firm and halted the enemy who continued to fire until we finally retired a few hundred yards into the wood.

The accounts above by Newman of the 11th, and the 61st's *Digest*, concur that they both changed front to the right, to attack the flank of the French on the ridge and who had just repelled the Portuguese. In this sense, one could argue that there were two phases to Clinton's attack, certainly when looked at from the French point of view. What is common to British and French accounts is a failure of the Portuguese; we must remain unsure, however, whether Ferey made a last stand on the tree line, behind the ridge. Newman firmly states that once the hill was carried 'this was the last of the engagement'; but a fallback would certainly be in the spirit of his orders. He had clearly gained time for the Army of Portugal to make best speed for the Tormes.

What does emerge in accounts generally is some unhappiness with the way the 6th Division's attack on Ferey was conducted, specifically their being held static, under gunfire, and allowed/ordered to engage in volley firing. This episode was variously located as 'when advanced about halfway' (Leith Hay) and 'deployed at the bottom of a hill' (Royal Military Panorama, December 1812). Wherever, since both refer to the subsequent firing of regular volleys, it could not have been more than 100 paces from Ferey's line. Yet, as we saw earlier, various accounts gave the length of the halt between 'a long time' (Napier), 'for nearly three quarters of an hour' (61st *Digest*) and 'about an hour and a half' (Thomas Hamilton). Surely not, when volleying 100 paces away? So there must have been two such halts: first and for the longest, at a distance and under gunfire, probably while his Lordship co-ordinated his plan; second at 100 yards or less when the fire fight continued, volley against volley.

Now this, of course, was against Peninsular practice. Leith Hay spoke for all when he wrote after the war:

> It was owing to the 6th Division halting and firing at the enemy that our loss was so great. Those Divisions who rushed upon the enemy without hesitation not only did not lose nearly so many men, but did the business much better, and nowhere did the French columns stand for an instant when fairly attacked with the bayonet.

Or as he put it in his book: 'The only way is to get at them at once with the bayonet, that they can never stand, but as to firing they would do that as long as you like, and fire much better than we do.' That this view was widely held resulted from innumerable occasions in the Peninsula when we know the volley-cheer–charge progression was more than adequate to do the business, as Leith Hay put it. The *Panorama* of December 1812 wrote 'The 6th Division ... deployed at the bottom of a hill, of easy ascent, and then began to fire regular volleys. In consequence, they suffered very severely, for the French, it is well known, will exchange shots with you as much as you please.'

Which practice by eight battalions in line could only have been ordered by Clinton, and may well account for later criticism in letters, like George Bingham's, that Clinton's 'conduct on the day of the action was such as does not add to his popularity'. We may suppose the previous year's lessons learnt on Albuera's 'fatal hill' had been widely talked of and absorbed. Salamanca was the next such set-piece battle to follow and neither Pakenham's 3rd Division nor Leith's 5th had indulged in continuous volley firing; Cole's 4th (all of whose five British battalions had been present at Albuera) when invited to so indulge knew better than to accept. They turned and ran.

The argument that Sir Henry Clinton had nothing to do with it but rather that eight battalions simultaneously faltered and stopped at volley range does seem unlikely. Tired they were, and thinned by the earlier pause within cannon range, and undoubtedly Ferey's men above them would be a novel sight to all: Frenchmen in a three-deep line! Yes, there would be three volleys coming down the slope from ready primed muskets, fired as quickly as they like. But after that it was up to the rear rank loaders. People like Leith Hay would have taken their companies forward through the three volleys taking the losses, halted, fired, cheered and charged.

As it was, Clinton's casualties were twice as heavy as anyone else's, which is no surprise. The advance against Clausel, the pause under fire, the exchange of volleys, were all exposure enough to flying lead. Various brigade losses in the centre, expressed as percentages, are Hulse sixty per cent, Ellis twenty-eight per cent, Hinde twenty-four per cent, Stubbs and Rezende's Portuguese both nineteen per cent and Pack's Independent Portuguese fourteen per cent. Hulse was the big loser and we are fortunate that we have had several accounts of the severity of the fighting, involving the 1st/11th and the 1st/61st. The 2nd/53rd were left with just 199 men, say four companies worth, and did not take part in the second phase; the 1st/61st ended with 180 men and the 1st/11th with 176 – say each three companies worth. Indeed, if amalgamated they would still scarcely have formed a decent battalion. Their losses represented sixty-seven per cent and sixty-six per cent of their strength as at the State of 15 July – two in every three men were out of it. The 2nd/53rd's were forty-two per cent, nearly half the battalion. Taken together, Hulse's brigade had effectively become a composite battalion, and it was surely Hulse's men that lay everywhere wounded, described by John Douglas of the 1st (Royal Scots) coming up behind:

> near sunset, which appeared as red as sunset through the dense clouds of smoke ... the casualties so thick, while we passed on in pursuit, striving to avoid treading on the wounded, who were calling out for a little water for God's sake ... they pleaded 'don't trample on us'.

Ellis's Fusiliers, to the left of Hulse, had of course already suffered in their abortive assault on Clausel. The right of the line was hit hardest, whether from the latter or from Ferey we don't know. From left to right (1st/48th, 1st/23rd and 1st/7th) the losses were nineteen per cent, twenty-four per cent and forty per cent. (At Albuera they were sixty-six per cent, forty-six per cent and fifty-five per cent.) To the left of the 48th was Major Wackholtz's Brunswickers, who reported little opposition from Ferey, so it would seem the allied line extended on the left beyond Ferey's – hence the casualties being heavier to the right. This proposition is largely confirmed by the 4th Division's AQMG (Charles Vere) who wrote:

> The Fusilier brigade (commanded by Lieutenant Colonel Wilson, 48th) moved up the heights under a heavy fire, without returning a shot, and drove the enemy in its front from his ground. The brigade then brought up its left for the purpose of assisting General Hulse, by a flank and raking movement. But the formation was no sooner effected than the enemy gave way before the General and the defeat was completed.

While Claud-Francois Ferey, Baron de Rosengath, was himself mortally wounded, his Division's casualties were surprisingly quite light. Lamartiniere's return lists 1,001 men, which is a seventeen per cent rate. According to Ross-Lewin, as we have seen, the French chose to open fire 'within 200 yards', which effectively wasted the first and even the second volley. One must hope Clinton did not reply at that range. The onset of darkness as well as the usual smoke would certainly have much reduced marksmanship on both sides; the only other clue to the paucity of French losses is again something said by Ross-Lewin (not that it applied to battalions other than his own) 'The fire of musketry began . . . Our men came down to the charging position, and commenced firing from that level.' It is an odd phrase. Surely it is not credible that volleys would ever have been fired from the hip, but what else is meant? How does the rear rank fire?!

Putting Bonnet, Clausel and Ferey together, and Cole, Pack and Clinton together, on one side the losses were 4,299 and on the other 3,175. Some of the former of course occurred during the subsequent retreat. These figures for the five divisions involved which clashed in the centre of the field are much closer, as we shall see, than those for the entire field, and that says two things of note. Firstly, that the French commanders gave nearly as good as they got, shown by the repulse of Pack and Cole, the subsequent exploitation and Ferey's dogged last stand. Secondly, that Pack's losses were inevitable given Bonnet outnumbered him nearly three to one on and around the Greater Arapile, and he should never have been sent to capture it. The potential threat to Cole's left flank by Bonnet's 6,500 men required stronger protection, and that would have been the case even had Wellington sent Clinton rather than Cole, (whose men being largely under new management were especially vulnerable to pressure).

The last few men, inevitably the wounded and the lame, disappeared into the darkness of the tree line around 8.30pm. They went as quick as they could through the last formed body of the 31st Léger. Its two battalions, perhaps 1,000 bayonets, stayed formed as an inadequate blocking force within the wood, enough anyway to stop Clinton. It is said he had been ordered to pursue, but he did not, his exhausted battalions going but a little way into the wood before lighting their fires. It did not really matter, of course, for was not the bridge at Alba blocked by 2,000 Spaniards of Espana's? The pursuit was the other way, to the east then to the north-east, to the fords at Huerta and Encinas, already used by Marmont to cross the previous day. His Lordship had first to push Foy out of the way, who had pulled back to a ravine in front of the wood: 'I arrived at the edge of the wood half an hour before sunset,' said Foy.

> The battle continued to be extremely bloody; one could hear nothing above the continuous musketry and cannon fire. The French took flight. I decided not to enter the wood but to take a position very nearby, behind a ravine, in order to cover the retreat of the army. There was time; the victorious enemy was advancing towards Alba de Tormes between Calvarrasa and the wood, with two strong bodies of infantry, six cannon and 1,500 cavalry. I sent my skirmishers to delay their advance and they engaged them with artillery and musketry. Night saved my division and those I was protecting; without it I would probably have been broken and the enemy would have arrived at Alba de Tormes before the remains of our seven broken divisions. For an hour after sunset the English cavalry continued its charges on my regiments formed alternately in line and en masse. I had the good fortune to have my division in hand at all times and maintain its good order, although many of the broken units coming onto our left threatened to carry disorder into our ranks. The enemy's pursuit stopped near Utero de Maria Ascensio, and all our forces found their way to Alba de Tormes where the army was gathered about 10 at night.

So Wellington must seize the Huerta crossings, and he would then have the Army of Portugal trapped inside the Tormes. Well before dark, he sent orders to Major General Charles Alten, commanding the Light Division. This account is by Lieutenant John Cooke, 43rd:

> At seven, one of the Duke's aides-de-camp rode up and ordered our division to move on the left to attack. We moved towards the Table Mountain, right brigade in front, in open column; having passed it, we then closed to column of quarter distance. The enemy's skirmishers soon advanced, and opened a brisk fire. The shades of evening now approached, and the flashes of cannon and small arms in the centre and on the heights were still vivid, while the enemy were making their last struggle for victory. An English officer of General Pack's brigade

passed us, covered with dust and perspiration; he complained of the rough usage of the French. They allowed the Portuguese to approach nearly to the summit of the point of attack, then charged them, and used the bayonet without remorse, taking that part of the field under their especial protection.

The enemy's light infantry increased, and retired very deliberately; the ascent was gentle. The first brigade deployed, supported by the second; the first division was marching in reserve. Our skirmishers were obliged to give ground to the obstinacy of the enemy. The line of the 43rd was one of the finest specimens of discipline I ever saw – as steady as rocks, with Colonel William Napier twenty yards in front of the corps, alone; he was the point of direction. Our skirmishers ceased firing, and the line marched over them, dead and alive. I expected to see our chief unhorsed, and carried away in a blanket.

Appearances indicated a severe fight, for we were near the enemy's reserves. The Duke of Wellington was within fifty yards of the front, when the enemy's lines commenced firing. I thought he was exposing himself unnecessarily, the more so, as I heard he had put every division into action that day. The Duke ordered us to halt within two hundred yards of the enemy. They gave us two volleys with cheers, while our cavalry galloped forward to threaten their right flank. At this time I heard that a musket-ball had perforated the Duke's cloak, folded in front of his saddle. As we were about to charge, the enemy disappeared. This advance was beautifully executed. Night coming on, the firing died away. We bivouacked round a village.

The ability to change formation, depending upon the going and the enemy is well shown by George Hennell, 43rd:

By this time it was quite dark [and] our skirmishers [3rd Caçadores] opened upon them upon the brow of a hill and the French immediately returned it which passed mostly over our heads. We had express orders not to fire until ordered. Our regiment was well prepared to give them an excellent charge but they had received another lesson that afternoon that they will not forget in a twelvemonth. Had they stayed still till we came up twenty yards further they might have given us a most destructive volley but they rapidly fired a volley or two that passed mostly over our heads and they ran away.

We advanced in line ½ a mile over corn and ploughed land. Then [we] formed sections of a company, keeping our distance & marched 2 or 3 miles over bushes and ploughed lands. On passing a wood our skirmishers, who were always about 300 yards in advance, opened a fire. We were in a good line in 5 minutes (it was only a few cavalry in a wood) & advanced dressing by the Colours over horrid roads with numerous pebbles another league. We halted and slept.

Cooke's reference to the 1st Division being in rear is confirmed by their commander Henry Campbell:

[The French] Right then formed on a Hill and made a last effort, where they were attacked, just as the Moon was rising, by the Light Division in two Lines supported by the 1st (Division). They kept up a smart fire as we ascended the Hill, but on some Guns opening from a Hill on our Left they turned and ran for it, and must have made very good play for we followed them in the same order, the Light Division in two Lines, and the first (Division) in two Columns, one on each of its Flanks to support it, till near 1 o'clock in the Morning, going all the time at a rate of near 4 miles an hour, without overtaking more than a very few stragglers and wounded, but as a great deal of our way was thro' a very thick wood, we must have passed a great many that were picked up by others in our Rear. It is the first time I suppose, that ever Troops marched in Line for four hours across Country in the night, and they were in a very good Line when they halted, and our Columns also were in order to have wheeled into Line directly. We halted about one near the Village of Calvarrasa de Abajo.

On the right of Campbell, Wellington positioned the Fusiliers and Anson's brigades from Cole, whose assistance Clinton no longer needed. Campbell, of course, gets his details awry, since 4mph for four hours hardly equates to the seven miles a crow would fly to Calvarrasa de Abajo; but other sources put his Division in support, with the whole halting at midnight. During the advance, as the route converged on that assumed to be Marmont's, the lack of stragglers and discarded baggage would have become apparent. Foy had quietly side-stepped sometime before. As John Mills, 1st Coldstream, put it, 'We were for some time at their heels, but they desisted from firing, and the wood was so thick we could not see them so we lost them.' Some encouragement that they were on the right road, however, came from incidents like Napier's

Squadron of French dragoons bursting from the woods in front of the advancing troops soon after dark, firing their pistols and then [they] passed at full gallop towards the ford at Huerta, thus indicating great confusion in the defeated army, and confirming the notion that its final retreat would be in that direction.

To settle the nagging doubts, Cotton was sent forward to the ford (and on his return was badly wounded by a Portuguese sentry) and Arentschildt was sent to Alba. The latter returned with the unwelcome news that the Spanish had gone, and the French were busy passing the Tormes.

What a bitter blow to his Lordship! One can but poorly picture his anger, although he was later reported to have described Espana's action as 'a little misfortune'. Tomkinson says Espana had ordered his garrison out of Alba castle before the battle, but deigned not to tell Lord Wellington, and then:

> Before the action Don Carlos asked if he should not take his troops out of Alba – after he had done it – hoping for an order. Lord Wellington said 'Certainly not'; and the Don was afraid to tell what he had done. Lord Wellington of course acted as if it was in our possession.

From Ferey's ridge to the bridge at Alba is nearly six miles for our crow, or probably three hours for most Frenchmen that night, some in small parties, mostly individuals, few in formed bodies, and naturally all convinced British and German dragoons would any moment burst upon them. Lemonnier-Delafosse noted:

> A shapeless mass of soldiery rolling down the road like a torrent – infantry, cavalry, artillery, wagons, carts, baggage-mules, the reserve park of artillery drawn by oxen, all mixed up. The men shouting, swearing, running, were out of all order, each one looking after himself alone – a complete stampede. The panic was inexplicable to one who, coming from the extreme rear, knew that there was no pursuit by the enemy to justify the terror shown. But alas! I know well that if the French have boldness and extreme impetuosity in attack, if they fail they are then shameless and irresponsible in flight. It is the fear of being captured that gives our soldiers wings. I had to stand off far from the road, for if I had got near it, I should have been swept off by the torrent in spite of myself.

But there was no cavalry, nor any immediate fit infantry, to catch the French. It was all very well for his Lordship, in a letter to Graham of 25 July, to say, 'When I lost sight of them in the dark I marched upon Huerta and Encinas, and they went by Alba. If I had known there had been no garrison in Alba, I should have marched there and should probably have had the whole.' That was wishful thinking. Several thousand more prisoners, maybe, certainly all the slow-moving wounded, but the light-travelling mass had too great a start by the time the 7th Division or Espana could have been brought forward. Indeed, even if Alba had not been abandoned, it is arguable that some part of the Army of Portugal would then have turned north up the road to the ford at Encinas: the Light and 1st Divisions, from midnight, were sleeping four miles away at Calvarrasa de Albajo.

We quit this chapter, and the narrative of the battle, with a French account of the final crossing of the Tormes, at dawn on 23 July. It is by Colonel Girard, Chief of Staff to Maucune:

> We ourselves were almost completely hors de combat and in a most critical situation for our only line of retreat was across the Tormes a little below Alba. The enemy might easily have seized the bridge. Fortunately he spent the night collecting his forces and preparing to pursue on the following day. General Clausel took advantage of this to get his troops across the river, and in order to ensure that this was achieved without confusion, he placed General Maucune at the head of the bridge until the army was assembled on the further bank.
>
> In order to protect the passage, General Maucune and I – the only senior officers remaining! – had with great effort collected a thousand or 1,200 men and Blanzat's battery, now reduced to ten guns. Our advanced posts were so close to the enemy that we heard their voices. Wellington might, in the course of the night, have got some of his cavalry across the Tormes and attacked us simultaneously at both ends of the bridge. But fortunately he did nothing. It was dawn before his advance guard prepared to attack us. Our army was safely across the river, but it had not had enough time to reform and be ready for battle. General Maucune told me to cross the river and help rally the bulk of our troops. I asked to leave this until we had halted the enemy's advance by our volleys and artillery fire, and so forced him to deploy. We would still have time to disengage and retreat across the bridge, while our cannonade would alert the general that the enemy had begun their advance. Maucune accepted all my suggestions, and it turned out as I predicted.

CHAPTER 14

Salamanca
Casualties and Comment

Earlier chapters covering the different divisional actions have given most of the detailed casualty figures and, so far as these have been helpful, we have attempted to draw deductions as to the intensity of the fighting and what happened generally. It is, of course, impossible to venture far down this road since, on both sides, such figures cover a timescale where some of the brigades or divisions took part in more than one action. For example, what did Cole suffer at the hands of Clausel, or Bonnet and Boyer, and what next, helping Leith against Ferey? On the French side, what of Thomières's overall losses were down to Ned Pakenham's muskets and what to Le Marchant's sabres? Such unknowns, however, need not discourage healthy speculation!

As to the provenance of the figures, your author has taken the Morning States of 15 July for both Armies as set out by Charles Oman. The losses are those shown in the Return annexed to Wellington's despatch, and the official Return of French casualties made out by Marmont's Chief of Staff, General Lamartiniere. Unfortunately, these latter cover the period 18 July to 8 August i.e. including the fighting on the Guarena and (see later chapter) at Garcia Hernandez. A great many pertinent observations on both these sources are included in Rory Muir's excellent *Salamanca*, whose tireless efforts in this regard seem quite definitive and surely cannot be surpassed. I pay him the compliment of following his calculations, rather than Oman's, and certainly not of attempting any of my own.

Marmont took the field with 46,700 all ranks, of whom a quarter were returned killed or captured, wounded or missing. The importance of the first category is that these men were lost to the Army for all purposes, unlike those wounded who recuperated, or the missing, many of whom straggled in eventually. Killed and captured totalled 7,691 all ranks, wounded 4,099 and missing 645: a total of 12,435 all ranks, of whom 394 were officers. These figures are Lamartiniere's which, of course, can be endlessly argued over as variously 'fudged' or distorted; but Oman (and Muir) come to fairly similar figures, by alternative calculations.

Of the officer losses, 162 were killed or taken, and this roughly equates to the leadership of seven battalions, virtually a whole division. (For example,

Maucune's 5th Division had 165 officers, Taupin's 6th Division had 179.) With a further 232 officers wounded – and let us suppose they were all taken to the rear – it is no exaggeration, therefore, to say that of Marmont's seventy-two infantry battalions, he would lack all officers for the equivalent of eighteen of them. They would be entirely commanded by NCOs. Such figures allow us to understand Clausel's major difficulties towards the end of the battle.

Compounding this cull to the regimental leadership, was the loss among his formation commanders. Thomières and Ferey were killed (the latter not instantly), Bonnet and Marmont himself were severely wounded, Clausel slightly, and Foy and Ferey both lost brigadiers. That is, half the Army of Portugal functioned under replacement divisional commanders, and the very top changed hands twice, with Bonnet standing in for Clausel until the latter, now wounded, was brought forward. That all occurred after Thomières had over-stepped his side-stepping, and Le Marchant's hurricane was hovering. It is difficult to imagine a worse time for Marmont to be carried off the field, nor for poor Clausel to be elevated. His own division, far from being quietly in reserve, was coming up into the thick of it. In the event, Clausel surely added to his reputation, on both sides: there are indications that his repulse and pursuit of Cole and Pack in tandem with Bonnet, earned English admiration (if not from the Portuguese).

The French lost an astonishing number of prisoners, getting on for 6,000 (and more the next day), many of whom were unwounded, and there is little doubt the mass of these came once Le Marchant, with follow-up infantry, got on to the Monte de Azan amongst the now-unformed bodies belonging to Thomières, Maucune and Taupin. A thousand dragoons are simply too many to argue with, when you are unformed or in bunches. It is no surprise that their presence on Marmont's left saw that part of his army suffer the heaviest losses: Thomières's fifty per cent, Maucune's thirty-four per cent and Taupin nearly that, but with two of his three 22nd battalions virtually destroyed. The worst regimental figures were both Thomières. The 101st Ligne, whose point battalion had to contend not only with being charged and dispersed by D'Urban's 1st Dragoons, but later by Le Marchant's, suffered eighty-two per cent casualties; while his 62nd suffered seventy-seven per cent (and their Eagle – or was it the 101st's?).

Clausel, Bonnet and Ferey in the centre were all similar at twenty-six, twenty-three and seventeen per cent respectively, while Sarrut's eight per cent was as noteworthy as Foy's four per cent (Muir's reasonable guess). Foy we can understand, but not Sarrut, which seems astonishingly low. Amongst his total loss of 384 all ranks, he had just five wounded officers – five out of 203! One really does wonder if his emergence from the woods to appear on the Monte de Azan simply coincided with that period following Le Marchant's death, when the cavalry were blown, and when most infantry efforts were on gathering and escorting prisoners. This was before Clinton's second push, at Ferey. It is certain that during this lengthy period Pakenham and Leith were not actively aggressive; and once Sarrut fell back behind the left of Ferey, of course, he was out of it. Marmont's cavalry remained largely intact, with just over 400 casualties amongst the twenty-four squadrons – say seventeen men out of an average squadron strength around 150, or eleven per cent. Both Boyer and Curto were similar, being rather notably absent from the battle's various phases, except for Boyer's assistance to Bonnet. We should recall perhaps a quarter of Curto's horses, and a fifth of Boyer's, were unschooled hacks, taken from the infantry. Even so, the 53rd (Shropshires) certainly had cause to remember French dragoons.

A dozen guns were lost, according to Lamartinière, (eleven in Wellington's Return of Ordnance) out of the seventy-eight deployed. His Despatch however says 'It is believed 20 have fallen into our hands', which would seem nearer the mark. For Bonnet's battery was mostly man-packed onto the Greater Arapiles, and Colonel Bouthmy surely never got them down in time as he fled Campbell's German skirmishers; and it is hard to see Thomières' battery getting away. We can see why Lamartiniere might not wish to overstate to Napoleon the number of French guns lost, but not our own Ordnance Return. Apart from guns, the capture of which are always highly prized, other trophies included two Eagles and six battalion Colours or fannions. So much for Marmont's force.

Wellington took the field with a force 51,937 strong, of whom 30,578 or fifty-nine per cent of the whole were British or KGL. That was 5,200 more than his opponent, say an extra ten per cent or the equivalent of another infantry division. Wellington lost 5,220, of whom 694 were killed, 4,270 were wounded and 256 missing – these figures from the Return. Both British and Portuguese lost similarly (ten and eleven per cent), the British 3,176 men from their 30,578 and the Portuguese 2,038 from their 17,999. The estimated 3,360 Spaniards, who were not used in any meaningful way, suffered just six men hit, two fatally (0.2 per cent). Thus the British paid sixty per cent of the price of victory, their Portuguese allies the other forty per cent, the Spanish nothing.

Henry Campbell's 1st Division and John Hope's 2nd Division were little involved in the battle proper, except at the end and the beginning, and their paltry casualties reflect a quiet day: 153 men and 142 men respectively, which are rates of two and three per cent. Bradford's Portuguese brigade similarly were effectively unused, losing seventeen men out of 1,894. It is a measure, therefore, of his Lordship's 'spare capacity' that he had therein some 13,500 men, in twenty-one battalions, untouched and available. Plus of course the Spaniards.

Edward Pakenham's 3rd Division marched, volleyed and charged hard and received their just return of (relatively) light casualties, bearing in mind what they achieved. Their modest price was seventy-four killed and 460 men wounded. The 88th Connaught Rangers' enthusiasm and the 5th Northumberlands' tangle with the chasseurs accounted for 261 or half the bill. Pakenham's Portuguese brigade under Power escaped lightly, with just seventy-six casualties or three per cent.

Lowry Cole's 4th Division, of course, had a busy day attacking Clausel, retreating, attacking Clausel; attacking Ferey with Clinton; then on the right of Campbell attacking Foy in the dark. Perhaps the loss of one man in every five after all that is not too excessive? Among his five British battalions the extremes were just eight men lost to the 3rd/27th (one per cent) as the static garrison on the Lesser Arapile, to 195 men (forty per cent) for the 7th Royal Fusiliers, who as right of the line caught just about the worst of each phase. My own regiment, the 1st/48th (Northamptons) lost seventy-nine men or nineteen per cent, of whom ten were officers – half the leadership, and three of whom were still recovering from wounds collected at Badajoz! Cole's Portuguese brigade under Stubbs lost a similar proportion of nineteen per cent.

In Leith's 5th Division, the lead brigade (Greville's) suffered nearly four times the casualties (400) of Pringle in the second line (105). This was in effect a spectacular large brigade attack by five battalions, of some 2,800 bayonets, and it broke Maucune's nine battalions of 4,800 bayonets: sufficiently anyway for Le Marchant then to run through them. Leith was, of course, lucky to catch Maucune in half-formed squares and columns. Without the dragoons, however, Maucune would probably have reformed, and no doubt Pringle's and Spry's Portuguese would then have had to help Greville. Leith's total casualties were 628 or nine per cent, a very cost-effective attack thanks partly to the proximity of Le Marchant, partly to Maucune's unprepared formations, and partly to Leith's aggressively quick assault.

Clinton's 6th Division took on Bonnet, Clausel and Ferey, so not surprisingly was the most knocked-about division, with a total of 1,680 casualties, or nearly a third of his force. Hulse's brigade of the 1st/11th, 2nd/53rd and 1st/61st between them accounting for 849 losses, the remainder being split between Hinde and Rezende's Portuguese. Gunfire from Ferey's ridge and the Greater Arapiles undoubtedly caused havoc in the lull, but the puzzling business of a continuing exchange of volleys, rather than closing to charge, probably laid many men low. It was John Douglas, 3rd/1st, part of Leith's follow-up division, who noted: 'Our poor fellows [6th Division in front] having to bear up against the united fire of cannon or musketry, their ranks thinned ere they commenced to climb the hill . . . Never saw British casualties so thick, while we passed on in pursuit, striving to avoid treading upon the wounded.'

Cotton's cavalry generally were little troubled in their work, which was largely that of cutting at men on the ground, not those in a saddle. The 5th Dragoon Guards came off worst, probably at the hands of Maucune's 15th Ligne on the left, losing a troop's worth of fifty-six men out of their six troops (seventeen per cent); the 3rd and 4th Dragoons, roughly half a troop each, a total of 105 men for Le Marchant's brigade, of whom twenty-three were killed. Anson's Light Dragoons lost only three dead and two wounded; Victor Alten three dead and twenty-eight wounded; and D'Urban seven dead and thirty wounded and missing. Bock's KGL dragoons and Julian Sanchez's two Spanish lancer regiments got off scot-free. While one can understand the need for Bock to cover the left flank of the army, especially in the early stages, the addition to Le Marchant of 1,000 vengeful Spanish Lancers might have been interesting. It would also have been a diplomatic act of inclusion towards our otherwise disregarded ally; one doubts however that his Lordship ever over-concerned himself with such considerations. The British cavalry losses overall have been put at 178, a paltry four per cent.

What was not so paltry were the injuries both permanent and temporary to his commanders: Le Marchant dead, Beresford, Cole, Cotton, Leith and Alten carried away with severe wounds, so, too, two commanders of Portuguese brigades (Collins and Rezende). Wellington himself was mildly bruised late in the day by a spent ball; had he been taken off the scene earlier, presumably Beresford would have assumed the command. He in turn was carted away during Cole's embarrassing movement, then Cotton was next in line. He being wounded that evening, the pursuit next day would subsequently have fallen upon Henry Clinton. (The prospect of which would no doubt have seen gallopers urgently despatched to fetch up Hill from Estremadure.) That none of this was to happen is little short of amazing, considering the constant exposure our 'Atty seemed to embrace. Not for him a snug post on a hill, telescope positioned ready, a queue of mounted ADCs waiting to relay orders. He was reportedly everywhere, and for once here is a battle when his movements can be reasonably well traced. Their main feature was their appropriateness to the action; for while a general commanding in a defensive position can indeed put himself under a prominent tree, and largely stay there, in attack he must be wherever the shifting pressure points occur, preferably five minutes before they do.

We know he rushed three miles to Pakenham and there delivered a personalised instruction, the exact words have been variously reported but the manner appeared firm, clear and decisive; we know he had first caught up with Brigadier D'Urban, and briefed him; we know he then went to speak near Las Torres with Le Marchant; and then onto Leith; and then with Cole. So all the major opening phases of the action were personally generated by Lord Wellington. Earlier, having lost the race for the Greater Arapile, and aware of the pivotal importance of the Lesser, he impressed upon Colonel MacLean, 3rd/27th, 'You must defend this position so long as you have a man'. Then later he was said to ride behind Leith's first line, and then to be present with (or close behind) the dragoons, allowing him to make the anecdotal remark to Cotton 'By God, Cotton, I never saw anything more beautiful in my life! The day is yours!'; and again towards the end 'The Duke of Wellington was within 50 yards of the front, when the enemy's lines commenced firing ... He ordered us to halt ... etc.' (John Cooke, 43rd) And 'when we came under the hill the enemy were upon, Lord Wellington passed us and said "Come fix your bayonets, my brave fellows".' (George Hennell)

This manner of personal presence at critical points can be criticised. It was always a fine conceit of Montgomery that he went to bed once he had issued his orders. Certainly too close a contact with events can take the mind off the bigger picture. However, who would argue that the 4th Division and Pack's Portuguese were saved by the 6th Division marching through, to take up the burden of the day? That was possible because Wellington had ordered Clinton forward before the repulse, as he read the developing situation, and which he was only able to do because he was on the spot. It also helped that Wellington's dispositions were based on his interior lines, while Marmont suffered from exterior: that is, the theoretical concentration from one decisive spot on the enemy's front, to another, involved a shorter period of time than that taken by the enemy's reserves, between the same two points. Now, of course, it is true our scenario does not precisely fit that definition, but the 6th and 7th Divisions could undoubtedly be brought forward to assist Cole or Leith quicker than Marmont could bring forward Foy, Ferey or Sarrut.

One reason Wellington did seem constantly adjacent to his advancing troops was his fear they would get carried away, and become vulnerable to counter-attack. 'Lord Wellington ... Had always expressed himself as afraid of the impetuosity of the British troops in attack, carrying them forward in disorder after the first driving of the enemy, and giving them the only chance they can possibly have of defeating us.' (John Burgoyne) This fear, based on little actual precedent in the infantry, but fuelled by the mounted arm, proved groundless apart from a certain enthusiasm on the Monte by Wallis and the 88th 'whose impetuosity was found most difficult to restrain.' Had Leith's 5th Division felt so inclined, of course, they were largely prevented by the sudden arrival of Le Marchant's dragoons, so we shall never know; neither did such opportunity arise for Cole's 4th Division, or for Pack's Portuguese; and Clinton's 6th were hardly likely to go blundering off in ill-disciplined pursuit, into a dark wood, after what they had been through.

In this regard only a part of the allied army was tested. Maybe if the 1st, 7th and Light Divisions (and Bradford's Portuguese) had had an opportunity to show 'impetuosity', they might have obliged? For in truth the battle was fought between forty-one battalions (twenty-six British and fifteen Portuguese) – some 26,000 men, and sixty-four French battalions or 38,000. The negligible losses amongst Wellington's three unused divisions gave him some 15,000 *spare* men – three times what Clausel could similarly claim in Foy's division. This raises two thoughts: firstly, with that numerical advantage remaining at the end of the day, could not Wellington have done even better? Did he under-use his resources? Especially having chosen not to use the 1st or 7th rather than Cole's 4th and Pack to take on Clausel and Bonnet; or to assist Clinton against Ferey: it is as if having carefully saved them, he then forgot them.

The answer lies at Alba, surely. They were not forgotten, they remained out of action precisely because Wellington wished to have fresh troops for the pursuit he hoped he could engineer. He led them himself, the Light and 1st Divisions, supposing that (round the next corner) he would surely come upon his limping prey. But this final flourish was denied him by Espana.

The second deduction from the disparity of troops actually engaged must be that his soldiers fought better than Marmont's. That is not to belittle the French in any particular, who saw off Cole and a ridiculously outnumbered Pack in easy fashion, and much reduced Clinton; while Ferey and Foy were instrumental in the final holding action, showing fine discipline when many would have joined the sauve-qui-peut. Even Thomières's rout on the Pico we can blame on him, not his soldiers, for never was a division caught misformed so inappropriately for the terrain. And along a similar fault line, Maucune's men also may be absolved from responsibility, which lay rather with their commanders, for more inappropriate misformations. If we are correct, that is, to assume Maucune was preparing to meet Leith in columns. He must have had twenty minutes warning. Perhaps he planned a downhill charge in columns? But then, as John Douglas noted, coming up over the crest the 'French seem to be taken by surprise as (British cavalry) advanced with us on our right ... The enemy seemed to be rather in confusion ... The cavalry were to them a puzzle. [They] seem to have formed parts of squares and parts of lines.' No wonder Leith's volley, in response to Maucune's, delivered a far harder punch, and in the confusion of muddled, misformed ranks the approaching charge was never going to be held. Once out of formation, there is no hope against 1,000 sabres. But it was hardly the fault of the poor *poilu*.

The morale of infantry – their spirit – makes or breaks opportunities, overcomes or buckles beneath difficulties, and owes everything to their immediate leaders. Confidence in the subaltern, respect for the sergeant, perhaps a certain pride in the company commander's eccentricities, enough food and certainly drink, spare flints and a settled comradeship with their long-term mates – and yes, that includes the few female mates allowed to tag along – all are ingredients for a good spirit. The Fusilier Brigade showed they had it, in the way they bounced back from trouble: '[They] were furious with themselves for having allowed the enemy to gain the advantage. In about five minutes they were formed in perfect order at a short distance below, and they then re-ascended the hill most gallantly.' (John Burgoyne) The fact that the overtaking 6th Division might have shouted out 'Be ashamed, Fusiliers!' would no doubt have stiffened their resolve; but with the largely second-eleven leadership touched on earlier, a major problem shared only by the Light Division, it says much for the underlying spirit of Cole's troops. Morale, like individual courage, has been likened to a bank deposit account, which can be added to, and drawn upon. This day's work unquestionably saw a substantial British cheque paid in, to both the infantry and cavalry sub-accounts.

Poor Marshal Marmont, we fear, ended rather over-drawn. As Frederick Ponsonby commented 'He had outmanoeuvred himself.' He blamed Thomières and Maucune, of course, which was hardly fair. He himself had become more than a little bedazzled at out-marching and out-turning this man Wellington. Outmanoeuvred the fellow from the Douro back to Salamanca, taunted him, invited him to stand and fight, increasingly convinced his dance partner was a passive defender. After all, the man in five years had never once attacked a single French position (forgetting the mere bagatelle of Roliça). Once across the Tormes, and with that dust cloud over towards the Rodrigo road, he knew he had him. The aborted attack on the Greater Arapile confirmed it. He could relax. A push and a shove and Wellington would be off. He, Marmont, would descend upon his rear guard, and by the way let's send young Thomières ahead, to slip around their flank, and we'll all be back in Salamanca in time for supper tonight.

Into that rather relaxed frame of mind came no inkling of the reverse rapidly approaching. Reverse in the sense both of disaster, and also in that his own flanking movement was about to be outflanked. At no point did he seem fearful, which is a half-brother to caution, and certainly not related to arrogance. It is worth repeating his words to Berthier nine days later:

> My object was, in taking up this position, to prolong my movement to the left, in order to dislodge the enemy from the neighbourhood of Salamanca, and to fight him at a greater advantage. I calculated on taking up a good defensive position, against which the enemy could make no offensive move, and intended to press near enough to him to be able to profit from the first fault that he might make, and to attack him with vigour.

Oman adds a telling sentence from his *Memoires*: 'I considered that our respective positions would bring on not a battle, but an advantageous rearguard action, in which, using my full force late in the day, with a part only of the British army left in front of me, I should probably score a point.' For Wellington was indeed all set to go towards Rodrigo, if the day produced no opening for an attack. But that was a big 'if' for Marmont to risk with a man like his Lordship. As Foy wrote 'The wily Wellington was ready to give battle – the greater part of his host was collected, masked behind the line of heights. He was waiting for our movement.'

Wellington did indeed do a lot of waiting. His patience did wear thin that day, but that was because it really was his last chance, after a prolonged spell of waiting. Waiting is not a common trait of those born to power and deference (except perhaps those who cut their teeth in the slow motion of British India). The Salamanca Forts, the San Cristoval Ridge, the Douro, back-pedalling to the affairs at Castrejon and Castillo, the parallel march, all these would have eaten away at a lesser man, since Marmont gave no opening for the devastating attack his Lordship sought. The odds had to be right, and they were not right. And that carried on into the day of the battle, with the low point for the Peer surely the realisation that Beresford's caution around midday was correct, and his own intended attack on the Greater Arapile was wrong. How he must have hated countermanding his previous order to Henry Campbell! Even if kicking Bonnet off the ridge was intended to be no more than delivering Marmont a limited bloody nose, he was big enough to swallow his pride, along with his long-simmering frustration – but he kept looking for the best chance. That's the point. He had not given up. His tenacity and his patience were very strong. So what inner excitement and determination must have accompanied that cry of 'By God, that will do!', when he saw Thomières's columns march beyond the point of no return.

There seems no doubt Pakenham was sent to lie up in Aldea Tejaea for a double purpose: firstly for its proximity to securing the heights beside the Tormes, covering the Rodrigo road; and secondly should the required 'advantageous terms' at last arise, to be equally on hand as an unexpected right hook. It was a decision perfectly demonstrating Wellington's ability to plan ahead, allowing for both caution and for hope. This one conscious decision, more than any other, allowed for his glorious victory.

It is hard to see what Marmont or Clausel could have done to prevent it, once the band began to play. They, their dispositions, their infantry and their cavalry, all were outclassed. Of course, some phases did not go well – Cole and Pack's retreat, and the pursuit – but for the first time in five years Wellington's army had taken the fight to the French, and won hands down. As Napier put it: 'In former actions the French had been repulsed, here they were driven head long as it were before a mighty wind.' We cannot not quote Foy's words, handsomely entered in his diary six days after the battle:

> This battle is the most cleverly fought, the largest in scale, the most important in results, of any the English have won in recent times. It brings up Lord Wellington's reputation almost to that of Marlborough. Up to this day we knew his prudence, his eye for choosing good positions, and the skill with which he used them. But at Salamanca he has shown himself a great and able master of manoeuvring. He kept his dispositions hidden nearly all the day: he allowed us to develop our movement before he pronounced his own: he played a close game; he utilised the 'oblique order' in the style of Frederick the Great ... The catastrophe of the Spanish War has come – for six long months we ought to have seen that it was quite probable.

The results were far-reaching. We will describe below how the news of victory was received in England, but the Government there immediately benefited from the silencing of the Opposition. In return they raised the Earl to the rank of Marquis (to which apparently he asked 'What the devil is the use of making me a Marquis?', showing rather more interest in the gift of the Manor of Wellington and £100,000). Spain had already given him a Golden Fleece. In France a corresponding shock of belittling magnitude was delivered to national pride, and to their Army's spirit. The caution which in future their Marshals would show when in Wellington's presence was to affect their plans and reactions in quite a major way. Commanders lacking confidence are halfway beaten, knowing which no doubt accounts for a rapid blaming of Marmont, who just as rapidly had already blamed General Maucune and the late Thomières. The French had been comprehensively whipped, and whilst one can talk of the effect of this victory on the situation in England or Russia or Paris, or in Andalucia or Castille, or in Madrid or amongst the partisans, the prime effect was the emergence of a supreme fighting machine. British soldiers have always been good in defence; in the Peninsula a consistent narrative had developed over four years or so wherein the individual man in the ranks expected to hold whatever piece of ground his officers chose. Going forwards up a breach or up scaling ladders, however, while certainly an attack upon the enemy, was not remotely like the advance in the open of two or three brigades in line, closing and disposing of Johnny Frog. And that was something the British soldier had never done until today, bar the Fusilier Brigade at Albuera. No wonder that night 'When they [the 6th Division] were ordered to halt for the night ... So tired ... Yet they sat up through the night, talking over the action, each recalling to his comrade the events that had happened.' (Tomkinson)

There was indeed much to talk about, but some slept for a while:

> The troops that had gained the victory lay buried in sleep until two o'clock of the morning following, when the arrival of the mules carrying rum aroused them from their slumber, but the parties sent out in search of water had not yet reached the field. The soldiers, with parching lips, their tongues cleaving to their mouths from thirst, their limbs benumbed with cold, and their bodies enfeebled by a long abstinence from food, and the exertion of the former day, ran to the casks, and each man drank a fearful quantity.

(Needless to say, Grattan's *bhoys* of the 88th Connaught.) What a way to end such a day – drunk again!

In London, rumours of all this grew during the first days of August, with *The Times* stopping their press at 1am on Thursday 6th to announce:

> That an Officer arrived at the Admiralty late last night, with dispatches from the North coast of Spain. We understand that he has brought a confirmation of the Ferrol account of the victory gained by Lord Wellington near Salamanca on the 22nd ult. We have not heard the particulars; but we believe they put the fact of his Lordship's success beyond all doubt.

An earlier dispatch from Sir Home Popham had reached Falmouth, but fog had descended upon the Admiralty telegraph, to great frustration in the capital. Ten days were to pass with only unofficial and unconfirmed news crossing the briny, with details forever changing:

> The victory obtained by Lord Wellington was within two leagues of Salamanca. He made a false retreat of fourteen leagues, which fairly took in MARMONT, who was completely defeated leaving according to one dispatch 8,000 killed and wounded and 4,000 prisoners, the greatest part of his artillery, cavalry and baggage; but the second report mentions their having left 12,000 killed and wounded, with 4,000 prisoners, and there being a most disorderly retreat. Eight Eagles are said to have been taken, etc. (*The Times*, 11 August)

Then on the 15th Captain Lord Clinton, his Lordship's chosen man from amongst his ADCs, was reported to have passed Cuidad Rodrigo with despatches three weeks previously; a copy of the *Corunna Gazette* talked of Te Deums performed both there and at Salamanca, with 'The highest exultation spread through the country'. All lay agog, until Clinton's chaise and four rattled the very next day out of the blue to Lord Bathurst's house in Mansfield Street, for a late breakfast.

> The drivers and horses were decorated with laurel. The eagles and flags were displayed out of the windows of the chaise. One of the eagles is besmeared with blood, supposed to be in consequence of the Ensign's head who held it being shot away. His Lordship drove to Lord Bathurst's residence, in Mansfield street. The state of the chaise soon spread the report throughout the neighbourhood, and a great concourse of people were collected in a few minutes. The glad tidings spread to Lady Wellington's, who resides near the spot, in Harley street. Her Ladyship ran with all possible speed to Lord Bathurst's house, with a naturally anxious desire to enquire after the welfare of her husband. Lord Clinton of course paid every possible attention to her Ladyship's enquiries; and on her receiving a satisfactory account, she was so much overwhelmed with joy, that she nearly fainted. The eagles and flags were left in Lord Bathurst's house.

From Bathurst's house, Clinton was taken to the War Department in Downing Street, and then across the park to Carlton House, to see the Prince Regent. They went on foot, with a growing crowd of Sunday idlers cheering away in their wake, and from there the news spread widely. Next day *The Times* printed extracts from the despatch, and arrangements were promptly put in hand so that (as an early example of psychological warfare) 'Details of the victory of Salamanca are circulated on the Continent as widely as possible, particularly in the Russian territories,' with copies of the *Gazette* to be sent immediately to the Baltic 'to be distributed on its coasts.'

Within hours that Monday, astonishingly rapid efforts on the part of private citizens and government offices ensured the late evening dusk of London was richly illuminated with an entertaining spectacle for the populous. There were back-lit silhouettes depicting variously his Lordship, the crown, wreaths, anchors, stars, the letters G.R., Britannia, eagles and even, in Spring Gardens, a

> Well-portrayed transparency of Lord Wellington driving Bonaparte and the French out of the Peninsula, while Britannia appears on one side consoling and upraising a drooping female representing Spain, and in the clouds were the figures of Julius Caesar, the Duke of Marlborough and Charles V. The illuminations last night were general. All the houses in the great leading lines of streets, from the East to the West End, were illuminated; and the illumination varied with occasional transparencies, mottes in lamps, and devices equally brilliant and appropriate to an occasion so justly entitled to call out the strongest expression of natural rejoicing.
>
> The space from Temple Bar to Charing Cross was one continuous train of light; the whole bright, but parts of it eminently splendid. The Navy office exhibited a star and anchor, composed of lamps of the most brilliant effect, while the pillars that support the cupola of the building were decorated with variegated festoons of the most luminous description. The Navy Pay office was ornamented with a profusion of light, and contained a display of two anchors placed transversely, and the letters G R in shining characters. The illumination at the Admiralty was on a grand and extensive scale, for which the magnitude of the building is excellently calculated. The screen facing the street was covered with a profusion of variegated lamps and flambeaux. The name of 'WELLINGTON' was placed conspicuously over the entrance, and surmounted by the Crown, star, a wreath, and anchor, producing a handsome effect. Nor was the exhibition at the Horse Guards less grand and imposing. The name of WELLINGTON was eminently bright, and accompanied with the letters G R and G P R. The Treasury displayed a well-executed transparency of George III, attended by Britannia and other emblematical figures. The illuminations at the Council office, and the other government offices, though not so grand, were elegant and tasteful. At the Secretary of State for War and Colonies, in Downing Street, were exhibited the Eagles and Colours taken at the Battle of Salamanca. The office was brilliantly illuminated.

Pall Mall, Carlton House, the Ordnance Office, the Portuguese and Spanish Embassies, Apsley House, East India House, the Bank, the Mansion House and many private dwellings were all brightly lit that night. But Lady Wellington's house at number 11 Harley Street, was described, somewhat meanly, as 'Plainly illuminated with a few lamps.'

Politically all this was splendid news for the weak and embattled government of Lord Liverpool, who promptly called an election. The results strengthened his position somewhat, and correspondingly reduced that of his Whig opponents; however, it is possible, had Wellington lost at Salamanca or been caused to retreat to Rodrigo, that Liverpool's administration would have been ousted, the result of which it is now hard to contemplate, not only domestically but upon the continuance of the campaign in Spain. Such an outcome had no doubt been ever present in Wellington's mind as he and Marmont manoeuvred for advantage. 'By God, that will do!' had had much wider implications than on a dusty Spanish plain.

In Russia the laborious five-week journey eastwards of Marmont's despatch at last found Napoleon, four marches from Moscow, at a place called Borodino, with other pressures on his mind. He is reported to have dismissed the news with 'The English have their hands full there: they cannot leave Spain and go to make trouble for me in France and Germany. That is all that matters.' In Paris, the Regency Council, unable quickly to consult the Emperor, recalled Massena from retirement, to replace Marmont, but the wily fox managed to fall ill on arrival in Bayonne, and resigned. While the Council's extreme fears of an invasion in Napoleon's absence were neither realistic nor immediately realised, the general effect of the news was decidedly detrimental to civilian morale. Doubts spread, inevitably. News of 30,000 French dead at Borodino, and the occupation of Moscow a week later by the 95,000 remnant of the original quarter million strong Army were not reasons for untrammelled joy, the humiliating retreat five weeks later being a disastrous reminder of that smaller version in Spain.

In London on the last day of September the Army put on a show for the Royal family and the populace – who turned out in their thousands – with a parade to lay up the captured Eagles and Colours. Five Eagles and four flags (including the garrison flag of Badajoz 'a great part of it red with human blood') were on parade, together with three regiments of Foot Guards and two of Life Guards, under the unlikely command of old Sir Harry Burrard of Vimeiro fame. *The Times*:

> Four of the Eagles are numbered 13, 22, 39, 51 ... Two of them taken at the Battle of Salamanca, were very much mutilated; two others, taken at Madrid ... And the fifth we understand was found in the channel of a stream near Ciudad Rodrigo into which it was thrown when the rear of Massena's army was closely pressed by the British cavalry, on its retreat from Portugal.

The 22nd's Eagle we know about, but neither the 12th (Wellington's despatch incorrectly named it as the 13th) nor 51st were at Salamanca. The latter fought in Albuera village in Godinot's brigade, but escaped with modest casualties, with no loss of an Eagle as far as we know. The 39th were with Foy at Salamanca, but lacking their 1st Battalion and, therefore, the Regimental Eagle. And anyway the 12th were in Russia and had never set foot in Spain. It leaves one puzzled.

The Queen, her Princesses and the Duchess of York watched from Horse Guards' Levee room as a white charger carried the Prince Regent from Carlton House onto parade, accompanied by the Dukes of York and Kent. The Colours having been trooped, the French Eagles and Standards were brought out, and the carrying parties proceeded round the square to the tune of the 'Grenadiers March', the trophies being lowered before the Prince and Royal Family 'Amid the acclamation of the thousands of spectators.' Then it was off to Whitehall Chapel to hear Divine Service. As *The Times* noted:

> The concourse of people assembled on the occasion was immense, and the spectacle altogether was of the most gratifying description. It was impossible to view without feelings of exaltation, these trophies which bore witness to the prowess of British soldiers, and which were won from no despicable enemy, but from troops whose military reputation stands so high in Europe.

CHAPTER 15

Salamanca
The Sad Field of Battle

The foregoing story of the battle has necessarily concerned the movement of men en masse. This chapter touches on individuals. We are fortunate that so many veterans wrote of their experiences, presumably out of an understandable mixture of pride in their part in a notable event and a profound relief at surviving. It is also natural that common recollections were the sights and plights of the wounded and of the dead. After all, on this field of battle, on which 100,000 men and 8,000 horses had manoeuvred – a space some three miles long and a couple deep at most – there now lay the blood of between 17,000 and 18,000 men killed, wounded or taken prisoner and nearly 1,000 horses killed, wounded or running loose. Many thousands lay where they were hit. Unlike a successful British defensive battle, where the winner stays put and can succour his wounded whilst the retreating French must abandon theirs, here the pursuit took the Army forwards, leaving the wounded of both sides to fend for themselves.

It was fortunate Salamanca was so near. The village of Las Torres, such as it was, provided the first habitations in rear, and became a natural focus for casualties, along with the rather battered hovels of Arapiles. The latter being five miles from Salamanca, where hospitals were being prepared, a flow soon commenced on Spanish carts, wagons and traps driven by sightseers and the more charitably minded, with generous stocks of water, food and dressings. The main hospital was the Irish College at the university, presided over by Dr Patrick Curtis, Regius Professor of Astronomy and Natural History, and an invaluable informant into Wellington's personal ear. He had the ready help of many citizens who, as Leith Hay reported, 'Showed their gratitude . . . by sincere and zealous exertion to provide for the wants of the wounded, and assistance in furnishing the large hospitals.' The inhabitants, said John Aitchinson:

> Came forward after the battle both high and low as became them, and even ladies of birth went to the field of battle and lent all their delicate assistance at removing the wounded into their houses and

administering every comfort in their power – this lasted the whole night and they have since assisted at the hospitals.

Grattan too recorded the Spanish help:

> The inhabitants of Salamanca, who had a clear view of what was passing hastened to the spot, to afford all the relief in their power. Several cars, most of them loaded with provisions, reached the field of battle before morning; and it is but due to those people to state, that their attentions were unremitting, and of the most disinterested kind, for they sought no emolument. They brought fruit, and even quantities of water, well knowing how distant the river was from us, and how scantily the countryside around was provided with so necessary a relief to men who had not tasted a drop for so many hours, under a burning sun, and oppressed with the fatigue they had endured during the fight.

The individual regimental hospitals, or aid posts, were under cover in the villages, each manned in theory by the regiment's three surgeons and their mates. Company commanders detailed search and carrying parties, whose job it was to get the casualties back to the aid posts, as Green of the 68th tells us:

> We encamped on that part of the field where the carnage had been most dreadful, and actually piled our arms amongst the dead and dying. We immediately sent six men from each company to collect the wounded, and carry them to a small village, where doctors were in attendance to dress their wounds.

Charity beginning at home, the losers were not top priority. William Warre, ADC to Beresford, and who got his wounded boss to Salamanca by 11pm: 'After having his wounds dressed on the road', expressed a common morale dilemma:

> Owing to the Army having advanced and the few means of transport, many of the wounded, particularly of the French, have suffered horribly, for, three days after, I saw a great many still lying, who had received no assistance or were likely to till next day, and had lain scorching in the sun without a drop of water or the least shade. It was a most dreadful sight. These are the horrid miseries of war. No person who has not witnessed them can possibly form any idea of what they are. Many of the poor creatures have crawled to this. Many made crutches of the barrels of the firelocks and their shoes. Cruel and villainous as they are themselves, and even were during the action to our people, one cannot help feeling for them and longing to be able to assist them. But our own people have suffered almost as much, and they are our first care.

Lieutenant John Cooke was another man who had misgivings, especially for the treatment doled out by the Spanish to the vanquished French. During the pursuit, he says:

> As we passed onwards, lying by the side of the road were numerous objects to remind us of the miseries of war in all its horrors: many French soldiers lay dead. The scorching rays of the sun had so blistered their faces and swelled their bodies that they scarcely represented human forms; they looked like huge and horrible monsters. It is impossible to convey an adequate idea of such spectacles. These now inanimate objects had marched over sandy plains without a tree to shelter them, suffering from fatigue, sore feet, and want of water. Crowding into the battle under a scorching sun, covered with dust, they had received severe wounds. Enduring excruciating torture, they were finally dragged, or carried from the scene of action on rudely-constructed bearers then left to perish by the side of the road, or on stubble land, with their parched tongues cleaving to the roof of their mouths. And then, before breathing their last sight, they would behold, with glazed and half-closed eyes, the uplifted hand of a Spanish assassin, armed with a knife to put an end to their existence. These dreadful fates awaited the defeated French soldiers in Spain, and it was impossible to gaze on their mutilated bodies without feelings of deep commiseration for fellow-creatures who, a day or two previously, had been alive like ourselves, and perhaps the admiration of their comrades.

On Salamanca field any prisoner or casualty, of either side, was liable to be plundered or worse, whether by men in blue or red or brown, or by civilians or by the wives. The search was for drink, food, clothing, boots, coin, gold or silver or, occasionally from an officer, the chance of a rich keepsake – a watch, or ring, a fancy sword or bullion epaulettes. That worthy man of the 51st, William Wheeler, nonchalantly noted:

> Having examined a few dead French men for money etc. we collected what dead bodies were near and made a kind of wall with them. We did this to break the wind which was very cutting as we were very damp with sweat. Under this shelter we slept very sound until morning.

Apart from the practical use of corpses, we notice the 'etc.' added to the search for money, and which presumably stood for just about any item of value, in bodily comfort or profit.

Douglas of the 1st got something for his stomach, boiling in a kettle, and then nearly got a lead ball in the same place:

We halted for the night on the ground occupied by the enemy during the morning and sent out parties for water, having nearly 5 miles to travel before it was found, and then it was as green as the water you may have seen during the heat of summer in a stagnant pond. However, it went down with a fine relish. The only piece of plunder either I or my comrade had got happened to be a leg of mutton off a Frenchman's knapsack, which I put down in a kettle to boil, having made a fire of French firelocks. I was sitting on a stone watching the fire, musing over the day's work, when, rising up to look into the kettle, one of the pieces went off, the ball passing between my legs. This was the nearest visible escape I had, for if providence had not so ordered it that I rose at the instant, the contents would have been through my body. The breaking up of the ammunition wagons might be heard at a great distance as the men wanted firewood for cooking.

Douglas's references to water parties having to march long distances is repeated frequently elsewhere; the extreme heat of the day, combined with the saltpetre in the black powder of their cartridges, and the dust of the plain, created a furious thirst – another reason to search all knapsacks, and rattle all canteens.

The stripping of bodies, alive or dead, was partly to acquire the clothing, especially trousers and boots, as replacements – and boots often held money; it was also done to search for body belts and what lay therein. Greene of the 68th:

It really was distressing to hear the cries and moans of the wounded and dying, whose sufferings were augmented by the Portuguese plunderers stripping several of them naked. We took a poor Frenchman who had been stripped by an unfeeling Portuguese: the adjutant gave him a shirt, an old jacket and trousers, and sent him to the village hospital.

Another witness to Portuguese opportunism was Lieutenant Frederic Monro: 'I found myself amongst the dead and dying, and to the shame of human nature be it said, both stripped, some half naked, others quite so; and this done principally by those infernal devils in mortal shape, the cruel, cowardly Portuguese camp-followers, unfeeling ruffians.'

And our own camp-followers were not far behind and were rated highly by his Lordship in the plundering way: 'It is well known that in all armies the women are at least as bad, if not worse, than the men as plunderers!' Murder, too, according to Lieutenant Thomas Browne, DAAG:

All ideas of conduct or decency had disappeared – plunder & profligacy seemed their sole object, & the very Soldiers their Husbands evidently estimated them in proportion to their proficiency in these vices. They covered in number the ground of the field of battle when the action was over, & were seen stripping & plundering friend and foe alike. It is not doubted that they gave the finishing blow to many an Officer who was struggling with a mortal wound; & Major Offley of the 23rd Regiment, who lay on the ground, unable to move, but not dead, is said to have fallen victim to this unheard of barbarity. The daring & enterprise of these creatures, so transformed beyond anything we have heard of in man, is not to be described.

Walking wounded stood a chance, of course. It was those with leg injuries who became immobile attractions, easy meat. Charles Synge, Pack's ADC, had a broken thigh bone and lay under the rocky ledge of the Greater Arapile. In rich Hussar trappings, he had been rapidly stripped by the 120th Ligne as they briefly charged past; he then decided his death was imminent:

> I could not perceive that any near me were alive. It was some time too before I could realise the particulars of my own situation. I was a prisoner. I was wounded. I was naked. An open artery was bleeding fast. I was drying. Could this be death? There could be no doubt about it, and in a few moments I should be dead. Having come to that conclusion I lay down to die, and, having said my prayers, waited with composure for the last struggle. After lying some little time expecting faintness and some of the usual symptoms of death, my attention was attracted by some cannon shot. The balls were literally ploughing the ground all about me. They were from our own Artillery, who were in reserve on the other hill of the Arapiles, and who had opened their guns on those with whom my body lay. I thought it probable that one of those balls must hit me, and I am afraid I must acknowledge that I sat up and stretched my head as high as I could in the hope of a friendly ball ending my misery. But it was not to be. God in His mercy willed it otherwise. I began to think that I should be a long time dying, for, though I had lost much blood, I still felt no faintness. Then, for the first time, it came into my head that somehow I might have 'a chance', and I have often since thought of that 'trying to put my head in the way of a friendly ball.'

Poor Harry Ross-Lewin, hit later in the day on Ferey's ridge, could walk (his wound was to his left arm and shoulder) but got lost in the dark – and was found, miraculously, by his own servant:

> I had nearly reached the French position when a musket ball struck me, and, from the loss of blood, I soon found it requisite to go to the rear for surgical assistance; but, as it was already dusk, I wandered about, ignorant whether I was or was not taking the right direction for a village. I had walked for some time in this state of perplexity,

when I suddenly heard the trampling of horses, and, on calling out to know who went there, I found, to my great satisfaction, that the party belonged to my own regiment, and that my batman was one of their number. They conducted me to the village of Arapiles, where we found the men breaking open the houses for the admittance of wounded officers, seven of whom were of my regiment. All the habitations and outhouses, even to the very pigsties, were speedily filled with wounded men, whose cries to have the dead taken away from them were incessant throughout the whole night.

It is not clear if Marshal Beresford was treated in Arapiles village or Las Torres – or even back in Salamanca. William Warre just said he had his wound 'dressed on the road' there. The following surgeon's account does not sound quite like a mere dressing for poor Beresford:

> The Marshal was lying on his back dressed in a blue frock coat with a white waistcoat. Just below the left breast was a star of blood, bright and defined as a star of knighthood. It was about the size of that chivalrous decoration, and occupied the exact spot where it is usually fixed. There was a small rent in its centre, black and round. The eyes were half closed; the countenance in perfect repose, perhaps a little paler than when I had last seen it. In an instant the marshal's dress was torn open, and my forefinger, that best of probes, was deep in his side. Not a muscle moved, not a sound was uttered. I felt the rib, smooth and resisting below, while the track of the bullet led downward and backwards, round the cavity of his ample chest. I now spoke for the first time, and said, 'General, your wound is not mortal.' This observation of mine seemed to have been heard with perfect indifference; for without taking the slightest notice, he looked up and asked, 'How does the day go?' 'Well,' I replied, 'the enemy has begun to give way.' 'Hah!' rejoiced the marshal, 'it has been a bloody day.' I proceeded to cut out the bullet. My knife was already buried deep in the flesh, its point grating against the lead, when the marshal, feeling I had ceased to cut, and calculating, perhaps, that my steadiness as an operator might be influenced by the rank of my patient, again turned round and with as much sang-froid as if he had been merely a spectator, said in an encouraging tone, 'Cut boldly, doctor; I never fainted in my life': almost at the same moment I placed the bullet in his hand.

Ned Costello, 95th, was in the overcrowded Salamanca hospital, not from a new wound, but from a worsening in the one he got at Badajoz. His ward was in the charge of Sergeant Michael Connelly, an Irishman much concerned that all those dying in his care should depart quietly, and not disgrace either their regiment or their country in front of the foreigners present – Johnny Frog. Connelly fatally over-anaesthetised himself on drink, and although his funeral has nothing to do with our battle, it is a nice story:

> While lying in hospital – at all times a wretched place, from the groans of the numerous sufferers – I was placed under the immediate attendance of Sergeant Michael Connelly who, having recovered sufficiently from a slight wound, had been appointed sergeant to the hospital, and was in charge of our ward. He was one of the most singular characters I ever met with. If an awkward person and uncouth face had gained him the preferment, then his match could not be found anywhere.
>
> Mike was exceedingly attentive to the sick, and particularly anxious that the dying British soldier should hold out a pattern of firmness to the Frenchmen, who lay intermixed with us. 'Hold your tongue, ye blathering devil,' he would say, in a low tone. 'Don't be after disgracing your country in the teeth of these 'ere furriners by dying hard. You are not at Elvas to be thrown into a hole like dog. You'll be buried in a shroud and coffin; you'll have the company at your burial, won't you? You'll have the drums beating and the guns firing over you, won't you? Marciful God! what more do you want? For God's sake, die like a man before these 'ere Frenchers.'
>
> Mike, however, had a great failing – he drank like a whale, and as he did not scruple to adopt as gifts or legacies, the wine rations of the dying and the dead, he drank himself out of the world. As his patients remarked, he died like a beast.
>
> The news of Mike's death spread like wildfire, and all his old friends, and the convalescents, crowded around to do honour to his remains. The funeral of the Duke himself could not have made a greater stir. The coffin carrying the deceased sergeant, borne by four bearers, and with the usual complement of soldiers with the arms reversed, slowly wound its way through the city of Salamanca. Cavalier and foot soldier, drum boy and trumpeter, and all the women, children and camp followers in the locality, flocked to follow his remains. The town became unusually alive with the variegated throng, and many a jest made the streets ring with laughter. They reached the burial ground, near the French battery, which had been taken by us some time previously. The bearers were about to enter the gateway, when they were suddenly aroused by a slight cry. It came from within the coffin, and was accompanied by the kind of scraping noise. They halted, paused, and listened. Surely it was Mike scraping! On they moved again doubtfully, but for the second time they heard the voice.

'Whist!' ejaculated the bearers, their caps moving almost off their heads.

'Oh blood and guns!' said the voice. 'Where am I? Oh, bad luck to yer souls! Let me out, won't you? Oh, merciful Jasus, I'm smothered.' The bearers bolted out from under the coffin, and in an instant a dozen bayonets were sunk under the lid to lift it. The crowd crushed forward to take a look. There lay Sergeant Michael Connelly, as stiff as a fugleman, but somewhat colder. One of the bearers was that blackguard Josh Hetherington, the cockney ventriloquist, and he joined in the astonishment as 'innocent' as you please! He winked at me, and I winked back. 'Ned,' he said, 'I'm blessed if I think he's dead. Why don't some of them there chaps go for a doctor?' 'To be sure,' cried the crowd, 'send for the doctor.'

Meanwhile a regular rush was made to press Mike to swallow some of his favourite liquor, but his teeth so obstinately opposed the draught, that when the doctor arrive, they pronounced that poor Mike was 'not himself'.

Costello and many others who survived their wounds stayed in Salamanca to convalesce, and to regain their strength. He was there for two months, re-joining the 1st/95th near Madrid. About the same time, Harry Ross-Lewis visited the field of Salamanca and

found a long line of vultures on the battle-ground; these ill-omened birds stand quite erect, and might be mistaken by a distant spectator for a regiment drawn up in a single rank. Here was a fine field for them; the bodies of men and horses, which an attempt had been made to burn, lay everywhere in heaps, only half-consumed. After the action, wherever the carcase of a horse was found, such human bodies as had fallen near were collected and thrown over it, and these again were covered with branches of trees, which, being quite green, made too weak a fire to reduce them to ashes; consequently the air had become very offensive, and the whole scene was extremely revolting. A vast number of pigs, which had been driven hither by their owners, also roamed the field, and shared the loathsome feast with the vultures.

Modern readers, now well accustomed to the new system of repatriation of bodies back to Britain, with all the respect and ceremony rightly due, may raise an eyebrow at pyramids of massed half-burnt bodies, men and horses inter-mingled, littering yet another Spanish plain. It says much for the common view two centuries ago, essentially practical and unsentimental, to leave affairs to what has been called the Spanish national undertaker – the vulture. It is also perhaps relevant, in wondering whether the grateful Spanish citizens of

Salamanca might themselves have done the decent thing by their allies, with picks and shovels, to recall that twenty years later 6,000 Spanish troops were quartered in the town for two months, yet 'Not one man or officer had ever been to visit the battlefield.' (Richard Ford, 1832) It will be interesting to discover how the civic authorities of Salamanca in 2012 propose to mark the 200th anniversary of the battle, if at all.

CHAPTER 16

Salamanca
Garcia Hernandez
23 July 1812

The most dashing and successful attack made by any of Wellington's cavalry during the whole war.

Oman

The name of Garcia Hernandez will always be included amongst the great achievements of cavalry in the history of the world.

Fortescue

I have never witnessed a more gallant charge.

Wellington

* * *

Major-General Eberhard, Baron Bock commanded the 1st and 2nd Dragoons KGL. We do not know quite how many sabres he took forward next morning as part of Wellington's advance guard – Tomkinson tells us Bock and Anson combined 'did not amount to 800, being so weakened by detaching squadrons during the night'. Bock's troopers had had a dismally quiet Wednesday on the Salamanca plain. With such good going underfoot it had been doubly frustrating to hear of Le Marchant's glorious afternoon. His own men were equally eager to even things up, given half a chance. With not a single man or horse returned killed or wounded in the whole of the great battle of the 22nd, it is unlikely they were even involved, later that evening, in the obligatory charges which pushed back Foy's rearguard. The Germans almost certainly were out to the left, not really in harm's way, and then were finally on the road to the fords at Huerta, searching in vain for the Army of Portugal.

Next morning, it was five miles from the bivouac at Pelabravo to the fords south of Encinos; crossing there after first light they were brought down to join Wellington and Anson's dragoon squadrons, who had crossed at Alba. The quantities of abandoned baggage and wounded, and the limping stragglers, clearly indicated the Army had used the road through Garcia Hernandez east towards Penaranda. Wellington, Anson and Bock converged on the former village around 2pm. The 1st and Light Divisions were some miles behind, the bulk of the army resting still.

Anson's patrols reported French water parties at the village wells, a battery of horse artillery, a chasseur brigade, and various battalions both in the village and formed on the Penaranda road in rear. This was Foy's division, the rear-guard, and at the appearance of the horsemen, Foy clearly not proposing to argue, a general movement commenced to continue the withdrawal. The chasseurs moved to a covering position on slightly higher ground behind the village. They blocked Wellington's line of sight, for in their rear were two of Foy's four regiments, the 6th Léger and the 76th Ligne, drawn up a little to the flank on higher slopes – a rearguard to the rearguard – while the 39th and 69th Ligne legged it for all they were worth. Wellington immediately ordered Anson to charge the chasseurs with what was to hand, Bock's dragoons being across to the left. Anson had four squadrons, two each of the 11th and 16th Light Dragoons, and went straight at the chasseurs, most of whom promptly turned tail on the spot, and in panic and confusion withdrew; but with two squadrons – doing the decent thing – moving a little up the slopes, as some protection to the 76th Ligne's square.

Baron Bock now thundered onto the scene, doubtless squinting at the possibilities for glory (he was said to be very shortsighted). He was at the head of Captain Haltorff's squadron, the first of three of the 1st Dragoons, crashing in column through a defile along the Caballero brook on the outskirts of the village. Emerging into open ground and seeing the two French squadrons, he went straight for them, forming line as they went, only to be hammered in the left flank by a volley from the unseen 76th. The two chasseur squadrons turned to join their fellows, pursued by Haltorff and Bock, whose second and third squadrons were similarly greeted with musketry from their left. Captain Gustavus von der Decken, commanding the third squadron, in a twinkling wheeled left and charged the battalion square. At eighty yards von Decken and others were hit by the first volley. His knee was shattered, his balance gone, and over he went (and died of the wound six weeks later) but, the lead passing to Captain von Usslar Gleichen, the squadron tore on into a second volley at close range.

There now occurred a stroke of luck, and a mischance for the poor 76th; the impetus of one horse, brought down in that final volley, carried him onto the kneeling front rank of the square. Rolling on over, the flailing legs and hooves cleared a passageway to the inside. Instantly seizing their chance, troopers dashed through and began hacking away at the inside of the breaking square. Resistance could not have been lengthy, for afterwards many of the 76th's muskets were found lying in neat rows. Most surrendered, and quickly at that. This was an astonishing collapse of some 500 formed men, facing not more than 100 horsemen, and brought about solely by the battering effect of a falling horse. Charles Oman has found the names of twenty-two officers of this battalion (surely the full complement), only seven of whom were wounded, but with fourteen taken prisoner unwounded. It is his reckoning that not above fifty men escaped.

Now such figures surely indicate a lack of serious resistance. This is all the stranger – or is it just a case of experienced men knowing when resistance is useless? – for the 76th were an immensely veteran regiment who had fought at Ulm, Jena, Eylau, Friedland, Essling, Wagram and, in the Peninsula, at Busaco and Fuentes. So too had Foy's 39th and 69th. But Colonel Molard's 6th had not a single battle to their credit, virgins to the slaughter indeed. It is widely known that three or four ranks of men – whether with bayonets or not – will stop any horse, not so much that they recognise and fear danger in the bayonet itself, rather that by nature a horse will not risk its vulnerable legs in treading on moving bodies. No cavalryman charges expecting to force his way past solidly massed bodies. Indeed, since a horse, no matter how fast it is ridden at a square, will swerve or put in a 'stop' at the very last, there is always a high chance of the rider being ejected – on to the bayonets! Hence he rides a moderate pace where he can sit tight, especially in the last few strides. Now, of course, what he hopes for and why he charges at all, is an ill-formed square comprising poorly spirited defenders, perhaps not shoulder to shoulder, with a chance of frightening some to waver and draw back. Decken's squadron was presented with the best of all: an open door.

In full view of this catastrophe, and of Bock's other squadrons threateningly below them, Colonel Molard of the 6th ordered his two battalions, who were in column, not to form square. He made the astonishing decision, instead, to make for the higher ground – the heights are indeed fairly precipitous in places, and effectively immune to cavalry. But first you have got to get there. The voices of the officers were heard shouting 'Allongez le pas, gagnons la hauteur' and one cannot but feel sympathy, given the broiling heat of the afternoon sun, for these two columns, each 500 men, struggling to keep their tight formations as they doubled upwards, knowing the next order would be to form square – if they could get high enough, quickly enough. Below them the approaching thuds and jingling equipment of several hundred horses closed rapidly. The squadron under Captain von Reizenstein was almost upon the rear battalion when the last two companies under Captain Philippe halted and, facing about, fired a ragged and no doubt ill-aimed volley. Two subalterns and several troopers were hit, but the dragoons simply rode through them – 100 on foot, 100 on horse – so each dragoon could pick his man, who either dropped his musket and raised his hands, or was cut down. Philippe, however, had gained a little time, enough for some of the leading files of the other four companies to climb the hill and join the square now nearly formed by their sister battalion on the crest. The lagging files were cut down. Next to the new square stood one of the chasseur squadrons, fugitives from Anson's earlier charge.

Passing through the carnage next came two squadrons of the 2nd Dragoons (Marschalak's and Furnetty's), spurring up the slope to the second square. Once again the chasseurs turned and moved away, but no fallen horse was needed this time to bring success: the 6th's square just disintegrated. Its rapid formation was said to be disturbed by the fugitives from the broken battalion coming up behind and, in truth, even without them the formation was hurried and therefore slipshod. Many men surrendered and others ran off down the slopes for the safety of the other regiments on the road. These were the 39th and 69th Ligne, which Foy had now got into squares, unlimbering guns, and just in time. For the Germans made for their third square of the day, that of the 69th, cutting at the fugitives of the 6th as they roared past, the horsemen in some disorder now and a mixture of the KGL squadrons. The square fired competent volleys, killing Captain von Uslar who, with Marschalak, had led this charge, and enough troopers for the dragoons to shear off. Foy was allowed to go his way, there being neither allied infantry nor artillery to hand. And that was that.

In this splendid cavalry action, the French lost in entirety the battalion of the 76th first set upon, some twenty-two officers and about 600 other ranks killed, wounded or taken, leaving perhaps five officers and fifty men – a small company, if that. The 6th Léger of two battalions lost Colonel Molard (who subsequently died of his wounds), six other officers captured and eight more wounded, with about 500 men lost one way or the other. Add some chasseurs, and Foy had thus been blooded to the extent of about 1,100 men – a fifth of his division.

It was not a cheap victory. Bock lost 127 men, of whom fifty-two were killed. Taken as a squadron level action, which it truly was, the Germans showed excellent leadership: seizing opportunities, acting instantly, yet acting in concert of squadrons, and clearly manoeuvring swiftly. This was not an action of premeditation at regimental level. There was no forming up on a start line, no planned supports, no marked axis of advance. It was a pure encounter battle of the sort a later generation of German cavalrymen would dub *blitzkrieg* (the battle honour 'Garcia Hernandez' was still, quite rightly, emblazoned on the guidons of two Hanoverian cavalry regiments in 1914). Wellington had nothing to do with it, and neither did Bock, neither did the Colonels of the 1st and 2nd Dragoons. It was the work of four captains and their 400 men, and especially of von Decken, whose instant success spread shock, panic and despair amongst the French and inspired emulation in Von Reizenstein, Marschalak and Furnetty. Yet, if that horse had not fallen as it did, none of this might have happened and, as usual, cavalry would again have failed against the experienced 76th's square. Yet perhaps Colonel Molard might still have tried to run for it, and Von Reizenstein and Marschalak might still have overcome him?

Your author, whose life has happily combined much foot soldiering and much hunting, has always found difficulty in knowing which to admire more on 22/23 July 1812 – his old 48th on their feet (even if we were in a fusilier brigade), or the swifter dragoons, whether British or German. But Le Marchant, surely, had he lived, would have given the Salamanca cavalry honours to Baron Bock. For while he himself had charged troops not in square, and who were already devastated and beaten by British infantry, Bock's men beat two formed squares and rode down a column, overcoming three times their own strength, in the face of (what should not be forgotten) a chasseur brigade hovering nearby some 800 strong. Shame on that brigade, and of whom we also saw very little the previous day. It was all over in forty minutes, they say, much as it took to determine the previous day's work. Taken together, the British and German cavalry had made a truly memorable contribution to his Lordship's trouncing of Marmont's Army of Portugal.

CHAPTER 17

Madrid and Burgos
12 August–21 October 1812

Immediately after the drubbing on Salamanca field, Clausel said he was down to 22,000 men, half of Marmont's original army, although thousands more were straggling in, despite the attentions of lurking Spanish peasants. Naturally the men's morale was entirely – for the moment – as low as could be. That did not prevent them marching with their usual unencumbered vigour. When on 24 July the British vanguard reached Penaranda, twenty-five miles from Alba, they had disappeared up the Valladolid road. Wellington followed sedately, which did not please all his supporters, reaching that place on the 30th, another sixty miles in easy marches with one rest day. In Valladolid he captured 1,000 sick in the hospital, seventeen guns and much ammunition. During this movement some cavalry prisoners were brought in from Joseph Bonaparte's small Army of the Centre who, in ignorance of the situation, had marched to help Marmont and had so very nearly fallen under Wellington's hand. With 14,000 men Joseph had left Madrid the day before the great battle; then learning the news on the night of the 24th, not far from Penaranda, he about-turned post haste to Madrid.

It was open to Wellington to continue to follow Clausel. He was after all now astride one of the four main roads between Madrid and France; could he but reach Burgos, another eighty miles, then he would also be astride the direct second road from Madrid, which place then could rely only on the third via Zaragoza, or the fourth, impossibly lengthy, via Valencia. However, that extra eighty miles to Burgos would so lengthen the allied line of communication back to Ciudad Rodrigo that even Joseph might descend upon it. The more cautious course of action was therefore to capture Madrid, 100 miles away, which had much in its favour politically, and possibly meet up with Hill's 18,000 men when, combined, they could cope with Joseph and Soult, should the latter join.

So leaving Anson's light brigade and two divisions of the Spanish under Santocildes at Valladolid and along the line of the Douro, to watch for Clausel, Wellington himself moved to Cuellar, thirty miles to the east. There he left Clinton's 6th Division and a stores depot. In addition, Clinton was given five battalions badly in need of rest and acclimatisation, all being new in theatre and all with Walcheren in their blood, the 2nd/4th, 1st/5th, 1st/38th, 1st/42nd and 1st/82nd (the latter had missed the battle at Salamanca).

But there was more than Clausel and Joseph to consider, and Wellington halted for a few days at Cuellar, to consider further the options open to him. He knew Marshal Soult had been ordered, with his Army of the South, to reinforce the king, though whether he would obey was the question; and there was Suchet's Army of Valencia. It was therefore a pleasure to hear from an intercepted despatch that the latter now seemed fully concerned with Lord William Bentinck's expedition on the Spanish coast, long delayed. So his Lordship set out for Madrid on 7 August. Behind him, on one road through the mountains of the Guadarrama, threaded 36,000 men in six infantry divisions, two independent Portuguese brigades, three cavalry brigades, Espana's Spanish and Julian Sanchez's lancers, and it all made for an exceptionally long column and a tiresomely slow passage. Any complacency, however, was shattered on 11 August, seven miles from Madrid at a place called Majalahonda, when D'Urban's seven vanguard squadrons – some 700 men – were rudely awakened at their 4pm siesta by three French dragoon regiments and one of lancers, three times their strength. Fortunately for the Portuguese, KGL cavalry and a KGL light battalion was in close support. A fierce fight developed, both sides losing about 200 men, with the Portuguese twice turning and running, and leaving their officers unsupported in the French ranks. It was a bad to-do, and Wellington afterwards wrote, 'I shall not place Portuguese dragoons again in situations in which, by their misconduct, they can influence the safety of other troops.'

Joseph Bonaparte quit Madrid with a huge convoy of 2,000 carts and, it was said, 10,000 civilian fugitives who, for various reasons, feared for their lives. A dreadful 250 mile journey in appalling conditions ensued, to Valencia, on the coast. It was to take three weeks. Many of the so-called Afrancesados – the collaborators and hangers-on – sought shelter wherever they could en route, hoping no doubt to be able to return to Madrid before too long, given a change of fortune (and which indeed turned out to be the case).

Madrid welcomed Lord Wellington and his men in properly hearty fashion. Three years before at Talavera, he had approached to within sixty miles of the Spanish capital but, of course, with no prospect of reaching it. The welcome was everything the army and its commanders could wish for – and indeed quite rightly expected, given the blood, sweat and tears expended since 1808 to remove the French yoke. The liberation of an ally's capital city is a military milestone in any campaign, a sign of success, reward, hope and encouragement, and the reverse of all these things to the ejected occupiers; in addition (with a bit of luck) there will be vast stocks of food, clothing, shoes, guns, muskets, powder, saddlery, workshops, armouries and barracks, not all of which in a hurry can be carted off or destroyed by the rightful owners.

Joseph's token garrison of 2,000 men having surrendered after a day or so, and with over 400 sick in hospital, the captured store houses were found to contain 180 brass guns and two Eagles (the 51st Ligne and 12th Léger), 20,000 muskets, 14,000 uniforms, 900 barrels of gunpowder, 40,000 pairs of shoes, and rations etc., all of which was most welcome, especially the shoes: blue coats were issued to the light dragoons and artillery men, to be cut down into jackets, and the 68th (amongst others) according to William Wheeler 'was fortunate enough to fall in with the clothing and well stocked themselves with new shirts, stockings and shoes'. Wheeler's account of the 7th Division's entry into the city is particularly well drawn, including being kissed by men with garlic moustaches soaked in snuff:

> Our division marched right in front, and as our Regiment is on the right of the division we were the first regiment that entered Madrid. I never before witnessed such a scene. At the distance of five miles from the gates we were met by the inhabitants, each had brought out something, viz. laurel, flowers, bread, wine, grapes, lemonade, aquedente, tobacco, sweetmeats etc. etc. etc. The road represented a moving forest, from the great multitude of people carrying boughs. The intervals of our subdivisions soon became filled up with men, women and children. In one place would be a brawny Spaniard with a pigskin of wine, filling vessels for us to drink, then another with a basket full of bread distributing it around, then a pretty palefaced black-eyed maid would modestly offer a nosegay or sprig of parma or of olive, while others of the sex more bold would dash into our ranks take off our caps and place a sprig of laurel, then without ceremony seize our arm and sing some martial air to the memory of some immortal patriot who had fallen in the good cause. The immortal names of Crauford and others would also sound in Spanish song.
>
> Thus we slowly moved on, amidst the sweet voices of thousands of the most bewitching and interesting little devils I had ever seen, at least I then thought so. But as we approached the city the crowd increased, the people were mad with joy. They called us 'their deliverours, their Saviours.' And by a thousand other names. The poor Virgin Mary was forgotten, at least for that day. The air was rent with the deafening shouts of 'Vivi Wellington, Vivi les Angolese, Vivi les Ilandos' and by ten thousand other Vivis, I cannot think on. Wellington was at the head of the column. When we entered the city the shouting increased tenfold, every bell that had got a clapper was set ringing, the windows were ornamented with rich drapery embroidered with gold and silver, such as is only used on great festivals when the Host is carried. The whole of the windows and tops of the houses were crowded with Spanish beauty, waving white handkerchiefs. The people endeavoured to drag us into their houses. Suffice it to say, that we were several hours going to the convent

where we were to be quartered, that under ordinary circumstances might have been walked in fifteen minutes. But amidst all this pleasure and happiness we were obliged to submit to a custom so unenglish that I cannot but feel disgust now I am writing. It was to be kissed by the men. What made it still worse, their breath was so highly seasoned with garlick, then their huge mustaches stiffened with sweat, dust and snuff, it was like having a hair broom pushed into ones face that had been daubed in a dirty gutter.

Major the Hon. Somers Cocks had also (more happily)

Never been kissed by so many pretty girls in a day in all his life, nor did he ever expect to be again ... the inhabitants testified their joy by hanging all their curtains, tapestries etc. out of the windows which had a very pretty effect and was greatly increased for three nights by a splendid illumination with immense candles. On the third night they gave a Ball to the army, which affords me an opportunity of seeing more splendid clothes than I ever saw before. The women are beautiful, very fond of the English ...

Others had eyes for a different kind of bargain:

You would be delighted to see the fine collection of Pictures both here, and in private houses, I scarce do anything else; and am now become well acquainted with the style of every master. There are Good Pictures to be bought, and I think if I can procure one or two very good Murillos I shall buy them for you, but I shall not go further than from £50 to £100. I shall confine myself to this master as one cannot be mistaken in his paintings, and I certainly think him the best of the Painters of his day. There is one however who has painted much here who I also think delightful, and is not known in England, Mengs. There are a number of Titians & Rubens to be seen, and procured here, but I cannot say I esteem generally the works of the latter ... Velasquez is certainly the first Portrait painter of the Spanish style ... You might if you were here pick up a number of fine things as almost everything is to be sold, I understand there are some find Greek & Roman Antiques & statues to be had.

(Lieutenant Colonel Alexander Gordon) One must comment that 1812's £50 to £100 would then buy one a second-rate horse; it seems a Morillo, Titian, Rubens or Velasquez were not much more!

Whilst his army enjoyed genuine Spanish hospitality, and put on a bit of fat, the Peer had much to ponder while sitting through bullfights, balls and receptions. Throughout August he remained busy but immobile, not straying far from his headquarters, to which surely must soon come news on which to act. For he was in a quandary over quite what to do for the best. It really turned on Marshal Soult's decision, to stay or quit his fiefdom of Andalucia. Stay, and his garrison commitments and the containment of Ballesteros and his Spaniards, and of the partisans, would mean he could march with fewer than 25,000 to join Joseph's 15,000. That Wellington and Hill could cope with. But evacuate Andalucía entirely, and the joint force 65,000 strong would be a different kettle of fish. 'Any other but a modern French army would now leave the province of Andalucía,' Wellington had written to Bathurst four days before Salamanca 'As they have now absolutely no communications of any kind with France or with any other French army ... yet I suspect Soult will not stir til I force him out.' To do that, Wellington must turn his back on Clausel, and possibly Joseph, and it would be a hideously long march; not really something to be contemplated.

Then things started to fall into place: it became clear that Valencia and Suchet were the objects of Joseph's retreat, which surely made it certain Soult must march there also; and by 25 August Wellington had indeed enough unconfirmed reports to suggest Soult 'is about to make a general movement ... it is supposed in the direction of Granada and Valencia [and] that all persons belonging to the civil departments were to march with the army.' That is, an evacuation. All this must take time – some few weeks – and his Lordship resolved to use that time to deal with Clausel and then 'return to this part of the country [Madrid] and hope I shall be here and shall be joined by the troops under Sir Rowland Hill, before Soult can have made much progress to form his junction with the King.' (to Bathurst, 30 August) For that junction was the prime problem Wellington saw he must face: the next few weeks of what has been called the Burgos campaign, thus were regarded as a side-issue, in a time frame probably closing at the end of September. Hill had been ordered to set out to Madrid only once Soult's force under Drouet had definitely disappeared towards the east. This took place on 26 August. Thanks to the lack of food in the Tagus valley, however, it was a slow march to join but, nevertheless, Hill was to reach Toledo, two marches south of the capital, by the end of the month. He was joined in front of Madrid by Colonel Skerrett with some 4,000 men from around Seville. So together Hill commanded 21,000 men, half British half Portuguese. In addition, around Madrid, were the 3rd, 4th and Light Divisions, and Espana's 3,000, with Alten's and D'Urban's light dragoons – another 17,000 men making 38,000 under Hill about the capital. Wellington took with him to Valladolid the 1st, 5th, 6th and 7th Divisions, with Pack and Bradford's Portuguese, and Boch and Ponsonby's dragoons – a separate force of 30,000 men. (We must bear in mind that the hospital State of 25 August showed 20,000 marked not on duty.)

Now this decision is hard to understand, except as a cautious compromise, if he had decided he could well deal with Clausel and get back in time before Joseph and Soult could come up. That is, to denude himself to leave such a force under Hill. But he really could not be sure of Clausel's current strength (it was in fact 40,000), nor of likely reinforcements to it (might Caffarelli lend him two divisions?). We say that, of course, with hindsight; similarly, Hill really could no more hold a combined Joseph/Soult force of 60,000 with his reinforced 38,000 than he could with his own 21,000. Neither wing of the allied army was strong enough to cope with the potential threats; nor collectively if they combined Joseph/Soult/Suchet should come together – what, 85,000 strong? Nor if, perish the thought, supposing Napoleon returns triumphant from Russia, that the man was to descend upon Spain with sizeable intentions and additional forces. So the burden on Wellington's shoulders, and his alone, weighed heavily and that he was not as confident as his outward demeanour required, is shown in a downbeat letter to his brother of 23 August:

> Though I still hope to be able to maintain our position in Castille, and even to improve our advantages, I shudder when I reflect upon the enormity of the task which I have undertaken, with inadequate powers myself to do anything, and without assistance of any kind from the Spaniards ... I am apprehensive that all this will turn out but ill for the Spanish cause. If, for any cause, I should be over-powered, or should be obliged to retire, what will the world say? What will the people of England say? What will those in Spain say?

He left Madrid on 31 August, having set out his purpose the previous day to Bathurst: 'I prepare to establish a secure communication between this army and the army of Galicia; and to drive off the parties of the Army of Portugal which have come forward to the Douro.' He was forever looking over his shoulder, however. A week later, when he was in Valladolid, the French being on the road to Burgos, he wrote, 'I shall follow them as far as I can; but I must attend to the south, where it is reported Soult is in movement.' That day for the first time he talks of capturing Burgos, 'There is a storm brewing up from the south, for which I am preparing by driving the detachments of the Army of Portugal away from the Douro; and I propose, if I have time, to take Burgos from them.' Then to Hill the next day:

> I came here to drive Marmont's parties to a greater distance preparatory to the events likely to occur about Madrid and the Tagus. I have waited here to receive accounts of the Army of Galicia, and shall move on tomorrow; but I shall return to Madrid as soon as I shall hear that the plot thickens to the southward.

Predictably, the 11,000-strong Galician army was slow to join. Four days later (13 September) it was still one march adrift, and Burgos still four marches ahead. Wellington had covered forty miles in the last four days, admitting to Bathurst 'I have not pressed them as hard as I might,' dawdling as he did to let the Galicians catch up. Burgos was not reached until 18 September: eighty miles in eleven gentle days. Two days later he was again explaining (this time to Edward Paget, fresh from England) why he was there: 'To remove to a distance all embarrassments existing on this side, preparatory to the events that might be expected on the Tagus [for]) whenever Soult should connect himself with Suchet and the King. We should be pressed a little ... on the Tagus.' As to Burgos Castle, 'I am a little apprehensive that I have not the means to take it (although) if I could get it, I think I might take some of the force southward, and I must still endeavour to do so, even though I should not succeed in taking the Castle.' In these letters we see a man somewhat torn – not that it would perturb him unduly: he clearly wanted to be where he felt his major role required, back with Hill; yet he had not resolved 'The embarrassment existing on this side', and how could he? He seemed not to be looking to engage Clausel in battle, and yet his wish to 'work the French beyond the Ebro' would require ten more days there and back. And there was the small matter of the Army of the North, since Burgos came under General Caffarelli (it was his 2,200 men who formed the garrison). It was all very well hoping Commodore Home Popham could go on being annoying along the coast, but that was not to be relied upon. Clausel could well soon get help. Wellington had already heard 7,000 conscripts had come down the great road from France for the Army of Portugal and, further, that his old foe Massena had been sent to command it once more. In fact, by early September Clausel handed over to General Joseph Souham – and that appointment was to last only a few weeks. In addition, the Army of Portugal had picked up around 4,000 men from the depot in Valladolid, collected earlier from the smaller outposts during the retreat. Taken together, these two groups very nearly replaced his Salamanca losses. So if Wellington could seize and garrison Burgos Castle, which sat above the bridges, a resurgent Army of Portugal would have to deal with it on any new move to the south; and it might even be temptation enough for another battle.

The overall position when he got to Burgos was, of course, known to him with a two week delay. When he made his first move, Soult had been reported on 8 September as being still in Granada, and Joseph in Valencia, presumably waiting for Soult to join. This excellent slow progress anchored the King on the coast yet awhile, and presented Wellington with a little more time.

So the decision was made, not one of his Lordship's best. Men were to die, in the end with nothing to show for it and with his own reputation definitely diminished. Since our earlier chapters have fully considered two successful sieges – three, if we count the Salamanca forts – it is but fair to our French friends not to dodge, via a brief passing note, the Burgos fiasco. As at Badajoz, here they are led by an energetic and resourceful garrison commander. Napoleon once said 'fortresses alone will not win a war but a successful defence will retard the movements of an enemy.' How true. But while General Dubreton's sturdy defence is one prime reason for English failure, we cannot hide that the wounds generally were self-inflicted. At least, however, we shall be spared too many graphic reminders of a comprehensively botched job, since fewer participants later described their recollections than was normal after victorious outcomes.

It was agreed afterwards that the job was much harder than anticipated. Otherwise, one of the divisions experienced in siege work – the 3rd, 4th, 5th or Light – would have been used. The 5th were present with Wellington, but he had sent them forward as part of the covering force. No provision had been made for heavy guns or adequate ammunition and powder – merely the three iron 18-pounders used against the Salamanca forts, and five 24-pounder howitzers, whose feeble accuracy and kinetic energy is useless against masonry. There were just four engineer officers under Burgoyne, including John Jones, also now a half colonel, with eight artificers, plus ten volunteer officers and eighty-one men from the regiments with carpentry, masonry, mining etc. skills. Even the supply of picks and shovels was scarcely enough for one battalion. We can only suppose either that the operation was not foreseen, or that (as with Salamanca) the available intelligence on the nature of the fortress buildings was incorrect. Once seen, however, it was pretty plain: 'We have had a view of the castle, which appears a more tough job than we might have supposed.' (Lieutenant Colonel Robe, commanding the artillery)

The reason was obvious – the place had walls. Now you can blast a breach in walls, or climb a ladder over them, or explode mines underneath and make a breach that way. With just the three 18-pounders, only the second two methods were available, and both of which depended entirely upon surprise and experienced practitioners, whether in wielding picks, or providing covering musketry; and while Wellington could make his own surprise, he could not make instant miners, nor marksmen out of men lumbered with the Brown Bess.

The castle fortress was quite small, on a knoll towering in places 400 feet above the lower parts of the city, which lay mainly to the east. The knoll was just 200 paces long by 100 wide. The various lines of defensive walls down the steep slopes encompassed a much larger acreage. Immediately to the south lay the river Arlanzon, with three bridges; to the north a deep ravine, beyond which rose another knoll. This was flatter but of the same height, and only distant some 300 paces, the ravine being quite steep: this was the hill of San Miguel. Just as at Ciudad Rodrigo the Greater Teson had the Renault Redoubt situated upon it, for much the same reason San Miguel had been crowned by a hornwork. It was in clear view and range of a battery of eight heavy cannon on the keep, which was on the castle site across the ravine, together with the magazines. The guns also covered a palisaded fenceline and the slopes to it, at the hornwork's rear. The west end contained the ruined church of Santa Maria la Blanca – the white house, where provisions were stored. A covered way connected the church with the Keep.

The map shows a double line of walls around the whole, with a third line of wall below the white house, where the ground beneath it falls away more gently and was, therefore, a good deal more inviting of attack than elsewhere. The garrison comprised two battalions of the 34th Ligne and one of the 130th, 1,600 bayonets altogether, with an artillery company to work the 9-, 12- and 16-pounders (eight being on the keep) eleven field guns (seven being on the hornwork) and six mortars and howitzers. In command was Brigadier General Dubreton, reputedly the equal of Badajoz's Phillipon, and as we shall see, certainly no less energetic. He had two big insoluble problems but which, again, Wellington was ill-equipped to exploit: firstly the lack of overhead cover within the confines of the final walls. Only the keep and the white house had roofs, so the great mass of Dubreton's 2,000 men necessarily bivouacked in the open, and were vulnerable to mortar fire which, had such weapons been available, must surely have seen the fortress rapidly become untenable. Secondly, so steep were the slopes upon which the various walls stood, that in many places the outer line quite failed to prevent shot striking an inner, especially fired from the near-commanding level of the hornwork. The latter's capture, therefore, was a pre-requisite, especially since there was thought to be an area just to the right of it, near the gorge, which might provide a defilade gun position, able to engage the north-westerly walls across the ravine but protected by a swell in the ground from fire from the battery on the keep.

Wellington's plan of assault on the hornwork was put together that very day of arrival, 19 September, and successfully executed that night. It bore various fraternal similarities to the previous assaults on both the Renault Redoubt and Fort Picurina, including being made after last light and without preliminary artillery programmes. It was, however, a costly success, and one has to note again the Portuguese element, from Pack's brigade – not for the last time – were a little shy. What happened was that soon after 8pm, two ladder parties supplied by the 1st/42nd (Black Watch) and led by Lieutenant Pitts crept to the two demi-bastions which formed the ends of the hornwork's north face. The Black Watch also provided two forlorn hopes. They were followed by two Portuguese storming parties, whilst a Black Watch firing party of 150 men should have advanced to the edge of the ditch, to keep French heads down while the storm proceeded. John Mills, Coldstream, wrote 'The Portuguese who thought to raise their spirits by it, began to shout at 200 yards distance and thereby drew the enemy's fire upon them.' In the moonlight, the Highlanders were then spotted also, and engaged with a heavy fire – it is said at 150 yards – from where the Highlanders then pointlessly began firing their own muskets. They advanced firing, to the ditch, where they stayed under fire for a quarter of an hour. The ladders up against both demi-bastions were found to be rather short, but the forlorn hopes managed the climb, albeit without support, for neither Portuguese storming party could be availed upon to enter the ditch, let alone to mount. They again remained under fire for some minutes before pulling back, along with the 42nd. What saved the day was a force led by Major Somers Cocks, now 79th, comprising the three light companies of the 1st/42nd

(Black Watch), 1st/24th (Warwicks) and 1st/79th (Camerons). His role was to prevent reinforcements coming from the castle and to make a false attack on the gorge – and convert it for real if he could. He took them round the horn-work, and clambered over the seven-foot palisades at the rear, overcoming the surprisingly light opposition. Opening the gateway, he got inside with about 140 men, and his appearance caused a mass exodus by the garrison, assisted by a bayonet charge which, Tomkinson says, accounted for fifty Frenchmen 'and making as many more as prisoners.' John Jones says the French 'literally ran over the party left to oppose them (at the gorge gate) and mostly escaped into the Castle.' The French garrison was a battalion of the 34th, some 500 strong. Their losses were about a third: six officers and 137 men killed and wounded, of whom sixty were captured – about two companies worth. British losses were however six officers and sixty-five men killed and fifteen officers and 334 men wounded, with the Black Watch accounting for 204 of the losses, the Portuguese the remainder. In return for this heavy bill Wellington obtained seven field guns, and the necessary first key to unlock Burgos Castle; he also obtained widespread grumbling as to the part not played by the Portuguese, and which was to resurface and get worse almost immediately.

Over the next three days a battery position for five guns was constructed next to the hornwork, two 18-pounders and three howitzers being put in on the night of the 22nd. At midnight an attempted escalade was made on the outer wall, on the north-western slopes beneath the white house. Here the wall ran straight for 200 yards, was about twenty-four feet high and had a shallow ditch. A covered approach from the suburb of San Pedro, next to the river, was provided by a sunken lane. It lay in dead ground to the garrison's guns and view, and led to within sixty paces of the wall. The result of the escalade was a disaster, another 158 all ranks killed and wounded, for a dozen or so French. Wellington blamed the officer he appointed and personally briefed, but as we shall see, that was only fair to a degree: some of his own decisions were obviously questionable. Four months later, in a letter to Liverpool, he wrote:

> They did not take the line because Major Laurie, the field officer who commanded, did that which is too common in our army. He paid no attention to his orders, notwithstanding the pains I took in writing them; and in reading and explaining them to him twice over. He made none of the dispositions ordered; and instead of regulating the attack as he ought, he rushed on as if he had been the leader of a forlorn hope, and fell, together with many of those who went with him. He had my instructions in his pocket; and as the French got possession of his body, and were made acquainted with the plan, the attack could never be repeated. When he fell, nobody having received orders what to do, nobody could give any to the troops. I was in the trenches, however, and ordered them to withdraw. Our time and

ammunition were then expended, and our guns destroyed in taking this line; than which at former sieges we had taken many stronger by assault.

'The plan was for a 200-strong storming party taken from volunteers out of the entire 1st Division, with five ladders, should attempt the wall by coup-de-main after a short run from the concealed lane, covered by a firing party, also 200 strong, who were to line up along the bank above the lane. The wall to be assaulted had a thick earthen parapet, and their fire thus sweeping the parapet, should allow the storm to proceed unhindered. The range was said by Jones to be fifty yards.

The storming party was divided into ten groups of an officer and twenty men. Five ladders were to be placed, for the sole use of the first group to go forward, that is four men to shin up each ladder. On their reaching the parapet, another group would advance to the ladders, and so on. When all twenty groups had climbed, the firing party was then to become a working party, tasked with demolishing the wall sufficiently to make a ramp. As a diversion, the 9th Caçadores from the 6th Division were to attempt the wall 200 yards farther along, on the south-western corner, where Dubreton had positioned a small guard. Unfortunately, the Portuguese failed to reach even the ditch, let alone the wall, being deterred by the guards' musketry; the firing party failed to line the bank, remaining with the stormers on the sunken lane. Gallant attempts were made by the forlorn hope to mount the five ladders successfully placed (the French counted forty dead bodies in the ditch the next day) but it is clear chaos reigned supreme. A flavour of this is contained in John Mills' letter home the next day:

> A party of 130 of the Brigade of Guards led the way with the ladders. The enemy opened a tremendous fire, on which the Germans filed off to the right and the Scotch followed them. Our men got the ladders up with some difficulty under a heavy fire from the top of the wall, but were unable to get to the top. Hall of the 3rd Regiment [3rd Foot Guards] who mounted first was knocked down. Frazer tried and was shot in the knee. During the whole of this time they kept up a constant fire from the top of the wall and threw down bags of gunpowder and large stones. At last, having been twenty-five minutes in the ditch and not seeing anything of the other parties they retired having lost half their numbers in killed and wounded. Three officers were wounded. The Portuguese failed in their attempts. Thus ended the attack which was almost madness to attempt.

Apparently the 400 volunteers had been moved along the lane from San Pedro in a column of fours, and in the process become strung out. Major Laurie of the 79th having issued few if any clear orders then being fatally hit, the matter was at a stand. The entire column seems to have left the cover of the lane while standing around waiting for someone to tell them what to do. Jones says 'the whole remained for above a quarter of an hour under the destructive efforts of the garrison.' The Peer said it was he who then called them back, leaving nearly half their number dead or lying wounded under the wall.

Laurie aside, the mixing of volunteers from various regiments was not a good idea for a night operation, nor the successive waves of just twenty men and five ladders rather than a mass assault with multiple ladders, thereby stretching the defences. The accounts mention the parapet being stood upon to hurl 4lb shot and 'Much burning composition which caused many of the men's pouches to explode' and that was precisely why the firing party had been ordered to line the bank. In short, the sunken lane was an asset utterly wasted through appalling organisation and execution on the part of Laurie, with an overall plan by his General which was overly optimistic: the equivalent of two strong infantry companies, with five ladders, was hardly a serious approach.

His Lordship now changed tactics, having wasted three days. Unfortunately his remaining means were also by nature slow. A further week passed in preparation: the digging of a tunnel to lay an explosive mine under the walls. A gallery three feet wide and four feet high was commenced at the end of a sap pushed out from the hollow lane, the wall being a cricket pitch away. The workmen had to make do with the large English pickaxes available – and of course as infantrymen they largely learned as they went along. The mine would be placed near to the earlier escalade, which had failed. A second gallery was commenced for another mine, nearer to the San Pedro suburb. At midday on 29 September the miners reported that they had reached large blocks of masonry. A chamber was hollowed out and stocked with 1,090 pounds of powder. It was decided to attack at midnight.

During the previous week, whilst the tunnels had been slowly driven forwards, a serious of saps and approaches zigzagged between the hornwork and San Pedro, allowing musketry firing trenches, and a second battery (in the gorge) to be positioned. The garrison's guns proved lethal at such short range, so too their musketry, and in places the tossing of shells and hand grenades, which as Jones described 'being thrown over the parapet at a high angle from small distance of 20 or 25 yards, had much the appearance in descending of cricket balls.' The trenches necessarily were deep and lined above by gabions: nonetheless the plunging fire from the walls made movement vulnerable, with several marksmen making a name for themselves. There was also great danger from fused shells being rolled down the slopes or, a variant for the trenches beneath the hornwork, shells which overshot and pitched above the trench would roll back down into it.

When the mine went up at midnight, under cover of a firing party, the stormers closed on the wall and the forlorn hope sent ahead a sergeant and three men. They found the facing stones brought down, but with the earth rampart behind largely still standing. They managed to reach the top and 'were some minutes on the top of the parapet before the garrison recovered from their surprise' (Jones). Whereupon they were forced down at the point of the bayonet. The main body of the hope, with no engineer officer to guide them, then went too far right, found no damaged wall and decided the mine had failed. The report that the wall was intact saw the whole party withdraw back to the trenches. By the time the sergeant had had his say, showing bruises and bayonet wounds to prove his point, it was too late to go back: the garrison had formed a parapet behind the breach, which now bristled with obstacles.

Wellington's loss this time was only twenty-nine killed and wounded. The loss to morale generally, however, was more serious. To the generals, ten days effort went unrewarded, and frustrating wider, more important matters. For the junior officers and the men, ten days of hard physical work and daily danger had now three times seen plans not work, either totally or in part. The lack of proper artillery and trained engineers was obvious to the thickest skull, and would point to inadequate planning somewhere. Yet blaming the staff could not hide the undoubted sense that in several instances – not all involving the poor Portuguese – attacks had not been pressed home robustly, nor opportunities seized. It was all becoming rather disheartening.

The next plan was more of the same, plus an artillery aspect. The second gallery was progressing slowly, but should be ready to blow in a few days. Wellington decided to re-position his three 18-pounders very close to the wall of the first mine, and batter it and the new parapet into a practicable breach, thus providing two entry points. Battery No. 3 was prepared just in front of the hollow lane, at sixty-five yards range; but the French artillery reacted with great and immediate violence. Before a single ball was fired at the wall, the battery position was in ruins, with two guns knocked over, one with a trunnion blasted off, and the third hit eleven times and with a split muzzle. (The three guns were subsequently christened 'Thunder', 'Lightning' and 'Nelson' – the one with only one trunnion.) Nothing daunted, a better protected site nearby was prepared, but was again to become untenable to very accurate plunging fire and the guns, now with a third change of position, were sent back to their original battery, next to the hornwork. That night, the working parties, with the exception of the Guards, shirked their tasks, choosing with their officers' connivance to shelter from the appalling weather. This shirking was not the first, and was a measure of the general loss of morale. However, two of the guns were reported ready on 4 October, as was the mine. About 9am the pitiful battery of two repaired 18-pounders and three howitzers opened fire, and by 4pm the breach was much improved, being held practicable for a width of about twenty yards. The mine had 1,080 pounds of powder, and was fired at 5pm. It was to be a daylight attack by the 2nd/24th on both breaches, five companies or half of the battalion on each and, the mine working splendidly, both were instantly carried. John Mills, Coldstream, watched near the horn-work with a crowd of spectators:

> The troops rushed forward from the place where they were con-cealed. A Grenadier officer of the 24th led that regiment in the most gallant style. He was first on to the breach but when near the top appeared to find great difficulty in getting up, the ground slipping from under his feet. Just at this moment about ten Frenchmen appeared; they seemed quite confounded and not to know what was going on. Two or three ran to the old breach, one fired close to the officer but missed him, the men then peered over and the French ran off as fast as they could into the fort. The 24th advanced and hid themselves behind a pile of shot from whence they commenced firing. Thus far the French seemed taken quite unawares. The explosion of the mine and the storming were so instantaneous that they had not time to do anything before the men were in and then it was too late.

The 24th's attack was well planned and controlled, and executed robustly and at speed – a proper justification for giving the job not to a mixture of units but to one battalion. The 24th lost just sixty-eight men killed and wounded, the supporting work parties about 120. The garrison lost sixty-nine. So Wellington was at last within the outer or third wall. The 24th then faced a palisaded ditch, and the day was spent sapping forwards – sufficiently to provoke General Dubreton to launch a 300-strong sortie at midnight. It overran the working parties (the two sides were but another cricket pitch apart), and reached the breach (the one the artillery had improved); there the protective gabions were overthrown, the trenches back-filled and the tools taken. They inflicted 150 casualties and withdrew when counter-attacked, no doubt very pleased with themselves. Several more days passed in desperate close work, which both sides' great-great-grandsons would have recognised in later trench warfare, including the atrocious rains, the mud and the floods. Duckboards were almost certainly invented in Burgos in 1812.

Four days later, a second and bigger sortie of 400 men erupted at 3am on 8 October. The working parties that day were Pack's Portuguese, with the 1st Division's Germans as their covering parties. Both were entirely surprised and ejected; the works again were levelled and tools taken, at the laughable cost of thirty-three casualties to the French. Wellington suffered 184 losses, mostly KGL and the counter-attack saw its leader, Major Somers Cocks, that most valuable soldier, shot and killed. He was clearly a man thought to be cut out for great things, whose many friends rated his personal qualities rather as was Nelson by his frigate captains, while it is certain his sad death touched Wellington himself profoundly. The death of Somers Cocks was certainly not the last at Burgos Castle, but in a melancholy way it marked the effective end of the siege. All ammunition had to be rationed, French cannonballs had to be picked up and re-used, heavy naval guns were belatedly sent for from Santander, and more powder barrels – even red hot shot was tried – but all to no avail. Ten days later the guns were still firing, and another escalade was attempted on the second line, there was another mine, another bloody repulse with the dead this time Germans and guardsmen. John Mills of the Coldstream described the attack:

> At three o'clock it was communicated to us that the place was to be stormed at 4 o'clock. The signal was the explosion of the mine, on which a flag was to be held up on the hill. The mine exploded – the explosion was attended with so little noise that though we were anxiously expecting it, we could hear no noise. The earth shook a little, we looked to the hill and saw the flag. The 300 Germans stormed the breach and got well up it. They then attempted the third line, by a place in the wall which was broken down. It ended with their being beat out of the whole with the loss of 7 officers and a great many men. Our party was to escalade the wall in front. Burgess ran forward with 30 men, Walpole and myself followed with fifty each and ladders. Burgess got up without much difficulty, Walpole and myself followed. The place we stood on was a ledge in the wall about three feet from the top. A most tremendous fire opened upon us from every part which took us in front and rear. They poured down fresh men and ours kept falling down into the ditch, dragging and knocking down others. We were so close that they fairly put their muskets into our face, and we pulled one of their men through an embrasure. Burgess was killed and Walpole severely wounded. We had hardly any men left on the top and at last we gave way. How we got over the palisades I know not. They increased their fire as we retreated, and we came off with the loss of more than half our party and all the badly wounded were left in the ditch. Burgess behaved nobly – he was the first up the ladder and waved his hat on the top. I found him lying there wounded. He begged me to get my men up and in the act of speaking a stone hit him, he fell on the ledge and was shot dead. The time we were on the wall was not more than six minutes. The fire was tremendous, shot, shells, grape, musketry, large stones, hand grenades and every missile weapon was used against us.

On 20 October Wellington admitted defeat. Even the withdrawal on the night of the 21st went awry, with the bullocks too few and weak to draw the old battered 18-pounders and howitzers. The former were therefore made useless and abandoned, being described by Wellington in his despatch as 'destroyed by the enemy's fire', which was only half true. Even the plan to blow up the hornwork failed, through the powder barrels going to the wrong place. A sorry month-long saga, in which in total twenty-four officers and 485 men had been killed, sixty-eight officers and 1,445 wounded and forty-two men missing, a total bill of 2,064 all ranks. During the siege the day-after-day casualty list had ground remorselessly on, keeping the doctors forever busy. While the four storms cost 973 men, and the two French sorties 326 men, for each of the other twenty-six days of 'inaction' on average twenty-nine men were hit, which is a measure of French gunnery and marksmanship in the trenches.

The conduct of the siege can be criticised on several levels, and one must firstly quote the Commander's own limited self-criticism:

> The fault of which I was guilty in the expedition to Burgos was, not that I undertook the operation with inadequate means, but that I took there the most inexperienced instead of the best troops. I left at Madrid the 3rd, 4th and Light Divisions, who had been with myself always before; and I brought with me that were good the 1st Division, and they were inexperienced.

He went on in this letter to Lord Liverpool, as we quoted earlier, to blame Major Laurie of the 79th. Had Laurie succeeded in that very first attempt, he said 'we had means sufficient to take the place.' What nonsense! Neither his artillery nor his engineers were anything like adequate, and whose fault was that? Yes, had he had a dozen 24-pounders and no engineers the place would have fallen; yes, had he engineers to guide and proper miners to dig but no guns, the same can be said, and was indeed later said by Dickson, Burgoyne and Jones, polishing their own axes thereby. No, his Lordship's scant early intelligence on the castle gave him no hint to be cautious. He was in no position to be cautious, he needed to get on, and get back: no time for guns to be fetched from Santander or Madrid, let's get the ladders up and get in. Yet at the same time there was also a continuing reluctance to commit the overpowering numbers such an approach required, and this was so amateurish a mistake, we can only assume he was strongly influenced by his losses in the ditch at Badajoz. This reticence led to a rather half-hearted atmosphere by all concerned, including those due to climb the ladders: there is nothing like being more numerous than your enemy. Burgoyne, who after all was his Chief Engineer, tried to persuade him to use more men. 'Why' he said in reply 'expose more men that can ascend the ladders or enter the work at any one time, when by this mode the support is ordered to be up in time to follow the tail of the preceding party close?' Yet the supports were not always there, tight behind, when needed, and when men look around and see no-one, it's a bit grim. The final assault on 18 October was notably unfunded. For their escalade, 300 guardsmen were to move up in successive waves of a forlorn hope of twenty men, then six storm parties of fifty men: but these were not to leave cover until the previous party had reached a certain point. For their breach, 300 Germans with a similar tiny hope and a support of fifty men – but these were not to move until the hope's twenty men had reached the lip of the breach. A reserve of 200 men were to stay in their trench until the fifty-man support were well established on the rampart. Well, such a proceeding is clearly not remotely related to the 4th and Light Divisions – thousands in each! – each being given a breach at Badajoz! Why, they had more in their forlorn hopes than here the Guards and KGL had in their entirety!

A lack of endeavour was also noticed among the working parties, as Burgoyne wrote:

> Our undertaking, every night that we broke ground, appeared most pitiful: there was scarcely a single instance where at least double the work was not projected, with sufficient men and tools collected, that was afterwards executed, owing to the neglect and misconduct of the working parties. It was seldom that the men could be induced to take out their gabions and set to work, and I myself placed at different times hundreds of gabions with my own hands, and then entreated the men to go and fill them, to no purpose. The engineers blamed the men – the men blamed the engineers, who, as they grumbled, were by unskilful direction 'sending them out to be butchered'.

This regrettable attitude was surely not helped by Wellington's own doubts, set out in letters at an early point, as we have seen. These might well have been known in Headquarters and, if so, gossip would have done the rest, down the officer chain, and the men would eavesdrop. Also on his shoulders was the use of ad hoc groupings of men, from whichever men were on duty in the trenches, especially if men were allocated away from their own officers and sergeants. Nothing like a proper spirit would exist in such circumstances, a fact of life known by the merest green subaltern, and it is to be wondered at, that his Lordship allowed it. It is one thing to ask for 200 volunteers from a division, another to make men wearing nine different cap badges work in harmony. They can't, for they just don't know the next man from Adam. Or their officer, probably. It is no coincidence that the cleanest, cheapest and quickest storm was that of 4 October, by the 2nd/24th.

What cannot be placed on Wellington's shoulders, yet affected the outcome, was the appalling weather – both the heat and the torrents. Nor the skill and energy of his enemy and, in particular, the leadership of General Dubreton. Nor the Portuguese, who more than once were said to have been shy. Burgoyne was one of those who had no time for them, and he urged Wellington to 'brigade them', that is use them at all times in conjunction with British battalions or companies. However, their rather poor showing at Salamanca, and now for whatever reason in siegework, cannot be blamed upon Wellington; except, one supposes, in so far as he could have chosen not to use them.

Perhaps in the end we must simply blame Badajoz. The recent memory of what can follow full-blooded measures taken against a good enemy, dictated half measures this time. The snatching of Indian hill-forts, the Renault Redoubt, and Fort Picurina encouraged him in his belief in the coup-de-main use of ladders; indeed, had not Badajoz fallen in the end to those same devices, and the indomitable fighting qualities of the British soldier? But now it was October and the men were stale, and tired. They needed rest. No more miracles, for a while. Which was not a good starting point for a humiliating month-long march backwards of 200 grim miles. Many said what they now faced was worse than that other retreat four years back, to the ships at Corunna.

CHAPTER 18

Back to Portugal
22 October–19 November 1812

John Aitchison, 3rd Guards, wrote to his father on the last day of October:

> The enemy had collected towards the beginning of this month a very considerable force in our front, and they gradually advanced towards Burgos as they found our inability to take it; on the 19th they were within one day's march of it in force and Wellington then judged it proper to raise the siege and move forward to meet them. Accordingly on the 20th, soon after daybreak, the whole allied army was assembled in position about 7 miles from Burgos, on a range of hills covering the high road from Vitoria; in the afternoon the enemy came down upon us with a large body of Cavalry and about 15,000 Infantry, but being uncertain of the points occupied by us, they exposed their own right flank in their advance upon our right, and this error was instantly taken advantage of by Wellington – he quitted the heights with the left of the army, and advanced on the plain and gained considerably towards the rear of their right – but night came on and they effected their retreat, and we returned to our position about 9 o'clock.

We remained looking at each other throughout the whole of 21st, the enemy bringing up fresh troops and we making preparations for a retreat. As soon as the sun set we began to move, and notwithstanding it was fine moonlight we passed under the guns of the Castle within range of grape shot without being discovered, and before daybreak on the 22nd the whole of our army was three leagues in rear of Burgos. The next day we made a short march of a league and a half but we were compelled to quicken our pace on the 23rd.

The Army of Portugal had passed briefly into the hands of General Joseph Souham on 3 October, five weeks or so before King Joseph sacked him. He inherited an Army much improved in numbers and morale since 22 July. With 10,000 men in two divisions and 1,600 cavalry from Caffarelli's Army of the North, and drafts of new men, he had some 51,000 men, whereas Wellington here had just 21,000 Anglo–Portuguese and 11,000 Spaniards, and was clearly not adequately placed. He must surely now have regretted leaving 17,000 in and around Madrid, to combine with Hill.

Yet Hill needed the 17,000 men also: news from him arrived on 21 October, as Wellington was being tested by Souham after his last abortive attempt on the castle; 'The King, Soult, and Suchet having united their armies are on the frontiers of Murcia and Valencia, and appear to be moving this way. It is certain that a considerable force is advancing towards Madrid.' That was the news that broke the siege, for the king's combined strength, which Wellington judged to be 'Not less than 50,000 men,' put Hill also in jeopardy: it was imperative Wellington and Hill closed their 150-mile separation. Hill had accordingly been instructed to quit the Tagus and march north. He was to head for Arevalo, seventy miles north-west of Madrid, but in extremis to march west along the Tagus. So it was about-turn for all. Soult and the king were already at Ocana and Taracon, fifty miles below Madrid.

One of the 1st (Royal) Dragoons' surgeons was George Burroughs. In a letter home he gives an account of the first two days of the retreat:

I had scarcely reposed an hour in my tent, and it was eleven o'clock at night, when my servant came to inform me the regiment was ordered to march. I arose hastily and dressed myself, the thunders of the artillery of the castle vibrating in my ears. My tent was instantly struck, and the baggage thrown upon the mule. The distant sounds of the artillery rattling on the roads, the buzzing murmurs of the passing soldiery, and the angry lightning from the cannon of the besieged castle, could not fail of inspiring sublimity even in the most vacant mind.

Having mounted my horse, I directed my way to Villa Toro, a very small and insignificant village, about two miles from Burgos, where the headquarters of the army had been established during the siege. As the narrow road (which from the late rains, was rendered heavy) led through the mountains, and lay out of the range of the shot of the castle; the spare artillery and hospital waggons, commissariat mules, and baggage of the army, proceeded by it. The throng presently became so great, that the cargoes of the mules were overturned, and in proportion to the opposition, did the desire of pushing forward increase. Everything was at a stand and in disorder. In one place were two or three sick soldiers bolstered up by their comrades' knapsacks lying on a bullock car, and surrounded by some less sick companions; in another, bags of biscuit trodden under feet, and casks of rum stove in; here an artillery waggon had sunk axle-tree high in mud, the leading horses of which, having exhausted their strength to drag it out, were lying prostrate and panting in the road, so that it was with much difficulty I could proceed, and then only by striking out a path over the mountain.

Having entered Villa Toro, which presented one scene of bustle, I found the flying artillery of the Spanish army passing, and the streets so narrow and dirty, and so blocked up with beasts of burden of every sort, that the officers' servants, of headquarters, were unable to load their mules with baggage, and the commissaries were in a like situation with regard to their supplies. Some considerable time elapsed before I got clear of this village, and had scarcely done so, when I overtook one of the eighteen-pounders, which had been employed on the horn-work of Saint Michael against the castle of Burgos. An extraordinary number of horses were endeavouring to drag the carriage through the muddy ground, but the resistance offered was so great, that it was ordered to be spiked and left behind.

I had now approached a village, and feeling an ague coming on, dismounted from my horse, at the door of a house which was open. On entering, quantities of burnt straw lay on the floor, with some wood, which seemed recently to have supplied a fire. Having ordered my baggage to be unloaded, and a fire to be kindled, I wrapped myself up in my cloak, and laid down, prepared to encounter the paroxysm. This hovel, which from its exterior, looked as decent as any in the place, was entirely divested of everything in the shape of furniture. The slender partitions which separated the upper rooms with the flooring, was removed, and only the central beam, that from its size had resisted every attempt, was remaining. Stores of all kinds and baggage continued to pass by, and the Portuguese soldiers were frequently entering my quarters to light their paper segars. As soon as break of day, I arose, and almost the first object that presented itself, was the 5th division and Spanish army, marching over the mountains which run northward through Old Castile, and which are a continuation of those forming the northern boundary to the kingdom of Leon.

A party of German hussars marching by, informed me the whole of the infantry had passed the skirts of the village, and that the cavalry would arrive presently. Having re-mounted, and marched about three miles, I overtook the 6th division, and proceeded with it to Celada del Camino, where the headquarters of our second in command, the Honourable Sir Edward Paget, was established; and, at some little distance, the column was encamped. These troops had arrived here about two hours before, and were cooking their dinners. I had but just come to my regiment, when the route was announced. The column was soon under arms, and proceeded to Vallefena, which after several halts we did not reach until dark. Vallefena is a

small village, distance eight leagues from Burgos; and is situated on
the Pisuerga river, over which a good stone bridge is thrown. There
is much inconvenience suffered in coming to a bivouac at night,
particularly in the present instance, as it was upon vineyard grounds,
so that at every step we sunk deep in the soft ground surrounding the
trunk of the vines, or else were thrown down by their long branches
curling round our limbs. The tents were pitched, and the camp soon
began to blaze with our fires. Our horses felt this night the want of
straw; indeed, what little could be obtained, was always allotted to
the cavalry and artillery horses.

There is in this account that whiff of confusion, ignorance and mild
resignation which is a forerunner to the fear which characterises all retreats.
And there in the want of straw lay a first hint of breakdown in supplies, which
turned this retreat sour in spirit, and expensively wasteful in men and horses.
On 23 October the French vanguard was pushing hard and, with nearly
6,000 horsemen available, it was all Wellington's skinny rearguard could do
to keep them off the marching infantry. Anson's and Bock's brigades, and
1,000 of Julian Sanchez's lancers, totalled no more than 2,000. They and two
light battalions of the KGL had scampered over a tributary of the Arlanzon at
Venta del Pozo, near the village of Villodrigo, having already held the French
and gained precious time at a similar stream. The bridge gave Cotton a chance
to emulate Lumley at Usagre in May 1811, that is, to catch the French as they
crossed and were busy reforming. Unfortunately they were too close on Anson's
heels, whose squadrons whilst themselves reforming above the bridge masked
the fire of Cotton's horse artillery. French squadrons thus crossing without
hindrance, a strong force quickly built up, and by the time Bock's dragoons,
supported by Anson, charged, they had missed their chance. The French were
too numerous, and too boisterous, especially Boyer's dragoons who crashed
into the flank of the light cavalry. 'Then' wrote Napier, 'the British ranks were
broken, the regiments got inter-mixed and all went to the rear in confusion ...
The swiftness of the English horses alone prevented a terrible catastrophe',
while the KGL squares with a 'tempest of bullets emptied the French saddles
by scores ... After three fruitless attempts to charge, [they]) reined up and
drew off to the hills.' This affair is partly covered by Surgeon Burroughs:

About half-past four o'clock on the morning of the 23rd of October,
an aide-de-camp of Sir Edward Paget's, came to our ground, and
ordered the tents to be struck, and the baggage to be sent off; but
it was six o'clock before the column was in motion and clear of the
village. We continued our march, without interruption for several
hours, along a very fine and level road, which seemed to lengthen, as
we advanced. The 7th division, under the command of the Earl of

Dalhousie, with the cavalry, formed the rear of the army; and as these troops approached the village of Toquemada, the French cavalry, chiefly composed of the Gendarmerie of Paris, began to display themselves. The Spanish army, under General Castanos, was retiring by Palencia, with the Spanish cavalry, under that meritorious officer, Don Julian de la Sanchez; but these cavalry were unequal, both from the size of their horses, and the paucity of their numbers compared to that of the enemy, either to make a charge, or to resist one. And the French having encountered and put them into disorder, they came flying upon the British cavalry, mixed with the enemy, in pursuit. Here the difference of language, with the similarity of the Spanish to the French uniform, created much confusion; and our light dragoons, under Sir Stapleton Cotton, (now Lord Combermere) having done everything bravery could effect, were overpowered by numbers, and obliged to retire. At this critical moment, the 7th division, composed for the most part of Foreign soldiers, was halted, and formed a square. In this square, the commander of the forces with his staff was observed; when the enemy endeavouring to charge the square, was foiled in the attempt, and kept at a respectable distance afterwards.

But Surgeon Burroughs heard it as second hand; Lieutenant William Smith, 11th Light Dragoons, was there and gives a brief picture of the confusion:

The Enemy came up with us at day break a Cannonading for some time they then charged our skirmishers and pressed us so hard that one Squadron of the 16 Lt Drgs and our Regt were obliged to charge in front of Celada-del Camino some confusion and retired behind the Hormasa on which were placed L Col Ackett's [Halkett's two light battalions of King's German Legion] Infantry when we again got in order and retreated a Squadron occasionally charging. The German Brigade of heavy dragoons joined us near Venta del Pozo they charged came back in disorder, our Brigade also charged got intermixed and the confusion all together not to be described, had the Enemy behaved well that day they must have played the devil with us.

Wellington himself got caught up in the melee and took hurried cover in one of the KGL squares from where, according to Colonel J. Stanhope, who had just come out with Edward Paget, 'The riflemen brought the enemy down as if they had been partridges.' Caffarelli was another senior present, who apparently later complained that, had Boyer tried harder, the allied cavalry must have been quite overrun, such was the disparity of numbers. Fortescue calculated Anson and Bock at not above 1,000, in five weak regiments; the French engaging with a dozen regiments for certain, possibly sixteen, and with between 3,000 to 5,000 sabres. Thomas Sydenham wrote a few days later:

> I twice thought that Anson's brigade (which is weak in numbers and exhausted by constant service) would have been annihilated, and I believe we owe the preservation of that and of the German heavy brigade to Halkett's two light German battalions. Anson's brigade had only 460 sabres in the field ... The French had 1,600–2,000 swords against them. We have literally to fight our way for four miles.

Both sides lost about 300 troopers, with the French, of course, the moral victors.

When that night they tumbled into the villages around Torquemada, after a punishing twenty-seven-mile march, it was to find by a most welcome coincidence that the annual grape harvest had just been got in, and indeed was already in barrels. The cellars everywhere were stuffed with them. Napier heard reports that '12,000 men were to be seen in a state of helpless inebriety,' while William Wheeler later saw

> Long strings of mules carrying drunken soldiers to prevent them falling into the hands of the enemy ... The sides of the roads were strewed with soldiers as if dead, not so much by fatigue as by wine ... I remember seeing a soldier fully accoutred with his knapsack on in a large tank, he had either fallen in or had been pushed in by his comrades, there he lay dead. I saw a dragoon fire his pistol into a large vat containing several thousands of gallons, in a few minutes we were up to our knees in wine fighting like tigers for it.

Douglas of the 1st (Royal Scots) measured that day's march at ten leagues, over thirty miles, ending at 2am. At dawn, having

> Made best use of our time as far as good wine and a sound sleep would go, though the latter was rather short ... A great many were in no condition to receive such early visitors, and uninvited, as the enemy were entering the camp ... Colonel Campbell I think was actually mad, seeing the state the men were in and the enemy at hand. He fairly jumped on them as they lay there; but he resumed his temper, as not a man fell out on the [later] march.

Another regiment to be slow starters that day were, surprisingly, the Coldstream Guards. John Mills wrote on 24 October:

> The men were in such a state in the morning that it was impossible to do anything with them. There were scarce a sober man in the army – how they got through the day's march I know not. Officers of every

regiment and a strong rearguard were left behind to force the men on. 500 stragglers were taken this day.

It is said the new wine harvest was also well sampled by Souham's men: the drunk chasing the drunk.

Further rearguard actions were fought at Villa Muriel and Palencia, with Wellington holding Cabezon on 26 October – only ten miles from Valladolid and seventy miles now from Burgos. Souham, however, bypassed Cabezon, reaching Valladolid on the 28th and sending Foy ahead one more march to Tordesillas. The crossing of the Douro at that place seemed blocked, with the bridge's main arch broken and all the boats burned. However, a daring raid was carried out by Captain Guingret and fifty-five soldiers of the 6th Léger, who swam the swift river towing and pushing their muskets on a raft, while Foy's gun battery engaged the tower at the end of the bridge. Inside was a half company picquet of the Brunswickers, whose battalion was back several hundred yards, in a wood. Guingret and his naked men found only a dozen Germans, the rest having fled after no very prolonged resistance; to add more incompetence, their battalion commander made no counter-attack, but sent off for orders! The bridge being rapidly if roughly repaired, Foy's battalions began crossing the Douro. Wellington, in response, concentrated opposite the crossing with his three divisions, his artillery well dug in within a mile of the river. This stop-gap coincided with a stroke of luck, and which was to provide him with a relatively peaceful interlude for the next six days.

For Caffarelli suddenly withdrew his two divisions and his horse, having received day by day more disturbing news from the north. Souham, without these 10,000 men, was reluctant to push his luck, deciding to wait upon evidence that Soult and the king were getting closer. So there was a pause, prompting his Lordship to write that 'I have got clear, in a handsome way, of the worst scrape I ever was in.' About this time, however, there is some first evidence of disenchantment among his officers concerning his leadership. Ensign John Mills, whose letters we have several times read, and who had become rather bitter about the waste of life at Burgos, wrote on the 28th:

> The Marquis has ruined his character, has lost 2,000 men in the siege, wasted two months of the most precious time and brought a most formidable army upon him. He has exposed his troops to five weeks' constant rain and brought on a great deal of sickness. Soult threatens Madrid with an immense army; Hill has an inferior and motley crew. In short, I think it all stands on the hazard of a die.

Sir Rowland Hill, meanwhile, had destroyed the bridge at Aranjuez; but with Soult closing from the south and D'Erlon from the east, and the Tagus anyway being fordable in several places, Hill prudently made tracks for Madrid. Wellington had ordered him to Villacastin and Arevalo, seventy miles beyond

Madrid and over the Guadarramas. Joseph Donaldson, 94th, in Pakenham's 3rd Division, writes that on 30 October, at Pinto,

> We were ordered to retreat upon Madrid, and passed our pontoons burning on the road side, having been set on fire to prevent them falling into the hands of the enemy. We supposed at first that we would again occupy Madrid, but when we came in sight of it the Retiro was in flames, and we could hear the report of cannon, which proceeded from the brass guns in the fort being turned on each other for the purpose of rendering them useless to the enemy; the stores of provision and clothing which we had previously taken were also burned, and every preparation made for evacuating the place. The staff officers were galloping about giving directions to the different divisions concerning their route; the inhabitants whom we met on the road were in evident consternation, and everything indicated an unexpected and hurried retreat: instead, therefore, of entering the city, we passed to the left of it. The enemy's cavalry by this time being close on our rear, and before ours had evacuated the town on the one side, the French had entered it on the other.

Beyond Madrid, the retreat aimed for the Escorial. William Paterson was a commissariat clerk caught up in it. He notes the exodus of Spanish citizens, fleeing refugees who perhaps too publicly had previously welcomed the liberators, and who now feared for their lives:

> The Army was now in full retreat every one pressing on in the best manner they could, and as the Escurial is a Town of no great extent it was not of course capable of containing the immense number of British, Spanish and Portuguese Troops which that evening entered it. Every hour was bringing in hundreds and the confusion for Quarters consequently every moment increased till at last all order and authority seemed to be at an end and every one availed himself of his own personal power to place himself in the best Quarter he could find. I obtained no less than [word missing] of four Billets, and by superior force was turned out of every one of them till at last tired and exhausted I was glad to go into a wood adjoining with a Spaniard who pitched a tent and afforded me a part of it.
>
>   During the whole of the night nothing but noise and Confusion was in the Town of Escurial, and even in our Distant retreat in the wood we heard Doors and windows breaking open attended with every other appalling circumstance which may be conceived to follow the regardless actions of retreating troops. Horses mules and asses were everywhere in crowding the highway, some conveying women and children others the most valuable of the poor creatures effects

and others led by boys were bearing grey headed men who hardly
were enabled to support themselves on the backs of the animals and
whose lives seemed so nearly worn to the last extremity that flying
from the French Army seemed only to be the means of shortening
their few days by the fatigue of a march which their exhausted frames
seemed incapable of supporting ...

Passage through the narrow Guadarrama Pass was obviously jampacked with
formed bodies of troops, individual parties of soldiers and straggling civilians,
columns of guns, mule trains, the wounded in carts and precious little to feel
good about.

On our march to this place [El Espinar, eighteen kilometres north-west
of El Escorial] we passed over the famous pass of the Guadarrama
which in some places is so narrow and the rocks on each side of the
road so steep and so rugged that more than six or eight men could
not go over abreast and as there is no other passable road for many
leagues round it comes a place of the utmost importance to an army,
particularly on a retreat, as it enables them, with a very small proportion of men, to defend the Narrow passage against any army,
however numerous. At this moment our Troops were in full retreat
and the whole extent of the pass as far as the Eye could carry was
covered with soldiers and as we were nearly in the rear it was some
hours until we could obtain the height of the Guadarrama mountains
so slow was the progress of the Troops in this Narrow and confined
way. (Joseph Donaldson)

Most fortunately for the good shepherd Hill and his retreating flock, the
pursuing wolves were not absolutely snapping at his heels; if anything they
were snapping and snarling at each other. For co-operation was not a word
widely understood amongst French marshals in Spain, and never had been. Yet
there was now some unity of purpose in their movements. Their field force
totalled near 100,000 men: 40,000 in Soult's Army of the South, 21,000 in the
king's Army of the Centre (now commanded by Soult's Drouet) and 40,000
in Souham's Army of Portugal. Suchet remained in Valencia. Wellington
together with Hill had perhaps 65,000 men, but that included 18,000 Spanish;
and the two wings of the army had yet to join. But by 4 November Hill was at
Villacastin, fifty miles from Rueda and the Peer, allowing messages to pass
between them in less than twelve hours. It was there he received orders to make
for Salamanca, seventy miles west, in the knowledge that Wellington himself
was en route to the same juncture.

For the big decision had been taken. No further active measures against the
French were to be commenced, and the stale and tired army was to be put to
bed for the winter. His Lordship was only too aware of his stewardship of the

only British force on the Continent and, unlike Napoleon, could not contemplate further losses. Rodrigo, Badajoz, Salamanca and Burgos, to say nothing of those now dropping daily by the roadside, prevented Wellington grasping the golden opportunity which fate was providing: any General's dream, that of being placed between two inferior enemy forces. The temptation to be self-indulgent was resistible, of course, to a man to whom duty came second only to breathing in and out. Quite what Napoleon would have done is, in detail, guess-work, but he surely would have joined with Hill and leapt with superior strength upon either Soult or Souham, turning then to the other. For Wellington, apart from the deteriorating season, the marched-out legs of his men and horses, the near-collapse of his supply chain, the number of the sick (17,000) and the message implied by the increase in straggling, the only way such a gamble could work would be a guarantee that the unengaged French force did not promptly counter-move against his rear, and his communications to Salamanca. In all the circumstances it was not a sensible proposition and so back they would go. Hope springing eternal, however, the French might yet oblige: it did happen once at Salamanca, it might again. His letter to Bathurst of 8 November is worth quoting, and noting particularly the hope expressed in the final sentence of engaging the French at San Cristoval.

> The two corps of this army, particularly that which has been in the North, are in want of rest. They have been continually in the field, and almost continually marching, since the month of January last; their clothes and equipments are much worn, and a period in canton-ments would be very useful to them. The cavalry likewise are weak in numbers, and the horses rather low in condition. I should wish to be able to canton the troops for a short time, and I should prefer the cantonments on the Tormes to those farther in the rear ... I propose therefore to wait at present on the Tormes, till I shall ascertain most exactly the extent of the enemy's force. If they should move forward, I can either bring the contest to a crisis on the positions of San Cristoval, or fall back to the Agueda, according to what I shall at the time consider to be best for the cause.

The retreat to Salamanca began in earnest on 5 November, without any serious pressure from either Souham or Soult, neither of whom were entirely sure they might not be facing a trap. After three leisurely marches, by the evening of 8 November Wellington's wing was positioned across the north-easterly approaches to the city, as they had been in June while the forts were being reduced. That same day Hill crossed the Tormes ten miles south at Alba. At last a combined force of some 52,000 men, plus 18,000 Spaniards, were together again under the Peer's immediate command. Approaching them came 90,000 Frenchmen who, also on the 8th, had made touch south of Rueda, closing on Alba two days later. Both Soult and Jourdan put forward plans of attack, the former's involving a crossing of the upper reaches of the Tormes, threatening Wellesley's right flank. This was designed to force him to adjust out of his prepared position. Jourdan's plan was more straightforward: a frontal crossing. The king decided in Soult's favour, giving him also command of the Army of the Centre, transferring D'Erlon to that of Portugal, and sacking Souham. A couple of days were spent relocating divisions further south, around Soult's crossing places at Lucinos and Galisancho and, at dawn on 14 November, the crossings commenced, unopposed. Once Wellington heard the French had gone from the Huerta fords and were crossing in strength at Galisancho, he was able to order the San Cristoval position to be abandoned. He rushed south with the 2nd Division and four brigades of cavalry to attack. However, on arrival at Mozarbes 'the enemy was already too strongly posted'; indeed by last light the entire French army was over the Tormes, including the two divisions under Maucune who had force-marched from Huerta.

Next day he drew up his army on the familiar battleground, stretching from Calvarrasa de Arriba in the north (4th Division), both Arapiles (2nd Division and Hamilton's Portuguese), then the 3rd Division and Morillo's Spanish out along the Monte de Azan; in second line lay the Light (on the left, which they knew well), Pack and Bradford, the Galicians, the 5th, 6th and 7th Divisions. The 1st reprised the 3rd Division's earlier role, on the right, at Aldea Tejada, together with most of the cavalry. It was said Bock's dragoons whilst moving around on 'Pakenham's Hill' set the French skulls rolling from the unburied skeletons. The divisions sent off their baggage half a march, and in Salamanca the magazines and stores were being emptied and back-loaded – but not via one of the three parallel direct roads to Ciudad Rodrigo, but way to the north through Rollan to San Felices (the latter twenty miles from Rodrigo). This choice of route by the QMG Colonel James Willoughby Gordon was a blunder of the very first class, resulting as we shall see in three days complete starvation for the Army, which was to travel to Rodrigo via the three more southerly routes. (Gordon's tenure lasted just five months, his Lordship regaining the service of George Murray.)

Early on 15 November Soult moved left and west, a mass of cavalry leading, but unlike Marmont four months earlier, without offering Wellington any opportunity to strike. Wellington accordingly around 2pm, and much to the annoyance of his army ('I never saw the men in such a bad humour' wrote Donaldson) issued the order to withdraw, and get upon the roads to Rodrigo, before Soult got there first. The drizzling rains turned to downpours, the land to mud, the Zurgain (beyond Aldea Tejada) became a tumbling torrent, and by darkness the divisions upon the three parallel routes had quit Salamanca by some ten miles, with forty more to go.

The day had not altogether heaped glory and honours upon the French commanders, whose later recriminations were bitter. The decision to adopt Soult's plan had made more likely that which had now happened: that Wellington, not being pinned frontally, should escape. Soult chose not to do any version of pinning, nor even to put his cavalry properly around Wellington's right. It is true that the heavens opened, closing down visibility, just as the red coats were withdrawing, but one wonders if Soult was recalling that other sullen wet day at Albuera? A French cavalryman wrote:

> The rain falling in deluge soon rendered the whole field of operations one vast and deep quagmire. The smallest dips in the ground became dangerous precipices. The darkness, continually growing blacker, soon added to the horror of the scene, and made us absolutely unable to act. The muskets of the infantry were no longer capable of being discharged. The cavalry was not only unable to manoeuvre, but even to advance on the slippery, sodden, and slimy soil ... We lay down on the field drenched by the rain, with the mud up to our knees.

So with a superiority of 20,000 men, and especially of horse, on blood-soaked ground where all French honour screamed out for revenge, it seems the gloom of the afternoon – Jourdan said it was dark by 4pm – had settled on their spirits. For the last few days of this sorry tale will see only mild pressure to Wellington's rearguard, a standard encouragement to retire across the border; no French intention now remained to bring him to a decisive battle. The Army of Portugal was detached to the city, and without it Soult would be reduced to capturing abandoned baggage and drunken stragglers. General Foy spoke for many in his *Memoirs*:

> We had an army stronger by a third than Wellington's, infinitely superior in cavalry and artillery. Confident expectations of victory were in every man's head. The chance had come of beating the English – perhaps of driving them from the peninsula. This fine opportunity, so splendid, so decisive, with so few adverse chances, has been let slip ... The King does not know how to show to advantage before his troops; he can speak with effect neither to his officers nor to the rank and file: he got absolutely wet through, rode home, and went to bed.

We are fortunate in having several accounts of the rigours of the next few days. This is almost certainly because of the widespread anger felt by all ranks at the notorious Memorandum subsequently written by Lord Wellington, and which we will come to in due course. That Memorandum being so unfairly critical of his officers and men's conduct, it encouraged the literary among them, in a form of self-defence, to pen their recollections of the circumstances. The best of the accounts, unsurprisingly, is that of William Grattan, who wrote with lightness and humour, and without that rather heavy Victorian sentimentality so frequently adopted. His is a long story, but it well conveys the robust approach to adversity we have come to admire in his writing.

The rain fell in torrents, almost without any intermission; the roads could no longer be so called, they were perfect quagmires; the small streams became rivers, and the rivers were scarcely fordable at any point. In some instances the soldiers were obliged to carry their ammunition boxes strapped on their shoulders to preserve them, while passing a ford which on our advance was barely ankle deep. The baggage and camp-kettles had left us; the former we never saw until we reached Rodrigo, and the latter rarely reached us until two o'clock in the morning, when the men, from fatigue, could make but little use of them. The wretched cattle had to be slaughtered, as our rations seldom arrived at their destination before the camp-kettles, and when both arrived, there was not one fire in our bivouac sufficient to boil a mess.

Officers as well as soldiers had no covering except the canopy of heaven; we had not one tent, and the army never slept in a village. We thus lay in the open country; our clothes saturated with rain, half the men and officers without shoes, nothing to eat, or, at all events, no means of cooking it. What then could be much worse than the situation in which the army was placed? But this was not the worst, because, from the nature of the retreat, and the pursuit, neither the cavalry nor artillery horses could be supplied with forage. The retreat each day generally began at four in the morning, in the dead dark of night; towards eight the army had gained perhaps a six mile, perhaps not five, start of the enemy. At ten they were at our heels. The rear, as a matter of necessity, for the preservation of the whole, was then obliged to face about and show a front, to enable the remainder to proceed on their retreat. The position taken up was, as a matter of course, according to the urgency of the moment, sometimes in a vast tract of ploughed land, where the troops were drawn up ankle deep in mud. In this position, those who were not fighting were obliged to remain, in their tattered uniforms, worn to rags after two years' service, scarcely a good pair of shoes or trousers on any, and the greater part without the former. The ague had also attacked the bulk of the army, and as the soldiers picked up the acorns that fell from the oak trees (these, by the way, are the property of the pigs in Spain, but the pigs, fortunately for themselves, had not yet appeared in the woods we now traversed), many were unable to eat them, so much were they enfeebled by the disorder.

Yet under all these privations, the soldiers, at least the 'Connaught Rangers', never lost their gaiety. Without shoes they fancied themselves 'at home', and there were few, I believe, who would not have wished themselves there in reality. Without food they were nearly at home, and without a good coat to their backs equally so! My man, Dan Carsons, came up to me, and with a broad grin said, 'By gor, Sir, this same place,' (at the time we were, and had been for hours before, standing in a wet ploughed field) 'puts me greatly in mind iv Madrid.' – 'Of Madrid! Why, Dan, no two places can be more unlike.' – 'By Jasus, Sir, they're as like as two paise, only that we want the houses, and the fires, and the mate, and the drink, and the women! But, excepting that, don't the jaws iv the boys with the ague, when they rattle so, put your honour greatly in mind iv the castonetts?' Dan's joke was not quite so palatable as it might have proved at a more fitting opportunity, or in a more fitting place, for at that moment I felt a queer sort of motion about my own jaws, which in less than an hour proved itself to be a confirmed attack of ague. On this night the rain never ceased; the rations could not be cooked, having arrived too late, and the army had no food except biscuit.

What I have related took place on the 16th. The following day matters became worse, the rain continued to come down in torrents, and in the passage of one river, out of ten that we forded, a woman and three children were lost, as likewise some baggage mules, which the women of the army, in defiance of the order against it, still contrived to smuggle into the line of retreat. The rations arrived alive (I mean the meat), as usual after midnight, but no kettles reached us for an hour after the poor famished brutes had been knocked on the head. Each man obtained his portion of the quivering flesh, but before any fires could be re-lighted, the order for march arrived, and the men received their meat dripping with water, but little, if anything, warmer than when it was delivered over to them by the butcher. The soldiers drenched with wet, greatly fatigued, nearly naked, and more than half asleep, were obliged either to throw away the meat, or put it with their biscuit into their haversacks, which from constant use, without any means of cleaning them, more resembled a beggarman's wallet than any part of the appointments of a soldier. In a short time the wet meat completely destroyed the bread, which became perfect paste, and the blood which oozed from the undressed beef, little better than carrion, gave so bad a taste to the bread that many could not eat it. Those who did were in general attacked with violent pains in their bowels, and the want of salt brought on dysentery. A number of cavalry and artillery horses died on this night, and fatigue and sickness had already obliged several men and officers to remain behind,

so that our ranks were now beginning to show that we had commenced, in downright earnest, a most calamitous retreat.

A circumstance occurred on this day that so strongly marks the
difference between the British soldiers and the soldiers of any other
nation on such a retreat as we were engaged in, that I cannot avoid
noticing it. I have already said that we had no means of cooking
our meat, and that the soldiers and officers, for all shared the same
privations alike, carried their meat raw, or nearly raw; consequently
it was not an additional supply of 'raw material' that we so much
needed as the means of dressing what we had. Nevertheless, towards
noon, while a portion of the army was engaged in a warm skirmish
with the enemy's advance, which lay through a vast forest of oak,
some hundreds of swine, nearly in a wild state, were discovered
feeding upon the acorns which had fallen from the trees the autumn
before. No flag of truce ever sent from the advance post of one army
to the advance of another had a more decisive effect. Our soldiers
immediately opened a murderous fire upon the pigs, who suffered
severely on the occasion, being closely pursued on the route, which
they followed with that stupid – and for them, on this occasion, fatal
– pertinacity which the pig tribe are so proverbial for, namely, going
to the rear when they ought to go straight forward. Had this herd of
swine deviated from the old beaten track of pigs in general – had
they, in short, gone forward instead of rearward – many valuable
lives, in the eyes of the owners at least, would have been saved,
because they would have soon reached the French advance, and our
fellows, once more placed vis a vis with the riflemen of the grande
nation, would have left off the pursuit – if for nothing else but to save
their bacon! This rencontre, one of the most curious that came within
my knowledge during my Peninsular campaigns, or indeed during
my soujourn in this world, led to consequences the most comic as
well as tragic. Colonel O'Shea, who commanded the cavalry of the
French advance ordered to support the tirailleurs, was astounded
when he saw the direction which the British fire took. He could not
be mistaken; the fire of the advance of his own soldiers had slackened
– ceased. It immediately occurred to him that some corps must have
got in rear of our advance, and he galloped up to the tirailleurs to
ascertain the real state of affairs. He was soon undeceived; but when
he learned the cause of the retrograde movement on the part of our
men, he could not avoid – and who could? – laughing heartily.

Meanwhile the discomfited and routed pigs fled, and soon got out
of the clutches of the advanced guard. The bulk of the fugitives took
the road to their right, but here they were again wrong. Had those ill-
fated animals known anything of the 'rules of the road', they would

have kept to the left. On the right they were encountered by a nearly famished brigade that had received no rations at all in the preceding twenty-four hours; and when they were, as has been seen, so roughly handled by men whose haversacks were amply stocked with meat, what chance had they – I ask the question fearlessly – of any mercy from a body of famished, ferocious fellows? The question I have just put is easily answered. They had none to expect, and none did they receive. Neither age nor sex was spared; and out of this fine herd of swine, scarcely one in one hundred escaped unhurt. No victory was ever more complete; and the grunting and squeaking of the wounded pigs and hogs throughout the forest was a sad contrast with the merriment of the soldiers, who toasted, on the points of their bayonets – intended for other and more noble game – the mangled fragments of their former companions.

Day was drawing to its close, and the 3rd Division, commanded by Sir Edward Pakenham, was about to retire from the ground it had held during several hours in face of the enemy, when a warm fire of musketry on our left led us to suppose we were outflanked. The officers of the staff galloped in the direction from whence the firing proceeded. Sir Edward did the same, but it was some time before they reached the scene of action. In the meantime the different regiments were so arranged as to be ready either to advance or retreat, as circumstances might require; and the French corps in our front made demonstrations of a similar kind. In this state of suspense we remained for nearly an hour, when at last Sir Edward returned, with the news that the firing was caused by a fresh attack on the pigs that had escaped the first brunt of the attack against them. He ordered the different advance posts to be placed, which he super-intended in person; the soldiers then prepared to fell timber for fires, and some ran to an uninhabited village – they were all uninhabited on the line of our march for that matter – for the purpose of getting dry wood, that is to say, the doors and roofs of the houses, to enable us to light up the green timber, which was the only fuel we could command. The soldiers and officers of all ranks were nearly exhausted from cold and wet; and had the village in question belonged to the kind of England, much less to a parcel of Spanish peasants, it would have shared the same fate as the one in question.

The party from the village soon arrived, some bringing doors, others articles of different kinds of household furniture, such as chairs, tables, and bedsteads; but nothing in the shape of food was to be found. No doubt, had it been day, something might be got at, but warmth was what we stood in need of more than food. Several of us still carried the parboiled beef of the night before, and, when the fires were lighted, we made a shift to roast it either on our swords, bayonets, or bits of sticks, which we formed into respectable skewers. This operation finished, the fire around which each group sat or stood, in order of companies, their arms regularly piled behind them, was replenished with green and dry timber, according to our supply of each or both. The soldiers then placed their knapsacks round the outer part of the circle, and, having given the best place to their officers inside the circle, all lay down together, or at their own choice, with their feet towards the heat of the fire. Some arranged in this manner, others did not lie down at all; and those who had captured a door, propped it up as a defence against the rains and winds. There were others who got a blanket and fixed it with branches of trees and stones against some uneven spot, and lay down in the mud. It was, in fact, all mud and wet; and in whatever manner we accommodated ourselves, according to circumstances, whether walking, standing, or sleeping, it was of little difference.

Thus ended the operations of this day; officers and soldiers were placed exactly, or nearly, as I have described. Many were so feeble as not to be capable of the least exertion: others, on the contrary, were hale and stout, and I myself was amongst the number of the latter. I had lain some time with my feet near the fire, but I dreaded an attack of ague, and I walked about to keep my body warm, which was but thinly clad.

The affair of the pigs featured in all the *Memoirs* of the 3rd and 4th Divisions who were lucky enough to be near the stampeding herds. Whole battalions broke ranks to chase what seems like each man his own pig, with bayonet or ball: Grattan's 88th were far from alone that night in dining on half-cooked pork. It is said two dragoons were wounded in the pig crossfire and so, too, his Lordship's sense of decorum, although whether there were truly two pig plunderers hanged is hard to ascertain. But this appropriation of Spanish goods was becoming far from unusual: Costello of the 95th tells us:

Fortune favoured a few of us when, towards the middle of the night, one or two of our men brought intelligence that several cars laden with spirits and biscuits for the Spanish army were stuck fast in the road. The temptation to our hungry maws could not be resisted. We left our fires, and screened by the darkness of the night, got up to the cars and managed to get a portion of both biscuits and aguardiente. But the Spanish guard discovered our fellows and commenced firing on them. This was quickly returned and several were, I believe, shot. The firing continued all night, which alarmed the chief part of our army. Had the offenders been discovered, it would not have been difficult to have foretold their fate, as the Duke's orders were particularly strict against plunder, even although all the carts, unable to be moved, fell into the hands of the French next morning. Such were my feelings this night that, were it not for the liquor I drank, I believe I should have expired.

Next morning, the 17th, French cavalry moved through the heavily wooded slopes down the flanks of the columns, at one stage capturing the baggage of the 7th Division including, wrote Costello several 'children in panniers carried by donkeys; one grief-stricken Irish woman in particular seemed inconsolable at the loss of her child. However, the French desired to be as little encumbered as ourselves, and a few days later sent them back with a flag of truce.' It is said the marauding dragoon squadrons got either side of the centre column through another blunder by QMG Gordon in sending back their covering cavalry screen ahead of the rearguard, the Light Division. Another casualty to the infiltrating French cavalry was the new commander of the 1st Division, the one-armed Edward Paget, who had ridden out with one orderly to investigate a widening gap between divisions. His capture by just three chasseurs was very sad, a stroke of luck for Soult, and a blow to the Allied cause. No wonder the intriguing semi-traitorous Colonel Gordon had few friends serving in the Peninsula, if rather more in the Whig Opposition at home, and Lord Grey particularly.

It was about this time that George Simmonds, 95th wrote:

> Numbers of men were left behind, and several died. The road was covered with carcases of all descriptions and at every deep slough were found horses, mules, donkeys and bullocks mingled together, some dead, others dying, all laden with baggage. It was a most disagreeable sight to a soldier to see everything going to rack and ruin without being able to prevent it.

Later that day the centre column at last quit the woods halfway between Salamanca and Rodrigo, around the town of San Munoz and the river Huebra. Again no rations were available, and the men necessarily made do with acorns and, the rain having eased, cooked pieces of beef from such skeletal oxen as had collapsed en route. It was on the high ground beyond the Huebra that Soult got up some infantrymen and threatened the Light and 7th Divisions now deployed to defend the crossing. The not-altogether-truthful marshal subsequently wrote to King Joseph, 'I had to give up the idea (of a combat of infantry and cavalry) the enemy showed us 20,000 men in position, including 3,000 horse and more than 20 guns.' The men of the Light Division saw it rather differently. George Simmons:

> Our company extended, and were the last to retire down the inclined plain towards the river Huebra, followed a short distance by the enemy's

skirmishers. The high ground was covered with masses of infantry and cavalry, which was fun for them, but death to us. The enemy got up guns and infantry, and as the Light Division descended to pass the ford, which was rapid and breast-high, their guns cannonaded us and killed several men and some officers.

Ned Costello was rather more specific:

This day we were hard pressed by the enemy's advanced guard, and I was in one of the two companies of ours which were ordered to cover the retreat of our Division. The French, confident in their numbers, pressed us vigorously, and we had difficulty checking their advance. Hotly engaged in skirmishing, I was about to take possession of a tree, when I beheld at the foot of it a poor woman. Unable to keep up with the regiment, she had sunk down exhausted. Poor soul! She seized my hands, and begged me to assist her; the enemy's balls were rapping into the tree that only partially screened us. I was obliged to leave her as there seemed every prospect of most of us being cut off. The assembly sounded, and away we dashed, 'devil take the hindmost', in upon the battalion.

Our illustrious chief [Wellington], who was generally to be found where danger was most apparent, saw us come puffing and blowing up to our column and called out to us in a cheering voice: 'Be cool, my lads; don't be in a hurry!' But, in faith, with all possible respect for his Lordship, we were in no greater haste that the occasion demanded, as the French were upon us. We were obliged to dash down the sides of the hill, where we halted for a moment – and his Lordship also – and then forded a river. The stream was much swollen by the late rains, and while we were crossing, a round-shot from the enemy, who were now peppering away at us, took off the head of Sergeant Fotheringham, of our battalion, and smashed the thigh of another man. On gaining the other side of the stream we turned to give a salute in return, but owing to the wet, our rifles were unserviceable.

And George Simmons again:

On getting through this ford we faced about and formed columns of battalions. The French tried to cross after them but met opposition from the Rifles and from some men of the 52nd, who were posted on picquet at that point. Not a Frenchman got across. That night, the Light Division bivouacked amid the cork trees on the steep bank of the river in miserable weather. The rain that had held off all day, started to fall heavily again after dark. Beef was served out, but there was no biscuit.

Then Johnny Kincaid, not his normal irrepressible self:

> We received the usual order 'to make ourselves comfortable for the
> night', and I never remember an instance in which we had so much
> difficulty in obeying it, for the ground we occupied was a perfect flat,
> flooded more than ankle deep with water, excepting here and there
> where the higher ground around the roots of trees presented circles
> of a few feet of visible earth, upon which we grouped ourselves.
> Some few fires were kindled, at which we roasted some bits of raw
> beef on the points of our swords, and eat them by way of a dinner.

That night by way of a last-hurrah, the French horse batteries shelled the
bivouacs, and 18 November brought welcome daylight again but marred by
heavy rain. Gradually the shelling ceased and the sun burst through the
thinning cloud. George Simmons can have the last word:

> The day was very fine, but the road extremely bad, and we were
> obliged to wade for miles in slush and water, which made the feet
> extremely tender. Also, not being able to see where to place them,
> made one hit the stumps of small trees, which gave great pain. I do
> not know when I suffered so much from a day's march, which was a
> very long one. Bivouacked upon the side of a mountain near Sancti-
> Spiritus . . . The enemy followed us on the 19th. Most of us walking
> barefooted, my shoes also having no bottoms, as well as my friends'.
> My legs and feet much frostbitten so could hardly crawl. Halted near
> Ciudad Rodrigo. Three days' bread served to us upon the spot.

The night of 18 November saw near-mutinous disregard of Wellington's
orders by three of his divisional commanders. This extraordinary happening
might be seen as a unique token at the top end, comparable to pig-shooting at
the bottom; that is, of the desperate situation all were confronting. Wellington
had ordered Stewart, Oswald and Dalhousie's 1st, 5th and 7th Divisions in the
centre column to cross a flooded stream over various fords, rather than by
the only bridge, which he allocated to the Spaniards. They demurred and took
their divisions to the bridge, where needless to say, a colossal traffic jam ensued
involving five divisions – the Light also being in the queue, which at one stage
was said to have involved a single file passage across a fallen tree. Wellington is
reported to have later told FitzRoy Somerset 'By God, it was too serious to
say anything' although to the three generals he managed a quiet, 'You see,
gentlemen, I know my own business best.' It was a week later, after the French
had given up and gone away, that all his generals received the Memorandum so
nicely described by Captain Jonathon Leach, 95th, (The Memorandum had
quickly become known to the entire army, and thence as quickly back into the
English newspapers,) 'as difficult to digest as the acorns in the woods of San
Munoz.'

The Memorandum, which is attached at Appendix 3, was obviously born of ill temper, caused no doubt by some immediate if minor irritant in Headquarters, following reflection on certain episodes of the journey back from Burgos: the drunkenness, straggling, the pig shoot, the robbing of store wagons, the apparent slackness in cooking, the ransacking of villages for food, the tossing aside of spare ammunition, and the general lack of cheerfulness amongst the ranks. But castigating all captains and subalterns for allowing such random indisciplines was only in order for certain ill-led regiments. While those guilty might be the first to so plead, for many others the criticisms were quite misplaced, and thus unfair. If there is one thing the British soldier hates more than going backwards (and digging holes), it is to be dealt with unfairly. Kipling put it nicely in his 'Norman and Saxon AD 1100' when the Norman baron offered his son some good advice:

> *The Saxon is not like us Normans. His manners are not so polite,*
> *But he never means anything serious, 'til he talks about Justice and Right.*
> *When he stands like an ox in the furrow, with his sullen eyes set on your own,*
> *And grumbles, 'This isn't fair dealing', my son – leave the Saxon alone.*

A mild example of the sullen Saxon is in the Journal kept by Lieutenant Edward Close, 48th, one of their few officer survivors of Soult's Polish Lancers at Albuera:

> We had only three-quarters of a pound of bread served out in seven days, yet we were severely reprehended by an order about this time for some irregularity that took place in search of food, and told we suffered no privations ... (whereas) the deprivations we suffered were severe; without bread or spirits, in cold rainy weather, the men, bare-footed, toiled along the road dispirited and discontented.

Wellington compounded the reaction, of course, by making light of the conditions, and by not acknowledging the failure of the commissaries and of his own staff, which led to most of the army receiving no rations for three or more days. The Memorandum was three pages long. In this it contrasted with the two sentence General Order expressing his thanks to the troops after the gloriously successful battle at Salamanca, the second sentence of which merely re-iterated that such success depends on the troops obeying their orders, and preserving their formation when in action. Verily, the man did not believe in spoiling the soldiery! The Memorandum was altogether a thoroughly ill-considered rant, rounding off an ill-considered venture – the Burgos outing was not our hero's finest hour, and for weeks afterwards Saxon sullenness continued: 'Lieutenant Wallis, 52nd regiment, refused this day after dinner to drink Ld. Wellington's health – I find he (Ld. W) is very much disliked by all the officers who have come from the army.' (letter home in early February 1813 from newly joined Lieutenant George Woodberry, 18th Hussars)

We should, however, temper criticism of the retreat itself by making two points that are easily overlooked. Firstly, it did actually succeed in removing the alliance's only joint Army from the closing jaws of a superior enemy; and, secondly, the remembered rigours were largely caused by the astonishingly bad weather, a mishap beyond Wellington's control. That said, of course, he was immensely aided by the ultracaution of Soult's slug-like pursuit, and would have been deeply in trouble had that not been the case; further, that the other ingredient in his soldiers' bitter recollections – the starvation – while the fault of the Commissariat's instructions from his QMG, would not have occurred without a lack of his own personal supervision. Coming from a man renowned for detailed micro-management, he seemed not to be aware that the planned supply route was to go via Ledesma, El Villar and San Felices or, if he knew, it is a puzzle that it was not promptly brought south. It is said that Gordon, like Espana over the withdrawal of the Alba garrison, refrained from telling him. That would be in character for Gordon. It was all a public relations disaster, both at home in London and to a lesser degree amongst his men, whose widespread admiration and belief in their illustrious Commander had thereby somewhat diminished.

At least the enemy could take no satisfaction in their role, and should have been ashamed that a joint force of 100,000 men belatedly got together for the sole purpose of catching and defeating their invader, had managed merely to chase him out. He would live to fight another day and they had missed the best chance in years – probably since Soult so nearly caught Wellington in the Tagus valley after Talavera.

Anyway, all were now mightily relieved to be well out of it, as the winter closed upon them. The immediate concerns on both sides were for solid shelter, solid food, new shoes, no mud, and horses with a bit of fat on them. The Army moved back into their familiar cantonments along the Portuguese border, and the French likewise dispersed in search of shelter and food. The year's campaigning was over.

The material achievements of the whole 1812 campaign are readily listed: some 20,000 prisoners of war taken and despatched to England (7,000 from Salamanca, 4,000 from Badajoz, 2,000 from Madrid, 2,000 from the various affairs on the Douro, the Guarena, via Hill in Estremadura, 1,300 from Astorga, 600 from the Salamanca Forts, 300 from those at Almaraz etc.), and (Oman calculates) nearly 3,000 guns from Rodrigo, Badajoz, Madrid Cadiz, Seville and many others taken in the field. The arsenals in these places, and the destruction of the contents of the storehouses, magazines and fortifications – where not usefully transferred to new ownership – was an immense loss to the French. And talking of losses, it has been calculated that the Armies of Portugal, of the Centre and of the South were 30,000 weaker at the end of the campaign than at the beginning, notwithstanding drafts totalling some 10,000. Napoleon's armies in Spain arguably now needed substantial reinforcements, but what of the snows of Russia? Of the 450,000 men in the Grande Armée who had marched east in June, nearer Christmas Ney's rearguard could barely muster a thousand, and the Armée itself under 40,000. There were no men for Spain, and certainly no conquering Emperor to give Wellington pause. What else? Just the liberation of Galicia, the Asturias, of Andalucía, of Granada, of Estremadura, of Seville and Cadiz and (briefly) Madrid, and in the withdrawal of their garrisons giving guerrillas elsewhere hope, reason and confidence to persevere.

But perhaps the greatest of all the material achievements of the year is that the removal of French forces from the south of Spain meant his Lordship could now at last turn his back on that direction. Hills' Corps no longer need be detached, at such a distance that it had become a separate army: separate outposts, supply lines, stores depots, reserve deployments and all the rest of it. The potential for the 1813 campaign was thereby immensely improved because simplified, and would allow the Commander's mind to consider much more ambitious projects.

The year's achievements also included aspects not so easily measured, but huge in everyone's mind. First amongst these for the French was the obvious: Wellington's fifth campaign is now over and he still has not been beaten on the field of battle. Burgos was a failure, not a defeat, and France had not a single marshal or general who would readily tangle with him. His perceived superiority was now a psychological factor the French had to overcome. Things have come to a pretty pass when an admiring French general can write things like:

> Wellington goes off unbeaten, with the glory of his laurels of the Arapiles untarnished, after having restored to the Spaniards all the lands south of the Tagus, after having forced us to destroy our own magazines and fortifications, and deprived us of all the resources that resulted from our former conquests. (Foy)

So French prestige was shattered, and the confidence that ought to run through an Army's nervous system, connecting the head and the hands, was greatly lessened. The men in blue coats had marched prodigious distances – just look at the map of Spain! Soult's men marched from Seville and Cadiz via Valencia to Madrid and Salamanca. That is the equivalent of marching from Inverness to London via Bristol and then back up to Liverpool! And they too suffered the same starvation, and the same weather, yet they could not seem to bring a smaller enemy to a stand and beat him. For the other concern was the discovery that the British army could manoeuvre and could attack. After four years repeatedly being repulsed by a volley-cheer-charge coming from two red ranks out of a reverse slope, Salamanca had shown that their enemy's foot and horse could now not only defend a hill but could climb one, and destroy them both ways. So the French had to fear Wellington's men's fighting qualities as well as his Generalship.

The latter survived the year with a few lapses. Given the careful preparations for capturing Rodrigo, for example, the expensive losses of time and men at the Salamanca Forts and at Burgos Castle, caused by the lack of siege guns (and which could have been got forward), were regrettable. The former possibly was justified as a lure to draw Marmont to battle; the latter had no strategic value apparent to us today, although one hesitates to call it a vanity project, coming so soon after the glory that was Salamanca. Further, at these two later sieges, it was noteworthy how few men he threw at the walls in the various escalades etc., and this self-defeating use of 'penny packets' can surely be a response to the Badajoz losses. A similar caution may have been involved at San Cristoval, during that brief period of numerical and ground superiority over Marmont, for which missed opportunity he has been much criticised. But, being convinced as he was that Marmont was about to attack, and knowing a defensive victory is always cheaper than victory through attack, only hindsight says he made the wrong choice. Ironically, it was the reverse sin – a lack of caution – that so nearly saw Wellington blot his copy book next to the Arapiles – saved by Beresford – who caused him to abort the 1st Division's attack on Bonnet. Bearing in mind the drubbing Bonnet later gave the 4th Division and Pack (with help by Clausel), the attack may well have stalled, had it begun. Preceding as it did Wellington's brilliant concept of battle starting with Pakenham's 3rd Division, it was hard to see what was in his mind here, beyond feeling better after the endless frustrations of parallel marching and, of course, the temporary joy of giving Marmont a passing bloody nose. That would have been fair justice, however, for what Marmont did to him the previous week up at Toro, and the crossings at Tordesillas. It may be Marmont could have better developed his feint and forward movement from the Douro, but for Wellington it involved a fair degree of nip and tuck by his standards, and rather too many hand to mouth moments under pressure.

There were two occasions when one might perhaps question Wellington's choice of troops for particular tasks. He had with him at Burgos the 5th Division, who had successfully escaladed Badajoz, and who had gained experience there in the trenches; yet he sent them forward as part of the covering force whereas, as we have seen, their expertise might have been preferably employed in the attempts on the castle. Secondly, in the breach at Badajoz the Light and 4th Divisions suffered appalling losses in their junior command positions. When at Salamanca he ordered Cole to attack Clausel, the companies were largely under an untried second eleven management of just three months standing. In this regard another division (he had the choice of three more) might have held Clausel a little more firmly.

Perhaps the final question we should fairly raise is the stupendous losses in the breach at Badajoz. His later tears were eloquent and the memory shaped future actions. But was it a mistake to launch two full divisions at three holes in a wall? Would he have done the same, ever again? Our difficulty in not being critical of this plan is not only that it did not work, but that not one but two of the escalade subsidiary attempts did work. It is therefore with hindsight extremely hard not to pontificate: serious false attacks on Trinidad and Santa Maria, the breaches of which would be so properly made to be thought entirely practicable, must have deserved the same response from the garrison, to the detriment of their deployment along the walls elsewhere, allowing Picton and Leith to escalade, as they did. Indeed, one of the great tragic errors of the night was undoubtedly the hour's delay in getting Leith his ladders. Had he been up and over by 11pm and not midnight, much would have been different, including the casualty lists.

It is in the nature of armchair generals like your author – and probably you, dear reader – to scratch around for such blemishes like those in the foregoing paragraphs, on the skin of their hero. It makes us feel less like the pygmies we undoubtedly are beside such a man, whose many qualities have appeared in these pages. His determination, foresight, energy, sagacity, patience, intelligence and sense of duty, can be seen repeatedly demonstrated in this campaign. As Commander of the Forces his leadership had long since established a respect, and Salamanca, in particular, now demanded the same of the wider world. It is true the affection felt for him by the men seemed to have about it a tinge of slight apprehension; it is remarkable to the modern soldier, bearing in mind the fearsome orders he had occasion to issue, that any hesitancy on their part was never more than in the mind. One can recall only those few days at Burgos, when the men came close to any collective obstinacy. Their complete willingness to do his bidding flowed naturally from the years of successful generalship behind him and them, and the usual embellished talk around the camp fires. They would not have missed, for example, his ready liking for the coup-de-main, an operation which has always appealed to the British soldier, especially where it both makes their enemy look silly, and short-cuts any need for more costly alternatives. The immediate seizure of the Renault Redoubt at Rodrigo, the capture of Fort Picurina at Badajoz, and the bridge at Almaraz, were all to their liking. Less high in their admiration (because unseen) would be his unrelenting attention to forward planning: the timely yet secret concentration under Dickson of the siege train for Rodrigo; the very careful analysis after Badajoz of the courses open and the prudent choice of Marmont and Salamanca rather than Soult and the south; the elaborate and detailed schemes then to occupy the French generally in Granada, Valencia, Catalonia, Galicia and the Cantabrian mountains, the involvement of the various Spanish forces, Lord Bentinck, and the partisans, were all designed to place Marmont in temporary isolation. While not all these Machiavellian schemes came to fruition, and some tardily so, enough did, to have the desired effect. There was also the wider achievement that came from this direction of the efforts of so many: it showed quite clearly the British controlling hand in these affairs, and at last brought some measure of co-operation to the many individual forces – so often squabbling – in the Peninsula.

Finally one has to return to that moment next to the Las Arapiles when 'By God, that will do!' set in train such an ambitious sequence. To that point the day – and the previous days – had passed in contemplating a rather shameful return to the Rodrigo road, whilst still looking for the opportunity that might yet break the deadlock. After an aborted false start, his staff (and Beresford!) were, perhaps, trusting that there would not be another. When he then galloped off to Pakenham it was obvious there was to be no turning back this time. What he had in mind we can know only by the development of subsequent events. There was to be an inevitable time gap of around an hour before Pakenham could close on Thomières. He did not wish Leith or Cole to move forward during the gap, until Thomières was engaged to the west with Pakenham, lest he swing north to threaten Leith's flank. Reducing the plan to the simplicity of a boxing ring, we may say Wellington was to deliver a right hook (Pakenham), a pair of straight lefts (Leith followed by Cole) and then a right upper cut (Le Marchant). The latter was to be the intended killer blow. We know Wellington was present and watched, and it is said, later complimented Cotton; so he was certainly in a position to have himself decided when to give the nod to release the Heavy Brigade. It was, of course, Le Marchant's job then to take them forward, and to regulate the direction and pace. Wellington's timing was perfect, allowing Leith's assault to have developed and to have turned Maucune's regiments such that the dragoons were presented with their ideal target: largely ill-formed groups and individuals. After that the day was in no doubt. It had been a classic exhibition of how matured military experience can provide a sound base for just one sparking, inspired moment of decision. It required high moral courage and a fine judgement, and in both regards his Lordship met the challenge. It also required resolute physical courage and a robust fighting spirit, and in both those regards his men and their officers readily gave of their best.

This story of a year's campaigning, a year whose two halves are somewhat at odds one with another, we may safely say shows the achievements listed earlier did together render Napoleon's Spanish policy vulnerable and therefore with time running out, as is a tree to a gusting wind, whose roots have started to rot. There is now a growing inevitability of a crash. The only prevention is for the tree to be propped up with reinforcing timbers, but after Russia the Emperor had none to spare. Indeed, the contemporary ruin of the huge army he took there would, on the contrary, require replacement drafts from Spain, as from everywhere else. The knowledge of the extent of the retreat from Moscow, and French losses, would not become known much before Christmas, and the consequences to the European allies would not take shape much before Easter 1813. Thereby was provided, for our thin worn-out men in tattered red coats, a few months of rest, dedicated to keeping warm, dry and safe, and well topped up with rum and rations. For they would be on the march again. When they did so, Wellington paused at the frontier into Spain, turned his horse, took off his hat and with a dramatic flourish completely out of character, cried 'Farewell, Portugal! I shall never see you again.' Nor did he, but he did see France.

Further Reading

With few exceptions, my hundred or so eyewitness accounts are available in the Reading Room of the National Army Museum in Chelsea, London. Anything published after about mid-1840, however, should be read in the knowledge that the author would have had at his elbow William Napier's six-volume *History of the War in the Peninsula*, for the next sixty years the pre-eminent general history, which naturally inspired many veterans' memoirs. It also provided a ready-made solution for veterans with memory loss concerning particular events, such as those at which they were not actually present. Napier's words were accordingly well borrowed – frequently verbatim.

However, with no disrespect to Napier, Sir Charles Oman's seven-volume *History of the Peninsular War*, first published between 1902 to 1930, must remain the academic bible of ultimate reference. Volume V covers Ciudad Rodrigo, Badajoz and Salamanca, Volume VI covers Burgos. Oman's immense research into sources and battlefield investigations produced a massive definitive work, which surely, warts and all, will never now be superseded by a single author. His nearest rival is his contemporary Sir John Fortescue, whose thirteen-volume *History of the British Army* devotes no fewer than seven volumes to the Peninsula – Volume VIII covers 1812.

The prime sources for the sieges are Colonel John Jones's *Journal of the Sieges etc.* (1814) and Sir Alexander Dickson's *The Dickson Manuscripts* (1908). Both have been used to great effect, together with individual Memoirs and Letters etc., by Frederick Myatt's *British Sieges of the Peninsular War* (1987) and Ian Fletcher's *In Hell before Daylight* (1984). The latter's account of Badajoz is particularly colourful, with revealing modern photographs; while the garrison's problems are covered by their Chief Engineer, Colonel Lamare, in his *Account of the Second Siege etc.* (1824).

Salamanca itself is well brought to life by Lawford and Young's *Wellington's Masterpiece* (1973) and Ian Fletcher's *Salamanca* in the Osprey series (1997), the latter again presenting excellent photography of the battlefield. The pamphlet *The Salamanca Campaign* written in 1906 by Captain A.H. Marindin, Black Watch, is by nature essentially just a Staff College crammer, but includes some thoughtful comment. Very far from a pamphlet is Rory Muir's excellent *Salamanca 1812* (2001) for which the description 'comprehensive' is inadequate by half: his scholarship and the breadth of his research puts this work in a class of its own. Similarly ground breaking in its depth and detail is *Galloping at Everything* (1999) by (again) Ian Fletcher, which does long-overdue justice to the British cavalry so unfairly slighted by both Oman and the Duke himself, yet whose finest and most decisive Peninsular outing was at Salamanca – and of course, the following day, for the dragoons of the King's German Legion at Garcia Hernandez.

At one's side, when reading any of these accounts, must surely be the 2011 *Atlas of the Peninsular War* by Ian Robertson. His cartographer Martin Brown has succeeded brilliantly in producing uncluttered battle plans, in colour and in beautiful detail, the whole much enhanced of course by Robertson's reliable narrative.

Memoirs, Journals and Letters etc.
quoted in the Text

Aitchison, Lieutenant John, 3rd Guards, *Ensign in the Peninsular War, Letters etc.*, 1981

Anon, Officer of the 5th, Maxwell's Sketches, 1844

Anon, Officer, Ellis's Fusilier Brigade, Letter (National Army Museum)

Anon, Officer of the 77th, Maxwell's Sketches, 1844

Anon, Officer of the 94th, Maxwell's Sketches, 1844

Anon, Officer (C.J.T.S) attached 77th, *United Services Journal*, Oct 1832

Anon, Soldier of the 42nd, *Personal Narrative of a Private Soldier*, 1821

Anon, Soldier of the 38th, Letter (National Army Museum)

'A.Z.' *United Services Journal*, Nov 1833

Arentschildt, Lieutenant Colonel F. von, Quoted in *History of the K.G.L.* (Beamish)

Bainbrigge, Captain Philip, *United Services Journal*, 1878

Bell, Ensign George, 34th, *Rough Notes of an Old Soldier*, 1867

Bingham, Lieutenant Colonel George, 53rd, *The Bingham Manuscripts*, 1948

Blakeney, Captain Robert, 28th, *A Boy in the Peninsular War*, 1899

Bragge, Captain William, 3rd Dragoons, *Peninsular Portrait*, 1963

Brazill, Sergeant Pat, 88th, Letter to *United Services Journal*, August 1843

Browne, Lieutenant Thomas, 23rd, *Journal*

Burgoyne, Major John, R.E., *Life & Correspondence*, 1873

Burroughs, Surgeon George, *Retreat from Burgos*, 1814

Cameron, Lieutenant Colonel John, 9th, Letter to Napier, 1827

Cameron, Lieutenant Donald, 7th, Quoted in Regimental History

Campbell, Major General Henry, Letter in Luffness Papers

Campbell, Captain James, *The British Army As It Was*, 1840

Carss, Lieutenant John, 53rd, Quoted in History of the 53rd, 1970

Cathcart, Lieutenant Colonel Charles, Letter to Graham (Lynedock Papers)

Close, Lieutenant Edward, 48th, his Journal

Cocks, Major Edward Somers, 16th Light Dragoons, Letters and Diaries 1986

Colborne, Lieutenant Colonel John, 52nd, *The Life of John Colborne*, 1903

Cooke, Lieutenant John, 43rd, *Memoirs of the Late War*, 1831

Cooper, Sergeant John, 7th, *Rough Notes*, 1869

Costello, Rifleman Edward, 95th, *The Peninsular and Waterloo Campaigns*, 1852

Cotton, Lieutenant General Sir Stapleton, *Memoirs and Correspondence*, 1866

D'Arcy, Lieutenant John, 88th, Quoted in Regimental History

D'Hautpol, Captain Alfonse, 59th Ligne, *Memoirs* etc., 1906

D'Urban, Major General Benjamin, *The Peninsular Journal*, 1930

Dickson, Major Alexander RA, *The Dickson Manuscripts*, 1908

Dobbs, Captain John, 52nd, *Recollections of an old 52nd Man*, 1863

Douglas, Corporal John, 1st, *Tale of the Peninsular*

Dyneley, Captain Thomas RA, Letters

Ewart, Captain John, 52nd, *Journal*, 1905

Fergusson, Captain James, 43rd, Letter Quoted by Napier

Foy, General Maximilian, *History of the War of the Peninsular under Napoleon*, 1827

Foy, General Maximilian, *His Military Life*, 1900

Freer, Ensign George, 38th, Quoted in Regimental History

Garretty, Sergeant Thomas, 43rd, *Memoirs of a Sergeant*, 1835

Girard, Colonel Etienne-Francois, *Les Cahiers du Colonel Girard*, 1951

Gomm, Major William, 9th, Letters and Journals, 1881

Grattan, Ensign William, 88th, *Adventures with the Connaught Rangers*, 1847

Green, Private John, 68th, *The Vicissitudes of a Soldier's Life*, 1827

Green, Bugler William, 95th, *The Travels and Adventures of William Green*, 1857

Hale, Sergeant James, 9th, *Journal*, 1826

Harvey, Brigadier General William, *At Rodrigo*, Quoted by Napier

Hay, Captain Andrew Leith, 29th, *Narrative of the Peninsular War*, 1831

Hennell, Volunteer George, *A Gentleman Volunteer – Letters*

Henry, Surgeon Walter, *Events of a Military Life*, 1843

Hill, Lieutenant General Sir Rowland, *Life and Letters*, 1845

Hodenberg, Lieutenant Carl von, KGL, *Letters*, ed. Oman, 1913

Hopkins, Captain Edward, 4th, Letter Quoted by Napier

History of the 1st (Royal) Dragoons (Atkinson)

History of the 4th Dragoons (Scott Daniell) 1959

History of the 5th Dragoon Guards (Cannon)

History of the 12th Lancers (Stewart) 1950

History of the 13th Hussars (Barrett)

History of the 1st (Royal Scots) (Brander) 1921

History of the 4th (Cowper) 1939

History of the 5th (Walker) 1919

History of the 7th (Wheater) 1875

History of the 9th (Cannon) 1848

History of the 11th (Cannon) 1845

History of the 23rd (Cary and McCance)

History of the 30th (Bannatyne) 1923
History of the 38th (Jones) 1923
History of the 43rd (Levinge) 1868
History of the 44th (Carter) 1887
History of the 45th (Wylly) 1929
History of the 52nd (Moorson) 1860
History of the 71st
History of the 88th (Cannon) 1838
History of the Rifle Brigade (Verner) 1912
History of the King's German Legion (Beamish) 1832
History of the 61st (Regimental Digest of Service)
Jones, Major John, RE, *Journal of the Sieges*, 1846
Jones, Sergeant John, 5th, Letter to *United Services Journal*, 1843
Kempt, Major General James, Letter Quoted by Napier, 1833
Kincaid, Captain John, 95th, *Adventures in the Rifle Brigade*
Kincaid, Captain John, *Random Shots from a Rifleman*, 1835
Kingsmill, Lieutenant Parr, 88th, Journal and Correspondence
Knowles, Lieutenant Robert, 7th, *The War in the Peninsular: Some Letters*, 1913
Lamare, Colonel, *Account of the Second Defence of Badajoz*, 1824
Landsheit, Sergeant Norbert, 'The Hussar', 1844
Lawrence, Sergeant William, 40th, *The Autobiography of Sergeant William Lawrence*, 1886
Leach, Captain John Anthon, 95th, *Rough Sketches*, 1831
Le Monnier-Delafosse, Captain J-B, 31st Léger, *Souvenirs Militaire*, 1850
Lightfoot, Captain Thomas, 45th, *Regimental History*
Lillie, Major John, Letter to Napier
Luard, Lieutenant John, 4th Dragoons, Letters in Scarlet Lancer, 1964
Marmont, Marshal, Duc de Ragusa, *Memoirs etc.* 1857
Marchant, Major General John Le, *Memoirs etc.* 1841
Massey, Lieutenant John, 3rd Dragoons, Letter in National Army Museum, August 1812
Mills, Lieutenant John, Coldstream, Letters and Diaries
Money, Colonel Archibald, 11th Light Dragoons, Quoted in Napier
Moriarty, Lieutenant Thomas, 88th, Quoted in Regimental History
Morley, Sergeant Stephen, 5th, *Memoirs*, 1842
MacCarthy, Captain James, 50th, *Recollections of the Storming of Badajoz*, 1836
McGrigor, Surgeon James, *Autobiography and Services*, 1861
Napier, Major General Sir William, *History of the War in the Peninsular*, Volume IV, 1834
Newman, Major Frederick, 11th, Quoted in Life of Napier (Brace)
Norcliffe, Lieutenant N., 4th Dragoons, Quoted in *Cavalry Journal*, 1912
Pack, Brigadier General Dennis, *Blackwoods* magazine, 1946
Pakenham, Major General The Hon. Edward, *The Pakenham Letters etc.*, 1914

Parquin, Captain Charles (of Marmont's Escort), *Napoleon's Army*, 1969

Paterson, William, Commissariat Clerk, Letters in National Army Museum

Patterson, Captain John, 50th, *The Adventures of etc.*, 1837

Ponsonby, Colonel Frederick, 12th Light Dragoons, Letters in Leveson Gower, 1916

Ridge, Major Henry, 5th, Letter of 24 January, 1812

Ridge, Major Henry, *Peninsular Sketches* (Maxwell), 1844

Ross-Lewin, Lieutenant Harry, 32nd, *With the 32nd in the Peninsular*, 1904

Simmons, Lieutenant George, 95th, *A British Rifleman: Journals and Correspondence*, 1899

Smith, Lieutenant Harry, 95th, *Autobiography*, 1910

Smith, Lieutenant William, 11th Light Dragoons, Letter at National Army Museum

Somerset, Lieutenant Colonel Lord Fitzroy, *Greville Memoirs*, 1838

Stanhope, Captain James, 1st Guards, Journal

Surtees, Quartermaster William, 95th, *Twenty Five Years in the Rifle Brigade*, 1833

Synge, Lieutenant Charles, 10th Light Dragoons, *19th Century and After*, 1912

Tomkinson, Captain William, 16th Light Dragoons, *Diary of a Cavalry Officer*, 1894

Vere, Major Charles, *Marches etc. of the 4th Division*, 1841

Warre, Lieutenant Colonel William, *Letters from the Peninsular*, 1909

Wellington, General Arthur, Earl of,

Wellington, General Arthur, *The Dispatches of FM, The Duke of Wellington*, 1844–47

Wellington, General Arthur, *Supplementary Dispatches and Memoranda*, 1858–72

Wheeler, Private William, 51st, *Letters*, ed. Liddell Hart, 1952

APPENDIX 1

Orders for the Attack on Ciudad Rodrigo 19 January 1812

The attack upon Ciudad Rodrigo must be made this evening at 7 o'clock.

The light infantry company of the 83rd regiment will join Lieutenant Colonel O'Toole at sunset.

Lieutenant Colonel O'Toole, with the 2nd Caçadores, and the light company of the 83rd regiment, will, 10 minutes before 7, cross the Agueda by the bridge, and make an attack upon the outwork in front of the castle. The object of this attack is to drive the artillerymen from two guns in that outwork, which bear upon the entrance into the ditch, at the junction of the counterscarp with the main wall of the place: if Lieutenant Colonel O'Toole can get into the outwork, it would be desirable to destroy these guns. Major Sturgeon will show Lieutenant Colonel O'Toole his point of attack. Six ladders, 12 feet long each, will be sent from the engineer park to the old French guardroom, at the mill on the Agueda, for the use of this detachment.

The 5th regiment will attack the entrance of the ditch at the point above referred to; Major Sturgeon will likewise show them the point of attack; they must issue from the right of the convent of Santa Cruz; they must have 12 axes to cut down the gate by which the ditch is entered, at the junction of the counterscarp with the body of the place. The 5th regiment are likewise to have 12 scaling ladders, 25 feet long, and immediately on entering the ditch, are to scale the *fausse-braie* wall, and are to proceed along the *fausse-braie*, in order to clear it of the enemy's posts on their left, towards the principal breach.

The 77th regiment are to be in reserve on the right of the convent of Santa Cruz, to support the first party, which will have entered the ditch.

The ditch must besides be entered on the right of the breach by two columns, to be formed on the left of the convent of Santa Cruz, each to consist of five companies of the 94th regiment. Each column must have three ladders, 12 feet long, by which they are to descend into the ditch, and they are to have 10 axes to cut down any palisades which may be placed in the ditch to impede the communication along it.

The detachment of the 94th regiment, when descended into the ditch, is to turn to its left to the main breach.

The 5th regiment will issue from the convent of Santa Cruz 10 minutes before 7.

At the same time a party consisting of 180 sappers, carrying bags containing hay, will move out of the second parallel, covered by a fire of the 83rd regiment, formed in the second parallel, upon the works of the place, which bags are to be thrown into the ditch, so as to enable the troops to descend the counterscarp to the attack of the breach: they are to be followed immediately by the storming party of the great breach, which is to consist of the troops of Major General McKinnon's brigade. Major General McKinnon's brigade is to be formed in the first parallel, and in the communications between the first and second parallel, ready to move up to the breach immediately in rear of the sappers with bags. The storming party of the great breach must be provided with six scaling ladders, 12 feet long each, and with 10 axes.

The ditch must likewise be entered by a column on the left of the great breach, consisting of three companies of the 95th regiment, which are to issue from the right of the convent of St Francisco. This column will be provided with three ladders, 12 feet long, with which they are to descend into the ditch, at a point which will be pointed out to them by Lieutenant Wright: on descending into the ditch, they are to turn to their right, and to proceed towards the main breach; they are to have 10 axes, to enable them to cut down the obstacles which may have been erected to impede the communication along the ditch on the left of the breach.

Another column, consisting of Major General Vandeleur's brigade, will issue out from the left of the convent of St Francisco, and are to attack the breach to the left of the main breach; this column must have 12 ladders, each 12 feet long, with which they are to descend into the ditch, at a point which will be shown them by Captain Ellicombe: on arriving in the ditch, they are to turn to their left, to storm the breach in the *fausse-braie*, on their left, of the small ravelin, and thence to the breach in the tower of the body of the place: as soon as this body will have reached the top of the breach, in the *fausse-braie* wall, a detachment of five companies are to be sent to the right, to cover the attack of Major General McKinnon's brigade, by the principal breach, and as soon as they have reached the top of the tower, they are to turn to their right, and communicate with the rampart of the main breach: as soon as this communication can be established, endeavour should be made to open the gate of Salamanca.

The Portuguese brigade in the 3rd division will be formed in the communication to the first parallel and behind the hill of St Francisco (upper Teson), and will move up to the entrance of the second parallel, ready to support Major General McKinnon's brigade.

Colonel Barnard's brigade will be formed behind the convent of St Francisco, ready to support Major General Vandeleur's brigade; all these columns will have detached parties especially appointed to keep up a fire on the defences during the above.

The men with ladders, and axes, and bags, must not have their arms; those who are to storm, must not fire.

Brigadier General Pack, with his brigade, will make a false attack upon the outwork of the gate of St Jago, and upon the works towards La Caridad.

The different regiments and brigades to receive ladders are to send parties to the engineers' depot to receive them, three men for each ladder.

(Wellington)

APPENDIX 2

Orders for the Attack on Badajoz
6 April 1812

There may be some alteration in this plan, which will be communicated by reference to the number of the paragraph altered.

1. The fort of Badajos is to be attacked at 10 o'clock this night.
2. The attack must be made on three points; the castle, the face of the bastion of La Trinidad, and the flank of the bastion of Sta. Maria.
3. The attack of the castle to be by escalade; that of the two bastions by the storm of the breaches.
4. The troops for the storm of the castle, consisting of the third division of infantry, should move out from the right of the first parallel at a little before 10 o'clock, but not to attack till 10 o'clock.
5. They should cross the river Rivillas below the broken bridge over that river, and attack that part of the castle which is on the right, looking from the trenches, and in the rear of the great battery constructed by the enemy to fire on the bastion of La Trinidad.
6. Having arrived within the castle, and having secured the possession of it, parties must be sent to the left along the rampart, to fall on the rear of those defending the great breach in the bastion of La Trinidad, and to communicate with the right of the attack on that bastion.
7. The troops for this attack must have all the long ladders in the engineers' park, and six of the lengths of the engineers' ladders. They must be attended by twelve carpenters with axes, and by six miners with crowbars, &c.
8. The 4th division, with the exception of the covering party in the trenches, must make the attack on the face of the bastion of La Trinidad, and the light division on the flank of the bastion of Sta. Maria.
9. These two divisions must parade in close columns of divisions at 9 o'clock. The light division, with the left in front; the 4th division with its advanced guard, with the left in front; the remainder with the right in front. The 4th division must be on the right of the little stream, near the picquet of the 4th division, and the light division must have the river on their right.

10. The light division must throw 100 men forward into the quarries, close to the covered-way of the bastion of Sta. Maria, who, as soon as the garrison are disturbed, must keep down by their fire the fire from the face of the bastion of Sta. Maria, and that from the covered-way.

11. The advance of both divisions must consist of 500 men from each, attended by twelve ladders; and the men of the storming party should carry sacks filled with light materials, to be thrown into the ditch, to enable the troops to descend into it. Care must be taken that these bags are *not* thrown into the covered-way.

12. The advance of the light division must precede that of the 4th division; and both must keep as near the inundation as they possibly can.

13. The advance of both divisions must be formed into firing parties and storming parties. The firing parties must be spread along the crest of the glacis to keep down the fire of the enemy; while the men of the storming party who carry bags will enter the covered-way at the place d'armes, under the breached face of the bastion of La Trinidad; those attached to the 4th division on its right, those to the light division on its left, looking from the trenches or the camp.

14. The storming party of the advance of the light division will then descend into the ditch, and turning to its left, storm the breach in the flank of the bastion of Sta. Maria, while the storming party of the 4th division will likewise descend into the ditch, and storm the breach in the face of the bastion of La Trinidad.

   The firing parties are to follow immediately in the rear of their respective storming parties.

15. The heads of the two divisions will follow their advanced guards, keeping nearly together, but they will not advance beyond the shelter afforded by the quarries on the left of the road till they will have seen the heads of the advanced guards ascend the breaches: they will then move forward to the storm in double quick time.

16. If the light division should find the bastion of Sta. Maria intrenched, they will turn the right of the intrenchment by moving along the parapet of the bastion. The 4th division will do the same by an intrenchment which appears in the left face, looking from the trenches of the bastion of La Trinidad.

17. The light division, as soon as they are in possession of the rampart of Sta. Maria, are to turn to their left, and to proceed along the rampart to their left, keeping always a reserve at the breach.

18. The advance guard of the 4th division are to turn to their left, and to keep up the communication with the light division. The 4th division are to turn to their right, and to communicate with the 3rd division, by the bastion of St Pedro, and the demi-bastion of St Antonio, taking care to keep a reserve at the bastion of La Trinidad.

19. Each (the 4th and light) division must leave 1,000 men in reserve in the quarries.
20. The 4th division must endeavour to get open the gate of La Trinidad; the light division must do the same by the gate called Puerto del Pillar.
21. The soldiers must leave their knapsacks in camp.
22. In order to aid these operations, the howitzers in No. 12 are to open fire upon the batteries, constructed by the enemy to fire upon the breach, as soon as the officers will observe that the enemy are aware of the attack, which they must continue till they see that the 3rd division are in possession of the castle.
23. The commanding officer in the trenches is to attack the ravelin of St Roque with 200 of the covering party, moving from the right of the second parallel, and round the right of the ravelin, looking from the trenches, and attacking the barriers and gates of communication between the ravelin and the bridge, while 200 men, likewise of the covering party, will rush from the right of the sap into the salient angle of the covered-way of the ravelin, and keep up a fire on its faces. These last should not advance from the sap, till the party to attack the gorge of the ravelin will have turned it. That which will move into the covered-way on the right of the ravelin looking from the trenches, ought not to proceed further down than the angle formed by the face and the flank.
24. The remainder of the covering party to be a reserve in the trenches. The working parties in the trenches are to join their regiments at half-past seven o'clock.
    Twelve carpenters with axes, and ten miners with crow-bars, must be with each (the 4th and light) division. A party of one officer and 20 artillerymen must be with each division.
25. The 5th division must be formed, one brigade on the ground occupied by the 48th regiment; one brigade on the Sierra del Viento; and one brigade in the low grounds extending to the Guadiana, now occupied by the pickets of the light division.
26. The pickets of the brigades on the Sierra del Viento, and that in the low grounds towards the Guadiana, should endeavour to alarm the enemy during the attack by firing at the Pardaleras, and at the men in the covered-way of the works towards the Guadiana.
27. The Commander of the Forces particularly request the General Officers commanding divisions and brigades, and the Commanding Officers of regiments, and the Officers commanding companies, to impress upon their men the necessity of their keeping together, and formed as a military body after the storm, and during the night. Not only the success of the operation, and the honour of the army, but their own individual safety, depend upon their being in a situation to repel any attack by the enemy, and to overcome

all resistance which they may be inclined to make, till the garrison have been completely subdued.

(Wellington)

Note upon the 6th Paragraph – It is recommended that the attack of the 3rd division should be kept clear of the bastion of St Antonio, at least till the castle, which is able and commands that bastion, will be carried.

Note upon the 9th Paragraph – This arrangement of the columns is made in order that the light division may extend along the ramparts to the left; and that the 4th division, with the exception of the advanced guard, which is to communicate by its left with the light division, might extend along the ramparts to the right. It may be necessary, however, for these divisions mutually to support each other, and attention must in this case be paid to the formations.

No. 13 will run thus: – after the words 'while the men of the storming party who carry bags will enter the covered way,' insert, 'those of the light division, at the place d'armes on the left, looking from camp, of the unfinished ravelling; those of the 4th division, on the right of that ravelin, at the place d'armes under the breached face of the bastion of La Trinidad.'

No. 14 General Colville will observe that a part of the advance of the 4th division must be allotted to storm the new breach in the curtain.

Note on No. 15 – The place here pointed out may be too distant. The heads of the columns should be brought as near as they can without being exposed to fire.

Note on No. 19 – It will be necessary for the commanding officer of the light division to attend to the ditch on his left as he will make his attack. He should post a detachment in the ditch towards the salient angle of the bastion of Santa Maria, so as to be covered by the angle from the fire of the next bastion on its left, looking from the trenches.

Note upon No. 22 – Some signal must be arranged between the commanding officer of the artillery and the officer who will command the attack on the castle, for ceasing the fire in No. 12.

Note upon No. 23 – It would be better that this attack should move from the right of the sap. The commanding officer in the trenches must begin it as soon as he will observe that the attack of the 3rd division on the castle is perceived by the enemy.

No. 26 The commanding officer of the light division will attend to this. General Power will likewise make a false attack on the tête-de-pont. (19)

APPENDIX 3

A Memorandum Critical to his Army

General the Marquis of Wellington, K.B., to Officers Commanding Divisions and Brigades

Freneda, 28th November, 1812

Gentlemen,

I have ordered the army into cantonments, in which I hope that circumstances will enable me to keep them for some time, during which the troops will receive their clothing, necessaries &c., which are already in progress by different lines of communication to the several divisions of Brigades.

But besides these objects, I must draw your attention in a very particular manner to the state of discipline of the troops. The discipline of every army, after a long and active campaign, becomes in some degree relaxed, and requires the utmost attention on the part of the general and other officers to bring it back to the state in which it ought to be for service; but I am concerned to have to observe that the army under my command has fallen off in this respect in the late campaign to a greater degree than any army with which I have ever served, or of which I have ever read. Yet this army has met with no disaster; it has suffered no privations which but trifling attention on the part of the officers could not have prevented, and for which there existed no reason whatever in the nature of the service; nor has it suffered any hardships excepting those resulting from the necessity of being exposed to the inclemencies of the weather at a moment when they were most severe.

It must be obvious however to every officer, that from the moment the troops commenced their retreat from the neighbourhood of Burgos on the one hand, and from Madrid on the other, the officers lost all command over their men. Irregularities and outrages of all descriptions were committed with impunity, and losses have been sustained which ought never to have occurred. Yet the necessity for retreat existing, none was ever made on which the troops made such short marches; none on which they made such long and repeated halts; and none on which the retreating armies were so little pressed on their rear by the enemy.

We must look therefore for the existing evils, and for the situation in which we now find the army, to some cause besides those resulting from the operations in which we have been engaged.

I have no hesitation in attributing these evils to the habitual inattention of the Officers of the regiments to their duty, as prescribed by the standing regulations of the service, and by the orders of this army.

I am far from questioning the zeal, still less the gallantry and spirit of the Officers of the army; and I am quite certain that if their minds can be convinced of the necessity of minute and constant attention to understand, recollect, and carry into execution the orders which have been issued for the performance of their duty, and that the strict performance of this duty is necessary to enable the army to serve the country as it ought to be served, they will in future give their attention to these points.

Unfortunately the inexperience of the Officers of the army has induced many to consider that the period during which an army is on service is one of relaxation from all rule, instead of being, as it is, the period during which of all others every rule for the regulation and control of the conduct of the soldier, for the inspection and care of his arms, ammunition, accoutrements, necessaries, and field equipments, and his horse and horse appointments; for the receipt and issue and care of his provisions; and the regulation of all that belongs to his food and the forage for his horse, must be most strictly attended to by the officers of his company or troop, if it is intended that an army, a British army in particular, shall be brought into the field of battle in a state of efficiency to meet the enemy on the day of trial.

These are the points then to which I most earnestly intreat you to turn your attention, and the attention of the officers of the regiments under your command, Portuguese as well as English, during the period in which it may be in my power to leave the troops in their cantonment. The Commanding Officers of regiments must enforce the orders of the army regarding the constant inspection and superintendence of the officers over the conduct of the men of their companies in their cantonments; and they must endeavour to inspire the noncommissioned officers with a sense of their situation and authority; and the noncommissioned officers must be forced to do their duty by being constantly under the view and superintendence of the officers. By these means the frequent and discreditable recourse to the authority of the provost, and to punishments by the sentence of courts martial, will be prevented, and the soldiers will not dare to commit the offences and outrages of which there are too many complaints, when they well know that their officers and their non-commissioned officers have their eyes and attention turned towards them.

The Commanding Officers of regiments must likewise enforce the orders of the army regarding the constant, real inspection of the soldiers' arms, ammunition, accoutrements, and necessaries, in order to prevent at all times the shameful waste of ammunition, and the sale of that article and of the soldiers' necessaries. With this view both should be inspected daily.

In regard to the food of the soldier, I have frequently observed and lamented in the late campaign, the facility and celerity with which the French soldiers cooked in comparison with those of our army.

The cause of this disadvantage is the same with that of every other description, the want of attention of the officers to the orders of the army, and the conduct of their men, and the consequent want of authority over their conduct. Certain men of each company should be appointed to cut and bring in wood, others to fetch water, and others to get the meat, &c. to be cooked; and it would soon be found that if this practice was daily enforced, and a particular hour for seeing the dinners, and for the men dining, named, as it ought to be, equally as for parade, that cooking would no longer require the inconvenient length of time which it has lately been found to take, and that the soldiers would not be exposed to the privation of their food at the moment at which the army may be engaged in operations with the enemy.

You will of course give your attention to the field exercise and discipline of the troops. It is very desirable that the soldiers should not lose the habits of marching, and the division should march 10 or 12 miles twice in each week, if the weather should permit, and the roads in the neighbourhood of the cantonments of the division should be dry.

But I repeat, that the great object of the attention of the General and Field Officers must be to get the Captains and Subalterns of the regiments to understand and perform the duties required from them, as the only mode by which the discipline and efficiency of the army can be restored and maintained during the next campaign.

I have the honour to be, &c.

(Wellington)

To Officers Commanding Divisions and Brigades

Index